FREE Study Skills Videos/DVD Offer

Dear Customer,

Thank you for your purchase from Mometrix! We consider it an honor and a privilege that you have purchased our product and we want to ensure your satisfaction.

As part of our ongoing effort to meet the needs of test takers, we have developed a set of Study Skills Videos that we would like to give you for <u>FREE</u>. These videos cover our *best practices* for getting ready for your exam, from how to use our study materials to how to best prepare for the day of the test.

All that we ask is that you email us with feedback that would describe your experience so far with our product. Good, bad, or indifferent, we want to know what you think!

To get your FREE Study Skills Videos, you can use the **QR code** below, or send us an **email** at <u>studyvideos@mometrix.com</u> with *FREE VIDEOS* in the subject line and the following information in the body of the email:

- The name of the product you purchased.
- Your product rating on a scale of 1-5, with 5 being the highest rating.
- Your feedback. It can be long, short, or anything in between. We just want to know your impressions and experience so far with our product. (Good feedback might include how our study material met your needs and ways we might be able to make it even better. You could highlight features that you found helpful or features that you think we should add.)

If you have any questions or concerns, please don't hesitate to contact me directly.

Thanks again!

Sincerely,

Jay Willis
Vice President
<u>jay.willis@mometrix.com</u>
1-800-673-8175

Praxis

Mathematics (5165)

Secrets Study Guide

Exam Review and Practice Test
for the Praxis Subject Assessments

Written and edited by Mometrix Test Prep

Printed in the United States of America

This paper meets the requirements of ANSI/NISO Z39.48-1992 (Permanence of Paper).

Mometrix offers volume discount pricing to institutions. For more information or a price quote, please contact our sales department at sales@mometrix.com or 888-248-1219.

Mometrix Media LLC is not affiliated with or endorsed by any official testing organization. All organizational and test names are trademarks of their respective owners.

Paperback
ISBN 13: 978-1-5167-2029-3
ISBN 10: 1-5167-2029-6

DEAR FUTURE EXAM SUCCESS STORY

First of all, **THANK YOU** for purchasing Mometrix study materials!

Second, congratulations! You are one of the few determined test-takers who are committed to doing whatever it takes to excel on your exam. **You have come to the right place.** We developed these study materials with one goal in mind: to deliver you the information you need in a format that's concise and easy to use.

In addition to optimizing your guide for the content of the test, we've outlined our recommended steps for breaking down the preparation process into small, attainable goals so you can make sure you stay on track.

We've also analyzed the entire test-taking process, identifying the most common pitfalls and showing how you can overcome them and be ready for any curveball the test throws you.

Standardized testing is one of the biggest obstacles on your road to success, which only increases the importance of doing well in the high-pressure, high-stakes environment of test day. Your results on this test could have a significant impact on your future, and this guide provides the information and practical advice to help you achieve your full potential on test day.

Your success is our success

We would love to hear from you! If you would like to share the story of your exam success or if you have any questions or comments in regard to our products, please contact us at **800-673-8175** or **support@mometrix.com**.

Thanks again for your business and we wish you continued success!

Sincerely,
The Mometrix Test Preparation Team

Need more help? Check out our flashcards at:
http://MometrixFlashcards.com/PraxisII

TABLE OF CONTENTS

Introduction

Thank you for purchasing this resource! You have made the choice to prepare yourself for a test that could have a huge impact on your future, and this guide is designed to help you be fully ready for test day. Obviously, it's important to have a solid understanding of the test material, but you also need to be prepared for the unique environment and stressors of the test, so that you can perform to the best of your abilities.

For this purpose, the first section that appears in this guide is the **Secret Keys**. We've devoted countless hours to meticulously researching what works and what doesn't, and we've boiled down our findings to the five most impactful steps you can take to improve your performance on the test. We start at the beginning with study planning and move through the preparation process, all the way to the testing strategies that will help you get the most out of what you know when you're finally sitting in front of the test.

We recommend that you start preparing for your test as far in advance as possible. However, if you've bought this guide as a last-minute study resource and only have a few days before your test, we recommend that you skip over the first two Secret Keys since they address a long-term study plan.

If you struggle with **test anxiety**, we strongly encourage you to check out our recommendations for how you can overcome it. Test anxiety is a formidable foe, but it can be beaten, and we want to make sure you have the tools you need to defeat it.

Secret Key #1 – Plan Big, Study Small

There's a lot riding on your performance. If you want to ace this test, you're going to need to keep your skills sharp and the material fresh in your mind. You need a plan that lets you review everything you need to know while still fitting in your schedule. We'll break this strategy down into three categories.

Information Organization

Start with the information you already have: the official test outline. From this, you can make a complete list of all the concepts you need to cover before the test. Organize these concepts into groups that can be studied together, and create a list of any related vocabulary you need to learn so you can brush up on any difficult terms. You'll want to keep this vocabulary list handy once you actually start studying since you may need to add to it along the way.

Time Management

Once you have your set of study concepts, decide how to spread them out over the time you have left before the test. Break your study plan into small, clear goals so you have a manageable task for each day and know exactly what you're doing. Then just focus on one small step at a time. When you manage your time this way, you don't need to spend hours at a time studying. Studying a small block of content for a short period each day helps you retain information better and avoid stressing over how much you have left to do. You can relax knowing that you have a plan to cover everything in time. In order for this strategy to be effective though, you have to start studying early and stick to your schedule. Avoid the exhaustion and futility that comes from last-minute cramming!

Study Environment

The environment you study in has a big impact on your learning. Studying in a coffee shop, while probably more enjoyable, is not likely to be as fruitful as studying in a quiet room. It's important to keep distractions to a minimum. You're only planning to study for a short block of time, so make the most of it. Don't pause to check your phone or get up to find a snack. It's also important to **avoid multitasking**. Research has consistently shown that multitasking will make your studying dramatically less effective. Your study area should also be comfortable and well-lit so you don't have the distraction of straining your eyes or sitting on an uncomfortable chair.

 The time of day you study is also important. You want to be rested and alert. Don't wait until just before bedtime. Study when you'll be most likely to comprehend and remember. Even better, if you know what time of day your test will be, set that time aside for study. That way your brain will be used to working on that subject at that specific time and you'll have a better chance of recalling information.

Finally, it can be helpful to team up with others who are studying for the same test. Your actual studying should be done in as isolated an environment as possible, but the work of organizing the information and setting up the study plan can be divided up. In between study sessions, you can discuss with your teammates the concepts that you're all studying and quiz each other on the details. Just be sure that your teammates are as serious about the test as you are. If you find that your study time is being replaced with social time, you might need to find a new team.

Secret Key #2 – Make Your Studying Count

You're devoting a lot of time and effort to preparing for this test, so you want to be absolutely certain it will pay off. This means doing more than just reading the content and hoping you can remember it on test day. It's important to make every minute of study count. There are two main areas you can focus on to make your studying count.

Retention

It doesn't matter how much time you study if you can't remember the material. You need to make sure you are retaining the concepts. To check your retention of the information you're learning, try recalling it at later times with minimal prompting. Try carrying around flashcards and glance at one or two from time to time or ask a friend who's also studying for the test to quiz you.

To enhance your retention, look for ways to put the information into practice so that you can apply it rather than simply recalling it. If you're using the information in practical ways, it will be much easier to remember. Similarly, it helps to solidify a concept in your mind if you're not only reading it to yourself but also explaining it to someone else. Ask a friend to let you teach them about a concept you're a little shaky on (or speak aloud to an imaginary audience if necessary). As you try to summarize, define, give examples, and answer your friend's questions, you'll understand the concepts better and they will stay with you longer. Finally, step back for a big picture view and ask yourself how each piece of information fits with the whole subject. When you link the different concepts together and see them working together as a whole, it's easier to remember the individual components.

Finally, practice showing your work on any multi-step problems, even if you're just studying. Writing out each step you take to solve a problem will help solidify the process in your mind, and you'll be more likely to remember it during the test.

Modality

Modality simply refers to the means or method by which you study. Choosing a study modality that fits your own individual learning style is crucial. No two people learn best in exactly the same way, so it's important to know your strengths and use them to your advantage.

For example, if you learn best by visualization, focus on visualizing a concept in your mind and draw an image or a diagram. Try color-coding your notes, illustrating them, or creating symbols that will trigger your mind to recall a learned concept. If you learn best by hearing or discussing information, find a study partner who learns the same way or read aloud to yourself. Think about how to put the information in your own words. Imagine that you are giving a lecture on the topic and record yourself so you can listen to it later.

For any learning style, flashcards can be helpful. Organize the information so you can take advantage of spare moments to review. Underline key words or phrases. Use different colors for different categories. Mnemonic devices (such as creating a short list in which every item starts with the same letter) can also help with retention. Find what works best for you and use it to store the information in your mind most effectively and easily.

3

Secret Key #3 – Practice the Right Way

Your success on test day depends not only on how many hours you put into preparing, but also on whether you prepared the right way. It's good to check along the way to see if your studying is paying off. One of the most effective ways to do this is by taking practice tests to evaluate your progress. Practice tests are useful because they show exactly where you need to improve. Every time you take a practice test, pay special attention to these three groups of questions:

- The questions you got wrong
- The questions you had to guess on, even if you guessed right
- The questions you found difficult or slow to work through

This will show you exactly what your weak areas are, and where you need to devote more study time. Ask yourself why each of these questions gave you trouble. Was it because you didn't understand the material? Was it because you didn't remember the vocabulary? Do you need more repetitions on this type of question to build speed and confidence? Dig into those questions and figure out how you can strengthen your weak areas as you go back to review the material.

Additionally, many practice tests have a section explaining the answer choices. It can be tempting to read the explanation and think that you now have a good understanding of the concept. However, an explanation likely only covers part of the question's broader context. Even if the explanation makes perfect sense, **go back and investigate** every concept related to the question until you're positive you have a thorough understanding.

As you go along, keep in mind that the practice test is just that: practice. Memorizing these questions and answers will not be very helpful on the actual test because it is unlikely to have any of the same exact questions. If you only know the right answers to the sample questions, you won't be prepared for the real thing. **Study the concepts** until you understand them fully, and then you'll be able to answer any question that shows up on the test.

It's important to wait on the practice tests until you're ready. If you take a test on your first day of study, you may be overwhelmed by the amount of material covered and how much you need to learn. Work up to it gradually.

On test day, you'll need to be prepared for answering questions, managing your time, and using the test-taking strategies you've learned. It's a lot to balance, like a mental marathon that will have a big impact on your future. Like training for a marathon, you'll need to start slowly and work your way up. When test day arrives, you'll be ready.

Start with the strategies you've read in the first two Secret Keys—plan your course and study in the way that works best for you. If you have time, consider using multiple study resources to get different approaches to the same concepts. It can be helpful to see difficult concepts from more than one angle. Then find a good source for practice tests. Many times, the test website will suggest potential study resources or provide sample tests.

Practice Test Strategy

If you're able to find at least three practice tests, we recommend this strategy:

UNTIMED AND OPEN-BOOK PRACTICE

Take the first test with no time constraints and with your notes and study guide handy. Take your time and focus on applying the strategies you've learned.

TIMED AND OPEN-BOOK PRACTICE

Take the second practice test open-book as well, but set a timer and practice pacing yourself to finish in time.

TIMED AND CLOSED-BOOK PRACTICE

Take any other practice tests as if it were test day. Set a timer and put away your study materials. Sit at a table or desk in a quiet room, imagine yourself at the testing center, and answer questions as quickly and accurately as possible.

Keep repeating timed and closed-book tests on a regular basis until you run out of practice tests or it's time for the actual test. Your mind will be ready for the schedule and stress of test day, and you'll be able to focus on recalling the material you've learned.

Secret Key #4 – Pace Yourself

Once you're fully prepared for the material on the test, your biggest challenge on test day will be managing your time. Just knowing that the clock is ticking can make you panic even if you have plenty of time left. Work on pacing yourself so you can build confidence against the time constraints of the exam. Pacing is a difficult skill to master, especially in a high-pressure environment, so **practice is vital**.

Set time expectations for your pace based on how much time is available. For example, if a section has 60 questions and the time limit is 30 minutes, you know you have to average 30 seconds or less per question in order to answer them all. Although 30 seconds is the hard limit, set 25 seconds per question as your goal, so you reserve extra time to spend on harder questions. When you budget extra time for the harder questions, you no longer have any reason to stress when those questions take longer to answer.

Don't let this time expectation distract you from working through the test at a calm, steady pace, but keep it in mind so you don't spend too much time on any one question. Recognize that taking extra time on one question you don't understand may keep you from answering two that you do understand later in the test. If your time limit for a question is up and you're still not sure of the answer, mark it and move on, and come back to it later if the time and the test format allow. If the testing format doesn't allow you to return to earlier questions, just make an educated guess; then put it out of your mind and move on.

On the easier questions, be careful not to rush. It may seem wise to hurry through them so you have more time for the challenging ones, but it's not worth missing one if you know the concept and just didn't take the time to read the question fully. Work efficiently but make sure you understand the question and have looked at all of the answer choices, since more than one may seem right at first.

Even if you're paying attention to the time, you may find yourself a little behind at some point. You should speed up to get back on track, but do so wisely. Don't panic; just take a few seconds less on each question until you're caught up. Don't guess without thinking, but do look through the answer choices and eliminate any you know are wrong. If you can get down to two choices, it is often worthwhile to guess from those. Once you've chosen an answer, move on and don't dwell on any that you skipped or had to hurry through. If a question was taking too long, chances are it was one of the harder ones, so you weren't as likely to get it right anyway.

On the other hand, if you find yourself getting ahead of schedule, it may be beneficial to slow down a little. The more quickly you work, the more likely you are to make a careless mistake that will affect your score. You've budgeted time for each question, so don't be afraid to spend that time. Practice an efficient but careful pace to get the most out of the time you have.

Secret Key #5 – Have a Plan for Guessing

When you're taking the test, you may find yourself stuck on a question. Some of the answer choices seem better than others, but you don't see the one answer choice that is obviously correct. What do you do?

The scenario described above is very common, yet most test takers have not effectively prepared for it. Developing and practicing a plan for guessing may be one of the single most effective uses of your time as you get ready for the exam.

In developing your plan for guessing, there are three questions to address:

- When should you start the guessing process?
- How should you narrow down the choices?
- Which answer should you choose?

When to Start the Guessing Process

Unless your plan for guessing is to select C every time (which, despite its merits, is not what we recommend), you need to leave yourself enough time to apply your answer elimination strategies. Since you have a limited amount of time for each question, that means that if you're going to give yourself the best shot at guessing correctly, you have to decide quickly whether or not you will guess.

Of course, the best-case scenario is that you don't have to guess at all, so first, see if you can answer the question based on your knowledge of the subject and basic reasoning skills. Focus on the key words in the question and try to jog your memory of related topics. Give yourself a chance to bring the knowledge to mind, but once you realize that you don't have (or you can't access) the knowledge you need to answer the question, it's time to start the guessing process.

It's almost always better to start the guessing process too early than too late. It only takes a few seconds to remember something and answer the question from knowledge. Carefully eliminating wrong answer choices takes longer. Plus, going through the process of eliminating answer choices can actually help jog your memory.

Summary: Start the guessing process as soon as you decide that you can't answer the question based on your knowledge.

How to Narrow Down the Choices

The next chapter in this book (**Test-Taking Strategies**) includes a wide range of strategies for how to approach questions and how to look for answer choices to eliminate. You will definitely want to read those carefully, practice them, and figure out which ones work best for you. Here though, we're going to address a mindset rather than a particular strategy.

Your odds of guessing an answer correctly depend on how many options you are choosing from.

Number of options left	5	4	3	2	1
Odds of guessing correctly	20%	25%	33%	50%	100%

You can see from this chart just how valuable it is to be able to eliminate incorrect answers and make an educated guess, but there are two things that many test takers do that cause them to miss out on the benefits of guessing:

- Accidentally eliminating the correct answer
- Selecting an answer based on an impression

We'll look at the first one here, and the second one in the next section.

To avoid accidentally eliminating the correct answer, we recommend a thought exercise called **the $5 challenge**. In this challenge, you only eliminate an answer choice from contention if you are willing to bet $5 on it being wrong. Why $5? Five dollars is a small but not insignificant amount of money. It's an amount you could afford to lose but wouldn't want to throw away. And while losing

$5 once might not hurt too much, doing it twenty times will set you back $100. In the same way, each small decision you make—eliminating a choice here, guessing on a question there—won't by itself impact your score very much, but when you put them all together, they can make a big difference. By holding each answer choice elimination decision to a higher standard, you can reduce the risk of accidentally eliminating the correct answer.

The $5 challenge can also be applied in a positive sense: If you are willing to bet $5 that an answer choice *is* correct, go ahead and mark it as correct.

Summary: Only eliminate an answer choice if you are willing to bet $5 that it is wrong.

Which Answer to Choose

You're taking the test. You've run into a hard question and decided you'll have to guess. You've eliminated all the answer choices you're willing to bet $5 on. Now you have to pick an answer. Why do we even need to talk about this? Why can't you just pick whichever one you feel like when the time comes?

The answer to these questions is that if you don't come into the test with a plan, you'll rely on your impression to select an answer choice, and if you do that, you risk falling into a trap. The test writers know that everyone who takes their test will be guessing on some of the questions, so they intentionally write wrong answer choices to seem plausible. You still have to pick an answer though, and if the wrong answer choices are designed to look right, how can you ever be sure that you're not falling for their trap? The best solution we've found to this dilemma is to take the decision out of your hands entirely. Here is the process we recommend:

Once you've eliminated any choices that you are confident (willing to bet $5) are wrong, select the first remaining choice as your answer.

Whether you choose to select the first remaining choice, the second, or the last, the important thing is that you use some preselected standard. Using this approach guarantees that you will not be enticed into selecting an answer choice that looks right, because you are not basing your decision on how the answer choices look.

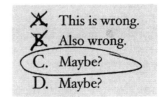

This is not meant to make you question your knowledge. Instead, it is to help you recognize the difference between your knowledge and your impressions. There's a huge difference between thinking an answer is right because of what you know, and thinking an answer is right because it looks or sounds like it should be right.

Summary: To ensure that your selection is appropriately random, make a predetermined selection from among all answer choices you have not eliminated.

Test-Taking Strategies

This section contains a list of test-taking strategies that you may find helpful as you work through the test. By taking what you know and applying logical thought, you can maximize your chances of answering any question correctly!

It is very important to realize that every question is different and every person is different: no single strategy will work on every question, and no single strategy will work for every person. That's why we've included all of them here, so you can try them out and determine which ones work best for different types of questions and which ones work best for you.

Question Strategies

⊘ READ CAREFULLY

Read the question and the answer choices carefully. Don't miss the question because you misread the terms. You have plenty of time to read each question thoroughly and make sure you understand what is being asked. Yet a happy medium must be attained, so don't waste too much time. You must read carefully and efficiently.

⊘ CONTEXTUAL CLUES

Look for contextual clues. If the question includes a word you are not familiar with, look at the immediate context for some indication of what the word might mean. Contextual clues can often give you all the information you need to decipher the meaning of an unfamiliar word. Even if you can't determine the meaning, you may be able to narrow down the possibilities enough to make a solid guess at the answer to the question.

⊘ PREFIXES

If you're having trouble with a word in the question or answer choices, try dissecting it. Take advantage of every clue that the word might include. Prefixes can be a huge help. Usually, they allow you to determine a basic meaning. *Pre-* means before, *post-* means after, *pro-* is positive, *de-* is negative. From prefixes, you can get an idea of the general meaning of the word and try to put it into context.

⊘ HEDGE WORDS

Watch out for critical hedge words, such as *likely, may, can, sometimes, often, almost, mostly, usually, generally, rarely,* and *sometimes.* Question writers insert these hedge phrases to cover every possibility. Often an answer choice will be wrong simply because it leaves no room for exception. Be on guard for answer choices that have definitive words such as *exactly* and *always.*

⊘ SWITCHBACK WORDS

Stay alert for *switchbacks.* These are the words and phrases frequently used to alert you to shifts in thought. The most common switchback words are *but, although,* and *however.* Others include *nevertheless, on the other hand, even though, while, in spite of, despite,* and *regardless of.* Switchback words are important to catch because they can change the direction of the question or an answer choice.

10

⊘ Face Value

When in doubt, use common sense. Accept the situation in the problem at face value. Don't read too much into it. These problems will not require you to make wild assumptions. If you have to go beyond creativity and warp time or space in order to have an answer choice fit the question, then you should move on and consider the other answer choices. These are normal problems rooted in reality. The applicable relationship or explanation may not be readily apparent, but it is there for you to figure out. Use your common sense to interpret anything that isn't clear.

Answer Choice Strategies

⊘ Answer Selection

The most thorough way to pick an answer choice is to identify and eliminate wrong answers until only one is left, then confirm it is the correct answer. Sometimes an answer choice may immediately seem right, but be careful. The test writers will usually put more than one reasonable answer choice on each question, so take a second to read all of them and make sure that the other choices are not equally obvious. As long as you have time left, it is better to read every answer choice than to pick the first one that looks right without checking the others.

⊘ Answer Choice Families

An answer choice family consists of two (in rare cases, three) answer choices that are very similar in construction and cannot all be true at the same time. If you see two answer choices that are direct opposites or parallels, one of them is usually the correct answer. For instance, if one answer choice says that quantity x increases and another either says that quantity x decreases (opposite) or says that quantity y increases (parallel), then those answer choices would fall into the same family. An answer choice that doesn't match the construction of the answer choice family is more likely to be incorrect. Most questions will not have answer choice families, but when they do appear, you should be prepared to recognize them.

⊘ Eliminate Answers

Eliminate answer choices as soon as you realize they are wrong, but make sure you consider all possibilities. If you are eliminating answer choices and realize that the last one you are left with is also wrong, don't panic. Start over and consider each choice again. There may be something you missed the first time that you will realize on the second pass.

⊘ Avoid Fact Traps

Don't be distracted by an answer choice that is factually true but doesn't answer the question. You are looking for the choice that answers the question. Stay focused on what the question is asking for so you don't accidentally pick an answer that is true but incorrect. Always go back to the question and make sure the answer choice you've selected actually answers the question and is not merely a true statement.

⊘ Extreme Statements

In general, you should avoid answers that put forth extreme actions as standard practice or proclaim controversial ideas as established fact. An answer choice that states the "process should be used in certain situations, if…" is much more likely to be correct than one that states the "process should be discontinued completely." The first is a calm rational statement and doesn't even make a definitive, uncompromising stance, using a hedge word *if* to provide wiggle room, whereas the second choice is far more extreme.

11

⊘ Benchmark

As you read through the answer choices and you come across one that seems to answer the question well, mentally select that answer choice. This is not your final answer, but it's the one that will help you evaluate the other answer choices. The one that you selected is your benchmark or standard for judging each of the other answer choices. Every other answer choice must be compared to your benchmark. That choice is correct until proven otherwise by another answer choice beating it. If you find a better answer, then that one becomes your new benchmark. Once you've decided that no other choice answers the question as well as your benchmark, you have your final answer.

⊘ Predict the Answer

Before you even start looking at the answer choices, it is often best to try to predict the answer. When you come up with the answer on your own, it is easier to avoid distractions and traps because you will know exactly what to look for. The right answer choice is unlikely to be word-for-word what you came up with, but it should be a close match. Even if you are confident that you have the right answer, you should still take the time to read each option before moving on.

General Strategies

⊘ Tough Questions

If you are stumped on a problem or it appears too hard or too difficult, don't waste time. Move on! Remember though, if you can quickly check for obviously incorrect answer choices, your chances of guessing correctly are greatly improved. Before you completely give up, at least try to knock out a couple of possible answers. Eliminate what you can and then guess at the remaining answer choices before moving on.

⊘ Check Your Work

Since you will probably not know every term listed and the answer to every question, it is important that you get credit for the ones that you do know. Don't miss any questions through careless mistakes. If at all possible, try to take a second to look back over your answer selection and make sure you've selected the correct answer choice and haven't made a costly careless mistake (such as marking an answer choice that you didn't mean to mark). This quick double check should more than pay for itself in caught mistakes for the time it costs.

⊘ Pace Yourself

It's easy to be overwhelmed when you're looking at a page full of questions; your mind is confused and full of random thoughts, and the clock is ticking down faster than you would like. Calm down and maintain the pace that you have set for yourself. Especially as you get down to the last few minutes of the test, don't let the small numbers on the clock make you panic. As long as you are on track by monitoring your pace, you are guaranteed to have time for each question.

⊘ Don't Rush

It is very easy to make errors when you are in a hurry. Maintaining a fast pace in answering questions is pointless if it makes you miss questions that you would have gotten right otherwise. Test writers like to include distracting information and wrong answers that seem right. Taking a little extra time to avoid careless mistakes can make all the difference in your test score. Find a pace that allows you to be confident in the answers that you select.

12

⊘ KEEP MOVING

Panicking will not help you pass the test, so do your best to stay calm and keep moving. Taking deep breaths and going through the answer elimination steps you practiced can help to break through a stress barrier and keep your pace.

Final Notes

The combination of a solid foundation of content knowledge and the confidence that comes from practicing your plan for applying that knowledge is the key to maximizing your performance on test day. As your foundation of content knowledge is built up and strengthened, you'll find that the strategies included in this chapter become more and more effective in helping you quickly sift through the distractions and traps of the test to isolate the correct answer.

Now that you're preparing to move forward into the test content chapters of this book, be sure to keep your goal in mind. As you read, think about how you will be able to apply this information on the test. If you've already seen sample questions for the test and you have an idea of the question format and style, try to come up with questions of your own that you can answer based on what you're reading. This will give you valuable practice applying your knowledge in the same ways you can expect to on test day.

Good luck and good studying!

14

Number and Quantity and Algebra

Number and Quantity

CLASSIFICATIONS OF NUMBERS

Numbers are the basic building blocks of mathematics. Specific features of numbers are identified by the following terms:

Integer – any positive or negative whole number, including zero. Integers do not include fractions $\left(\frac{1}{3}\right)$, decimals (0.56), or mixed numbers $\left(7\frac{3}{4}\right)$.

Prime number – any whole number greater than 1 that has only two factors, itself and 1; that is, a number that can be divided evenly only by 1 and itself.

Composite number – any whole number greater than 1 that has more than two different factors; in other words, any whole number that is not a prime number. For example: The composite number 8 has the factors of 1, 2, 4, and 8.

Even number – any integer that can be divided by 2 without leaving a remainder. For example: 2, 4, 6, 8, and so on.

Odd number – any integer that cannot be divided evenly by 2. For example: 3, 5, 7, 9, and so on.

Decimal number – any number that uses a decimal point to show the part of the number that is less than one. Example: 1.234.

Decimal point – a symbol used to separate the ones place from the tenths place in decimals or dollars from cents in currency.

Decimal place – the position of a number to the right of the decimal point. In the decimal 0.123, the 1 is in the first place to the right of the decimal point, indicating tenths; the 2 is in the second place, indicating hundredths; and the 3 is in the third place, indicating thousandths.

The **decimal**, or base 10, system is a number system that uses ten different digits (0, 1, 2, 3, 4, 5, 6, 7, 8, 9). An example of a number system that uses something other than ten digits is the **binary**, or base 2, number system, used by computers, which uses only the numbers 0 and 1. It is thought that the decimal system originated because people had only their 10 fingers for counting.

Rational numbers include all integers, decimals, and fractions. Any terminating or repeating decimal number is a rational number.

Irrational numbers cannot be written as fractions or decimals because the number of decimal places is infinite and there is no recurring pattern of digits within the number. For example, pi (π) begins with 3.141592 and continues without terminating or repeating, so pi is an irrational number.

Real numbers are the set of all rational and irrational numbers.

NUMBERS IN WORD FORM AND PLACE VALUE

When writing numbers out in word form or translating word form to numbers, it is essential to understand how a place value system works. In the decimal or base-10 system, each digit of a number represents how many of the corresponding place value—a specific factor of 10—are contained in the number being represented. To make reading numbers easier, every three digits to the left of the decimal place is preceded by a comma. The following table demonstrates some of the place values:

Power of 10	10^3	10^2	10^1	10^0	10^{-1}	10^{-2}	10^{-3}
Value	1,000	100	10	1	0.1	0.01	0.001
Place	thousands	hundreds	tens	ones	tenths	hundredths	thousandths

For example, consider the number 4,546.09, which can be separated into each place value like this:

4: thousands
5: hundreds
4: tens
6: ones
0: tenths
9: hundredths

This number in word form would be *four thousand five hundred forty-six and nine hundredths*.

RATIONAL NUMBERS

The term **rational** means that the number can be expressed as a ratio or fraction. That is, a number, r, is rational if and only if it can be represented by a fraction $\frac{a}{b}$ where a and b are integers and b does not equal 0. The set of rational numbers includes integers and decimals. If there is no finite way to represent a value with a fraction of integers, then the number is **irrational**. Common examples of irrational numbers include: $\sqrt{5}$, $\left(1 + \sqrt{2}\right)$, and π.

THE NUMBER LINE

A number line is a graph to see the distance between numbers. Basically, this graph shows the relationship between numbers. So a number line may have a point for zero and may show negative numbers on the left side of the line. Any positive numbers are placed on the right side of the line. For example, consider the points labeled on the following number line:

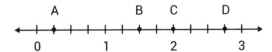

We can use the dashed lines on the number line to identify each point. Each dashed line between two whole numbers is $\frac{1}{4}$. The line halfway between two numbers is $\frac{1}{2}$.

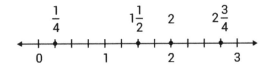

Review Video: The Number Line
Visit mometrix.com/academy and enter code: 816439

ABSOLUTE VALUE

A precursor to working with negative numbers is understanding what **absolute values** are. A number's absolute value is simply the distance away from zero a number is on the number line. The absolute value of a number is always positive and is written $|x|$. For example, the absolute value of 3, written as $|3|$, is 3 because the distance between 0 and 3 on a number line is three units. Likewise, the absolute value of –3, written as $|-3|$, is 3 because the distance between 0 and –3 on a number line is three units. So $|3| = |-3|$.

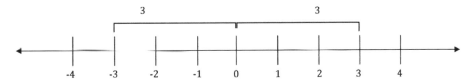

Review Video: Absolute Value
Visit mometrix.com/academy and enter code: 314669

OPERATIONS

An **operation** is simply a mathematical process that takes some value(s) as input(s) and produces an output. Elementary operations are often written in the following form: *value operation value*. For instance, in the expression $1 + 2$ the values are 1 and 2 and the operation is addition. Performing the operation gives the output of 3. In this way we can say that $1 + 2$ and 3 are equal, or $1 + 2 = 3$.

ADDITION

Addition increases the value of one quantity by the value of another quantity (both called **addends**). Example: $2 + 4 = 6$ or $8 + 9 = 17$. The result is called the **sum**. With addition, the order does not matter, $4 + 2 = 2 + 4$.

When adding signed numbers, if the signs are the same simply add the absolute values of the addends and apply the original sign to the sum. For example, $(+4) + (+8) = +12$ and $(-4) + (-8) = -12$. When the original signs are different, take the absolute values of the addends and

17

subtract the smaller value from the larger value, then apply the original sign of the larger value to the difference. Example: $(+4) + (-8) = -4$ and $(-4) + (+8) = +4$.

SUBTRACTION

Subtraction is the opposite operation to addition; it decreases the value of one quantity (the **minuend**) by the value of another quantity (the **subtrahend**). For example, $6 - 4 = 2$ or $17 - 8 = 9$. The result is called the **difference**. Note that with subtraction, the order does matter, $6 - 4 \neq 4 - 6$.

For subtracting signed numbers, change the sign of the subtrahend and then follow the same rules used for addition. Example: $(+4) - (+8) = (+4) + (-8) = -4$

MULTIPLICATION

Multiplication can be thought of as repeated addition. One number (the **multiplier**) indicates how many times to add the other number (the **multiplicand**) to itself. Example: $3 \times 2 = 2 + 2 + 2 = 6$. With multiplication, the order does not matter, $2 \times 3 = 3 \times 2$ or $3 + 3 = 2 + 2 + 2$, either way the result (the **product**) is the same.

If the signs are the same, the product is positive when multiplying signed numbers. Example: $(+4) \times (+8) = +32$ and $(-4) \times (-8) = +32$. If the signs are opposite, the product is negative. Example: $(+4) \times (-8) = -32$ and $(-4) \times (+8) = -32$. When more than two factors are multiplied together, the sign of the product is determined by how many negative factors are present. If there are an odd number of negative factors then the product is negative, whereas an even number of negative factors indicates a positive product. Example: $(+4) \times (-8) \times (-2) = +64$ and $(-4) \times (-8) \times (-2) = -64$.

DIVISION

Division is the opposite operation to multiplication; one number (the **divisor**) tells us how many parts to divide the other number (the **dividend**) into. The result of division is called the **quotient**. Example: $20 \div 4 = 5$. If 20 is split into 4 equal parts, each part is 5. With division, the order of the numbers does matter, $20 \div 4 \neq 4 \div 20$.

The rules for dividing signed numbers are similar to multiplying signed numbers. If the dividend and divisor have the same sign, the quotient is positive. If the dividend and divisor have opposite signs, the quotient is negative. Example: $(-4) \div (+8) = -0.5$.

> **Review Video: Mathematical Operations**
> Visit mometrix.com/academy and enter code: 208095

PARENTHESES

Parentheses are used to designate which operations should be done first when there are multiple operations. Example: $4 - (2 + 1) = 1$; the parentheses tell us that we must add 2 and 1, and then subtract the sum from 4, rather than subtracting 2 from 4 and then adding 1 (this would give us an answer of 3).

> **Review Video: Mathematical Parentheses**
> Visit mometrix.com/academy and enter code: 978600

EXPONENTS

An **exponent** is a superscript number placed next to another number at the top right. It indicates how many times the base number is to be multiplied by itself. Exponents provide a shorthand way to write what would be a longer mathematical expression, Example: $2^4 = 2 \times 2 \times 2 \times 2$. A number with an exponent of 2 is said to be "squared," while a number with an exponent of 3 is said to be "cubed." The value of a number raised to an exponent is called its power. So 8^4 is read as "8 to the 4th power," or "8 raised to the power of 4."

Review Video: **Introduction to Exponents**
Visit mometrix.com/academy and enter code: 600998

ROOTS

A **root**, such as a square root, is another way of writing a fractional exponent. Instead of using a superscript, roots use the radical symbol ($\sqrt{}$) to indicate the operation. A radical will have a number underneath the bar, and may sometimes have a number in the upper left: $\sqrt[n]{a}$, read as "the nth root of a." The relationship between radical notation and exponent notation can be described by this equation:

$$\sqrt[n]{a} = a^{\frac{1}{n}}$$

The two special cases of $n = 2$ and $n = 3$ are called square roots and cube roots. If there is no number to the upper left, the radical is understood to be a square root ($n = 2$). Nearly all of the roots you encounter will be square roots. A square root is the same as a number raised to the one-half power. When we say that a is the square root of b ($a = \sqrt{b}$), we mean that a multiplied by itself equals b: ($a \times a = b$).

A **perfect square** is a number that has an integer for its square root. There are 10 perfect squares from 1 to 100: 1, 4, 9, 16, 25, 36, 49, 64, 81, 100 (the squares of integers 1 through 10).

Review Video: **Roots**
Visit mometrix.com/academy and enter code: 795655
Review Video: **Square Root and Perfect Squares**
Visit mometrix.com/academy and enter code: 648063

WORD PROBLEMS AND MATHEMATICAL SYMBOLS

When working on word problems, you must be able to translate verbal expressions or "math words" into math symbols. This chart contains several "math words" and their appropriate symbols:

Phrase	Symbol
equal, is, was, will be, has, costs, gets to, is the same as, becomes	$=$
times, of, multiplied by, product of, twice, doubles, halves, triples	$\times$
divided by, per, ratio of/to, out of	$\div$
plus, added to, sum, combined, and, more than, totals of	$+$
subtracted from, less than, decreased by, minus, difference between	$-$
what, how much, original value, how many, a number, a variable	x, n, etc.

EXAMPLES OF TRANSLATED MATHEMATICAL PHRASES

- The phrase four more than twice a number can be written algebraically as $2x + 4$.

19

- The phrase half a number decreased by six can be written algebraically as $\frac{1}{2}x - 6$.
- The phrase the sum of a number and the product of five and that number can be written algebraically as $x + 5x$.
- You may see a test question that says, "Olivia is constructing a bookcase from seven boards. Two of them are for vertical supports and five are for shelves. The height of the bookcase is twice the width of the bookcase. If the seven boards total 36 feet in length, what will be the height of Olivia's bookcase?" You would need to make a sketch and then create the equation to determine the width of the shelves. The height can be represented as double the width. (If x represents the width of the shelves in feet, then the height of the bookcase is $2x$. Since the seven boards total 36 feet, $2x + 2x + x + x + x + x + x = 36$ or $9x = 36$; $x = 4$. The height is twice the width, or 8 feet.)

SUBTRACTION WITH REGROUPING

A great way to make use of some of the features built into the decimal system would be regrouping when attempting longform subtraction operations. When subtracting within a place value, sometimes the minuend is smaller than the subtrahend, **regrouping** enables you to 'borrow' a unit from a place value to the left in order to get a positive difference. For example, consider subtracting 189 from 525 with regrouping.

First, set up the subtraction problem in vertical form:

$$
\begin{array}{r}
525 \\
- \ 189 \\
\hline
\end{array}
$$

Notice that the numbers in the ones and tens columns of 525 are smaller than the numbers in the ones and tens columns of 189. This means you will need to use regrouping to perform subtraction:

$$
\begin{array}{rrr}
5 & 2 & 5 \\
- \ 1 & 8 & 9 \\
\hline
\end{array}
$$

To subtract 9 from 5 in the ones column you will need to borrow from the 2 in the tens columns:

$$
\begin{array}{rrr}
5 & 1 & 15 \\
- \ 1 & 8 & 9 \\
\hline
& & 6 \\
\end{array}
$$

Next, to subtract 8 from 1 in the tens column you will need to borrow from the 5 in the hundreds column:

$$
\begin{array}{rrr}
4 & 11 & 15 \\
- \ 1 & 8 & 9 \\
\hline
& 3 & 6 \\
\end{array}
$$

Last, subtract the 1 from the 4 in the hundreds column:

$$
\begin{array}{rrr}
4 & 11 & 15 \\
- \ 1 & 8 & 9 \\
\hline
3 & 3 & 6 \\
\end{array}
$$

> **Review Video: <u>Subtracting Large Numbers</u>**
> Visit mometrix.com/academy and enter code: 603350

ORDER OF OPERATIONS

The **order of operations** is a set of rules that dictates the order in which we must perform each operation in an expression so that we will evaluate it accurately. If we have an expression that includes multiple different operations, the order of operations tells us which operations to do first. The most common mnemonic for the order of operations is **PEMDAS**, or "Please Excuse My Dear Aunt Sally." PEMDAS stands for parentheses, exponents, multiplication, division, addition, and subtraction. It is important to understand that multiplication and division have equal precedence, as do addition and subtraction, so those pairs of operations are simply worked from left to right in order.

For example, evaluating the expression $5 + 20 \div 4 \times (2 + 3)^2 - 6$ using the correct order of operations would be done like this:

- **P:** Perform the operations inside the parentheses: $(2 + 3) = 5$
- **E:** Simplify the exponents: $(5)^2 = 5 \times 5 = 25$
  - The expression now looks like this: $5 + 20 \div 4 \times 25 - 6$
- **MD:** Perform multiplication and division from left to right: $20 \div 4 = 5$; then $5 \times 25 = 125$
  - The expression now looks like this: $5 + 125 - 6$
- **AS:** Perform addition and subtraction from left to right: $5 + 125 = 130$; then $130 - 6 = 124$

> **Review Video: Order of Operations**
> Visit mometrix.com/academy and enter code: 259675

The properties of exponents are as follows:

Property	Description
$a^1 = a$	Any number to the power of 1 is equal to itself
$1^n = 1$	The number 1 raised to any power is equal to 1
$a^0 = 1$	Any number raised to the power of 0 is equal to 1
$a^n \times a^m = a^{n+m}$	Add exponents to multiply powers of the same base number
$a^n \div a^m = a^{n-m}$	Subtract exponents to divide powers of the same base number
$(a^n)^m = a^{n \times m}$	When a power is raised to a power, the exponents are multiplied
$(a \times b)^n = a^n \times b^n$ $(a \div b)^n = a^n \div b^n$	Multiplication and division operations inside parentheses can be raised to a power. This is the same as each term being raised to that power.
$a^{-n} = \dfrac{1}{a^n}$	A negative exponent is the same as the reciprocal of a positive exponent

Note that exponents do not have to be integers. Fractional or decimal exponents follow all the rules above as well. Example: $5^{\frac{1}{4}} \times 5^{\frac{3}{4}} = 5^{\frac{1}{4} + \frac{3}{4}} = 5^1 = 5$.

> **Review Video: Properties of Exponents**
> Visit mometrix.com/academy and enter code: 532558

FACTORS AND GREATEST COMMON FACTOR

Factors are numbers that are multiplied together to obtain a **product**. For example, in the equation $2 \times 3 = 6$, the numbers 2 and 3 are factors. A **prime number** has only two factors (1 and itself), but other numbers can have many factors.

A **common factor** is a number that divides exactly into two or more other numbers. For example, the factors of 12 are 1, 2, 3, 4, 6, and 12, while the factors of 15 are 1, 3, 5, and 15. The common factors of 12 and 15 are 1 and 3.

A **prime factor** is also a prime number. Therefore, the prime factors of 12 are 2 and 3. For 15, the prime factors are 3 and 5.

The **greatest common factor** (GCF) is the largest number that is a factor of two or more numbers. For example, the factors of 15 are 1, 3, 5, and 15; the factors of 35 are 1, 5, 7, and 35. Therefore, the greatest common factor of 15 and 35 is 5.

> **Review Video: Factors**
> Visit mometrix.com/academy and enter code: 920086
>
> **Review Video: Prime Numbers and Factorization**
> Visit mometrix.com/academy and enter code: 760669
>
> **Review Video: Greatest Common Factor and Least Common Multiple**
> Visit mometrix.com/academy and enter code: 838699

MULTIPLES AND LEAST COMMON MULTIPLE

Often listed out in multiplication tables, **multiples** are integer increments of a given factor. In other words, dividing a multiple by the factor will result in an integer. For example, the multiples of 7 include: $1 \times 7 = 7, 2 \times 7 = 14, 3 \times 7 = 21, 4 \times 7 = 28, 5 \times 7 = 35$. Dividing 7, 14, 21, 28, or 35 by 7 will result in the integers 1, 2, 3, 4, and 5, respectively.

The **least common multiple** (**LCM**) is the smallest number that is a multiple of two or more numbers. For example, the multiples of 3 include 3, 6, 9, 12, 15, etc.; the multiples of 5 include 5, 10, 15, 20, etc. Therefore, the least common multiple of 3 and 5 is 15.

> **Review Video: Multiples**
> Visit mometrix.com/academy and enter code: 626738

FRACTIONS

A **fraction** is a number that is expressed as one integer written above another integer, with a dividing line between them $\left(\frac{x}{y}\right)$. It represents the **quotient** of the two numbers "x divided by y." It can also be thought of as x out of y equal parts.

The top number of a fraction is called the **numerator**, and it represents the number of parts under consideration. The 1 in $\frac{1}{4}$ means that 1 part out of the whole is being considered in the calculation. The bottom number of a fraction is called the **denominator**, and it represents the total number of equal parts. The 4 in $\frac{1}{4}$ means that the whole consists of 4 equal parts. A fraction cannot have a denominator of zero; this is referred to as "*undefined.*"

Fractions can be manipulated, without changing the value of the fraction, by multiplying or dividing (but not adding or subtracting) both the numerator and denominator by the same number. If you divide both numbers by a common factor, you are **reducing** or simplifying the fraction. Two fractions that have the same value but are expressed differently are known as **equivalent fractions**. For example, $\frac{2}{10}, \frac{3}{15}, \frac{4}{20}$, and $\frac{5}{25}$ are all equivalent fractions. They can also all be reduced or simplified to $\frac{1}{5}$.

When two fractions are manipulated so that they have the same denominator, this is known as finding a **common denominator**. The number chosen to be that common denominator should be the least common multiple of the two original denominators. Example: $\frac{3}{4}$ and $\frac{5}{6}$; the least common multiple of 4 and 6 is 12. Manipulating to achieve the common denominator: $\frac{3}{4} = \frac{9}{12}$; $\frac{5}{6} = \frac{10}{12}$.

> **Review Video: Overview of Fractions**
> Visit mometrix.com/academy and enter code: 262335

PROPER FRACTIONS AND MIXED NUMBERS

A fraction whose denominator is greater than its numerator is known as a **proper fraction**, while a fraction whose numerator is greater than its denominator is known as an **improper fraction**. Proper fractions have values *less than one* and improper fractions have values *greater than one*.

A **mixed number** is a number that contains both an integer and a fraction. Any improper fraction can be rewritten as a mixed number. Example: $\frac{8}{3} = \frac{6}{3} + \frac{2}{3} = 2 + \frac{2}{3} = 2\frac{2}{3}$. Similarly, any mixed number can be rewritten as an improper fraction. Example: $1\frac{3}{5} = 1 + \frac{3}{5} = \frac{5}{5} + \frac{3}{5} = \frac{8}{5}$.

> **Review Video: Improper Fractions and Mixed Numbers**
> Visit mometrix.com/academy and enter code: 211077

ADDING AND SUBTRACTING FRACTIONS

If two fractions have a common denominator, they can be added or subtracted simply by adding or subtracting the two numerators and retaining the same denominator. If the two fractions do not already have the same denominator, one or both of them must be manipulated to achieve a common denominator before they can be added or subtracted. Example: $\frac{1}{2} + \frac{1}{4} = \frac{2}{4} + \frac{1}{4} = \frac{3}{4}$.

> **Review Video: Adding and Subtracting Fractions**
> Visit mometrix.com/academy and enter code: 378080

MULTIPLYING FRACTIONS

Two fractions can be multiplied by multiplying the two numerators to find the new numerator and the two denominators to find the new denominator. Example: $\frac{1}{3} \times \frac{2}{3} = \frac{1 \times 2}{3 \times 3} = \frac{2}{9}$.

DIVIDING FRACTIONS

Two fractions can be divided by flipping the numerator and denominator of the second fraction and then proceeding as though it were a multiplication problem. Example: $\frac{2}{3} \div \frac{3}{4} = \frac{2}{3} \times \frac{4}{3} = \frac{8}{9}$.

> **Review Video: Multiplying and Dividing Fractions**
> Visit mometrix.com/academy and enter code: 473632

MULTIPLYING A MIXED NUMBER BY A WHOLE NUMBER OR A DECIMAL

When multiplying a mixed number by something, it is usually best to convert it to an improper fraction first. Additionally, if the multiplicand is a decimal, it is most often simplest to convert it to a fraction. For instance, to multiply $4\frac{3}{8}$ by 3.5, begin by rewriting each quantity as a whole number plus a proper fraction. Remember, a mixed number is a fraction added to a whole number and a decimal is a representation of the sum of fractions, specifically tenths, hundredths, thousandths, and so on:

$$4\frac{3}{8} \times 3.5 = \left(4 + \frac{3}{8}\right) \times \left(3 + \frac{1}{2}\right)$$

Next, the quantities being added need to be expressed with the same denominator. This is achieved by multiplying and dividing the whole number by the denominator of the fraction. Recall that a whole number is equivalent to that number divided by 1:

$$= \left(\frac{4}{1} \times \frac{8}{8} + \frac{3}{8}\right) \times \left(\frac{3}{1} \times \frac{2}{2} + \frac{1}{2}\right)$$

When multiplying fractions, remember to multiply the numerators and denominators separately:

$$= \left(\frac{4 \times 8}{1 \times 8} + \frac{3}{8}\right) \times \left(\frac{3 \times 2}{1 \times 2} + \frac{1}{2}\right)$$

$$= \left(\frac{32}{8} + \frac{3}{8}\right) \times \left(\frac{6}{2} + \frac{1}{2}\right)$$

Now that the fractions have the same denominators, they can be added:

$$= \frac{35}{8} \times \frac{7}{2}$$

Finally, perform the last multiplication and then simplify:

$$= \frac{35 \times 7}{8 \times 2} = \frac{245}{16} = \frac{240}{16} + \frac{5}{16} = 15\frac{5}{16}$$

DECIMALS

Decimals are one way to represent parts of a whole. Using the place value system, each digit to the right of a decimal point denotes the number of units of a corresponding *negative* power of ten. For example, consider the decimal 0.24. We can use a model to represent the decimal. Since a dime is worth one-tenth of a dollar and a penny is worth one-hundredth of a dollar, one possible model to represent this fraction is to have 2 dimes representing the 2 in the tenths place and 4 pennies representing the 4 in the hundredths place:

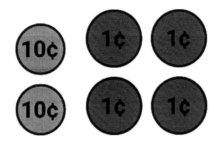

To write the decimal as a fraction, put the decimal in the numerator with 1 in the denominator. Multiply the numerator and denominator by tens until there are no more decimal places. Then simplify the fraction to lowest terms. For example, converting 0.24 to a fraction:

$$0.24 = \frac{0.24}{1} = \frac{0.24 \times 100}{1 \times 100} = \frac{24}{100} = \frac{6}{25}$$

Review Video: Decimals
Visit mometrix.com/academy and enter code: 837268

OPERATIONS WITH DECIMALS
ADDING AND SUBTRACTING DECIMALS

When adding and subtracting decimals, the decimal points must always be aligned. Adding decimals is just like adding regular whole numbers. Example: $4.5 + 2.0 = 6.5$.

If the problem-solver does not properly align the decimal points, an incorrect answer of 4.7 may result. An easy way to add decimals is to align all of the decimal points in a vertical column visually. This will allow you to see exactly where the decimal should be placed in the final answer. Begin adding from right to left. Add each column in turn, making sure to carry the number to the left if a column adds up to more than 9. The same rules apply to the subtraction of decimals.

Review Video: Adding and Subtracting Decimals
Visit mometrix.com/academy and enter code: 381101

MULTIPLYING DECIMALS

A simple multiplication problem has two components: a **multiplicand** and a **multiplier**. When multiplying decimals, work as though the numbers were whole rather than decimals. Once the final product is calculated, count the number of places to the right of the decimal in both the multiplicand and the multiplier. Then, count that number of places from the right of the product and place the decimal in that position.

For example, 12.3×2.56 has a total of three places to the right of the respective decimals. Multiply 123×256 to get 31,488. Now, beginning on the right, count three places to the left and insert the decimal. The final product will be 31.488.

Review Video: How to Multiply Decimals
Visit mometrix.com/academy and enter code: 731574

DIVIDING DECIMALS

Every division problem has a **divisor** and a **dividend**. The dividend is the number that is being divided. In the problem $14 \div 7$, 14 is the dividend and 7 is the divisor. In a division problem with decimals, the divisor must be converted into a whole number. Begin by moving the decimal in the divisor to the right until a whole number is created. Next, move the decimal in the dividend the same number of spaces to the right. For example, 4.9 into 24.5 would become 49 into 245. The decimal was moved one space to the right to create a whole number in the divisor, and then the same was done for the dividend. Once the whole numbers are created, the problem is carried out normally: $245 \div 49 = 5$.

> **Review Video: How to Divide Decimals**
> Visit mometrix.com/academy and enter code: 560690
>
> **Review Video: Dividing Decimals by Whole Numbers**
> Visit mometrix.com/academy and enter code: 535669

PERCENTAGES

Percentages can be thought of as fractions that are based on a whole of 100; that is, one whole is equal to 100%. The word **percent** means "per hundred." Percentage problems are often presented in three main ways:

- Find what percentage of some number another number is.
  - Example: What percentage of 40 is 8?
- Find what number is some percentage of a given number.
  - Example: What number is 20% of 40?
- Find what number another number is a given percentage of.
  - Example: What number is 8 20% of?

There are three components in each of these cases: a **whole** (W), a **part** (P), and a **percentage** (%). These are related by the equation: $P = W \times \%$. This can easily be rearranged into other forms that may suit different questions better: $\% = \frac{P}{W}$ and $W = \frac{P}{\%}$. Percentage problems are often also word problems. As such, a large part of solving them is figuring out which quantities are what. For example, consider the following word problem:

In a school cafeteria, 7 students choose pizza, 9 choose hamburgers, and 4 choose tacos. What percentage of student choose tacos?

To find the whole, you must first add all of the parts: $7 + 9 + 4 = 20$. The percentage can then be found by dividing the part by the whole $\left(\% = \frac{P}{W}\right)$: $\frac{4}{20} = \frac{20}{100} = 20\%$.

> **Review Video: Computation with Percentages**
> Visit mometrix.com/academy and enter code: 693099

CONVERTING BETWEEN PERCENTAGES, FRACTIONS, AND DECIMALS

Converting decimals to percentages and percentages to decimals is as simple as moving the decimal point. To *convert from a decimal to a percentage*, move the decimal point **two places to the right**. To *convert from a percentage to a decimal*, move it **two places to the left**. It may be helpful to remember that the percentage number will always be larger than the equivalent decimal number. Example:

$$0.23 = 23\% \qquad 5.34 = 534\% \qquad 0.007 = 0.7\%$$
$$700\% = 7.00 \qquad 86\% = 0.86 \qquad 0.15\% = 0.0015$$

To convert a fraction to a decimal, simply divide the numerator by the denominator in the fraction. To convert a decimal to a fraction, put the decimal in the numerator with 1 in the denominator. Multiply the numerator and denominator by tens until there are no more decimal places. Then simplify the fraction to lowest terms. For example, converting 0.24 to a fraction:

$$0.24 = \frac{0.24}{1} = \frac{0.24 \times 100}{1 \times 100} = \frac{24}{100} = \frac{6}{25}$$

Fractions can be converted to a percentage by finding equivalent fractions with a denominator of 100. Example:

$$\frac{7}{10} = \frac{70}{100} = 70\% \qquad \frac{1}{4} = \frac{25}{100} = 25\%$$

To convert a percentage to a fraction, divide the percentage number by 100 and reduce the fraction to its simplest possible terms. Example:

$$60\% = \frac{60}{100} = \frac{3}{5} \qquad 96\% = \frac{96}{100} = \frac{24}{25}$$

Review Video: Converting Fractions to Percentages and Decimals
Visit mometrix.com/academy and enter code: 306233

Review Video: Converting Percentages to Decimals and Fractions
Visit mometrix.com/academy and enter code: 287297

Review Video: Converting Decimals to Fractions and Percentages
Visit mometrix.com/academy and enter code: 986765

Review Video: Converting Decimals, Improper Fractions, and Mixed Numbers
Visit mometrix.com/academy and enter code: 696924

PROPORTIONS

A proportion is a relationship between two quantities that dictates how one changes when the other changes. A **direct proportion** describes a relationship in which a quantity increases by a set amount for every increase in the other quantity, or decreases by that same amount for every decrease in the other quantity. Example: Assuming a constant driving speed, the time required for a car trip increases as the distance of the trip increases. The distance to be traveled and the time required to travel are directly proportional.

An **inverse proportion** is a relationship in which an increase in one quantity is accompanied by a decrease in the other, or vice versa. Example: the time required for a car trip decreases as the speed

27

increases and increases as the speed decreases, so the time required is inversely proportional to the speed of the car.

> **Review Video: Proportions**
> Visit mometrix.com/academy and enter code: 505355

RATIOS

A **ratio** is a comparison of two quantities in a particular order. Example: If there are 14 computers in a lab, and the class has 20 students, there is a student to computer ratio of 20 to 14, commonly written as 20: 14. Ratios are normally reduced to their smallest whole number representation, so 20: 14 would be reduced to 10: 7 by dividing both sides by 2.

> **Review Video: Ratios**
> Visit mometrix.com/academy and enter code: 996914

CONSTANT OF PROPORTIONALITY

When two quantities have a proportional relationship, there exists a **constant of proportionality** between the quantities. The product of this constant and one of the quantities is equal to the other quantity. For example, if one lemon costs $0.25, two lemons cost $0.50, and three lemons cost $0.75, there is a proportional relationship between the total cost of lemons and the number of lemons purchased. The constant of proportionality is the **unit price**, namely $0.25/lemon. Notice that the total price of lemons, t, can be found by multiplying the unit price of lemons, p, and the number of lemons, n: $t = pn$.

WORK/UNIT RATE

Unit rate expresses a quantity of one thing in terms of one unit of another. For example, if you travel 30 miles every two hours, a unit rate expresses this comparison in terms of one hour: in one hour you travel 15 miles, so your unit rate is 15 miles per hour. Other examples are how much one ounce of food costs (price per ounce) or figuring out how much one egg costs out of the dozen (price per 1 egg, instead of price per 12 eggs). The denominator of a unit rate is always 1. Unit rates are used to compare different situations to solve problems. For example, to make sure you get the best deal when deciding which kind of soda to buy, you can find the unit rate of each. If soda #1 costs $1.50 for a 1-liter bottle, and soda #2 costs $2.75 for a 2-liter bottle, it would be a better deal to buy soda #2, because its unit rate is only $1.375 per 1-liter, which is cheaper than soda #1. Unit rates can also help determine the length of time a given event will take. For example, if you can paint 2 rooms in 4.5 hours, you can determine how long it will take you to paint 5 rooms by solving for the unit rate per room and then multiplying that by 5.

> **Review Video: Rates and Unit Rates**
> Visit mometrix.com/academy and enter code: 185363

SLOPE

On a graph with two points, (x_1, y_1) and (x_2, y_2), the **slope** is found with the formula $m = \frac{y_2 - y_1}{x_2 - x_1}$; where $x_1 \neq x_2$ and m stands for slope. If the value of the slope is **positive**, the line has an *upward direction* from left to right. If the value of the slope is **negative**, the line has a *downward direction* from left to right. Consider the following example:

A new book goes on sale in bookstores and online stores. In the first month, 5,000 copies of the book are sold. Over time, the book continues to grow in popularity. The data for the number of copies sold is in the table below.

# of Months on Sale	1	2	3	4	5
# of Copies Sold (In Thousands)	5	10	15	20	25

So, the number of copies that are sold and the time that the book is on sale is a proportional relationship. In this example, an equation can be used to show the data: $y = 5x$, where x is the number of months that the book is on sale. Also, y is the number of copies sold. So, the slope of the corresponding line is $\frac{\text{rise}}{\text{run}} = \frac{5}{1} = 5$.

> **Review Video: Finding the Slope of a Line**
> Visit mometrix.com/academy and enter code: 766664

FINDING AN UNKNOWN IN EQUIVALENT EXPRESSIONS

It is often necessary to apply information given about a rate or proportion to a new scenario. For example, if you know that Jedha can run a marathon (26.2 miles) in 3 hours, how long would it take her to run 10 miles at the same pace? Start by setting up equivalent expressions:

$$\frac{26.2 \text{ mi}}{3 \text{ hr}} = \frac{10 \text{ mi}}{x \text{ hr}}$$

Now, cross multiply and solve for x:

$$26.2x = 30$$
$$x = \frac{30}{26.2} = \frac{15}{13.1}$$
$$x \approx 1.15 \text{ hrs } or \text{ 1 hr 9 min}$$

So, at this pace, Jedha could run 10 miles in about 1.15 hours or about 1 hour and 9 minutes.

> **Review Video: Cross Multiply Fractions**
> Visit mometrix.com/academy and enter code: 893904

Algebra

TERMS AND COEFFICIENTS

Mathematical expressions consist of a combination of one or more values arranged in terms that are added together. As such, an expression could be just a single number, including zero. A **variable term** is the product of a real number, also called a **coefficient**, and one or more variables, each of which may be raised to an exponent. Expressions may also include numbers without a variable, called **constants** or **constant terms**. The expression $6s^2$, for example, is a single term where the coefficient is the real number 6 and the variable term is s^2. Note that if a term is written as simply a variable to some exponent, like t^2, then the coefficient is 1, because $t^2 = 1t^2$.

LINEAR EXPRESSIONS

A **single variable linear expression** is the sum of a single variable term, where the variable has no exponent, and a constant, which may be zero. For instance, the expression $2w + 7$ has $2w$ as the variable term and 7 as the constant term. It is important to realize that terms are separated by addition or subtraction. Since an expression is a sum of terms, expressions such as $5x - 3$ can be written as $5x + (-3)$ to emphasize that the constant term is negative. A real-world example of a single variable linear expression is the perimeter of a square, four times the side length, often expressed: $4s$.

In general, a **linear expression** is the sum of any number of variable terms so long as none of the variables have an exponent. For example, $3m + 8n - \frac{1}{4}p + 5.5q - 1$ is a linear expression, but $3y^3$ is not. In the same way, the expression for the perimeter of a general triangle, the sum of the side lengths $(a + b + c)$ is considered to be linear, but the expression for the area of a square, the side length squared (s^2) is not.

LINEAR EQUATIONS

Equations that can be written as $ax + b = 0$, where $a \neq 0$, are referred to as **one variable linear equations**. A solution to such an equation is called a **root**. In the case where we have the equation $5x + 10 = 0$, if we solve for x we get a solution of $x = -2$. In other words, the root of the equation is –2. This is found by first subtracting 10 from both sides, which gives $5x = -10$. Next, simply divide both sides by the coefficient of the variable, in this case 5, to get $x = -2$. This can be checked by plugging –2 back into the original equation $(5)(-2) + 10 = -10 + 10 = 0$.

The **solution set** is the set of all solutions of an equation. In our example, the solution set would simply be –2. If there were more solutions (there usually are in multivariable equations) then they would also be included in the solution set. When an equation has no true solutions, it is referred to as an **empty set**. Equations with identical solution sets are **equivalent equations**. An **identity** is a term whose value or determinant is equal to 1.

Linear equations can be written many ways. Below is a list of some forms linear equations can take:

- **Standard Form**: $Ax + By = C$; the slope is $\frac{-A}{B}$ and the y-intercept is $\frac{C}{B}$
- **Slope Intercept Form**: $y = mx + b$, where m is the slope and b is the y-intercept
- **Point-Slope Form**: $y - y_1 = m(x - x_1)$, where m is the slope and (x_1, y_1) is a point on the line
- **Two-Point Form**: $\frac{y - y_1}{x - x_1} = \frac{y_2 - y_1}{x_2 - x_1}$, where (x_1, y_1) and (x_2, y_2) are two points on the given line
- **Intercept Form**: $\frac{x}{x_1} + \frac{y}{y_1} = 1$, where $(x_1, 0)$ is the point at which a line intersects the x-axis, and $(0, y_1)$ is the point at which the same line intersects the y-axis

> **Review Video: Slope-Intercept and Point-Slope Forms**
> Visit mometrix.com/academy and enter code: 113216
>
> **Review Video: Linear Equations Basics**
> Visit mometrix.com/academy and enter code: 793005

SOLVING ONE-VARIABLE LINEAR EQUATIONS

Multiply all terms by the lowest common denominator to eliminate any fractions. Look for addition or subtraction to undo so you can isolate the variable on one side of the equal sign. Divide both sides by the coefficient of the variable. When you have a value for the variable, substitute this value into the original equation to make sure you have a true equation. Consider the following example:

Kim's savings are represented by the table below. Represent her savings, using an equation.

X (Months)	Y (Total Savings)
2	$1,300
5	$2,050
9	$3,050
11	$3,550
16	$4,800

The table shows a function with a constant rate of change, or slope, of 250. Given the points on the table, the slopes can be calculated as $\frac{(2,050-1300)}{(5-2)}$, $\frac{(3,050-2,050)}{(9-5)}$, $\frac{(3,550-3,050)}{(11-9)}$, and $\frac{(4,800-3,550)}{(16-11)}$, each of which equals 250. Thus, the table shows a constant rate of change, indicating a linear function. The slope-intercept form of a linear equation is written as $y = mx + b$, where m represents the slope and b represents the y-intercept. Substituting the slope into this form gives $y = 250x + b$. Substituting corresponding x- and y-values from any point into this equation will give the y-intercept, or b. Using the point, $(2, 1,300)$, gives $1,300 = 250(2) + b$, which simplifies as $b = 800$. Thus, her savings may be represented by the equation, $y = 250x + 800$.

RULES FOR MANIPULATING EQUATIONS
LIKE TERMS

Like terms are terms in an equation that have the same variable, regardless of whether or not they also have the same coefficient. This includes terms that *lack* a variable; all constants (i.e., numbers without variables) are considered like terms. If the equation involves terms with a variable raised to different powers, the like terms are those that have the variable raised to the same power.

For example, consider the equation $x^2 + 3x + 2 = 2x^2 + x - 7 + 2x$. In this equation, 2 and –7 are like terms; they are both constants. $3x$, x, and $2x$ are like terms, they all include the variable x raised to the first power. x^2 and $2x^2$ are like terms, they both include the variable x, raised to the second power. $2x$ and $2x^2$ are not like terms; although they both involve the variable x, the variable is not raised to the same power in both terms. The fact that they have the same coefficient, 2, is not relevant.

> **Review Video: Rules for Manipulating Equations**
> Visit mometrix.com/academy and enter code: 838871

CARRYING OUT THE SAME OPERATION ON BOTH SIDES OF AN EQUATION

When solving an equation, the general procedure is to carry out a series of operations on both sides of an equation, choosing operations that will tend to simplify the equation when doing so. The reason why the same operation must be carried out on both sides of the equation is because that leaves the meaning of the equation unchanged, and yields a result that is equivalent to the original equation. This would not be the case if we carried out an operation on one side of an equation and not the other. Consider what an equation means: it is a statement that two values or expressions are equal. If we carry out the same operation on both sides of the equation—add 3 to both sides, for example—then the two sides of the equation are changed in the same way, and so remain equal. If we do that to only one side of the equation—add 3 to one side but not the other—then that wouldn't be true; if we change one side of the equation but not the other then the two sides are no longer equal.

ADVANTAGE OF COMBINING LIKE TERMS

Combining like terms refers to adding or subtracting like terms—terms with the same variable—and therefore reducing sets of like terms to a single term. The main advantage of doing this is that it simplifies the equation. Often, combining like terms can be done as the first step in solving an equation, though it can also be done later, such as after distributing terms in a product.

For example, consider the equation $2(x + 3) + 3(2 + x + 3) = -4$. The 2 and the 3 in the second set of parentheses are like terms, and we can combine them, yielding $2(x + 3) + 3(x + 5) = -4$. Now we can carry out the multiplications implied by the parentheses, distributing the outer 2 and 3 accordingly: $2x + 6 + 3x + 15 = -4$. The $2x$ and the $3x$ are like terms, and we can add them together: $5x + 6 + 15 = -4$. Now, the constants 6, 15, and –4 are also like terms, and we can combine them as well: subtracting 6 and 15 from both sides of the equation, we get $5x = -4 - 6 - 15$, or $5x = -25$, which simplifies further to $x = -5$.

> **Review Video: Solving Equations by Combining Like Terms**
> Visit mometrix.com/academy and enter code: 668506

CANCELING TERMS ON OPPOSITE SIDES OF AN EQUATION

Two terms on opposite sides of an equation can be canceled if and only if they *exactly* match each other. They must have the same variable raised to the same power and the same coefficient. For example, in the equation $3x + 2x^2 + 6 = 2x^2 - 6$, $2x^2$ appears on both sides of the equation and can be canceled, leaving $3x + 6 = -6$. The 6 on each side of the equation *cannot* be canceled, because it is added on one side of the equation and subtracted on the other. While they cannot be canceled, however, the 6 and –6 are like terms and can be combined, yielding $3x = -12$, which simplifies further to $x = -4$.

It's also important to note that the terms to be canceled must be independent terms and cannot be part of a larger term. For example, consider the equation $2(x + 6) = 3(x + 4) + 1$. We cannot cancel the x's, because even though they match each other they are part of the larger terms $2(x + 6)$ and $3(x + 4)$. We must first distribute the 2 and 3, yielding $2x + 12 = 3x + 12 + 1$. Now we see that the terms with the x's do not match, but the 12s do, and can be canceled, leaving $2x = 3x + 1$, which simplifies to $x = -1$.

PROCESS FOR MANIPULATING EQUATIONS
ISOLATING VARIABLES

To **isolate a variable** means to manipulate the equation so that the variable appears by itself on one side of the equation, and does not appear at all on the other side. Generally, an equation or inequality is considered to be solved once the variable is isolated and the other side of the equation or inequality is simplified as much as possible. In the case of a two-variable equation or inequality, only one variable needs to be isolated; it will not usually be possible to simultaneously isolate both variables.

For a linear equation—an equation in which the variable only appears raised to the first power—isolating a variable can be done by first moving all the terms with the variable to one side of the equation and all other terms to the other side. (*Moving* a term really means adding the inverse of the term to both sides; when a term is *moved* to the other side of the equation its sign is flipped.)

Then combine like terms on each side. Finally, divide both sides by the coefficient of the variable, if applicable. The steps need not necessarily be done in this order, but this order will always work.

EQUATIONS WITH MORE THAN ONE SOLUTION

Some types of non-linear equations, such as equations involving squares of variables, may have more than one solution. For example, the equation $x^2 = 4$ has two solutions: 2 and –2. Equations with absolute values can also have multiple solutions: $|x| = 1$ has the solutions $x = 1$ and $x = -1$.

It is also possible for a linear equation to have more than one solution, but only if the equation is true regardless of the value of the variable. In this case, the equation is considered to have infinitely many solutions, because any possible value of the variable is a solution. We know a linear equation has infinitely many solutions if when we combine like terms the variables cancel, leaving a true statement. For example, consider the equation $2(3x + 5) = x + 5(x + 2)$. Distributing, we get $6x + 10 = x + 5x + 10$; combining like terms gives $6x + 10 = 6x + 10$, and the $6x$-terms cancel to leave $10 = 10$. This is clearly true, so the original equation is true for any value of x. We could also have canceled the 10s leaving $0 = 0$, but again this is clearly true—in general if both sides of the equation match exactly, it has infinitely many solutions.

EQUATIONS WITH NO SOLUTION

Some types of non-linear equations, such as equations involving squares of variables, may have no solution. For example, the equation $x^2 = -2$ has no solutions in the real numbers, because the square of any real number must be positive. Similarly, $|x| = -1$ has no solution, because the absolute value of a number is always positive.

It is also possible for an equation to have no solution even if does not involve any powers greater than one, absolute values, or other special functions. For example, the equation $2(x + 3) + x = 3x$ has no solution. We can see that if we try to solve it: first we distribute, leaving $2x + 6 + x = 3x$. But now if we try to combine all the terms with the variable, we find that they cancel: we have $3x$ on the left and $3x$ on the right, canceling to leave us with $6 = 0$. This is clearly false. In general, whenever the variable terms in an equation cancel leaving different constants on both sides, it means that the equation has no solution. (If we are left with the *same* constant on both sides, the equation has infinitely many solutions instead.)

FEATURES OF EQUATIONS THAT REQUIRE SPECIAL TREATMENT

LINEAR EQUATIONS

A linear equation is an equation in which variables only appear by themselves: not multiplied together, not with exponents other than one, and not inside absolute value signs or any other functions. For example, the equation $x + 1 - 3x = 5 - x$ is a linear equation; while x appears multiple times, it never appears with an exponent other than one, or inside any function. The two-variable equation $2x - 3y = 5 + 2x$ is also a linear equation. In contrast, the equation $x^2 - 5 = 3x$ is *not* a linear equation, because it involves the term x^2. $\sqrt{x} = 5$ is not a linear equation, because it involves a square root. $(x - 1)^2 = 4$ is not a linear equation because even though there's no exponent on the x directly, it appears as part of an expression that is squared. The two-variable equation $x + xy - y = 5$ is not a linear equation because it includes the term xy, where two variables are multiplied together.

Linear equations can always be solved (or shown to have no solution) by combining like terms and performing simple operations on both sides of the equation. Some non-linear equations can be solved by similar methods, but others may require more advanced methods of solution, if they can be solved analytically at all.

SOLVING EQUATIONS INVOLVING ROOTS

In an equation involving roots, the first step is to isolate the term with the root, if possible, and then raise both sides of the equation to the appropriate power to eliminate it. Consider an example equation, $2\sqrt{x+1} - 1 = 3$. In this case, begin by adding 1 to both sides, yielding $2\sqrt{x+1} = 4$, and then dividing both sides by 2, yielding $\sqrt{x+1} = 2$. Now square both sides, yielding $x + 1 = 4$. Finally, subtracting 1 from both sides yields $x = 3$.

Squaring both sides of an equation may, however, yield a spurious solution—a solution to the squared equation that is *not* a solution of the original equation. It's therefore necessary to plug the solution back into the original equation to make sure it works. In this case, it does: $2\sqrt{3+1} - 1 = 2\sqrt{4} - 1 = 2(2) - 1 = 4 - 1 = 3$.

The same procedure applies for other roots as well. For example, given the equation $3 + \sqrt[3]{2x} = 5$, we can first subtract 3 from both sides, yielding $\sqrt[3]{2x} = 2$ and isolating the root. Raising both sides to the third power yields $2x = 2^3$; i.e., $2x = 8$. We can now divide both sides by 2 to get $x = 4$.

> **Review Video: Solving Equations Involving Roots**
> Visit mometrix.com/academy and enter code: 297670

SOLVING EQUATIONS WITH EXPONENTS

To solve an equation involving an exponent, the first step is to isolate the variable with the exponent. We can then take the appropriate root of both sides to eliminate the exponent. For instance, for the equation $2x^3 + 17 = 5x^3 - 7$, we can subtract $5x^3$ from both sides to get $-3x^3 + 17 = -7$, and then subtract 17 from both sides to get $-3x^3 = -24$. Finally, we can divide both sides by –3 to get $x^3 = 8$. Finally, we can take the cube root of both sides to get $x = \sqrt[3]{8} = 2$.

One important but often overlooked point is that equations with an exponent greater than 1 may have more than one answer. The solution to $x^2 = 9$ isn't simply $x = 3$; it's $x = \pm 3$ (that is, $x = 3$ or $x = -3$). For a slightly more complicated example, consider the equation $(x - 1)^2 - 1 = 3$. Adding 1 to both sides yields $(x - 1)^2 = 4$; taking the square root of both sides yields $x - 1 = 2$. We can then add 1 to both sides to get $x = 3$. However, there's a second solution. We also have the possibility that $x - 1 = -2$, in which case $x = -1$. Both $x = 3$ and $x = -1$ are valid solutions, as can be verified by substituting them both into the original equation.

> **Review Video: Solving Equations with Exponents**
> Visit mometrix.com/academy and enter code: 514557

SOLVING EQUATIONS WITH ABSOLUTE VALUES

When solving an equation with an absolute value, the first step is to isolate the absolute value term. We then consider two possibilities: when the expression inside the absolute value is positive or when it is negative. In the former case, the expression in the absolute value equals the expression on the other side of the equation; in the latter, it equals the additive inverse of that expression—the expression times negative one. We consider each case separately and finally check for spurious solutions.

For instance, consider solving $|2x - 1| + x = 5$ for x. We can first isolate the absolute value by moving the x to the other side: $|2x - 1| = -x + 5$. Now, we have two possibilities. First, that $2x - 1$ is positive, and hence $2x - 1 = -x + 5$. Rearranging and combining like terms yields $3x = 6$, and hence $x = 2$. The other possibility is that $2x - 1$ is negative, and hence $2x - 1 = -(-x + 5) = x - 5$. In this case, rearranging and combining like terms yields $x = -4$. Substituting $x = 2$ and $x = -4$ back into the original equation, we see that they are both valid solutions.

Note that the absolute value of a sum or difference applies to the sum or difference as a whole, not to the individual terms; in general, $|2x - 1|$ is not equal to $|2x + 1|$ or to $|2x| - 1$.

SPURIOUS SOLUTIONS

A **spurious solution** may arise when we square both sides of an equation as a step in solving it or under certain other operations on the equation. It is a solution to the squared or otherwise modified equation that is *not* a solution of the original equation. To identify a spurious solution, it's useful when you solve an equation involving roots or absolute values to plug the solution back into the original equation to make sure it's valid.

CHOOSING WHICH VARIABLE TO ISOLATE IN TWO-VARIABLE EQUATIONS

Similar to methods for a one-variable equation, solving a two-variable equation involves isolating a variable: manipulating the equation so that a variable appears by itself on one side of the equation, and not at all on the other side. However, in a two-variable equation, you will usually only be able to isolate one of the variables; the other variable may appear on the other side along with constant terms, or with exponents or other functions.

Often one variable will be much more easily isolated than the other, and therefore that's the variable you should choose. If one variable appears with various exponents, and the other is only raised to the first power, the latter variable is the one to isolate: given the equation $a^2 + 2b = a^3 + b + 3$, the b only appears to the first power, whereas a appears squared and cubed, so b is the variable that can be solved for: combining like terms and isolating the b on the left side of the equation, we get $b = a^3 - a^2 + 3$. If both variables are equally easy to isolate, then it's best to isolate the independent variable, if one is defined; if the two variables are x and y, the convention is that y is the independent variable.

GRAPHICAL SOLUTIONS TO EQUATIONS

When equations are shown graphically, they are usually shown on a **Cartesian coordinate plane**. The Cartesian coordinate plane consists of two number lines placed perpendicular to each other and intersecting at the zero point, also known as the origin. The horizontal number line is known as the x-axis, with positive values to the right of the origin, and negative values to the left of the origin. The vertical number line is known as the y-axis, with positive values above the origin, and negative values below the origin. Any point on the plane can be identified by an ordered pair in the form (x, y), called coordinates. The x-value of the coordinate is called the abscissa, and the y-value of the coordinate is called the ordinate. The two number lines divide the plane into **four quadrants**: I, II, III, and IV.

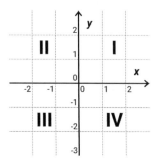

Note that in quadrant I $x > 0$ and $y > 0$, in quadrant II $x < 0$ and $y > 0$, in quadrant III $x < 0$ and $y < 0$, and in quadrant IV $x > 0$ and $y < 0$.

Recall that if the value of the slope of a line is positive, the line slopes upward from left to right. If the value of the slope is negative, the line slopes downward from left to right. If the y-coordinates are the same for two points on a line, the slope is 0 and the line is a **horizontal line**. If the x-coordinates are the same for two points on a line, there is no slope and the line is a **vertical line**. Two or more lines that have equivalent slopes are **parallel lines**. **Perpendicular lines** have slopes that are negative reciprocals of each other, such as $\frac{a}{b}$ and $\frac{-b}{a}$.

> **Review Video: Cartesian Coordinate Plane and Graphing**
> Visit mometrix.com/academy and enter code: 115173

GRAPHING EQUATIONS IN TWO VARIABLES

One way of graphing an equation in two variables is to plot enough points to get an idea for its shape and then draw the appropriate curve through those points. A point can be plotted by substituting in a value for one variable and solving for the other. If the equation is linear, we only need two points and can then draw a straight line between them.

For example, consider the equation $y = 2x - 1$. This is a linear equation—both variables only appear raised to the first power—so we only need two points. When $x = 0$, $y = 2(0) - 1 = -1$. When $x = 2$, $y = 2(2) - 1 = 3$. We can therefore choose the points $(0, -1)$ and $(2, 3)$, and draw a line between them:

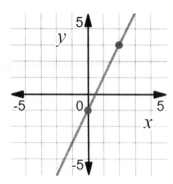

WORKING WITH INEQUALITIES

Commonly in algebra and other upper-level fields of math you find yourself working with mathematical expressions that do not equal each other. The statement comparing such expressions

with symbols such as $<$ (less than) or $>$ (greater than) is called an *inequality*. An example of an inequality is $7x > 5$. To solve for x, simply divide both sides by 7 and the solution is shown to be $x > \frac{5}{7}$. Graphs of the solution set of inequalities are represented on a number line. Open circles are used to show that an expression approaches a number but is never quite equal to that number.

> **Review Video: Solving Multi-Step Inequalities**
> Visit mometrix.com/academy and enter code: 347842
>
> **Review Video: Solving Inequalities Using All 4 Basic Operations**
> Visit mometrix.com/academy and enter code: 401111

Conditional inequalities are those with certain values for the variable that will make the condition true and other values for the variable where the condition will be false. **Absolute inequalities** can have any real number as the value for the variable to make the condition true, while there is no real number value for the variable that will make the condition false. Solving inequalities is done by following the same rules for solving equations with the exception that when multiplying or dividing by a negative number the direction of the inequality sign must be flipped or reversed. **Double inequalities** are situations where two inequality statements apply to the same variable expression. Example: $-c < ax + b < c$.

> **Review Video: Conditional and Absolute Inequalities**
> Visit mometrix.com/academy and enter code: 980164

DETERMINING SOLUTIONS TO INEQUALITIES

To determine whether a coordinate is a solution of an inequality, you can substitute the values of the coordinate into the inequality, simplify, and check whether the resulting statement holds true. For instance, to determine whether $(-2,4)$ is a solution of the inequality $y \geq -2x + 3$, substitute the values into the inequality, $4 \geq -2(-2) + 3$. Simplify the right side of the inequality and the result is $4 \geq 7$, which is a false statement. Therefore, the coordinate is not a solution of the inequality. You can also use this method to determine which part of the graph of an inequality is shaded. The graph of $y \geq -2x + 3$ includes the solid line $y = -2x + 3$ and, since it excludes the point $(-2,4)$ to the left of the line, it is shaded to the right of the line.

> **Review Video: Graphing Linear Inequalities**
> Visit mometrix.com/academy and enter code: 439421

FLIPPING INEQUALITY SIGNS

When given an inequality, we can always turn the entire inequality around, swapping the two sides of the inequality and changing the inequality sign. For instance, $x + 2 > 2x - 3$ is equivalent to $2x - 3 < x + 2$. Aside from that, normally the inequality does not change if we carry out the same operation on both sides of the inequality. There is, however, one principal exception: if we *multiply* or *divide* both sides of the inequality by a *negative number*, the inequality is flipped. For example, if we take the inequality $-2x < 6$ and divide both sides by –2, the inequality flips and we are left with $x > -3$. This *only* applies to multiplication and division, and only with negative numbers. Multiplying or dividing both sides by a positive number, or adding or subtracting any number regardless of sign, does not flip the inequality. Another special case that flips the inequality sign is when reciprocals are used. For instance, $3 > 2$ but the relation of the reciprocals is $\frac{1}{2} < \frac{1}{3}$.

COMPOUND INEQUALITIES

A **compound inequality** is an equality that consists of two inequalities combined with *and* or *or*. The two components of a proper compound inequality must be of opposite type: that is, one must be greater than (or greater than or equal to), the other less than (or less than or equal to). For instance, "$x + 1 < 2$ or $x + 1 > 3$" is a compound inequality, as is "$2x \geq 4$ and $2x \leq 6$." An *and* inequality can be written more compactly by having one inequality on each side of the common part: "$2x \geq 1$ and $2x \leq 6$," can also be written as $1 \leq 2x \leq 6$.

In order for the compound inequality to be meaningful, the two parts of an *and* inequality must overlap; otherwise, no numbers satisfy the inequality. On the other hand, if the two parts of an *or* inequality overlap, then *all* numbers satisfy the inequality and as such the inequality is usually not meaningful.

Solving a compound inequality requires solving each part separately. For example, given the compound inequality "$x + 1 < 2$ or $x + 1 > 3$," the first inequality, $x + 1 < 2$, reduces to $x < 1$, and the second part, $x + 1 > 3$, reduces to $x > 2$, so the whole compound inequality can be written as "$x < 1$ or $x > 2$." Similarly, $1 \leq 2x \leq 6$ can be solved by dividing each term by 2, yielding $\frac{1}{2} \leq x \leq 3$.

> **Review Video: Compound Inequalities**
> Visit mometrix.com/academy and enter code: 786318

SOLVING INEQUALITIES INVOLVING ABSOLUTE VALUES

To solve an inequality involving an absolute value, first isolate the term with the absolute value. Then proceed to treat the two cases separately as with an absolute value equation, but flipping the inequality in the case where the expression in the absolute value is negative (since that essentially involves multiplying both sides by –1.) The two cases are then combined into a compound inequality; if the absolute value is on the greater side of the inequality, then it is an *or* compound inequality, if on the lesser side, then it's an *and*.

Consider the inequality $2 + |x - 1| \geq 3$. We can isolate the absolute value term by subtracting 2 from both sides: $|x - 1| \geq 1$. Now, we're left with the two cases $x - 1 \geq 1$ or $x - 1 \leq -1$: note that in the latter, negative case, the inequality is flipped. $x - 1 \geq 1$ reduces to $x \geq 2$, and $x - 1 \leq -1$ reduces to $x \leq 0$. Since in the inequality $|x - 1| \geq 1$ the absolute value is on the greater side, the two cases combine into an *or* compound inequality, so the final, solved inequality is "$x \leq 0$ or $x \geq 2$."

> **Review Video: Solving Absolute Value Inequalities**
> Visit mometrix.com/academy and enter code: 997008

SOLVING INEQUALITIES INVOLVING SQUARE ROOTS

Solving an inequality with a square root involves two parts. First, we solve the inequality as if it were an equation, isolating the square root and then squaring both sides of the equation. Second, we restrict the solution to the set of values of x for which the value inside the square root sign is non-negative.

For example, in the inequality, $\sqrt{x - 2} + 1 < 5$, we can isolate the square root by subtracting 1 from both sides, yielding $\sqrt{x - 2} < 4$. Squaring both sides of the inequality yields $x - 2 < 16$, so $x < 18$. Since we can't take the square root of a negative number, we also require the part inside the square root to be non-negative. In this case, that means $x - 2 \geq 0$. Adding 2 to both sides of the inequality yields $x \geq 2$. Our final answer is a compound inequality combining the two simple inequalities: $x \geq 2$ and $x < 18$, or $2 \leq x < 18$.

Note that we only get a compound inequality if the two simple inequalities are in opposite directions; otherwise, we take the one that is more restrictive.

The same technique can be used for other even roots, such as fourth roots. It is *not*, however, used for cube roots or other odd roots—negative numbers *do* have cube roots, so the condition that the quantity inside the root sign cannot be negative does not apply.

> **Review Video: <u>Solving Inequalities Involving Square Roots</u>**
> Visit mometrix.com/academy and enter code: 800288

SPECIAL CIRCUMSTANCES

Sometimes an inequality involving an absolute value or an even exponent is true for all values of x, and we don't need to do any further work to solve it. This is true if the inequality, once the absolute value or exponent term is isolated, says that term is greater than a negative number (or greater than or equal to zero). Since an absolute value or a number raised to an even exponent is *always* non-negative, this inequality is always true.

GRAPHICAL SOLUTIONS TO INEQUALITIES

GRAPHING SIMPLE INEQUALITIES

To graph a simple inequality, we first mark on the number line the value that signifies the end point of the inequality. If the inequality is strict (involves a less than or greater than), we use a hollow circle; if it is not strict (less than or equal to or greater than or equal to), we use a solid circle. We then fill in the part of the number line that satisfies the inequality: to the left of the marked point for less than (or less than or equal to), to the right for greater than (or greater than or equal to).

For example, we would graph the inequality $x < 5$ by putting a hollow circle at 5 and filling in the part of the line to the left:

GRAPHING COMPOUND INEQUALITIES

To graph a compound inequality, we fill in both parts of the inequality for an *or* inequality, or the overlap between them for an *and* inequality. More specifically, we start by plotting the endpoints of each inequality on the number line. For an *or* inequality, we then fill in the appropriate side of the line for each inequality. Typically, the two component inequalities do not overlap, which means the shaded part is *outside* the two points. For an *and* inequality, we instead fill in the part of the line that meets both inequalities.

For the inequality "$x \leq -3$ or $x > 4$," we first put a solid circle at –3 and a hollow circle at 4. We then fill the parts of the line *outside* these circles:

GRAPHING INEQUALITIES INCLUDING ABSOLUTE VALUES

An inequality with an absolute value can be converted to a compound inequality. To graph the inequality, first convert it to a compound inequality, and then graph that normally. If the absolute value is on the greater side of the inequality, we end up with an *or* inequality; we plot the endpoints of the inequality on the number line and fill in the part of the line *outside* those points. If the absolute value is on the smaller side of the inequality, we end up with an *and* inequality; we plot the endpoints of the inequality on the number line and fill in the part of the line *between* those points.

For example, the inequality $|x + 1| \geq 4$ can be rewritten as $x \geq 3$ or $x \leq -5$. We place solid circles at the points 3 and –5 and fill in the part of the line *outside* them:

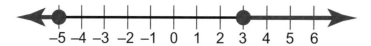

GRAPHING INEQUALITIES IN TWO VARIABLES

To graph an inequality in two variables, we first graph the border of the inequality. This means graphing the equation that we get if we replace the inequality sign with an equals sign. If the inequality is strict ($>$ or $<$), we graph the border with a dashed or dotted line; if it is not strict ($\geq$ or $\leq$), we use a solid line. We can then test any point not on the border to see if it satisfies the inequality. If it does, we shade in that side of the border; if not, we shade in the other side. As an example, consider $y > 2x + 2$. To graph this inequality, we first graph the border, $y = 2x + 2$. Since it is a strict inequality, we use a dashed line. Then, we choose a test point. This can be any point not on the border; in this case, we will choose the origin, (0,0). (This makes the calculation easy and is generally a good choice unless the border passes through the origin.) Putting this into the original inequality, we get $0 > 2(0) + 2$, i.e., $0 > 2$. This is *not* true, so we shade in the side of the border that does *not* include the point (0,0):

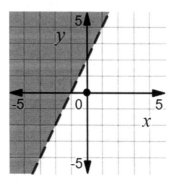

GRAPHING COMPOUND INEQUALITIES IN TWO VARIABLES

One way to graph a compound inequality in two variables is to first graph each of the component inequalities. For an *and* inequality, we then shade in only the parts where the two graphs overlap; for an *or* inequality, we shade in any region that pertains to either of the individual inequalities.

Consider the graph of "$y \geq x - 1$ and $y \leq -x$":

We first shade in the individual inequalities:

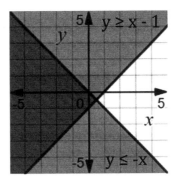

Now, since the compound inequality has an *and*, we only leave shaded the overlap—the part that pertains to *both* inequalities:

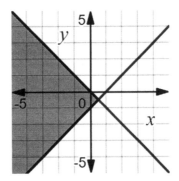

If instead the inequality had been "$y \geq x - 1$ or $y \leq -x$," our final graph would involve the *total* shaded area:

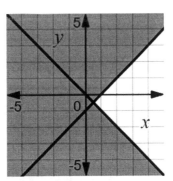

Review Video: Graphing Solutions to Inequalities
Visit mometrix.com/academy and enter code: 391281

SOLVING SYSTEMS OF EQUATIONS

A **system of equations** is a set of simultaneous equations that all use the same variables. A solution to a system of equations must be true for each equation in the system. **Consistent systems** are those with at least one solution. **Inconsistent systems** are systems of equations that have no solution.

SUBSTITUTION

To solve a system of linear equations by **substitution**, start with the easier equation and solve for one of the variables. Express this variable in terms of the other variable. Substitute this expression in the other equation and solve for the other variable. The solution should be expressed in the form (x, y). Substitute the values into both of the original equations to check your answer. Consider the following system of equations:

$$x + 6y = 15$$
$$3x - 12y = 18$$

Solving the first equation for x: $x = 15 - 6y$

Substitute this value in place of x in the second equation, and solve for y:

$$3(15 - 6y) - 12y = 18$$
$$45 - 18y - 12y = 18$$
$$30y = 27$$
$$y = \frac{27}{30} = \frac{9}{10} = 0.9$$

Plug this value for y back into the first equation to solve for x:

$$x = 15 - 6(0.9) = 15 - 5.4 = 9.6$$

Check both equations if you have time:

$$9.6 + 6(0.9) = 15 \qquad 3(9.6) - 12(0.9) = 18$$
$$9.6 + 5.4 = 15 \qquad 28.8 - 10.8 = 18$$
$$15 = 15 \qquad 18 = 18$$

Therefore, the solution is (9.6, 0.9).

ELIMINATION

To solve a system of equations using **elimination**, begin by rewriting both equations in standard form $Ax + By = C$. Check to see if the coefficients of one pair of like variables add to zero. If not, multiply one or both of the equations by a non-zero number to make one set of like variables add to zero. Add the two equations to solve for one of the variables. Substitute this value into one of the original equations to solve for the other variable. Check your work by substituting into the other equation. Now, let's look at solving the following system using the elimination method:

$$5x + 6y = 4$$
$$x + 2y = 4$$

If we multiply the second equation by -3, we can eliminate the y-terms:

$$5x + 6y = 4$$
$$-3x - 6y = -12$$

Add the equations together and solve for x:

$$2x = -8$$
$$x = \frac{-8}{2} = -4$$

Plug the value for x back in to either of the original equations and solve for y:

$$-4 + 2y = 4$$
$$y = \frac{4+4}{2} = 4$$

Check both equations if you have time:

$$5(-4) + 6(4) = 4 \qquad -4 + 2(4) = 4$$
$$-20 + 24 = 4 \qquad -4 + 8 = 4$$
$$4 = 4 \qquad 4 = 4$$

Therefore, the solution is $(-4, 4)$.

> **Review Video: The Elimination Method**
> Visit mometrix.com/academy and enter code: 449121

GRAPHICALLY

To solve a system of linear equations **graphically**, plot both equations on the same graph. The solution of the equations is the point where both lines cross. If the lines do not cross (are parallel), then there is **no solution**.

For example, consider the following system of equations:

$$y = 2x + 7$$
$$y = -x + 1$$

Since these equations are given in slope-intercept form, they are easy to graph; the y-intercepts of the lines are $(0,7)$ and $(0,1)$. The respective slopes are 2 and -1, thus the graphs look like this:

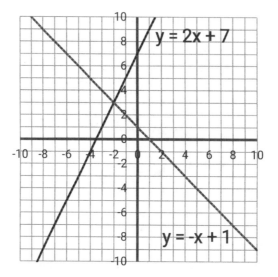

The two lines intersect at the point $(-2,3)$, thus this is the solution to the system of equations.

Solving a system graphically is generally only practical if both coordinates of the solution are integers; otherwise the intersection will lie between gridlines on the graph and the coordinates will be difficult or impossible to determine exactly. It also helps if, as in this example, the equations are in slope-intercept form or some other form that makes them easy to graph. Otherwise, another method of solution (by substitution or elimination) is likely to be more useful.

> **Review Video: Solving Systems by Graphing**
> Visit mometrix.com/academy and enter code: 634812

SOLVING SYSTEMS OF EQUATIONS USING THE TRACE FEATURE

Using the trace feature on a calculator requires that you rewrite each equation, isolating the y-variable on one side of the equal sign. Enter both equations in the graphing calculator and plot the graphs simultaneously. Use the trace cursor to find where the two lines cross. Use the zoom feature if necessary to obtain more accurate results. Always check your answer by substituting into the original equations. The trace method is likely to be less accurate than other methods due to the resolution of graphing calculators but is a useful tool to provide an approximate answer.

SOLVING A SYSTEM OF EQUATIONS CONSISTING OF A LINEAR EQUATION AND A QUADRATIC EQUATION

ALGEBRAICALLY

Generally, the simplest way to solve a system of equations consisting of a linear equation and a quadratic equation algebraically is through the method of substitution. One possible strategy is to solve the linear equation for y and then substitute that expression into the quadratic equation. After expansion and combining like terms, this will result in a new quadratic equation for x, which, like all quadratic equations, may have zero, one, or two solutions. Plugging each solution for x back into one of the original equations will then produce the corresponding value of y.

For example, consider the following system of equations:

$$x + y = 1$$
$$y = (x + 3)^2 - 2$$

We can solve the linear equation for y to yield $y = -x + 1$. Substituting this expression into the quadratic equation produces $-x + 1 = (x + 3)^2 - 2$. We can simplify this equation:

$$-x + 1 = (x + 3)^2 - 2$$
$$-x + 1 = x^2 + 6x + 9 - 2$$
$$-x + 1 = x^2 + 6x + 7$$
$$0 = x^2 + 7x + 6$$

This quadratic equation can be factored as $(x + 1)(x + 6) = 0$. It therefore has two solutions: $x_1 = -1$ and $x_2 = -6$. Plugging each of these back into the original linear equation yields $y_1 = -x_1 + 1 = -(-1) + 1 = 2$ and $y_2 = -x_2 + 1 = -(-6) + 1 = 7$. Thus, this system of equations has two solutions, $(-1,2)$ and $(-6,7)$.

It may help to check your work by putting each x- and y-value back into the original equations and verifying that they do provide a solution.

GRAPHICALLY

To solve a system of equations consisting of a linear equation and a quadratic equation graphically, plot both equations on the same graph. The linear equation will, of course, produce a straight line, while the quadratic equation will produce a parabola. These two graphs will intersect at zero, one, or two points; each point of intersection is a solution of the system.

For example, consider the following system of equations:

$$y = -2x + 2$$
$$y = -2x^2 + 4x + 2$$

The linear equation describes a line with a y-intercept of $(0,2)$ and a slope of -2.

To graph the quadratic equation, we can first find the vertex of the parabola: the x-coordinate of the vertex is $h = -\dfrac{b}{2a} = -\dfrac{4}{2(-2)} = 1$, and the y-coordinate is $k = -2(1)^2 + 4(1) + 2 = 4$. Thus, the vertex lies at $(1,4)$. To get a feel for the rest of the parabola, we can plug in a few more values of x to find more points; by putting in $x = 2$ and $x = 3$ in the quadratic equation, we find that the points

$(2,2)$ and $(3,-4)$ lie on the parabola; by symmetry, so must $(0,2)$ and $(-1,-4)$. We can now plot both equations:

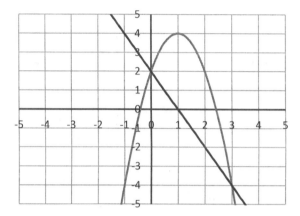

These two curves intersect at the points $(0,2)$ and $(3,-4)$, thus these are the solutions of the equation.

> **Review Video: Solving a System of Equations Consisting of a Linear Equation and Quadratic Equations**
> Visit mometrix.com/academy and enter code: 194870

CALCULATIONS USING POINTS

Sometimes you need to perform calculations using only points on a graph as input data. Using points, you can determine what the **midpoint** and **distance** are. If you know the equation for a line, you can calculate the distance between the line and the point.

To find the **midpoint** of two points (x_1, y_1) and (x_2, y_2), average the x-coordinates to get the x-coordinate of the midpoint, and average the y-coordinates to get the y-coordinate of the midpoint. The formula is: $\left(\frac{x_1+x_2}{2}, \frac{y_1+y_2}{2}\right)$.

The **distance** between two points is the same as the length of the hypotenuse of a right triangle with the two given points as endpoints, and the two sides of the right triangle parallel to the x-axis and y-axis, respectively. The length of the segment parallel to the x-axis is the difference between the x-coordinates of the two points. The length of the segment parallel to the y-axis is the difference between the y-coordinates of the two points. Use the Pythagorean theorem $a^2 + b^2 = c^2$ or $c = \sqrt{a^2 + b^2}$ to find the distance. The formula is $d = \sqrt{(x_2 - x_1)^2 + (y_2 - y_1)^2}$.

When a line is in the format $Ax + By + C = 0$, where A, B, and C are coefficients, you can use a point (x_1, y_1) not on the line and apply the formula $d = \frac{|Ax_1 + By_1 + C|}{\sqrt{A^2 + B^2}}$ to find the distance between the line and the point (x_1, y_1).

> **Review Video: Calculations Using Points on a Graph**
> Visit mometrix.com/academy and enter code: 883228

MONOMIALS AND POLYNOMIALS

A **monomial** is a single constant, variable, or product of constants and variables, such as 7, x, $2x$, or $x^3 y$. There will never be addition or subtraction symbols in a monomial. Like monomials have like variables, but they may have different coefficients. **Polynomials** are algebraic expressions that use addition and subtraction to combine two or more monomials. Two terms make a **binomial**, three terms make a **trinomial**, etc. The **degree of a monomial** is the sum of the exponents of the variables. The **degree of a polynomial** is the highest degree of any individual term.

Review Video: Polynomials
Visit mometrix.com/academy and enter code: 305005

SIMPLIFYING POLYNOMIALS

Simplifying polynomials requires combining like terms. The like terms in a polynomial expression are those that have the same variable raised to the same power. It is often helpful to connect the like terms with arrows or lines in order to separate them from the other monomials. Once you have determined the like terms, you can rearrange the polynomial by placing them together. Remember to include the sign that is in front of each term. Once the like terms are placed together, you can apply each operation and simplify. When adding and subtracting polynomials, only add and subtract the **coefficient**, or the number part; the variable and exponent stay the same.

Review Video: Adding and Subtracting Polynomials
Visit mometrix.com/academy and enter code: 124088

THE FOIL METHOD

In general, multiplying polynomials is done by multiplying each term in one polynomial by each term in the other and adding the results. In the specific case for multiplying binomials, there is a useful acronym, FOIL, that can help you make sure to cover each combination of terms. The **FOIL method** for $(Ax + By)(Cx + Dy)$ would be:

F	Multiply the *first* terms of each binomial	$(Ax + By)(Cx + Dy)$	ACx^2
O	Multiply the *outer* terms	$(Ax + By)(Cx + Dy)$	$ADxy$
I	Multiply the *inner* terms	$(Ax + By)(Cx + Dy)$	$BCxy$
L	Multiply the *last* terms of each binomial	$(Ax + By)(Cx + Dy)$	BDy^2

Then, add up the result of each and combine like terms: $ACx^2 + (AD + BC)xy + BDy^2$.

For example, using the FOIL method on binomials $(x + 2)$ and $(x - 3)$:

$$\text{First:} \quad (\boxed{x} + 2)(\boxed{x} + (-3)) \;\rightarrow\; (x)(x) = x^2$$
$$\text{Outer:} \quad (\boxed{x} + 2)(x + \boxed{(-3)}) \;\rightarrow\; (x)(-3) = -3x$$
$$\text{Inner:} \quad (x + \boxed{2})(\boxed{x} + (-3)) \;\rightarrow\; (2)(x) = 2x$$
$$\text{Last:} \quad (x + \boxed{2})(x + \boxed{(-3)}) \;\rightarrow\; (2)(-3) = -6$$

This results in: $(x^2) + (-3x) + (2x) + (-6)$

Combine like terms: $x^2 + (-3 + 2)x + (-6) = x^2 - x - 6$

Review Video: Multiplying Terms Using the FOIL Method
Visit mometrix.com/academy and enter code: 854792

DIVIDING POLYNOMIALS

Use long division to divide a polynomial by either a monomial or another polynomial of equal or lesser degree.

When **dividing by a monomial**, divide each term of the polynomial by the monomial.

When **dividing by a polynomial**, begin by arranging the terms of each polynomial in order of one variable. You may arrange in ascending or descending order, but be consistent with both polynomials. To get the first term of the quotient, divide the first term of the dividend by the first term of the divisor. Multiply the first term of the quotient by the entire divisor and subtract that product from the dividend. Repeat for the second and successive terms until you either get a remainder of zero or a remainder whose degree is less than the degree of the divisor. If the quotient has a remainder, write the answer as a mixed expression in the form:

$$\text{quotient} + \frac{\text{remainder}}{\text{divisor}}$$

For example, we can evaluate the following expression in the same way as long division:

$$\frac{x^3 - 3x^2 - 2x + 5}{x - 5}$$

$$
\begin{array}{r}
x^2 + 2x + 8 \\
x - 5 \overline{)\ x^3 - 3x^2 - 2x + 5} \\
-(x^3 - 5x^2) \\
\hline
2x^2 - 2x \\
-(2x^2 - 10x) \\
\hline
8x + 5 \\
-(8x - 40) \\
\hline
45
\end{array}
$$

$$\frac{x^3 - 3x^2 - 2x + 5}{x - 5} = x^2 + 2x + 8 + \frac{45}{x - 5}$$

When **factoring** a polynomial, first check for a common monomial factor, that is, look to see if each coefficient has a common factor or if each term has an x in it. If the factor is a trinomial but not a perfect trinomial square, look for a factorable form, such as one of these:

$$x^2 + (a + b)x + ab = (x + a)(x + b)$$
$$(ac)x^2 + (ad + bc)x + bd = (ax + b)(cx + d)$$

For factors with four terms, look for groups to factor. Once you have found the factors, write the original polynomial as the product of all the factors. Make sure all of the polynomial factors are prime. Monomial factors may be *prime* or *composite*. Check your work by multiplying the factors to make sure you get the original polynomial.

Below are patterns of some special products to remember to help make factoring easier:

- Perfect trinomial squares: $x^2 + 2xy + y^2 = (x + y)^2$ or $x^2 - 2xy + y^2 = (x - y)^2$
- Difference between two squares: $x^2 - y^2 = (x + y)(x - y)$

- Sum of two cubes: $x^3 + y^3 = (x + y)(x^2 - xy + y^2)$
  - Note: the second factor is *not* the same as a perfect trinomial square, so do not try to factor it further.
- Difference between two cubes: $x^3 - y^3 = (x - y)(x^2 + xy + y^2)$
  - Again, the second factor is *not* the same as a perfect trinomial square.
- Perfect cubes: $x^3 + 3x^2y + 3xy^2 + y^3 = (x + y)^3$ and $x^3 - 3x^2y + 3xy^2 - y^3 = (x - y)^3$

RATIONAL EXPRESSIONS

Rational expressions are fractions with polynomials in both the numerator and the denominator; the value of the polynomial in the denominator cannot be equal to zero. Be sure to keep track of values that make the denominator of the original expression zero as the final result inherits the same restrictions. For example, a denominator of $x - 3$ indicates that the expression is not defined when $x = 3$ and, as such, regardless of any operations done to the expression, it remains undefined there.

To **add or subtract** rational expressions, first find the common denominator, then rewrite each fraction as an equivalent fraction with the common denominator. Finally, add or subtract the numerators to get the numerator of the answer, and keep the common denominator as the denominator of the answer.

When **multiplying** rational expressions, factor each polynomial and cancel like factors (a factor which appears in both the numerator and the denominator). Then, multiply all remaining factors in the numerator to get the numerator of the product, and multiply the remaining factors in the denominator to get the denominator of the product. Remember: cancel entire factors, not individual terms.

To **divide** rational expressions, take the reciprocal of the divisor (the rational expression you are dividing by) and multiply by the dividend.

> **Review Video: Rational Expressions**
> Visit mometrix.com/academy and enter code: 415183

SIMPLIFYING RATIONAL EXPRESSIONS

To simplify a rational expression, factor the numerator and denominator completely. Factors that are the same and appear in the numerator and denominator have a ratio of 1. For example, look at the following expression:

$$\frac{x - 1}{1 - x^2}$$

The denominator, $(1 - x^2)$, is a difference of squares. It can be factored as $(1 - x)(1 + x)$. The factor $1 - x$ and the numerator $x - 1$ are opposites and have a ratio of -1. Rewrite the numerator as $-1(1 - x)$. So, the rational expression can be simplified as follows:

$$\frac{x - 1}{1 - x^2} = \frac{-1(1 - x)}{(1 - x)(1 + x)} = \frac{-1}{1 + x}$$

Note that since the original expression is only defined for $x \neq \{-1, 1\}$, the simplified expression has the same restrictions.

SOLVING QUADRATIC EQUATIONS

Quadratic equations are a special set of trinomials of the form $y = ax^2 + bx + c$ that occur commonly in math and real-world applications. The **roots** of a quadratic equation are the solutions that satisfy the equation when $y = 0$; in other words, where the graph touches the x-axis. There are several ways to determine these solutions including using the quadratic formula, factoring, completing the square, and graphing the function.

QUADRATIC FORMULA

The **quadratic formula** is used to solve quadratic equations when other methods are more difficult. To use the quadratic formula to solve a quadratic equation, begin by rewriting the equation in standard form $ax^2 + bx + c = 0$, where a, b, and c are coefficients. Once you have identified the values of the coefficients, substitute those values into the quadratic formula

$$x = \frac{-b \pm \sqrt{b^2 - 4ac}}{2a}$$

Evaluate the equation and simplify the expression. Again, check each root by substituting into the original equation. In the quadratic formula, the portion of the formula under the radical ($b^2 - 4ac$) is called the **discriminant**. If the discriminant is zero, there is only one root: $-\frac{b}{2a}$. If the discriminant is positive, there are two different real roots. If the discriminant is negative, there are no real roots; you will instead find complex roots. Often these solutions don't make sense in context and are ignored.

FACTORING

To solve a quadratic equation by factoring, begin by rewriting the equation in standard form, $x^2 + bx + c = 0$. Remember that the goal of factoring is to find numbers f and g such that $(x + f)(x + g) = x^2 + (f + g)x + fg$, in other words $(f + g) = b$ and $fg = c$. This can be a really useful method when b and c are integers. Determine the factors of c and look for pairs that could sum to b.

For example, consider finding the roots of $x^2 + 6x - 16 = 0$. The factors of -16 include, -4 and 4, -8 and 2, -2 and 8, -1 and 16, and 1 and -16. The factors that sum to 6 are -2 and 8. Write these factors as the product of two binomials, $0 = (x - 2)(x + 8)$. Finally, since these binomials multiply together to equal zero, set them each equal to zero and solve each for x. This results in $x - 2 = 0$, which simplifies to $x = 2$ and $x + 8 = 0$, which simplifies to $x = -8$. Therefore, the roots of the equation are 2 and -8.

COMPLETING THE SQUARE

One way to find the roots of a quadratic equation is to find a way to manipulate it such that it follows the form of a perfect square ($x^2 + 2px + p^2$) by adding and subtracting a constant. This process is called **completing the square**. In other words, if you are given a quadratic that is not a perfect square, $x^2 + bx + c = 0$, you can find a constant d that could be added in to make it a perfect square:

$$x^2 + bx + c + (d - d) = 0; \text{ \{Let } b = 2p \text{ and } c + d = p^2\}$$

then:

$$x^2 + 2px + p^2 - d = 0 \text{ and } d = \frac{b^2}{4} - c$$

Once you have completed the square you can find the roots of the resulting equation:

$$x^2 + 2px + p^2 - d = 0$$
$$(x + p)^2 = d$$
$$x + p = \pm\sqrt{d}$$
$$x = -p \pm \sqrt{d}$$

It is worth noting that substituting the original expressions into this solution gives the same result as the quadratic formula where $a = 1$:

$$x = -p \pm \sqrt{d} = -\frac{b}{2} \pm \sqrt{\frac{b^2}{4} - c} = -\frac{b}{2} \pm \frac{\sqrt{b^2 - 4c}}{2} = \frac{-b + \sqrt{b^2 - 4c}}{2}$$

Completing the square can be seen as arranging block representations of each of the terms to be as close to a square as possible and then filling in the gaps. For example, consider the quadratic expression $x^2 + 6x + 2$:

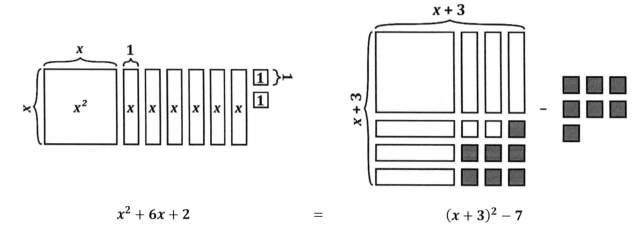

$$x^2 + 6x + 2 \qquad = \qquad (x+3)^2 - 7$$

> **Review Video: Completing the Square**
> Visit mometrix.com/academy and enter code: 982479

USING GIVEN ROOTS TO FIND QUADRATIC EQUATION

One way to find the roots of a quadratic equation is to factor the equation and use the **zero product property**, setting each factor of the equation equal to zero to find the corresponding root. We can use this technique in reverse to find an equation given its roots. Each root corresponds to a linear equation which in turn corresponds to a factor of the quadratic equation.

For example, we can find a quadratic equation whose roots are $x = 2$ and $x = -1$. The root $x = 2$ corresponds to the equation $x - 2 = 0$, and the root $x = -1$ corresponds to the equation $x + 1 = 0$.

These two equations correspond to the factors $(x - 2)$ and $(x + 1)$, from which we can derive the equation $(x - 2)(x + 1) = 0$, or $x^2 - x - 2 = 0$.

Any integer multiple of this entire equation will also yield the same roots, as the integer will simply cancel out when the equation is factored. For example, $2x^2 - 2x - 4 = 0$ factors as $2(x - 2)(x + 1) = 0$.

Functions and Calculus

Algebraic Theorems

ALGEBRAIC THEOREMS

According to the **fundamental theorem of algebra**, every non-constant, single-variable polynomial has exactly as many roots as the polynomial's highest exponent. For example, if x^4 is the largest exponent of a term, the polynomial will have exactly 4 roots. However, some of these roots may have multiplicity or be complex numbers. For instance, in the polynomial function $f(x) = x^4 - 4x + 3$, the only real root is 1, though it has multiplicity of 2 – that is, it occurs twice. The other two roots, $(-1 - i\sqrt{2})$ and $(-1 + i\sqrt{2})$, are complex, consisting of both real and non-real components.

The **remainder theorem** is useful for determining the remainder when a polynomial is divided by a binomial. The remainder theorem states that if a polynomial function $f(x)$ is divided by a binomial $x - a$, where a is a real number, the remainder of the division will be the value of $f(a)$. If $f(a) = 0$, then a is a root of the polynomial.

The **factor theorem** is related to the remainder theorem and states that if $f(a) = 0$ then $(x - a)$ is a factor of the function.

According to the **rational root theorem,** any rational root of a polynomial function $f(x) = a_n x^n + a_{n-1} x^{n-1} + \cdots + a_1 x + a_0$ with integer coefficients will, when reduced to its lowest terms, be a positive or negative fraction such that the numerator is a factor of a_0 and the denominator is a factor of a_n. For instance, if the polynomial function $f(x) = x^3 + 3x^2 - 4$ has any rational roots, the numerators of those roots can only be factors of 4 (1, 2, 4), and the denominators can only be factors of 1 (1). The function in this example has roots of 1 (or $\frac{1}{1}$) and –2 (or $\frac{-2}{1}$).

Basic Functions

FUNCTION AND RELATION

When expressing functional relationships, the **variables** x and y are typically used. These values are often written as the **coordinates** (x, y). The x-value is the independent variable and the y-value is the dependent variable. A **relation** is a set of data in which there is not a unique y-value for each x-value in the dataset. This means that there can be two of the same x-values assigned to different y-values. A relation is simply a relationship between the x- and y-values in each coordinate but does not apply to the relationship between the values of x and y in the data set. A **function** is a relation where one quantity depends on the other. For example, the amount of money that you make depends on the number of hours that you work. In a function, each x-value in the data set has one unique y-value because the y-value depends on the x-value.

FUNCTIONS

A function has exactly one value of **output variable** (dependent variable) for each value of the **input variable** (independent variable). The set of all values for the input variable (here assumed to be x) is the domain of the function, and the set of all corresponding values of the output variable (here assumed to be y) is the range of the function. When looking at a graph of an equation, the easiest way to determine if the equation is a function or not is to conduct the vertical line test. If a vertical line drawn through any value of x crosses the graph in more than one place, the equation is not a function.

DETERMINING A FUNCTION

You can determine whether an equation is a **function** by substituting different values into the equation for x. You can display and organize these numbers in a data table. A **data table** contains the values for x and y, which you can also list as coordinates. In order for a function to exist, the table cannot contain any repeating x-values that correspond with different y-values. If each x-coordinate has a unique y-coordinate, the table contains a function. However, there can be repeating y-values that correspond with different x-values. An example of this is when the function contains an exponent. Example: if $x^2 = y$, $2^2 = 4$, and $(-2)^2 = 4$.

> **Review Video: Definition of a Function**
> Visit mometrix.com/academy and enter code: 784611

FINDING THE DOMAIN AND RANGE OF A FUNCTION

The **domain** of a function $f(x)$ is the set of all input values for which the function is defined. The **range** of a function $f(x)$ is the set of all possible output values of the function—that is, of every possible value of $f(x)$, for any value of x in the function's domain. For a function expressed in a table, every input-output pair is given explicitly. To find the domain, we just list all the x-values and to find the range, we just list all the values of $f(x)$. Consider the following example:

x	–1	4	2	1	0	3	8	6
$f(x)$	3	0	3	–1	–1	2	4	6

In this case, the domain would be $\{-1, 4, 2, 1, 0, 3, 8, 6\}$ or, putting them in ascending order, $\{-1, 0, 1, 2, 3, 4, 6, 8\}$. (Putting the values in ascending order isn't strictly necessary, but generally makes the set easier to read.) The range would be $\{3, 0, 3, -1, -1, 2, 4, 6\}$. Note that some of these values appear more than once. This is entirely permissible for a function; while each value of x must be matched to a unique value of $f(x)$, the converse is not true. We don't need to list each value more than once, so eliminating duplicates, the range is $\{3, 0, -1, 2, 4, 6\}$, or, putting them in ascending order, $\{-1, 0, 2, 3, 4, 6\}$.

Note that by definition of a function, no input value can be matched to more than one output value. It is good to double-check to make sure that the data given follows this and is therefore actually a function.

> **Review Video: Domain and Range**
> Visit mometrix.com/academy and enter code: 778133
>
> **Review Video: Domain and Range of Quadratic Functions**
> Visit mometrix.com/academy and enter code: 331768

WRITING A FUNCTION RULE USING A TABLE

If given a set of data, place the corresponding x- and y-values into a table and analyze the relationship between them. Consider what you can do to each x-value to obtain the corresponding y-value. Try adding or subtracting different numbers to and from x and then try multiplying or dividing different numbers to and from x. If none of these **operations** give you the y-value, try combining the operations. Once you find a rule that works for one pair, make sure to try it with each additional set of ordered pairs in the table. If the same operation or combination of operations satisfies each set of coordinates, then the table contains a function. The rule is then used to write the equation of the function in "$y = f(x)$" form.

DIRECT AND INVERSE VARIATIONS OF VARIABLES

Variables that vary directly are those that either both increase at the same rate or both decrease at the same rate. For example, in the functions $y = kx$ or $y = kx^n$, where k and n are positive, the value of y increases as the value of x increases and decreases as the value of x decreases.

Variables that vary inversely are those where one increases while the other decreases. For example, in the functions $y = \frac{k}{x}$ or $y = \frac{k}{x^n}$ where k and n are positive, the value of y increases as the value of x decreases and decreases as the value of x increases.

In both cases, k is the constant of variation.

PROPERTIES OF FUNCTIONS

There are many different ways to classify functions based on their structure or behavior. Important features of functions include:

- **End behavior**: the behavior of the function at extreme values ($f(x)$ as $x \to \pm\infty$)
- **y-intercept**: the value of the function at $f(0)$
- **Roots**: the values of x where the function equals zero ($f(x) = 0$)
- **Extrema**: minimum or maximum values of the function or where the function changes direction ($f(x) \geq k$ or $f(x) \leq k$)

CLASSIFICATION OF FUNCTIONS

An **invertible function** is defined as a function, $f(x)$, for which there is another function, $f^{-1}(x)$, such that $f^{-1}(f(x)) = x$. For example, if $f(x) = 3x - 2$ the inverse function, $f^{-1}(x)$, can be found:

$$x = 3(f^{-1}(x)) - 2$$
$$\frac{x + 2}{3} = f^{-1}(x)$$

$$f^{-1}(f(x)) = \frac{3x - 2 + 2}{3}$$
$$= \frac{3x}{3}$$
$$= x$$

Note that $f^{-1}(x)$ is a valid function over all values of x.

In a **one-to-one function**, each value of x has exactly one value for y on the coordinate plane (this is the definition of a function) and each value of y has exactly one value for x. While the vertical line test will determine if a graph is that of a function, the horizontal line test will determine if a function is a one-to-one function. If a horizontal line drawn at any value of y intersects the graph in more than one place, the graph is not that of a one-to-one function. Do not make the mistake of using the horizontal line test exclusively in determining if a graph is that of a one-to-one function. A one-to-one function must pass both the vertical line test and the horizontal line test. As such, one-to-one functions are invertible functions.

A **many-to-one function** is a function whereby the relation is a function, but the inverse of the function is not a function. In other words, each element in the domain is mapped to one and only one element in the range. However, one or more elements in the range may be mapped to the same element in the domain. A graph of a many-to-one function would pass the vertical line test, but not the horizontal line test. This is why many-to-one functions are not invertible.

A **monotone function** is a function whose graph either constantly increases or constantly decreases. Examples include the functions $f(x) = x$, $f(x) = -x$, or $f(x) = x^3$.

An **even function** has a graph that is symmetric with respect to the y-axis and satisfies the equation $f(x) = f(-x)$. Examples include the functions $f(x) = x^2$ and $f(x) = ax^n$, where a is any real number and n is a positive even integer.

An **odd function** has a graph that is symmetric with respect to the origin and satisfies the equation $f(x) = -f(-x)$. Examples include the functions $f(x) = x^3$ and $f(x) = ax^n$, where a is any real number and n is a positive odd integer.

> **Review Video: Even and Odd Functions**
> Visit mometrix.com/academy and enter code: 278985

Constant functions are given by the equation $f(x) = b$, where b is a real number. There is no independent variable present in the equation, so the function has a constant value for all x. The graph of a constant function is a horizontal line of slope 0 that is positioned b units from the x-axis. If b is positive, the line is above the x-axis; if b is negative, the line is below the x-axis.

Identity functions are identified by the equation $f(x) = x$, where every value of the function is equal to its corresponding value of x. The only zero is the point (0,0). The graph is a line with a slope of 1.

In **linear functions**, the value of the function changes in direct proportion to x. The rate of change, represented by the slope on its graph, is constant throughout. The standard form of a linear equation is $ax + cy = d$, where a, c, and d are real numbers. As a function, this equation is commonly in the form $y = mx + b$ or $f(x) = mx + b$ where $m = -\frac{a}{c}$ and $b = \frac{d}{c}$. This is known as the slope-intercept form, because the coefficients give the slope of the graphed function (m) and its y-intercept (b). Solve the equation $mx + b = 0$ for x to get $x = -\frac{b}{m}$, which is the only zero of the function. The domain and range are both the set of all real numbers.

> **Review Video: Linear Functions**
> Visit mometrix.com/academy and enter code: 699478

Algebraic functions are those that exclusively use polynomials and roots. These would include polynomial functions, rational functions, square root functions, and all combinations of these functions, such as polynomials as the radicand. These combinations may be joined by addition, subtraction, multiplication, or division, but may not include variables as exponents.

> **Review Video: Common Functions**
> Visit mometrix.com/academy and enter code: 629798

ABSOLUTE VALUE FUNCTIONS

An **absolute value function** is in the format $f(x) = |ax + b|$. Like other functions, the domain is the set of all real numbers. However, because absolute value indicates positive numbers, the range is limited to positive real numbers. To find the zero of an absolute value function, set the portion inside the absolute value sign equal to zero and solve for x. An absolute value function is also known as a piecewise function because it must be solved in pieces—one for if the value inside the absolute value sign is positive, and one for if the value is negative. The function can be expressed as:

$$f(x) = \begin{cases} ax + b & \text{if } ax + b \geq 0 \\ -(ax + b) & \text{if } ax + b < 0 \end{cases}$$

This will allow for an accurate statement of the range. The graph of an example absolute value function, $f(x) = |2x - 1|$, is below:

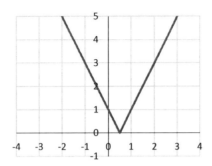

PIECEWISE FUNCTIONS

A **piecewise function** is a function that has different definitions on two or more different intervals. The following, for instance, is one example of a piecewise-defined function:

$$f(x) = \begin{cases} x^2, & x < 0 \\ x, & 0 \leq x \leq 2 \\ (x-2)^2, & x > 2 \end{cases}$$

To graph this function, you would simply graph each part separately in the appropriate domain. The final graph would look like this:

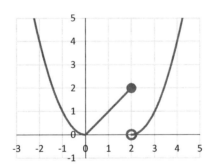

Note the filled and hollow dots at the discontinuity at $x = 2$. This is important to show which side of the graph that point corresponds to. Because $f(x) = x$ on the closed interval $0 \leq x \leq 2$, $f(2) = 2$. The point $(2, 2)$ is therefore marked with a filled circle, and the point $(2,0)$, which is the endpoint of the rightmost $(x - 2)^2$ part of the graph but *not actually part of the function*, is marked with a hollow dot to indicate this.

Review Video: Piecewise Functions
Visit mometrix.com/academy and enter code: 707921

QUADRATIC FUNCTIONS

A **quadratic function** is a function in the form $y = ax^2 + bx + c$, where a does not equal 0. While a linear function forms a line, a quadratic function forms a **parabola**, which is a u-shaped figure that either opens upward or downward. A parabola that opens upward is said to be a **positive quadratic function,** and a parabola that opens downward is said to be a **negative quadratic function**. The shape of a parabola can differ, depending on the values of a, b, and c. All parabolas contain a **vertex**, which is the highest possible point, the **maximum**, or the lowest possible point, the **minimum**. This is the point where the graph begins moving in the opposite direction. A quadratic function can have zero, one, or two solutions, and therefore zero, one, or two x-intercepts. Recall that the x-intercepts are referred to as the zeros, or roots, of a function. A quadratic function will have only one y-intercept. Understanding the basic components of a quadratic function can give you an idea of the shape of its graph.

Example graph of a positive quadratic function, $x^2 + 2x - 3$:

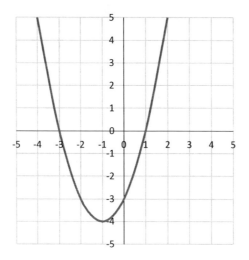

POLYNOMIAL FUNCTIONS

A **polynomial function** is a function with multiple terms and multiple powers of x, such as:

$$f(x) = a_n x^n + a_{n-1} x^{n-1} + a_{n-2} x^{n-2} + \cdots + a_1 x + a_0$$

where n is a non-negative integer that is the highest exponent in the polynomial and $a_n \neq 0$. The domain of a polynomial function is the set of all real numbers. If the greatest exponent in the polynomial is even, the polynomial is said to be of even degree and the range is the set of real numbers that satisfy the function. If the greatest exponent in the polynomial is odd, the polynomial is said to be odd and the range, like the domain, is the set of all real numbers.

RATIONAL FUNCTIONS

A **rational function** is a function that can be constructed as a ratio of two polynomial expressions: $f(x) = \frac{p(x)}{q(x)}$, where $p(x)$ and $q(x)$ are both polynomial expressions and $q(x) \neq 0$. The domain is the set of all real numbers, except any values for which $q(x) = 0$. The range is the set of real numbers that satisfies the function when the domain is applied. When you graph a rational function, you will have vertical asymptotes wherever $q(x) = 0$. If the polynomial in the numerator is of lesser degree than the polynomial in the denominator, the x-axis will also be a horizontal asymptote. If the numerator and denominator have equal degrees, there will be a horizontal asymptote not on the x-axis. If the degree of the numerator is exactly one greater than the degree of the denominator, the

58

graph will have an oblique, or diagonal, asymptote. The asymptote will be along the line $y = \frac{p_n}{q_{n-1}}x + \frac{p_{n-1}}{q_{n-1}}$, where p_n and q_{n-1} are the coefficients of the highest degree terms in their respective polynomials.

SQUARE ROOT FUNCTIONS

A **square root function** is a function that contains a radical and is in the format $f(x) = \sqrt{ax + b}$. The domain is the set of all real numbers that yields a positive radicand or a radicand equal to zero. Because square root values are assumed to be positive unless otherwise identified, the range is all real numbers from zero to infinity. To find the zero of a square root function, set the radicand equal to zero and solve for x. The graph of a square root function is always to the right of the zero and always above the x-axis.

Example graph of a square root function, $f(x) = \sqrt{2x + 1}$:

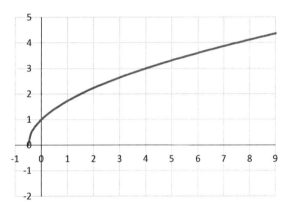

Basic Trigonometric Functions

BASIC TRIGONOMETRIC FUNCTIONS
SINE

The **sine** (sin) function has a period of $360°$ or 2π radians. This means that its graph makes one complete cycle every $360°$ or 2π. Because $\sin 0 = 0$, the graph of $y = \sin x$ begins at the origin, with the x-axis representing the angle measure, and the y-axis representing the sine of the angle. The graph of the sine function is a smooth curve that begins at the origin, peaks at the point $\left(\frac{\pi}{2}, 1\right)$, crosses the x-axis at $(\pi, 0)$, has its lowest point at $\left(\frac{3\pi}{2}, -1\right)$, and returns to the x-axis to complete one cycle at $(2\pi, 0)$.

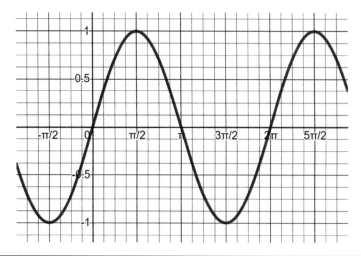

Review Video: Sine
Visit mometrix.com/academy and enter code: 193339

COSINE

The **cosine** (cos) function also has a period of 360° or 2π radians, which means that its graph also makes one complete cycle every 360° or 2π. Because $\cos 0° = 1$, the graph of $y = \cos x$ begins at the point $(0, 1)$, with the x-axis representing the angle measure, and the y-axis representing the cosine of the angle. The graph of the cosine function is a smooth curve that begins at the point $(0,1)$, crosses the x-axis at the point $\left(\frac{\pi}{2}, 0\right)$, has its lowest point at $(\pi, -1)$, crosses the x-axis again at the point $\left(\frac{3\pi}{2}, 0\right)$, and returns to a peak at the point $(2\pi, 1)$ to complete one cycle.

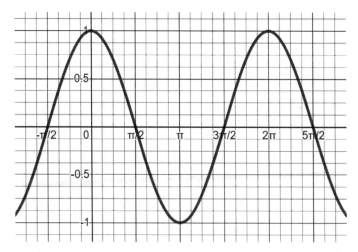

Review Video: Cosine
Visit mometrix.com/academy and enter code: 361120

TANGENT

The **tangent** (tan) function has a period of 180° or π radians, which means that its graph makes one complete cycle every 180° or π radians. The x-axis represents the angle measure, and the y-axis

60

represents the tangent of the angle. The graph of the tangent function is a series of smooth curves that cross the x-axis at every 180° or π radians and have an asymptote every $k \times 90$° or $\frac{k\pi}{2}$ radians, where k is an odd integer. This can be explained by the fact that the tangent is calculated by dividing the sine by the cosine, since the cosine equals zero at those asymptote points.

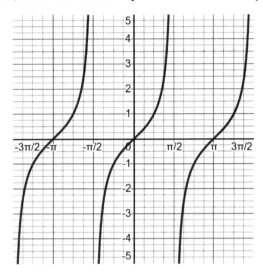

Review Video: Tangent
Visit mometrix.com/academy and enter code: 947639

Working with Functions

MANIPULATION OF FUNCTIONS

Translation occurs when values are added to or subtracted from the x- or y-values. If a constant is added to the y-portion of each point, the graph shifts up. If a constant is subtracted from the y-portion of each point, the graph shifts down. This is represented by the expression $f(x) \pm k$, where k is a constant. If a constant is added to the x-portion of each point, the graph shifts left. If a constant is subtracted from the x-portion of each point, the graph shifts right. This is represented by the expression $f(x \pm k)$, where k is a constant.

Stretching, compression, and reflection occur when different parts of a function are multiplied by different groups of constants. If the function as a whole is multiplied by a real number constant greater than 1, $(k \times f(x))$, the graph is stretched vertically. If k in the previous equation is greater than zero but less than 1, the graph is compressed vertically. If k is less than zero, the graph is reflected about the x-axis, in addition to being either stretched or compressed vertically if k is less than or greater than –1, respectively. If instead, just the x-term is multiplied by a constant greater than 1 $(f(k \times x))$, the graph is compressed horizontally. If k in the previous equation is greater than zero but less than 1, the graph is stretched horizontally. If k is less than zero, the graph is reflected about the y-axis, in addition to being either stretched or compressed horizontally if k is greater than or less than –1, respectively.

Review Video: Manipulation of Functions
Visit mometrix.com/academy and enter code: 669117

APPLYING THE BASIC OPERATIONS TO FUNCTIONS

For each of the basic operations, we will use these functions as examples: $f(x) = x^2$ and $g(x) = x$.

To find the sum of two functions f and g, assuming the domains are compatible, simply add the two functions together: $(f + g)(x) = f(x) + g(x) = x^2 + x$.

To find the difference of two functions f and g, assuming the domains are compatible, simply subtract the second function from the first: $(f - g)(x) = f(x) - g(x) = x^2 - x$.

To find the product of two functions f and g, assuming the domains are compatible, multiply the two functions together: $(f \times g)(x) = f(x) \times g(x) = x^2 \times x = x^3$.

To find the quotient of two functions f and g, assuming the domains are compatible, divide the first function by the second: $\frac{f}{g}(x) = \frac{f(x)}{g(x)} = \frac{x^2}{x} = x \; ; x \neq 0$.

The example given in each case is fairly simple, but on a given problem, if you are looking only for the value of the sum, difference, product, or quotient of two functions at a particular x-value, it may be simpler to solve the functions individually and then perform the given operation using those values.

The composite of two functions f and g, written as $(f \circ g)(x)$ simply means that the output of the second function is used as the input of the first. This can also be written as $f\big(g(x)\big)$. In general, this can be solved by substituting $g(x)$ for all instances of x in $f(x)$ and simplifying. Using the example functions $f(x) = x^2 - x + 2$ and $g(x) = x + 1$, we can find that $(f \circ g)(x)$ or $f\big(g(x)\big)$ is equal to $f(x + 1) = (x + 1)^2 - (x + 1) + 2$, which simplifies to $x^2 + x + 2$.

It is important to note that $(f \circ g)(x)$ is not necessarily the same as $(g \circ f)(x)$. The process is not always commutative like addition or multiplication expressions. It *can* be commutative, but most often this is not the case.

Advanced Functions

STEP FUNCTIONS

The double brackets indicate a step function. For a step function, the value inside the double brackets is rounded down to the nearest integer. The graph of the function $f_0(x) = [\![x]\!]$ appears on the left graph. In comparison $f(x) = 2 \left[\!\left[\frac{1}{3}(x - 1)\right]\!\right]$ is on the right graph. The coefficient of 2 shows that it's stretched vertically by a factor of 2 (so there's a vertical distance of 2 units between successive "steps"). The coefficient of $\frac{1}{3}$ in front of the x shows that it's stretched horizontally by a

62

factor of 3 (so each "step" is three units long), and the $x - 1$ shows that it's displaced one unit to the right.

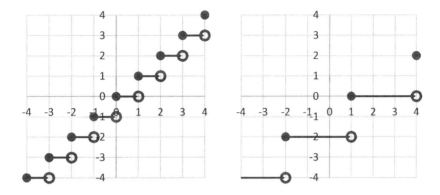

TRANSCENDENTAL FUNCTIONS

Transcendental functions are all functions that are non-algebraic. Any function that includes logarithms, trigonometric functions, variables as exponents, or any combination that includes any of these is not algebraic in nature, even if the function includes polynomials or roots.

EXPONENTIAL FUNCTIONS

Exponential functions are equations that have the format $y = b^x$, where base $b > 0$ and $b \neq 1$. The exponential function can also be written $f(x) = b^x$. Recall the properties of exponents, like the product of terms with the same base is equal to the base raised to the sum of the exponents $(a^x \times a^y = a^{x+y})$ and a term with an exponent that is raised to an exponent is equal to the base of the original term raised to the product of the exponents: $((a^x)^y = a^{xy})$. The graph of an example exponential function, $f(x) = 2^x$, is below:

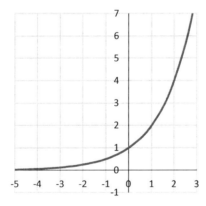

Note in the graph that the y-value approaches zero to the left and infinity to the right. One of the key features of an exponential function is that there will be one end that goes off to infinity and another that asymptotically approaches a lower bound. Common forms of exponential functions include:

Geometric sequences: $a_n = a_1 \times r^{n-1}$, where a_n is the value of the nth term, a_1 is the initial value, r is the common ratio, and n is the number of terms. Note that $a_1 \times r^{1-1} = a_1 \times r^0 = a_1 \times 1 = a_1$.

Population growth: $f(t) = ae^{rt}$, where $f(t)$ is the population at time $t \geq 0$, a is the initial population, e is the mathematical constant known as Euler's number, and r is the growth rate.

> **Review Video: Population Growth**
> Visit mometrix.com/academy and enter code: 109278

Compound interest: $f(t) = P\left(1 + \frac{r}{n}\right)^{nt}$, where $f(t)$ is the account value at a certain number of time periods $t \geq 0$, P is the initial principal balance, r is the interest rate, and n is the number of times the interest is applied per time period.

> **Review Video: Interest Functions**
> Visit mometrix.com/academy and enter code: 559176

General exponential growth or decay: $f(t) = a(1 + r)^t$, where $f(t)$ is the future count, a is the current or initial count, r is the growth or decay rate, and t is the time.

For example, suppose the initial population of a town was 1,200 people. The annual population growth is 5%. The current population is 2,400. To find out how much time has passed since the town was founded, we can use the following function:

$$2{,}400 = 1{,}200e^{0.05t}.$$

The general form for population growth may be represented as $f(t) = ae^{rt}$, where $f(t)$ represents the current population, a represents the initial population, r represents the growth rate, and t represents the time. Thus, substituting the initial population, current population, and rate into this form gives the equation above.

The number of years that have passed were found by first dividing both sides of the equation by 1,200. Doing so gives $2 = e^{0.05t}$. Taking the natural logarithm of both sides gives $\ln(2) = ln(e^{0.05t})$. Applying the power property of logarithms, the equation may be rewritten as $\ln(2) = 0.05t \times \ln(e)$, which simplifies as $\ln(2) = 0.05t$. Dividing both sides of this equation by 0.05 gives $t \approx 13.86$. Thus, approximately 13.86 years passed.

LOGARITHMIC FUNCTIONS

Logarithmic functions are equations that have the format $y = \log_b x$ or $f(x) = \log_b x$. The base b may be any number except one; however, the most common bases for logarithms are base 10 and base e. The log base e is the natural logarithm, or ln, expressed by the function $f(x) = \ln x$.

Any logarithm that does not have an assigned value of b is assumed to be base 10: $\log x = \log_{10} x$. Exponential functions and logarithmic functions are related in that one is the inverse of the other. If $f(x) = b^x$, then $f^{-1}(x) = \log_b x$. This can perhaps be expressed more clearly by the two equations: $y = b^x$ and $x = \log_b y$.

The following properties apply to logarithmic expressions:

Property	Description
$\log_b 1 = 0$	The log of 1 is equal to 0 for any base
$\log_b b = 1$	The log of the base is equal to 1
$\log_b b^p = p$	The log of the base raised to a power is equal to that power
$\log_b MN = \log_b M + \log_b N$	The log of a product is the sum of the log of each factor
$\log_b \dfrac{M}{N} = \log_b M - \log_b N$	The log of a quotient is equal to the log of the dividend minus the log of the divisor
$\log_b M^p = p\log_b M$	The log of a value raised to a power is equal to the power times the log of the value

The graph of an example logarithmic function, $f(x) = \log_2(x + 2)$, is below:

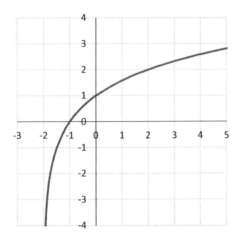

TRIGONOMETRIC FUNCTIONS

Trigonometric functions are periodic, meaning that they repeat the same form over and over. The basic trigonometric functions are sine (abbreviated 'sin'), cosine (abbreviated 'cos'), and tangent (abbreviated 'tan'). The simplest way to think of them is as describing the ratio of the side lengths of a right triangle in relation to the angles of the triangle.

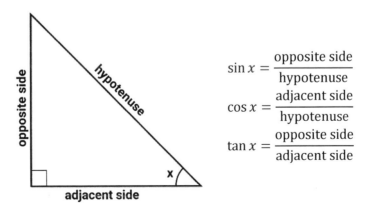

$$\sin x = \frac{\text{opposite side}}{\text{hypotenuse}}$$

$$\cos x = \frac{\text{adjacent side}}{\text{hypotenuse}}$$

$$\tan x = \frac{\text{opposite side}}{\text{adjacent side}}$$

Using sine as an example, trigonometric functions take the form $f(x) = A \sin(Bx + C) + D$, where the **amplitude** is simply equal to A. The **period** is the distance between successive peaks or troughs, essentially the length of the repeated pattern. In this form, the period is equal to $\frac{2\pi}{B}$. As for C, this is the **phase shift** or the horizontal shift of the function. The last term, D, is the vertical shift and determines the **midline** as $y = D$.

For instance, consider the function $f(x) = 2 + \frac{3}{2} \sin\left(\pi x + \frac{\pi}{2}\right)$. Here, $A = \frac{3}{2}$, $B = \pi$, $C = \frac{\pi}{2}$, and $D = 2$, so the midline is at $y = 2$, the amplitude is $\frac{3}{2}$, and the period is $\frac{2\pi}{\pi} = 2$. To graph this function, we center the sine wave on the midline and extend it to a height above and below the midline equal to the amplitude—so this graph would have a minimum value of $2 - \frac{3}{2} = \frac{1}{2}$ and a maximum of $2 + \frac{3}{2} = \frac{7}{2}$. So, the function would be graphed as follows:

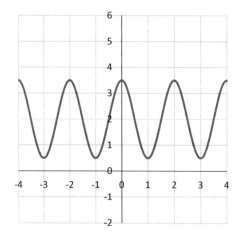

Complex Numbers

COMPLEX NUMBERS

Complex numbers consist of a real component and an imaginary component. Complex numbers are expressed in the form $a + bi$ with real component a and imaginary component bi. The imaginary unit i is equal to $\sqrt{-1}$. That means $i^2 = -1$. The imaginary unit provides a way to find the square root of a negative number. For example, $\sqrt{-25}$ is $5i$. You should expect questions asking you to add, subtract, multiply, divide, and simplify complex numbers. You may see a question that says, "Add $3 + 2i$ and $5 - 7i$" or "Subtract $4 + i\sqrt{5}$ from $2 + i\sqrt{5}$." Or you may see a question that says, "Multiply $6 + 2i$ by $8 - 4i$" or "Divide $1 - 3i$ by $9 - 7i$."

OPERATIONS ON COMPLEX NUMBERS

Operations with complex numbers resemble operations with variables in algebra. When adding or subtracting complex numbers, you can only combine like terms—real terms with real terms and imaginary terms with imaginary terms. For example, if you are asked to simplify the expression $-2 + 4i - (-3 + 7i) - 5i$, you should first remove the parentheses to yield $-2 + 4i + 3 - 7i - 5i$. Combining like terms yields $1 - 8i$. One interesting aspect of imaginary numbers is that if i has an exponent greater than 1, it can be simplified. Example: $i^2 = -1$, $i^3 = -i$, and $i^4 = 1$. When multiplying complex numbers, remember to simplify each i with an exponent greater than 1. For example, you might see a question that says, "Simplify $(2 - i)(3 + 2i)$." You need to distribute and multiply to get $6 + 4i - 3i - 2i^2$. This is further simplified to $6 + i - 2(-1)$, or $8 + i$.

SIMPLIFYING EXPRESSIONS WITH COMPLEX DENOMINATORS

If an expression contains an i in the denominator, it must be simplified. Remember, roots cannot be left in the denominator of a fraction. Since i is equivalent to $\sqrt{-1}$, i cannot be left in the denominator of a fraction. You must rationalize the denominator of a fraction that contains a complex denominator by multiplying the numerator and denominator by the conjugate of the denominator. The conjugate of the complex number $a + bi$ is $a - bi$. You can simplify $\frac{2}{5i}$ by simply multiplying $\frac{2}{5i} \times \frac{i}{i}$, which yields $-\frac{2}{5}i$. And you can simplify $\frac{5+3i}{2-4i}$ by multiplying $\frac{5+3i}{2-4i} \times \frac{2+4i}{2+4i}$. This yields $\frac{10+20i+6i-12}{4-8i+8i+16}$ which simplifies to $\frac{-2+26i}{20}$ or $\frac{-1+13i}{10}$, which can also be written as $-\frac{1}{10} + \frac{13}{10}i$.

Sequences

SEQUENCES

A **sequence** is an ordered set of numbers that continues in a defined pattern. The function that defines a sequence has a domain composed of the set of positive integers. Each member of the sequence is an element, or individual term. Each element is identified by the notation a_n, where a is the term of the sequence, and n is the integer identifying which term in the sequence a is.

There are two different ways to represent a sequence that contains the element a_n. The first is the simple notation $\{a_n\}$. The second is the expanded notation of a sequence: $a_1, a_2, a_3, \ldots a_n, \ldots$. Notice that the expanded form does not end with the nth term. There is no indication that the nth term is the last term in the sequence, only that the nth term is an element of the sequence.

ARITHMETIC SEQUENCES

An **arithmetic sequence**, or arithmetic progression, is a special kind of sequence in which a specific quantity, called the common difference, is added to each term to make the next term. The common difference may be positive or negative. The general form of an arithmetic sequence containing n terms is $a_1, a_1 + d, a_1 + 2d, \ldots, a_1 + (n-1)d$, where d is the common difference. The general formula for any term of an arithmetic sequence is $a_n = a_1 + (n-1)d$, where a_n is the term you are looking for and d is the common difference. To find the sum of the first n terms of an arithmetic sequence, use the formula $s_n = \frac{n}{2}(a_1 + a_n)$.

> **Review Video: Arithmetic Sequence**
> Visit mometrix.com/academy and enter code: 676885

MONOTONIC SEQUENCES

A **monotonic sequence** is a sequence that is either nonincreasing or nondecreasing. A **nonincreasing** sequence is one whose terms either get progressively smaller in value or remain the same. Such a sequence is always bounded above, that is, all elements of the sequence must be less than some real number. A **nondecreasing** sequence is one whose terms either get progressively larger in value or remain the same. Such a sequence is always bounded below, that is, all elements of the sequence must be greater than some real number.

RECURSIVE SEQUENCES

When one element of a sequence is defined in terms of a previous element or elements of the sequence, the sequence is a **recursive sequence**. For example, given the recursive definition

$a_1 = 1; a_2 = 1; a_n = a_{n-1} + a_{n-2}$ for all $n > 2$, you get the sequence 1,1,2,3,5,8, ... This is known as the Fibonacci sequence: a continuing sequence of numbers in which each number (after a_2) is the sum of the two previous numbers. The Fibonacci sequence can be defined as starting with either 1,1 or 0,1. Both definitions are considered correct in mathematics. Make sure you know which definition you are working with when dealing with Fibonacci numbers.

Sometimes in a recursive sequence, the terms can be found using a general formula that does not involve the previous terms of the sequence. Such a formula is called a **closed-form** expression for a recursive definition—an alternate formula that will generate the same sequence of numbers. However, not all sequences based on recursive definitions will have a closed-form expression. Some sequences will require the use of the recursive definition.

THE GOLDEN RATIO AND THE FIBONACCI SEQUENCE

The golden ratio is approximately 1.6180339887 and is often represented by the Greek letter phi, Φ. The exact value of Φ is $\frac{(1+\sqrt{5})}{2}$ and it is one of the solutions to $x - \frac{1}{x} = 1$. The golden ratio can be found using the Fibonacci sequence, since the ratio of a term to the previous term approaches Φ as the sequence approaches infinity:

n	a_n	a_{n-1}	$\dfrac{a_n}{a_{n-1}}$
3	2	1	2
4	3	2	1.5
5	5	3	$1.\overline{6}$
6	8	5	1.6
7	13	8	1.625
8	21	13	$1.\overline{615384}$
9	34	21	$1.\overline{619047}$
⋮	⋮	⋮	⋮
20	6,765	4,181	1.618033963 ...

GEOMETRIC SEQUENCES

A geometric sequence is a sequence in which each term is multiplied by a constant number (called the common ratio) to get the next term. Essentially, it's the same concept as an arithmetic sequence, but with multiplication instead of addition.

Consider the following example of a geometric sequence: Andy opens a savings account with $10. During each subsequent week, he plans to double the amount from the previous week.

Sequence: $10, 20, 40, 80, 160, ...$

Function: $a_n = 10 \times 2^{n-1}$

This is a geometric sequence with a common ratio of 2. All geometric sequences represent exponential functions. The nth term in any geometric sequence is $a_n = a_1 \times r^{n-1}$, where a_n represents the value of the nth term, a_1 is the initial term, r is the common ratio, and n is the number of terms. Thus, substituting the initial value of 10 and common ratio of 2 gives the function $a_n = 10 \times 2^{n-1}$.

Review Video: Geometric Sequences
Visit mometrix.com/academy and enter code: 140779

Advanced Sequences and Series

LIMIT OF A SEQUENCE

Some sequences will have a **limit**—a value the sequence approaches, or sometimes even reaches, but never passes. A sequence with a limit is called a **convergent** sequence because all the values of the sequence seemingly converge at that point. Sequences that do not converge at a particular limit are **divergent** sequences. The easiest way to determine whether a sequence converges or diverges is to find the limit of the sequence. If the limit is a real number, the sequence is convergent. If the limit is infinity, the sequence is divergent.

Remember the following rules for finding limits:

- $\lim_{n\to\infty} k = k$, for all real numbers k

- $\lim_{n\to\infty} \frac{1}{n} = 0$

- $\lim_{n\to\infty} n = \infty$

- $\lim_{n\to\infty} \frac{k}{n^p} = 0$, for all real numbers k and positive rational numbers p

- The limit of the sum of two sequences is equal to the sum of the limits of the two sequences: $\lim_{n\to\infty} (a_n + b_n) = \lim_{n\to\infty} a_n + \lim_{n\to\infty} b_n$

- The limit of the difference between two sequences is equal to the difference between the limits of the two sequences: $\lim_{n\to\infty} (a_n - b_n) = \lim_{n\to\infty} a_n - \lim_{n\to\infty} b_n$

- The limit of the product of two sequences is equal to the product of the limits of the two sequences: $\lim_{n\to\infty} (a_n \times b_n) = \lim_{n\to\infty} a_n \times \lim_{n\to\infty} b_n$

- The limit of the quotient of two sequences is equal to the quotient of the limits of the two sequences, with some exceptions: $\lim_{n\to\infty} \left(\frac{a_n}{b_n}\right) = \frac{\lim_{n\to\infty} a_n}{\lim_{n\to\infty} b_n}$. In the quotient formula, it is important that $b_n \neq 0$ and that $\lim_{n\to\infty} b_n \neq 0$.

- The limit of a sequence multiplied by a scalar is equal to the scalar multiplied by the limit of the sequence: $\lim_{n\to\infty} ka_n = k \lim_{n\to\infty} a_n$, where k is any real number

> **Review Video: Limit of a Sequence**
> Visit mometrix.com/academy and enter code: 847732

INFINITE SERIES

Both arithmetic and geometric sequences have formulas to find the sum of the first n terms in the sequence, assuming you know what the first term is. The sum of all the terms in a sequence is called a **series**. An **infinite series** is an infinite sum. In other words, it is what you get by adding up all the terms in an infinite sequence: $\sum_{n=1}^{\infty} a_n = a_1 + a_2 + a_3 + \cdots + a_n + \cdots$. This notation can be shortened to $\sum_{n=1}^{\infty} a_n$ or $\sum a_n$.

While we can't add up an infinite list of numbers one at a time, we can still determine the infinite sum. As we add the terms in a series, we can imagine an infinite sequence of partial sums, where the first partial sum is the first element of the series, the second partial sum is the sum of the first two elements of the series, and the nth partial sum is the sum of the first n elements of the series.

Every infinite sequence of partial sums (infinite series) either converges or diverges. As with the test for convergence in a sequence, finding the limit of the sequence of partial sums will indicate whether it is a converging series or a diverging series. If there exists a real number S such that $\lim_{n\to\infty} S_n = S$, where S_n is the sequence of partial sums, then the series converges. If the limit equals infinity, then the series diverges. If $\lim_{n\to\infty} S_n = S$ and S is a real number, then S is also the convergence value of the series.

To find the sum as n approaches infinity for the sum of two convergent series, find the sum as n approaches infinity for each individual series and add the results.

$$\sum_{n=1}^{\infty}(a_n + b_n) = \sum_{n=1}^{\infty} a_n + \sum_{n=1}^{\infty} b_n$$

The same idea works for subtraction.

$$\sum_{n=1}^{\infty}(a_n - b_n) = \sum_{n=1}^{\infty} a_n - \sum_{n=1}^{\infty} b_n$$

To find the sum as n approaches infinity for the product of a constant (also called a scalar) and a convergent series, find the sum as n approaches infinity for the series and multiply the result by the scalar.

$$\sum_{n=1}^{\infty} ka_n = k\sum_{n=1}^{\infty} a_n$$

Review Video: Infinite Series
Visit mometrix.com/academy and enter code: 271404

The nth **term test for divergence** means taking the limit of a sequence a_n as n goes to infinity $\left(\lim_{n\to\infty} a_n\right)$ and checking whether the limit is zero. If the limit is not zero, then the series $\sum a_n$ is a diverging series. This test only works to prove divergence, however. If the limit is zero, the test is inconclusive, meaning the series could be either convergent or divergent.

Review Video: Nth Term Test for Divergence
Visit mometrix.com/academy and enter code: 346400

The Unit Circle

DEGREES, RADIANS, AND THE UNIT CIRCLE

It is important to understand the deep connection between trigonometry and circles. Specifically, the two main units, **degrees** (°) and **radians** (rad), that are used to measure angles are related this way: 360° in one full circle and 2π radians in one full circle: (360° = 2π rad). The conversion factor relating the two is often stated as $\frac{180°}{\pi}$. For example, to convert $\frac{3\pi}{2}$ radians to degrees, multiply by the conversion factor: $\frac{3\pi}{2} \times \frac{180°}{\pi} = 270°$. As another example, to convert 60° to radians, divide by the conversion factor or multiply by the reciprocal: $60° \times \frac{\pi}{180°} = \frac{\pi}{3}$ radians.

Recall that the standard equation for a circle is $(x - h)^2 + (y - k)^2 = r^2$. A **unit circle** is a circle with a radius of 1 ($r = 1$) that has its center at the origin ($h = 0, k = 0$). Thus, the equation for the unit circle simplifies from the standard equation down to $x^2 + y^2 = 1$.

Standard position is the position of an angle of measure θ whose vertex is at the origin, the initial side crosses the unit circle at the point $(1, 0)$, and the terminal side crosses the unit circle at some other point (a, b). In the standard position, $\sin \theta = b$, $\cos \theta = a$, and $\tan \theta = \frac{b}{a}$.

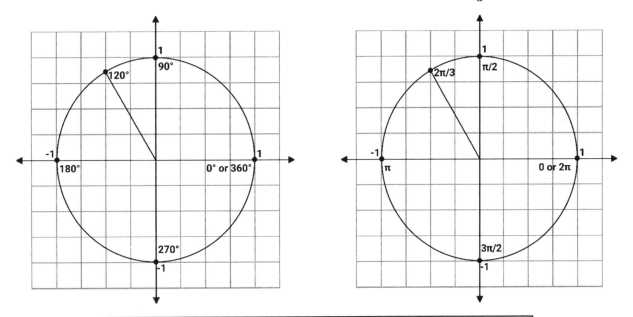

Review Video: Unit Circles and Standard Position
Visit mometrix.com/academy and enter code: 333922

TABLE OF COMMONLY ENCOUNTERED ANGLES

$0° = 0$ radians, $30° = \frac{\pi}{6}$ radians, $45° = \frac{\pi}{4}$ radians, $60° = \frac{\pi}{3}$ radians, and $90° = \frac{\pi}{2}$ radians

$\sin 0° = 0$	$\cos 0° = 1$	$\tan 0° = 0$
$\sin 30° = \frac{1}{2}$	$\cos 30° = \frac{\sqrt{3}}{2}$	$\tan 30° = \frac{\sqrt{3}}{3}$
$\sin 45° = \frac{\sqrt{2}}{2}$	$\cos 45° = \frac{\sqrt{2}}{2}$	$\tan 45° = 1$
$\sin 60° = \frac{\sqrt{3}}{2}$	$\cos 60° = \frac{1}{2}$	$\tan 60° = \sqrt{3}$
$\sin 90° = 1$	$\cos 90° = 0$	$\tan 90° =$ undefined
$\csc 0° =$ undefined	$\sec 0° = 1$	$\cot 0° =$ undefined
$\csc 30° = 2$	$\sec 30° = \frac{2\sqrt{3}}{3}$	$\cot 30° = \sqrt{3}$
$\csc 45° = \sqrt{2}$	$\sec 45° = \sqrt{2}$	$\cot 45° = 1$
$\csc 60° = \frac{2\sqrt{3}}{3}$	$\sec 60° = 2$	$\cot 60° = \frac{\sqrt{3}}{3}$
$\csc 90° = 1$	$\sec 90° =$ undefined	$\cot 90° = 0$

The values in the upper half of this table are values you should have memorized or be able to find quickly and those in the lower half can easily be determined as the reciprocal of the corresponding function.

Defined and Reciprocal Functions

DEFINED AND RECIPROCAL FUNCTIONS

The tangent function is defined as the ratio of the sine to the cosine: $\tan x = \frac{\sin x}{\cos x}$.

To take the reciprocal of a number means to place that number as the denominator of a fraction with a numerator of 1. The reciprocal functions are thus defined quite simply.

Cosecant	$\csc x$	$\frac{1}{\sin x}$
Secant	$\sec x$	$\frac{1}{\cos x}$
Cotangent	$\cot x$	$\frac{1}{\tan x}$

It is important to know these reciprocal functions, but they are not as commonly used as the three basic functions.

Review Video: <u>Defined and Reciprocal Functions</u>
Visit mometrix.com/academy and enter code: 996431

Inverse Trigonometric Functions

INVERSE FUNCTIONS

Each of the trigonometric functions accepts an angular measure, either degrees or radians, and gives a numerical value as the output. The inverse functions do the opposite; they accept a numerical value and give an angular measure as the output.

The inverse of sine, or arcsine, commonly written as either $\sin^{-1} x$ or arcsin x, gives the angle whose sine is x. Similarly:

The inverse of $\cos x$ is written as $\cos^{-1} x$ or arccos x and means the angle whose cosine is x.
The inverse of $\tan x$ is written as $\tan^{-1} x$ or arctan x and means the angle whose tangent is x.
The inverse of $\csc x$ is written as $\csc^{-1} x$ or arccsc x and means the angle whose cosecant is x.
The inverse of $\sec x$ is written as $\sec^{-1} x$ or arcsec x and means the angle whose secant is x.
The inverse of $\cot x$ is written as $\cot^{-1} x$ or arccot x and means the angle whose cotangent is x.

Review Video: <u>Inverse Trig Functions</u>
Visit mometrix.com/academy and enter code: 156054

IMPORTANT NOTE ABOUT SOLVING TRIGONOMETRIC EQUATIONS

When solving for an angle with a known trigonometric value, you must consider the sign and include all angles with that value. Your calculator will probably only give one value as an answer, typically in the following ranges:

- For $\sin^{-1} x$, $\left[-\frac{\pi}{2}, \frac{\pi}{2}\right]$ or $[-90°, 90°]$
- For $\cos^{-1} x$, $[0, \pi]$ or $[0°, 180°]$
- For $\tan^{-1} x$, $\left[-\frac{\pi}{2}, \frac{\pi}{2}\right]$ or $[-90°, 90°]$

It is important to determine if there is another angle in a different quadrant that also satisfies the problem. To do this, find the other quadrant(s) with the same sign for that trigonometric function and find the angle that has the same reference angle. Then check whether this angle is also a solution.

- In the first quadrant, all six trigonometric functions are positive.
- In the second quadrant, sin and csc are positive.
- In the third quadrant, tan and cot are positive.
- In the fourth quadrant, cos and sec are positive.

If you remember the phrase, "ALL Students Take Classes," you will be able to remember the sign of each trigonometric function in each quadrant. ALL represents all the signs in the first quadrant. The "S" in "Students" represents the sine function and its reciprocal in the second quadrant. The "T" in

"Take" represents the tangent function and its reciprocal in the third quadrant. The "C" in "Classes" represents the cosine function and its reciprocal.

Trigonometric Identities

TRIGONOMETRIC IDENTITIES
SUM AND DIFFERENCE

To find the sine, cosine, or tangent of the sum or difference of two angles, use one of the following formulas where α and β are two angles with known sine, cosine, or tangent values as needed:

$$\sin(\alpha \pm \beta) = \sin\alpha\cos\beta \pm \cos\alpha\sin\beta$$
$$\cos(\alpha \pm \beta) = \cos\alpha\cos\beta \mp \sin\alpha\sin\beta$$
$$\tan(\alpha \pm \beta) = \frac{\tan\alpha \pm \tan\beta}{1 \mp \tan\alpha\tan\beta}$$

HALF ANGLE

To find the sine or cosine of half of a known angle, use the following formulas where θ is an angle with a known exact cosine value:

$$\sin\left(\frac{\theta}{2}\right) = \pm\sqrt{\frac{(1-\cos\theta)}{2}}$$

$$\cos\left(\frac{\theta}{2}\right) = \pm\sqrt{\frac{(1+\cos\theta)}{2}}$$

To determine the sign of the answer, you must recognize which quadrant the given angle is in and apply the correct sign for the trigonometric function you are using. If you need to find an expression for the exact sine or cosine of an angle that you do not know, such as sine 22.5°, you can rewrite the given angle as a half angle, such as $\sin\left(\frac{45°}{2}\right)$, and use the formula above:

$$\sin\left(\frac{45°}{2}\right) = \pm\sqrt{\frac{(1-\cos(45°))}{2}} = \pm\sqrt{\frac{\left(1-\frac{\sqrt{2}}{2}\right)}{2}} = \pm\sqrt{\frac{(2-\sqrt{2})}{4}} = \pm\frac{1}{2}\sqrt{(2-\sqrt{2})}$$

To find the tangent or cotangent of half of a known angle, use the following formulas where θ is an angle with known exact sine and cosine values:

$$\tan\frac{\theta}{2} = \frac{\sin\theta}{1+\cos\theta}$$
$$\cot\frac{\theta}{2} = \frac{\sin\theta}{1-\cos\theta}$$

These formulas will work for finding the tangent or cotangent of half of any angle unless the cosine of θ happens to make the denominator of the identity equal to 0.

The Pythagorean theorem states that $a^2 + b^2 = c^2$ for all right triangles. The trigonometric identity that derives from this principle is stated in this way: $\sin^2 \theta + \cos^2 \theta = 1$.

Dividing each term by either $\sin^2 \theta$ or $\cos^2 \theta$ yields two other identities, respectively:

$$1 + \cot^2 \theta = \csc^2 \theta$$
$$\tan^2 \theta + 1 = \sec^2 \theta$$

> **Review Video: Sum and Difference Trigonometric Identities**
> Visit mometrix.com/academy and enter code: 468838

DOUBLE ANGLES

In each case, use one of the double angle formulas. To find the sine or cosine of twice a known angle, use one of the following formulas:

$$\sin(2\theta) = 2 \sin \theta \cos \theta$$

$$\cos(2\theta) = \cos^2 \theta - \sin^2 \theta$$
$$= 2 \cos^2 \theta - 1$$
$$= 1 - 2 \sin^2 \theta$$

To find the tangent or cotangent of twice a known angle, use the formulas where θ is an angle with known exact sine, cosine, tangent, and cotangent values:

$$\tan(2\theta) = \frac{2 \tan \theta}{1 - \tan^2 \theta}$$

$$\cot(2\theta) = \frac{\cot \theta - \tan \theta}{2}$$

PRODUCTS

To find the product of the sines and cosines of two different angles, use one of the following formulas where α and β are two unique angles:

$$\sin \alpha \sin \beta = \frac{1}{2}[\cos(\alpha - \beta) - \cos(\alpha + \beta)]$$

$$\cos \alpha \cos \beta = \frac{1}{2}[\cos(\alpha + \beta) + \cos(\alpha - \beta)]$$

$$\sin \alpha \cos \beta = \frac{1}{2}[\sin(\alpha + \beta) + \sin(\alpha - \beta)]$$

$$\cos \alpha \sin \beta = \frac{1}{2}[\sin(\alpha + \beta) - \sin(\alpha - \beta)]$$

> **Review Video: Half-Angle, Double Angle, and Product Trig Identities**
> Visit mometrix.com/academy and enter code: 274252

COMPLEMENTARY

The trigonometric cofunction identities use the trigonometric relationships of complementary angles (angles whose sum is 90°). These are:

$$\cos x = \sin(90° - x)$$
$$\csc x = \sec(90° - x)$$
$$\cot x = \tan(90° - x)$$

Domain, Range, and Asymptotes in Trigonometry

DOMAIN, RANGE, AND ASYMPTOTES IN TRIGONOMETRY

The domain is the set of all possible real number values of x on the graph of a trigonometric function. Some graphs will impose limits on the values of x.

The range is the set of all possible real number values of y on the graph of a trigonometric function. Some graphs will impose limits on the values of y.

Asymptotes are lines that the graph of a trigonometric function approaches but never reaches. Asymptotes exist for values of x in the graphs of the tangent, cotangent, secant, and cosecant. The sine and cosine graphs do not have any asymptotes.

DOMAIN, RANGE, AND ASYMPTOTES OF THE SIX TRIGONOMETRIC FUNCTIONS

The domain, range, and asymptotes for each of the trigonometric functions are as follows:

- In the **sine** function, the domain is all real numbers, the range is $-1 \leq y \leq 1$, and there are no asymptotes.
- In the **cosine** function, the domain is all real numbers, the range is $-1 \leq y \leq 1$, and there are no asymptotes.
- In the **tangent** function, the domain is $x \in \mathbb{R}$; $x \neq \frac{\pi}{2} + k\pi$, the range is all real numbers, and the asymptotes are the lines $x = \frac{\pi}{2} + k\pi$.
- In the **cosecant** function, the domain is $x \in \mathbb{R}$; $x \neq k\pi$, the range is $(-\infty, -1]$ and $[1, \infty)$, and the asymptotes are the lines $x = k\pi$.
- In the **secant** function, the domain is $x \in \mathbb{R}$; $x \neq \frac{\pi}{2} + k\pi$, the range is $(-\infty, 1]$ and $[1, \infty)$, and the asymptotes are the lines $x = \frac{\pi}{2} + k\pi$.
- In the **cotangent** function, the domain is $x \in \mathbb{R}$; $x \neq k\pi$, the range is all real numbers, and the asymptotes are the lines $x = k\pi$.

In each of the above cases, k represents any integer.

Rectangular and Polar Coordinates

RECTANGULAR AND POLAR COORDINATES

Rectangular coordinates are those that lie on the square grids of the Cartesian plane. They should be quite familiar to you. The polar coordinate system is based on a circular graph, rather than the square grid of the Cartesian system. Points in the polar coordinate system are in the format (r, θ), where r is the distance from the origin (think radius of the circle) and θ is the smallest positive angle (moving counterclockwise around the circle) made with the positive horizontal axis.

To convert a point from rectangular (x, y) format to polar (r, θ) format, use the formula (x, y) to $(r, \theta) \Rightarrow r = \sqrt{x^2 + y^2}$; $\theta = \arctan\frac{y}{x}$ when $x \neq 0$.

If x is positive, use the positive square root value for r. If x is negative, use the negative square root value for r. If $x = 0$, use the following rules:

- If $y = 0$, then $\theta = 0$.
- If $y > 0$, then $\theta = \frac{\pi}{2}$.
- If $y < 0$, then $\theta = \frac{3\pi}{2}$.

To convert a point from polar (r, θ) format to rectangular (x, y) format, use the formula (r, θ) to $(x, y) \Rightarrow x = r \cos \theta$; $y = r \sin \theta$.

DE MOIVRE'S THEOREM

De Moivre's theorem is used to find the powers of complex numbers (numbers that contain the imaginary number i) written in polar form. Given a trigonometric expression that contains i, such as $z = r \cos x + ir \sin x$, where r is a real number and x is an angle measurement in polar form, use the formula $z^n = r^n(\cos nx + i \sin nx)$, where r and n are real numbers, x is the angle measure in polar form, and i is the imaginary number $i = \sqrt{-1}$. The expression $\cos x + i \sin x$ can be written cis x, making the formula appear in the format $z^n = r^n$ cis nx.

Note that De Moivre's theorem is only for angles in polar form. If you are given an angle in degrees, you must convert to polar form before using the formula.

Calculus

CALCULUS

Calculus, also called analysis, is the branch of mathematics that studies the length, area, and volume of objects, and the rate of change of quantities (which can be expressed as slopes of curves). The two principal branches of calculus are differential and integral. **Differential calculus** is based on derivatives and takes the form,

$$\frac{d}{dx}f(x)$$

Integral calculus is based on integrals and takes the form,

$$\int f(x)dx$$

Some of the basic ideas of calculus were utilized as far back in history as Archimedes. However, its modern forms were developed by Newton and Leibniz.

LIMITS

The **limit of a function** is represented by the notation $\lim_{x \to a} f(x)$. It is read as "the limit of f of x as x approaches a." In many cases, $\lim_{x \to a} f(x)$ will simply be equal to $f(a)$, but not always. Limits are important because some functions are not defined or are not easy to evaluate at certain values of x.

The limit at the point is said to exist only if the limit is the same when approached from the right side as from the left: $\lim_{x \to a^+} f(x) = \lim_{x \to a^-} f(x))$. Notice the symbol by the a in each case. When x approaches a from the right, it approaches from the positive end of the number line. When x approaches a from the left, it approaches from the negative end of the number line.

If the limit as x approaches a differs depending on the direction from which it approaches, then the limit does not exist at a. In other words, if $\lim_{x \to a^+} f(x)$ does not equal $\lim_{x \to a^-} f(x)$, then the limit does not exist at a. The limit also does not exist if either of the one-sided limits does not exist.

Situations in which the limit does not exist include a function that jumps from one value to another at a, one that oscillates between two different values as x approaches a, or one that increases or decreases without bounds as x approaches a. If the limit you calculate has a value of $\frac{c}{0}$, where c is any constant, this means the function goes to infinity and the limit does not exist.

It is possible for two functions that do not have limits to be multiplied to get a new function that does have a limit. Just because two functions do not have limits, do not assume that the product will not have a limit.

DIRECT SUBSTITUTION

The first thing to try when looking for a limit is direct substitution. To find the limit of a function $\lim_{x \to a} f(x)$ by direct substitution, substitute the value of a for x in the function and solve. The following patterns apply to finding the limit of a function by direct substitution:

$$\lim_{x \to a} b = b, \text{ where } b \text{ is any real number}$$

$$\lim_{x \to a} x = a$$

$$\lim_{x \to a} x^n = a^n, \text{ where } n \text{ is any positive integer}$$

$$\lim_{x \to a} \sqrt{x} = \sqrt{a}; a > 0$$

$$\lim_{x \to a} \sqrt[n]{x} = \sqrt[n]{a}, \text{ where } n \text{ is a positive integer and } a > 0 \text{ for all even values of } n$$

$$\lim_{x \to a} \frac{1}{x} = \frac{1}{a}; a \neq 0$$

You can also use substitution for finding the limit of a trigonometric function, a polynomial function, or a rational function. Be sure that in manipulating an expression to find a limit that you do not divide by terms equal to zero.

In finding the limit of a composite function, begin by finding the limit of the innermost function. For example, to find $\lim\limits_{x \to a} f(g(x))$, first find the value of $\lim\limits_{x \to a} g(x)$. Then substitute this value for x in $f(x)$ and solve. The result is the limit of the original problem.

LIMITS AND OPERATIONS

When finding the limit of the sum or difference of two functions, find the limit of each individual function and then add or subtract the results. Example:

$$\lim_{x \to a} [f(x) \pm g(x)] = \lim_{x \to a} f(x) \pm \lim_{x \to a} g(x)$$

To find the limit of the product or quotient of two functions, find the limit of each individual function and then multiply or divide the results. Example:

$$\lim_{x \to a} [f(x) \times g(x)] = \lim_{x \to a} f(x) \times \lim_{x \to a} g(x)$$

$$\lim_{x \to a} \frac{f(x)}{g(x)} = \frac{\lim\limits_{x \to a} f(x)}{\lim\limits_{x \to a} g(x)}, \text{ where } g(x) \neq 0$$

$$\lim_{x \to a} g(x) \neq 0$$

When finding the quotient of the limits of two functions, make sure the denominator is not equal to zero. If it is, use differentiation or L'Hôpital's rule to find the limit.

To find the limit of a power of a function or a root of a function, find the limit of the function and then raise the limit to the original power or take the root of the limit. Example:

$$\lim_{x \to a} [f(x)]^n = \left[\lim_{x \to a} f(x) \right]^n$$

$$\lim_{x \to a} \sqrt[n]{f(x)} = \sqrt[n]{\lim_{x \to a} f(x)}, \text{ where } n \text{ is a positive integer}$$

$$\lim_{x \to a} f(x) > 0 \text{ for all even values of } n$$

To find the limit of a function multiplied by a scalar, find the limit of the function and multiply the result by the scalar. Example:

$$\lim_{x \to a} kf(x) = k \lim_{x \to a} f(x), \text{ where } k \text{ is a real number.}$$

> **Review Video: Limits**
> Visit mometrix.com/academy and enter code: 554961

L'HÔPITAL'S RULE

Sometimes solving $\lim\limits_{x \to a} \frac{f(x)}{g(x)}$ by the direct substitution method will result in the numerator and denominator both being equal to zero, or both being equal to infinity. This outcome is called an indeterminate form. The limit cannot be directly found by substitution in these cases. L'Hôpital's rule is a useful method for finding the limit of a problem in the indeterminate form. L'Hôpital's rule allows you to find the limit using derivatives. Assuming both the numerator and denominator are differentiable, and that both are equal to zero when the direct substitution method is used, take the derivative of both the numerator and the denominator and then use the direct substitution method. For example, if $\lim_{x \to a} \frac{f(x)}{g(x)} = \frac{0}{0}$, take the derivatives of $f(x)$ and $g(x)$ and then find $\lim_{x \to a} \frac{f'(x)}{g'(x)}$. If $g'(x) \neq 0$, then you have found the limit of the original function. If $g'(x) = 0$ and $f'(x) = 0$, L'Hôpital's rule may be applied to the function $\frac{f'(x)}{g'(x)}$, and so on until either a limit is found, or it can be determined that the limit does not exist.

Review Video: L'Hopital's Rule
Visit mometrix.com/academy and enter code: 624400

SQUEEZE THEOREM

The squeeze theorem is known by many names, including the sandwich theorem, the sandwich rule, the squeeze lemma, the squeezing theorem, and the pinching theorem. No matter what you call it, the principle is the same. To prove the limit of a difficult function exists, find the limits of two functions, one on either side of the unknown, that are easy to compute. If the limits of these functions are equal, then that is also the limit of the unknown function. In mathematical terms, the theorem is:

If $g(x) \leq f(x) \leq h(x)$ for all values of x where $f(x)$ is the function with the unknown limit, and if $\lim_{x \to a} g(x) = \lim_{x \to a} h(x)$, then this limit is also equal to $\lim_{x \to a} f(x)$.

To find the limit of an expression containing an absolute value sign, take the absolute value of the limit. If $\lim_{n \to \infty} a_n = L$, where L is the numerical value for the limit, then $\lim_{n \to \infty} |a_n| = |L|$. Also, if $\lim_{n \to \infty} |a_n| = 0$, then $\lim_{n \to \infty} a_n = 0$. The trick comes when you are asked to find the limit as n approaches from the left. Whenever the limit is being approached from the left, it is being approached from the negative end of the domain. The absolute value sign makes everything in the equation positive, essentially eliminating the negative side of the domain. In this case, rewrite the equation without the absolute value signs and add a negative sign in front of the expression. Example:

$$\lim_{n \to 0^-} |x| \text{ becomes } \lim_{n \to 0^-} (-x)$$

Review Video: Squeeze Theorem
Visit mometrix.com/academy and enter code: 383104

DERIVATIVES

The derivative of a function is a measure of how much that function is changing at a specific point, and is the slope of a line tangent to a curve at the specific point. The derivative of a function $f(x)$ is written $f'(x)$, and read, "f prime of x." Other notations for the derivative include $D_x f(x)$, y', $D_x y$, $\frac{dy}{dx}$, and $\frac{d}{dx}f(x)$. The definition of the derivative of a function is $f'(x) = \lim\limits_{h \to 0} \frac{f(x+h)-f(x)}{h}$. However, this formula is rarely used.

There is a simpler method you can use to find the derivative of a polynomial. Given a function $f(x) = a_n x^n + a_{n-1}x^{n-1} + a_{n-2}x^{n-2} + \cdots + a_1 x + a_0$, multiply each exponent by its corresponding coefficient to get the new coefficient and reduce the value of the exponent by one. Coefficients with no variable are dropped. This gives $f'(x) = na_n x^{n-1} + (n-1)a_{n-1}x^{n-2} + \cdots + a_1$, a pattern that can be repeated for each successive derivative.

> **Review Video: Definition of a Derivative**
> Visit mometrix.com/academy and enter code: 787269

Differentiable functions are functions that have a derivative. Some basic rules for finding derivatives of functions are:

$$f(x) = c \Rightarrow f'(x) = 0; \text{ where } c \text{ is a constant}$$
$$f(x) = x \Rightarrow f'(x) = 1$$
$$f(x) = x^n \Rightarrow f'(x) = nx^{n-1}; \text{ where } n \text{ is a real number}$$

$$(cf(x))' = cf'(x); \text{ where } c \text{ is a constant}$$
$$(f+g)'(x) = f'(x) + g'(x)$$
$$(fg)'(x) = f(x)g'(x) + f'(x)g(x)$$
$$\left(\frac{f}{g}\right)'(x) = \frac{f'(x)g(x) - f(x)g'(x)}{[g(x)]^2}$$
$$(f \circ g)'(x) = f'(g(x)) \times g'(x)$$

This last formula is also known as the **chain rule**. If you are finding the derivative of a polynomial that is raised to a power, let the polynomial be represented by $g(x)$ and use the chain rule. The chain rule is one of the most important concepts to grasp in the early stages of learning calculus. Many other rules and shortcuts are based upon the chain rule.

> **Review Video: Derivative Properties and Formulas**
> Visit mometrix.com/academy and enter code: 735227
>
> **Review Video: Product and Quotient Rule - When L'Hopital's Fails**
> Visit mometrix.com/academy and enter code: 649197
>
> **Review Video: The Chain Rule - An Integral Part of Calculus**
> Visit mometrix.com/academy and enter code: 938732

DIFFERENCE QUOTIENT AND DERIVATIVE

A secant is a line that connects two points on a curve. The **difference quotient** gives the slope of an arbitrary secant line that connects the point $(x, f(x))$ with a nearby point $(x+h, f(x+h))$ on the graph of the function f. The difference quotient is the same formula that is always used to determine a slope—the change in y divided by the change in x. It is written as $\frac{f(x+h)-f(x)}{h}$.

A tangent is a line that touches a curve at one point. The tangent and the curve have the same slope at the point where they touch. The derivative is the function that gives the slope of both the tangent and the curve of the function at that point. The derivative is written as the limit of the difference quotient, or:

$$\lim_{h \to 0} \frac{f(x + h) - f(x)}{h}$$

If the function is f, the derivative is denoted as $f'(x)$, and it is the slope of the function f at point $(x, f(x))$. It is expressed as:

$$f'(x) = \lim_{h \to 0} \frac{f(x + h) - f(x)}{h}$$

IMPLICIT FUNCTIONS

An **implicit function** is one where it is impossible, or very difficult, to express one variable in terms of another by normal algebraic methods. This would include functions that have both variables raised to a power greater than 1, functions that have two variables multiplied by each other, or a combination of the two. To differentiate such a function with respect to x, take the derivative of each term that contains a variable, either x or y. When differentiating a term with y, use the chain rule, first taking the derivative with respect to y, and then multiplying by $\frac{dy}{dx}$. If a term contains both x and y, you will have to use the product rule as well as the chain rule. Once the derivative of each individual term has been found, use the rules of algebra to solve for $\frac{dy}{dx}$ to get the final answer.

> ### Review Video: **Implicit Differentiation**
> Visit mometrix.com/academy and enter code: 102151

DERIVATIVES OF TRIGONOMETRIC FUNCTIONS

Trigonometric functions are any functions that include one of the six trigonometric expressions. The following rules for derivatives apply for all trigonometric differentiation:

$$\frac{d}{dx}(\sin x) = \cos x, \qquad \frac{d}{dx}(\cos x) = -\sin x, \qquad \frac{d}{dx}(\tan x) = \sec^2 x$$

For functions that are a combination of trigonometric and algebraic expressions, use the chain rule:

$$\frac{d}{dx}(\sin u) = \cos u \, \frac{du}{dx} \qquad \frac{d}{dx}(\sec u) = \tan u \sec u \, \frac{du}{dx}$$
$$\frac{d}{dx}(\cos u) = -\sin u \, \frac{du}{dx} \qquad \frac{d}{dx}(\csc u) = -\csc u \cot u \, \frac{du}{dx}$$
$$\frac{d}{dx}(\tan u) = \sec^2 u \, \frac{du}{dx} \qquad \frac{d}{dx}(\cot u) = -\csc^2 u \, \frac{du}{dx}$$

Functions involving the inverses of the trigonometric functions can also be differentiated.

$$\frac{d}{dx}(\sin^{-1} u) = \frac{1}{\sqrt{1-u^2}}\frac{du}{dx} \qquad \frac{d}{dx}(\csc^{-1} u) = \frac{-1}{|u|\sqrt{u^2-1}}\frac{du}{dx}$$

$$\frac{d}{dx}(\cos^{-1} u) = \frac{-1}{\sqrt{1-u^2}}\frac{du}{dx} \qquad \frac{d}{dx}(\sec^{-1} u) = \frac{1}{|u|\sqrt{u^2-1}}\frac{du}{dx}$$

$$\frac{d}{dx}(\tan^{-1} u) = \frac{1}{1+u^2}\frac{du}{dx} \qquad \frac{d}{dx}(\cot^{-1} u) = \frac{-1}{1+u^2}\frac{du}{dx}$$

In each of the above expressions, u represents a differentiable function. Also, the value of u must be such that the radicand, if applicable, is a positive number. Remember the expression $\frac{du}{dx}$ means to take the derivative of the function u with respect to the variable x.

> **Review Video: Derivatives of Trigonometry Functions**
> Visit mometrix.com/academy and enter code: 132724

DERIVATIVES OF EXPONENTIAL AND LOGARITHMIC FUNCTIONS

Exponential functions are in the form e^x, which has itself as its derivative: $\frac{d}{dx}e^x = e^x$. For functions that have a function as the exponent rather than just an x, use the formula $\frac{d}{dx}e^u = e^u\frac{du}{dx}$. The inverse of the exponential function is the natural logarithm. To find the derivative of the natural logarithm, use the formula $\frac{d}{dx}\ln u = \frac{1}{u}\frac{du}{dx}$.

If you are trying to solve an expression with a variable in the exponent, use the formula $a^x = e^{x\ln a}$, where a is a positive real number and x is any real number. To find the derivative of a function in this format, use the formula $\frac{d}{dx}a^x = a^x \ln a$. If the exponent is a function rather than a single variable x, use the formula $\frac{d}{dx}a^u = a^u \ln a \frac{du}{dx}$. If you are trying to solve an expression involving a logarithm, use the formula $\frac{d}{dx}(\log_a x) = \frac{1}{x\ln a}$ or $\frac{d}{dx}(\log_a |u|) = \frac{1}{u\ln a}\frac{du}{dx}; u \neq 0$.

> **Review Video: Derivatives of Exponential and Logarithmic Functions**
> Visit mometrix.com/academy and enter code: 594367

CONTINUITY

A function can be either continuous or discontinuous. A conceptual way to describe continuity is this: A function is continuous if its graph can be traced with a pen without lifting the pen from the page. In other words, there are no breaks or gaps in the graph of the function. However, this is only a description, not a technical definition. A function is continuous at the point $x = a$ if the three following conditions are met:

1. $f(a)$ is defined
2. $\lim_{x \to a} f(x)$ exists
3. $\lim_{x \to a} f(x) = f(a)$

If any of these conditions are not met, the function is discontinuous at the point $x = a$.

A function can be continuous at a point, continuous over an interval, or continuous everywhere. The above rules define continuity at a point. A function that is continuous over an interval $[a, b]$ is continuous at the points a and b and at every point between them. A function that is continuous everywhere is continuous for every real number, that is, for all points in its domain.

DISCONTINUITY

Discontinuous functions are categorized according to the type or cause of discontinuity. Three examples are point, infinite, and jump discontinuity. A function with a point discontinuity has one value of x for which it is not continuous. A function with infinite discontinuity has a vertical asymptote at $x = a$ and $f(a)$ is undefined. It is said to have an infinite discontinuity at $x = a$. A function with jump discontinuity has one-sided limits from the left and from the right, but they are not equal to one another, that is, $\lim_{x \to a^-} f(x) \neq \lim_{x \to a^+} f(x)$. It is said to have a jump discontinuity at $x = a$.

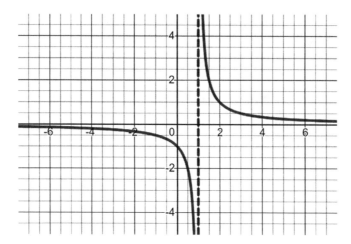

The function $f(x) = \sqrt{x}$ is not differentiable because its domain is $[0, \infty)$ and it has a discontinuity at $x = 0$. Therefore, a tangent could not be drawn at that point.

DIFFERENTIABILITY

A function is said to be differentiable at point $x = a$ if it has a derivative at that point, that is, if $f'(a)$ exists. For a function to be differentiable, it must be continuous because the slope cannot be defined at a point of discontinuity. Furthermore, for a function to be differentiable, its graph must not have any sharp turn for which it is impossible to draw a tangent line. The sine function is an example of a differentiable function. It is continuous, and a tangent line can be drawn anywhere along its graph.

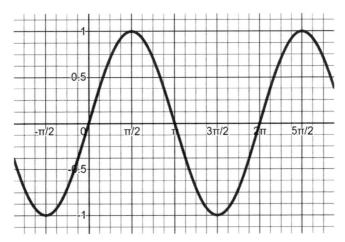

The absolute value function, $f(x) = |x|$, is an example of a function that is not differentiable:

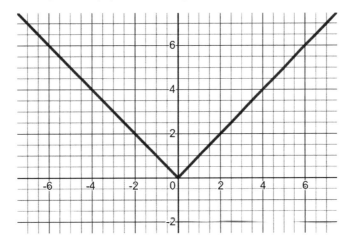

It is continuous, but it has a sharp turn at $x = 0$ which prohibits the drawing of a tangent at that point. All differentiable functions are continuous, but not all continuous functions are differentiable, as the absolute value function demonstrates.

The function $f(x) = \sqrt{x}$ is not differentiable because its domain is $[0, \infty)$ and it has a discontinuity at $x = 0$. Therefore, a tangent could not be drawn at that point.

APPROXIMATING A DERIVATIVE FROM A TABLE OF VALUES

The derivative of a function at a particular point is equal to the slope of the graph of the function at that point. For a nonlinear function, it can be thought of as the limit of the slope of a line drawn between two other points on the function as those points become closer to the point in question. Such a line drawn through two points on the function is called a **secant** of the function.

This definition of the derivative in terms of the secant allows us to approximate the derivative of a function at a point from a table of values: we take the slope of the line through the points on either side. That is, if the point lies between (x_1, y_1) and (x_2, y_2), the slope of the secant—the approximate derivative—is $\frac{y_2-y_1}{x_2-x_1}$. (This is also equal to the average slope over the interval $[x_1, x_2]$.)

For example, consider the function represented by the following table:

x	0	2	4	6	8	10
y	1	5	8	9	7	4

Suppose we want to know the derivative of the function when $x = 3$. This lies between the points $(2, 5)$ and $(4, 8)$; the approximate derivative is $\frac{8-5}{4-2} = \frac{3}{2}$.

POSITION, VELOCITY, AND ACCELERATION

Velocity is a specific type of rate of change. It refers to the rate of change of the position of an object with relation to a reference frame. **Acceleration** is the rate of change of velocity.

Average velocity over a period of time is found using the formula $\bar{v} = \frac{s(t_2)-s(t_1)}{t_2-t_1}$, where t_1 and t_2 are specific points in time and $s(t_1)$ and $s(t_2)$ are the distances traveled at those points in time.

Instantaneous velocity at a specific time, t, is found using the limit $v = \lim\limits_{h \to 0} \frac{s(t+h)-s(t)}{h}$, or $v = s'(t)$.

Remember that velocity at a given point is found using the first derivative, and acceleration at a given point is found using the second derivative. Therefore, the formula for acceleration at a given point in time is found using the formula $a(t) = v'(t) = s''(t)$, where a is acceleration, v is velocity, and s is displacement.

> **Review Video: Position, Velocity, and Acceleration**
> Visit mometrix.com/academy and enter code: 714040

USING FIRST AND SECOND DERIVATIVES

The **first derivative** of a function is equal to the **rate of change** of the function. The sign of the rate of change shows whether the value of the function is **increasing** or **decreasing**. A positive rate of change—and therefore a positive first derivative—represents that the function is increasing at that point. A negative rate of change represents that the function is decreasing. If the rate of change is zero, the function is not changing, i.e., it is constant.

For example, consider the function $f(x) = x^3 - 6x^2 - 15x + 12$. The derivative of this function is $f'(x) = 3x^2 - 12x - 15 = 3(x^2 - 4x - 5) = 3(x - 5)(x + 1)$. This derivative is a quadratic function with zeroes at $x = 5$ and $x = -1$; by plugging in points in each interval we can find that $f'(x)$ is positive when $x < -1$ and when $x > 5$ and negative when $-1 < x < 5$. Thus $f(x)$ is increasing in the interval $(-\infty, -1) \cup (5, \infty)$ and decreasing in the interval $(-1, 5)$.

EXTREMA

The **maximum** and **minimum** values of a function are collectively called the **extrema** of the function. Both maxima and minima can be local, also known as relative, or absolute. A local maximum or minimum refers to the value of a function near a certain value of x. An absolute maximum or minimum refers to the value of a function on a given interval.

The local maximum of a function is the largest value that the function attains near a certain value of x. For example, function f has a local maximum at $x = b$ if $f(b)$ is the largest value that f attains as it approaches b.

Conversely, the local minimum is the smallest value that the function attains near a certain value of x. In other words, function f has a local minimum at $x = b$ if $f(b)$ is the smallest value that f attains as it approaches b.

The absolute maximum of a function is the largest value of the function over a certain interval. The function f has an absolute maximum at $x = b$ if $f(b) \geq f(x)$ for all x in the domain of f.

The absolute minimum of a function is the smallest value of the function over a certain interval. The function f has an absolute minimum at $x = b$ if $f(b) \leq f(x)$ for all x in the domain of f.

CRITICAL POINTS

Remember Rolle's theorem, which states that if two points have the same value in the range that there must be a point between them where the slope of the graph is zero. This point is located at a peak or valley on the graph. A **peak** is a maximum point, and a **valley** is a minimum point. The relative minimum is the lowest point on a graph for a given section of the graph. It may or may not be the same as the absolute minimum, which is the lowest point on the entire graph. The relative maximum is the highest point on one section of the graph. Again, it may or may not be the same as the absolute maximum. A relative extremum (plural extrema) is a relative minimum or relative maximum point on a graph.

A **critical point** is a point $(x, f(x))$ that is part of the domain of a function, such that either $f'(x) = 0$ or $f'(x)$ does not exist. If either of these conditions is true, then x is either an inflection point or a point at which the slope of the curve changes sign. If the slope changes sign, then a relative minimum or maximum occurs.

In graphing an equation with relative extrema, use a sign diagram to approximate the shape of the graph. Once you have determined the relative extrema, calculate the sign of a point on either side of each critical point. This will give a general shape of the graph, and you will know whether each critical point is a relative minimum, a relative maximum, or a point of inflection.

FIRST DERIVATIVE TEST

Remember that critical points occur where the slope of the curve is 0. Also remember that the **first derivative** of a function gives the slope of the curve at a particular point on the curve. Because of this property of the first derivative, the first derivative test can be used to determine if a critical point is a minimum or maximum. If $f'(x)$ is negative at a point to the left of a critical number and $f'(x)$ is positive at a point to the right of a critical number, then the critical number is a relative minimum. If $f'(x)$ is positive to the left of a critical number and $f'(x)$ is negative to the right of a critical number, then the critical number is a relative maximum. If $f'(x)$ has the same sign on both sides, then the critical number is a point of inflection.

> **Review Video: First Derivative Test**
> Visit mometrix.com/academy and enter code: 205981

SECOND DERIVATIVE TEST

The **second derivative**, designated by $f''(x)$, is helpful in determining whether the relative extrema of a function are relative maximums or relative minimums. If the second derivative at the critical point is greater than zero, the critical point is a relative minimum. If the second derivative at the critical point is less than zero, the critical point is a relative maximum. If the second derivative at the critical point is equal to zero, you must use the first derivative test to determine whether the point is a relative minimum or a relative maximum.

There are a couple of ways to determine the concavity of the graph of a function. To test a portion of the graph that contains a point with domain p, find the second derivative of the function and evaluate it for p. If $f''(p) > 0$, then the graph is concave upward at that point. If $f''(p) < 0$, then the graph is concave downward at that point.

The **point of inflection** on the graph of a function is the point at which the concavity changes from concave downward to concave upward or from concave upward to concave downward. The easiest way to find the points of inflection is to find the second derivative of the function and then solve the equation $f''(x) = 0$. Remember that if $f''(p) > 0$, the graph is concave upward, and if $f''(p) < 0$, the graph is concave downward. Logically, the concavity changes at the point when $f''(p) = 0$:

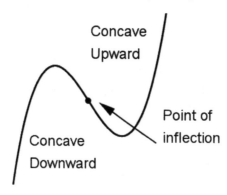

It is important to note in situations where $f'(p) = f''(p) = 0$ it is necessary to use the first derivative test to determine if p is an inflection point.

The derivative tests that have been discussed thus far can help you get a rough picture of what the graph of an unfamiliar function looks like. Begin by solving the equation $f(x) = 0$ to find all the zeros of the function, if they exist. Plot these points on the graph. Then, find the first derivative of the function and solve the equation $f'(x) = 0$ to find the critical points. Remember the numbers obtained here are the x portions of the coordinates. Substitute these values for x in the original function and solve for y to get the full coordinates of the points. Plot these points on the graph. Take the second derivative of the function and solve the equation $f''(x) = 0$ to find the points of inflection. Substitute in the original function to get the coordinates and graph these points. Test points on both sides of the critical points to test for concavity and draw the curve.

DERIVATIVE PROBLEMS

A derivative represents the rate of change of a function; thus, derivatives are a useful tool for solving any problem that involves finding the rate at which a function is changing. In its simplest form, such a problem might provide a formula for a quantity as a function of time and ask for its rate of change at a particular time.

If the temperature in a chamber in degrees Celsius is equal to $T(t) = 20 + e^{-\left(\frac{t}{2}\right)}$, where t is the time in seconds, then the derivative of the function represents the rate of change of the temperature over time. The rate of change is equal to $\frac{dT}{dt} = \frac{d}{dt}\left(20 + e^{-\left(\frac{t}{2}\right)}\right) = -\frac{1}{2}e^{-\left(\frac{t}{2}\right)}$, and the initial rate of change is $T'(0) = -\frac{1}{2}e^{-\left(\frac{0}{2}\right)} = -\frac{1}{2}\frac{°C}{s}$.

Suppose we are told that the net profit that a small company makes when it produces and sells x units of a product is equal to $P(x) = 200x - 20,000$. The derivative of this function would be the

88

additional profit for each additional unit sold, a quantity known as the marginal profit. The marginal profit in this case is $P'(x) = 200$.

SOLVING RELATED RATES PROBLEMS

A **related rate problem** is one in which one variable has a relation with another variable, and the rate of change of one of the variables is known. With that information, the rate of change of the other variable can be determined. The first step in solving related rates problems is defining the known rate of change. Then, determine the relationship between the two variables, then the derivatives (the rates of change), and finally substitute the problem's specific values. Consider the following example:

The side of a cube is increasing at a rate of 2 feet per second. Determine the rate at which the volume of the cube is increasing when the side of the cube is 4 feet long.

For the problem in question, the known rate of change can be expressed as $s'(t) = \frac{ds}{dt} = 2\frac{ft}{s}$, where s is the length of the side and t is the elapsed time in seconds. The relationship between the two variables of the cube is $v = s^3$, where v is the volume of the cube and s is the length of the side. The unknown rate of change to determine is the volume. As both v and s change with time, $v = s^3$ becomes $v(t) = [s(t)]^3$

Now, the chain rule is applied to differentiate both sides of the equation with respect to t.

$$d\frac{v(t)}{dt} = \frac{d[s(t)]^3}{dt}; \quad \frac{dv}{dt} = \frac{(3[s(t)]^2)ds}{dt}$$

Finally, the specific value of $s = 4$ feet is substituted, and the equation is evaluated.

$$\frac{dv}{dt} = \frac{(3[s(t)]^2)ds}{dt}$$

$$= 3(4)^2 \times 2 = 96\frac{ft^3}{s}$$

$$= 96 \text{ cubic} \frac{ft}{s}$$

Therefore, when a side of the cube is 4 feet long, the volume of the cube is increasing at a rate of 96 cubic $\frac{feet}{second}$.

> **Review Video: Solving Related Rates Problems**
> Visit mometrix.com/academy and enter code: 321959

SOLVING OPTIMIZATION PROBLEMS

An **optimization problem** is a problem in which we are asked to find the value of a variable that maximizes or minimizes a particular value. Because the maximum or maximum occurs at a critical point, and because the critical point occurs when the derivative of the function is zero, we can solve an optimization problem by setting the derivative of the function to zero and solving for the desired variable.

For example, suppose a farmer has 720 m of fencing, and wants to use it to fence in a 2 by 3 block of identical rectangular pens. What dimensions of the pens will maximize their area?

We can draw a diagram:

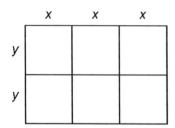

We want to maximize the area of each pen, $A(x, y) = xy$. However, we have the additional constraint that the farmer has only 720 m of fencing. In terms of x and y, we can count the number of segments of each length, 9 for x and 8 for y, so the total amount of fencing required will be $9x + 8y$. Our constraint becomes $9x + 8y = 720$; solving for y yields $y = -\frac{9}{8}x + 90$. We can substitute that into the area equation to get $A(x) = x\left(-\frac{9}{8}x + 90\right) = -\frac{9}{8}x^2 + 90x$. Taking the derivative yields $A'(x) = -\frac{9}{4}x + 90$; setting that equal to zero and solving for x yields $x = 40$. $y = -\frac{9}{8}(40) + 90 = 45$; thus, the maximum dimensions of the pen are 40 by 45 meters.

> **Review Video: Solving Optimization Problems**
> Visit mometrix.com/academy and enter code: 628734

CHARACTERISTICS OF FUNCTIONS (USING CALCULUS)

Rolle's theorem states that if a differentiable function has two different values in the domain that correspond to a single value in the range, then the function must have a point between them where the slope of the tangent to the graph is zero. This point will be a maximum or a minimum value of the function between those two points. The maximum or minimum point is the point at which $f'(c) = 0$, where c is within the appropriate interval of the function's domain. The following graph shows a function with one maximum in the second quadrant and one minimum in the fourth quadrant.

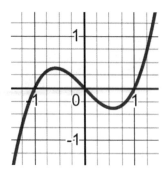

MEAN VALUE THEOREM

According to the **mean value theorem**, between any two points on a curve, there exists a tangent to the curve whose slope is parallel to the chord formed by joining those two points. Remember the formula for slope: $m = \frac{\Delta x}{\Delta y}$. In a function, $f(x)$ represents the value for y. Therefore, if you have two points on a curve, m and n, the corresponding points are $(m, f(m))$ and $(n, f(n))$. Assuming $m < n$, the formula for the slope of the chord joining those two points is $\frac{f(n)-f(m)}{n-m}$. This must also be the slope of a line parallel to the chord, since parallel lines have equal slopes. Therefore, there must be a value p between m and n such that $f'(p) = \frac{f(n)-f(m)}{n-m}$.

For a function to have continuity, its graph must be an unbroken curve. That is, it is a function that can be graphed without having to lift the pencil to move it to a different point. To say a function is continuous at point p, you must show the function satisfies three requirements. First, $f(p)$ must exist. If you evaluate the function at p, it must yield a real number. Second, there must exist a relationship such that $\lim_{x \to p} f(x) = f(p)$. Finally, the following relationship must be true:

$$\lim_{x \to p^+} F(x) = \lim_{x \to p^-} F(x) = F(p)$$

If all three of these requirements are met, a function is considered continuous at p. If any one of them is not true, the function is not continuous at p.

Review Video: <u>Mean Value Theorem</u>
Visit mometrix.com/academy and enter code: 633482

TANGENTS

Tangents are lines that touch a curve in exactly one point and have the same slope as the curve at that point. To find the slope of a curve at a given point and the slope of its tangent line at that point, find the derivative of the function of the curve. If the slope is undefined, the tangent is a vertical line. If the slope is zero, the tangent is a horizontal line.

A line that is normal to a curve at a given point is perpendicular to the tangent at that point. Assuming $f'(x) \neq 0$, the equation for the normal line at point (a, b) is: $y - b = -\frac{1}{f'(a)}(x - a)$. The easiest way to find the slope of the normal is to take the negative reciprocal of the slope of the tangent. If the slope of the tangent is zero, the slope of the normal is undefined. If the slope of the tangent is undefined, the slope of the normal is zero.

ANTIDERIVATIVES (INTEGRALS)

The antiderivative of a function is the function whose first derivative is the original function. Antiderivatives are typically represented by capital letters, while their first derivatives are represented by lower case letters. For example, if $F' = f$, then F is the antiderivative of f. Antiderivatives are also known as indefinite integrals. When taking the derivative of a function, any constant terms in the function are eliminated because their derivative is 0. To account for this possibility, when you take the indefinite integral of a function, you must add an unknown constant C to the end of the function. Because there is no way to know what the value of the original constant was when looking just at the first derivative, the integral is indefinite.

To find the indefinite integral, reverse the process of differentiation. Below are the formulas for constants and powers of x.

$$\int 0 \, dx = C$$

$$\int k \, dx = kx + C$$

$$\int x^n \, dx = \frac{x^{n+1}}{n+1} + C, \text{ where } n \neq -1$$

Recall that in the differentiation of powers of x, you multiplied the coefficient of the term by the exponent of the variable and then reduced the exponent by one. In integration, the process is reversed: add one to the value of the exponent, and then divide the coefficient of the term by this number to get the integral. Because you do not know the value of any constant term that might have been in the original function, add C to the end of the function once you have completed this process for each term.

> **Review Video: Indefinite Integrals**
> Visit mometrix.com/academy and enter code: 541913

Finding the integral of a function is the opposite of finding the derivative of the function. Where possible, you can use the trigonometric or logarithmic differentiation formulas in reverse, and add C to the end to compensate for the unknown term. In instances where a negative sign appears in the differentiation formula, move the negative sign to the opposite side (multiply both sides by -1) to reverse for the integration formula. You should end up with the following formulas:

$$\int \cos x \, dx = \sin x + C \qquad\qquad \int \sec^2 x \, dx = \tan x + C$$

$$\int \sec x \tan x \, dx = \sec x + C \qquad\qquad \int \csc^2 x \, dx = -\cot x + C$$

$$\int \sin x \, dx = -\cos x + C \qquad\qquad \int \frac{1}{x} \, dx = \ln |x| + C$$

$$\int \csc x \cot x \, dx = -\csc x + C \qquad\qquad \int e^x \, dx = e^x + C$$

Integration by substitution is the integration version of the chain rule for differentiation. The formula for integration by substitution is given by the equation

$$\int f\big(g(x)\big)g'(x)dx = \int f(u)du; \quad u = g(x) \text{ and } du = g'(x)dx$$

When a function is in a format that is difficult or impossible to integrate using traditional integration methods and formulas due to multiple functions being combined, use the formula shown above to convert the function to a simpler format that can be integrated directly.

Integration by parts is the integration version of the product rule for differentiation. Whenever you are asked to find the integral of the product of two different functions or parts, integration by parts can make the process simpler. Recall for differentiation $(fg)'(x) = f(x)g'(x) + g(x)f'(x)$. This can also be written $\frac{d}{dx}(u \times v) = u\frac{dv}{dx} + v\frac{du}{dx}$, where $u = f(x)$ and $v = g(x)$. Rearranging to integral form gives the formula:

$$\int u \, dv = uv - \int v \, du$$

$$\int f(x)g'(x) \, dx = f(x)g(x) - \int f'(x)g(x) \, dx$$

When using integration by parts, the key is selecting the best functions to substitute for u and v so that you make the integral easier to solve and not harder.

While the indefinite integral has an undefined constant added at the end, the definite integral can be calculated as an exact real number. To find the definite integral of a function over a closed interval, use the formula $\int_n^m f(x) \, dx = F(m) - F(n)$ where F is the integral of f. Because you have been given the boundaries of n and m, no undefined constant C is needed.

> **Review Video: Integration by Parts**
> Visit mometrix.com/academy and enter code: 459972
>
> **Review Video: Integration by Substitution**
> Visit mometrix.com/academy and enter code: 740649

FIRST FUNDAMENTAL THEOREM OF CALCULUS

The **first fundamental theorem of calculus** shows that the process of indefinite integration can be reversed by finding the first derivative of the resulting function. It also gives the relationship between differentiation and integration over a closed interval of the function. For example, assuming a function is continuous over the interval $[m, n]$, you can find the definite integral by using the formula

$$\int_m^n f(x) \, dx = F(n) - F(m)$$

To find the **average value** of the function over the given interval, use the formula:

$$\frac{1}{n-m}\int_m^n f(x) \, dx$$

> **Review Video: First Fundamental Theorem of Calculus**
> Visit mometrix.com/academy and enter code: 248431

SECOND FUNDAMENTAL THEOREM OF CALCULUS

The **second fundamental theorem of calculus** is related to the first. This theorem states that, assuming the function is continuous over the interval you are considering, taking the derivative of the integral of a function will yield the original function. The general format for this theorem for any point having a domain value equal to c in the given interval is:

$$\frac{d}{dx}\int_c^x f(t) \, dt = f(x)$$

For each of the following **properties of integrals** of function f, the variables $m, n,$ and p represent values in the domain of the given interval of $f(x)$. The function is assumed to be integrable across all relevant intervals.

Swapping the limits of integration:

$$\int_m^n f(x)\, dx = -\int_n^m f(x)\, dx$$

Function multiplied by a constant:

$$\int_m^n k f(x) dx = k \int_m^n f(x)\, dx$$

Separating the integral into parts:

$$\int_m^n f(x)\, dx = \int_m^p f(x)\, dx + \int_p^n f(x)\, dx$$

If the limits of integration are equivalent:

$$\int_n^n f(x)\, dx = 0$$

If $f(x)$ is an even function and the limits of integration are symmetric:

$$\int_{-m}^m f(x)\, dx = 2\int_0^m f(x)\, dx$$

If $f(x)$ is an odd function and the limits of integration are symmetric:

$$\int_{-m}^m f(x)\, dx = 0$$

> **Review Video: Second Fundamental Theorem of Calculus**
> Visit mometrix.com/academy and enter code: 524689

MATCHING FUNCTIONS TO DERIVATIVES OR ACCUMULATIONS

DERIVATIVES

We can use what we know about the meaning of a derivative to match the graph of a function with a graph of its derivative. For one thing, we know that where the function has a critical point, the derivative is zero. Therefore, at every x value at which the graph of a function has a maximum or minimum, the derivative must cross the *x-axis*—and conversely, everywhere the graph of the derivative crosses the x axis, the function must have a critical point: either a maximum, a minimum, or an inflection point. If this is still not enough to identify the correct match, we can also use the fact that the sign of the derivative corresponds to whether the function is increasing or decreasing: everywhere the graph of the derivative is above the x-axis, the function must be increasing (its slope is positive), and everywhere the graph of the derivative is below the x-axis, the function must be decreasing (its slope is negative).

For example, below are graphs of the function and its derivative. The maxima and minima of the function (left) are circled, and the zeroes of the derivative (right) are circled.

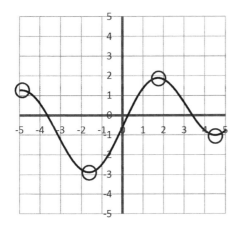 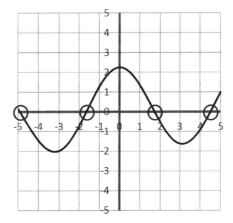

ACCUMULATIONS

The **accumulation** of a function is another name for its antiderivative, or integral. We can use the relationship between a function and its antiderivative to match the corresponding graphs. For example, we know that where the graph of the function is above the x-axis, the function is positive, thus the accumulation must be increasing (its slope is positive); where the graph of the function is below the x-axis, the accumulation must be decreasing (its slope is negative). It follows that where the function changes from positive to negative—where the graph crosses the x-axis with a negative slope—, its accumulation changes from increasing to decreasing—so the accumulation has a local maximum. Where the function changes from negative to positive—where its graph crosses the x-axis with a positive slope—, the accumulation has a local minimum.

For example, below are graphs of a function and its accumulation. The points on the function (left) where the graph crosses the x-axis are circled; the local minima and maxima of the accumulation (right) are circled.

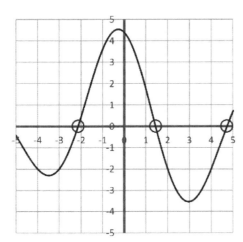 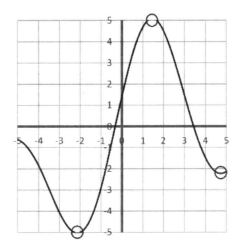

RIEMANN SUMS

A **Riemann sum** is a sum used to approximate the definite integral of a function over a particular interval by dividing the area under the function into vertical rectangular strips and adding the areas of the strips. The height of each strip is equal to the value of the function at some point within the

95

interval covered by the strip. Formally, if we divide the interval over which we are finding the area into n intervals bounded by the $n + 1$ points $\{x_i\}$ (where x_0 and x_n are the left and right bounds of the interval), then the Riemann sum is $\sum_{i=1}^{n} f(x_i^*)\Delta x_i$, where $\Delta x_i = x_i - x_{i-1}$ and x_i^* is some point in the interval $[x_{i-1}, x_i]$. In principle, any point in the interval can be chosen, but common choices include the left endpoint of the interval (yielding the **left Riemann sum**), the right endpoint (yielding the **right Riemann sum**), and the midpoint of the interval (the basis of the **midpoint rule**). Usually, it is convenient to set all the intervals to the same width, although the definition of the Riemann sum does not require this.

The following graphic shows the rectangular strips used for one possible Riemann sum of a particular function:

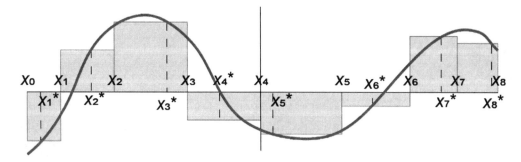

LEFT AND RIGHT RIEMANN SUMS

A **Riemann sum** is an approximation to the definite integral of a function over a particular interval performed by dividing it into smaller intervals and summing the products of the width of each interval and the value of the function evaluated at some point within the interval. The **left Riemann sum** is a Riemann sum in which the function is evaluated at the left endpoint of each interval. In the **right Riemann sum**, the function is evaluated at the right endpoint of each interval.

When the function is increasing, the left Riemann sum will always underestimate the function. This is because we are evaluating the function at the minimum point within each interval; the integral of the function in the interval will be larger than the estimate. Conversely, the right Riemann sum is evaluating the function at the maximum point within each interval, thus it will always overestimate the function. Consider the following diagrams, in which the area under the same increasing function is shown approximated by a left Riemann sum and a right Riemann sum:

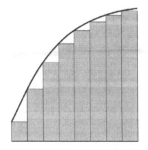 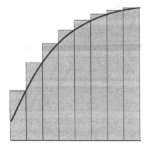

For a decreasing function these considerations are reversed: a left Riemann sum will overestimate the integral, and a right Riemann sum will underestimate it.

MIDPOINT RULE

The **midpoint rule** is a way of approximating the definite integral of a function over an interval by dividing the interval into smaller sub-intervals, multiplying the width of each sub-interval by the value of the function at the midpoint of the sub-interval, and then summing these products. This is a special case of the Riemann sum, specifying the midpoint of the interval as the point at which the function is to be evaluated. The approximation found using the midpoint rule is usually more accurate than that found using the left or right Riemann sum, though as the number of intervals becomes very large the difference becomes negligible.

For example, suppose we are asked to estimate by the midpoint rule the integral of $f(x) = \frac{1}{x}$ in the interval [2, 4]. We can divide this interval into four intervals of width $\frac{1}{2}$: [2, 2.5], [2.5, 3], [3, 3.5], and [3.5, 4]. (The more intervals, the more accurate the estimate, but we'll use a small number of intervals in this example to keep it simple.) The midpoint rule then gives an estimate of

$$\frac{1}{2}\big(f(2.25)\big) + \frac{1}{2}\big(f(2.75)\big) + \frac{1}{2}\big(f(3.25)\big) + \frac{1}{2}\big(f(3.75)\big) = \frac{1}{2}\left(\frac{4}{9}\right) + \frac{1}{2}\left(\frac{4}{11}\right) + \frac{1}{2}\left(\frac{4}{13}\right) + \frac{1}{2}\left(\frac{4}{15}\right) \approx 0.691,$$ not

far from the actual value of $\int_2^4 \frac{1}{x}\, dx = [\ln x]_2^4 \approx 0.693$.

> **Review Video: Midpoint Rule**
> Visit mometrix.com/academy and enter code: 790070

TRAPEZOID RULE

The **trapezoid rule** is a method of approximating the definite integral of a function by dividing the area under the function into a series of trapezoidal strips, the upper corners of the trapezoid touching the function, and adding the areas of the strips. The following diagram shows the use of the trapezoid rule to estimate the integral of the function $y = 2^x$ in the interval [0, 3]:

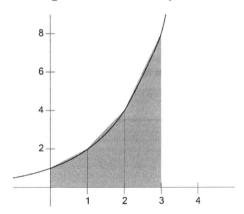

Mathematically, if we define the endpoints of the n subdivisions to be $\{x_{i-1}, x_i\}$: $(1 \le i \le n)$, where x_0 and x_n are the endpoints of the entire interval over which we are estimating the integral, then the result of the application of the trapezoid rule is equal to $\sum_{i=1}^{n} \left(\frac{f(x_{i-1}) + f(x_i)}{2}\right)(x_i - x_{i-1})$. For the example shown above, that yields $\left(\frac{2^1 + 2^0}{2}\right)(1 - 0) + \left(\frac{2^2 + 2^1}{2}\right)(2 - 1) + \left(\frac{2^3 + 2^2}{2}\right)(3 - 2) = \frac{21}{2}$, or

10.5—not far from the actual value of $\int_0^3 2^x dx = \int_0^3 e^{x \ln 2}\, dx = \left[\frac{2^x}{\ln 2}\right]_0^3 \approx 10.1$. (Of course, we could have achieved more accuracy by using smaller subdivisions.)

The trapezoid rule is related to the Riemann sum, but usually gives more accurate results than the left or right Riemann sum for the same number of intervals. In fact, it isn't hard to prove that the answer given by the trapezoid rule is equal to the average of the left and right Riemann sums using the same partition.

> **Review Video: Trapezoid Rule**
> Visit mometrix.com/academy and enter code: 170482

LIMIT OF RIEMANN SUMS

As the number of sub-intervals becomes larger, and the width of each sub-interval becomes smaller, the approximation becomes increasingly accurate, and at the limit as the number of sub-intervals approaches infinity and their width approaches zero, the value becomes exact. In fact, the definite integral is often defined as a limit of Riemann sums.

It's possible to find the definite integral by this method. Suppose we want to find the integral of $f(x) = x^2$ over the interval $[0, 2]$. We'll divide this interval into n sub-intervals of equal width and evaluate the function at the right endpoint of each sub-interval. (This choice is arbitrary; at the limit the answer would be the same if we chose the left endpoint, or any other point within the interval.)

Our Riemann sum becomes $\sum_{i=1}^{n} \frac{2}{n}\left(\frac{2}{n}i\right)^2 = \frac{8}{n^3}\sum_{i=1}^{n} i^2$, where $\sum_{i=1}^{n} i^2 = \frac{1}{6}n(n+1)(2n+1)$, thus this becomes $\frac{8}{n^3} \cdot \frac{1}{6}n(n+1)(2n+1) = \frac{4}{3}\left(1+\frac{1}{n}\right)\left(2+\frac{1}{n}\right)$. At the limit as $n \to \infty$, this becomes $\frac{4}{3}(1)(2) = \frac{8}{3}$. This is the same result as we get by integrating directly: $\int_0^2 x^2 dx = \left[\frac{1}{3}x^3\right]_0^2 = \frac{1}{3}(2)^3 - \frac{1}{3}(0)^3 = \frac{8}{3}$.

USES FOR INTEGRATION

CALCULATING DISTANCES

When given the velocity of an object over time, it's possible to find a distance by integration. The velocity is the rate of change of the position; therefore, the displacement is the accumulation of the velocity: that is, the integral of the velocity is the displacement. However, if asked to find the total distance traveled (as opposed to the displacement), it's important to take the sign into account: we must integrate not just the velocity, but the absolute value of the velocity, which essentially means integrating separately over each interval in which the velocity has a different sign.

For example, suppose we're asked to find the total distance traveled from $t = 0$ to $t = 8$ by an object moving with a velocity in meters per second given by the equation $v(t) = 2\sqrt{t} - t$. This function is zero when $2\sqrt{t} - t = 0 \Rightarrow \sqrt{t}(2 - \sqrt{t}) = 0 \Rightarrow t = 0$ or 4. $v(t)$ is positive when $0 < t < 4$ and negative when $t > 4$. Thus, the distance travelled is

$$\int_0^8 |v(t)|dt = \int_0^8 |2\sqrt{t} - t|dt$$

$$= \int_0^4 (2\sqrt{t} - t)dt - \int_4^8 (2\sqrt{t} - t)dt$$

$$= \left[\frac{4}{3}t^{\frac{3}{2}} - \frac{1}{2}t^2\right]_0^4 - \left[\frac{4}{3}t^{\frac{3}{2}} - \frac{1}{2}t^2\right]_4^8$$

$$= \left(\left[\frac{4}{3}(4)^{\frac{3}{2}} - \frac{1}{2}4^2\right] - \left[\frac{4}{3}(0)^{\frac{3}{2}} - \frac{1}{2}(0)^2\right]\right) - \left(\left[\frac{4}{3}(8)^{\frac{3}{2}} - \frac{1}{2}(8)^2\right] - \left[\frac{4}{3}(4)^{\frac{3}{2}} - \frac{1}{2}(4)^2\right]\right)$$

$$= \left(\left[\frac{32}{3} - 8\right] - 0\right) - \left(\left[\frac{64}{3}\sqrt{2} - 32\right] - \left[\frac{32}{3} - 8\right]\right)$$

$$= \frac{8}{3} - \frac{64}{3}\sqrt{2} + \frac{96}{3} + \frac{8}{3}$$

$$= \frac{8}{3}(1 - 8\sqrt{2} + 12 + 1)$$

$$= \frac{8}{3}(14 - 8\sqrt{2}) \approx 7.16 \text{ meters}$$

> **Review Video: Calculating Distances Using Integration**
> Visit mometrix.com/academy and enter code: 866719

CALCULATING AREAS

One way to calculate the area of an irregular shape is to find a formula for the width of the shape along the x direction as a function of the y coordinate, and then integrate over y, or vice versa. What this amounts to is dividing the area into thin strips and adding the areas of the strips—and then taking the limit as the width of the strips approaches zero.

For example, suppose we want to find the area enclosed by the functions $y_1 = x^2$ and $y_2 = (2 - x^2)$. The height of this enclosure is equal to $y_2 - y_1 = 2 - 2x^2$; we can find the area by integrating this height over x. The two shapes intersect at the points $(1, 1)$ and $(-1, 1)$, thus our limits of integration are –1 and 1. Thus the area can be found as:

$$\int_{-1}^1 (2 - 2x^2)dx = \left[2x - \frac{2}{3}x^3\right]_{-1}^1 = \left(2(1) - \frac{2}{3}(1)\right) - \left(2(-1) - \frac{2}{3}(-1)\right) = \frac{8}{3}$$

> **Review Video: Calculating Areas Using Integration**
> Visit mometrix.com/academy and enter code: 118949

CALCULATING VOLUMES

One way to calculate the volume of a three-dimensional shape is to find a formula for its cross-sectional area perpendicular to some axis and then integrate over that axis. Effectively, this divides the shape into thin, flat slices and adds the volumes of the slices—and then takes the limit as the thickness of the slices approaches zero.

For example, suppose we want to find the volume of the ellipsoid $4x^2 + 4y^2 + z^2 = 36$. If we take a cross-section perpendicular to the z-axis, this has the formula $4x^2 + 4y^2 = 36 - z^2$, or $x^2 + y^2 = 9 - \frac{z^2}{4}$; this is the formula of a circle with a radius of $\sqrt{9 - \frac{z^2}{4}}$, and thus has an area of $\pi\left(9 - \frac{z^2}{4}\right)$. To find the volume, we integrate this formula over z. The maximum and minimum values of z occur when $x = y = 0$, and then $z^2 = 36$, thus $z = \pm 6$; these are our limits of integration. Thus, the volume is:

$$
\int_{-6}^{6} \pi\left(9 - \frac{z^2}{4}\right) dz = \pi\left[9z - \frac{z^3}{12}\right]_{-6}^{6}
$$

$$
= \pi\left[\left(9(6) - \frac{6^3}{12}\right) - \left(9(-6) - \frac{(-6)^3}{12}\right)\right]
$$

$$
= \pi[(54 - 18) - (-54 + 18)]
$$

$$
= 72\pi \approx 226.2
$$

Review Video: <u>Calculating Volume Using Integration</u>
Visit mometrix.com/academy and enter code: 100341

Geometry

Rounding and Estimation

ROUNDING AND ESTIMATION

Rounding is reducing the digits in a number while still trying to keep the value similar. The result will be less accurate but in a simpler form and easier to use. Whole numbers can be rounded to the nearest ten, hundred, or thousand.

When you are asked to estimate the solution to a problem, you will need to provide only an approximate figure or **estimation** for your answer. In this situation, you will need to round each number in the calculation to the level indicated (nearest hundred, nearest thousand, etc.) or to a level that makes sense for the numbers involved. When estimating a sum **all numbers must be rounded to the same level**. You cannot round one number to the nearest thousand while rounding another to the nearest hundred.

> **Review Video: Rounding and Estimation**
> Visit mometrix.com/academy and enter code: 126243

Scientific Notation

SCIENTIFIC NOTATION

Scientific notation is a way of writing large numbers in a shorter form. The form $a \times 10^n$ is used in scientific notation, where a is greater than or equal to 1 but less than 10, and n is the number of places the decimal must move to get from the original number to a. Example: The number 230,400,000 is cumbersome to write. To write the value in scientific notation, place a decimal point between the first and second numbers, and include all digits through the last non-zero digit $(a = 2.304)$. To find the appropriate power of 10, count the number of places the decimal point had to move $(n = 8)$. The number is positive if the decimal moved to the left, and negative if it moved to the right. We can then write 230,400,000 as 2.304×10^8. If we look instead at the number 0.00002304, we have the same value for a, but this time the decimal moved 5 places to the right $(n = -5)$. Thus, 0.00002304 can be written as 2.304×10^{-5}. Using this notation makes it simple to compare very large or very small numbers. By comparing exponents, it is easy to see that 3.28×10^4 is smaller than 1.51×10^5, because 4 is less than 5.

> **Review Video: Scientific Notation**
> Visit mometrix.com/academy and enter code: 976454

Precision, Accuracy, and Error

PRECISION, ACCURACY, AND ERROR

Precision: How reliable and repeatable a measurement is. The more consistent the data is with repeated testing, the more precise it is. For example, hitting a target consistently in the same spot, which may or may not be the center of the target, is precision.

Accuracy: How close the data is to the correct data. For example, hitting a target consistently in the center area of the target, whether or not the hits are all in the same spot, is accuracy.

Note: it is possible for data to be precise without being accurate. If a scale is off balance, the data will be precise, but will not be accurate. For data to have precision and accuracy, it must be repeatable and correct.

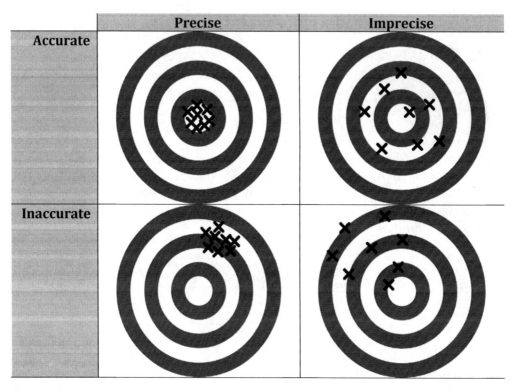

Approximate error: The amount of error in a physical measurement. Approximate error is often reported as the measurement, followed by the ± symbol and the amount of the approximate error.

Maximum possible error: Half the magnitude of the smallest unit used in the measurement. For example, if the unit of measurement is 1 centimeter, the maximum possible error is $\frac{1}{2}$ cm, written as ±0.5 cm following the measurement. It is important to apply significant figures in reporting maximum possible error. Do not make the answer appear more accurate than the least accurate of your measurements.

> **Review Video: Precision, Accuracy, and Error**
> Visit mometrix.com/academy and enter code: 520377

Parabolas

PARABOLA

A **parabola** is the set of all points in a plane that are equidistant from a fixed line, called the **directrix**, and a fixed point not on the line, called the **focus**. The **axis** is the line perpendicular to the directrix that passes through the focus.

For parabolas that open up or down, the standard equation is $(x - h)^2 = 4c(y - k)$, where h, c, and k are coefficients. If c is positive, the parabola opens up. If c is negative, the parabola opens down. The vertex is the point (h, k). The directrix is the line having the equation $y = -c + k$, and the focus is the point $(h, c + k)$.

For parabolas that open left or right, the standard equation is $(y - k)^2 = 4c(x - h)$, where k, c, and h are coefficients. If c is positive, the parabola opens to the right. If c is negative, the parabola opens to the left. The vertex is the point (h, k). The directrix is the line having the equation $x = -c + h$, and the focus is the point $(c + h, k)$.

Review Video: Parabolas
Visit mometrix.com/academy and enter code: 129187

Review Video: Vertex of a Parabola
Visit mometrix.com/academy and enter code: 272300

Metric and Customary Measurements

METRIC MEASUREMENT PREFIXES

Giga-	One billion	1 *giga*watt is one billion watts
Mega-	One million	1 *mega*hertz is one million hertz
Kilo-	One thousand	1 *kilo*gram is one thousand grams
Deci-	One-tenth	1 *deci*meter is one-tenth of a meter
Centi-	One-hundredth	1 *centi*meter is one-hundredth of a meter
Milli-	One-thousandth	1 *milli*liter is one-thousandth of a liter
Micro-	One-millionth	1 *micro*gram is one-millionth of a gram

---

Review Video: Metric System Conversion - How the Metric System Works
Visit mometrix.com/academy and enter code: 163709

MEASUREMENT CONVERSION

When converting between units, the goal is to maintain the same meaning but change the way it is displayed. In order to go from a larger unit to a smaller unit, multiply the number of the known amount by the equivalent amount. When going from a smaller unit to a larger unit, divide the number of the known amount by the equivalent amount.

For complicated conversions, it may be helpful to set up conversion fractions. In these fractions, one fraction is the **conversion factor**. The other fraction has the unknown amount in the numerator. So, the known value is placed in the denominator. Sometimes, the second fraction has the known value from the problem in the numerator and the unknown in the denominator. Multiply the two fractions to get the converted measurement. Note that since the numerator and the denominator of the factor are equivalent, the value of the fraction is 1. That is why we can say that the result in the new units is equal to the result in the old units even though they have different numbers.

It can often be necessary to chain known conversion factors together. As an example, consider converting 512 square inches to square meters. We know that there are 2.54 centimeters in an inch and 100 centimeters in a meter, and we know we will need to square each of these factors to achieve the conversion we are looking for.

$$\frac{512 \text{ in}^2}{1} \times \left(\frac{2.54 \text{ cm}}{1 \text{ in}}\right)^2 \times \left(\frac{1 \text{ m}}{100 \text{ cm}}\right)^2 = \frac{512 \text{ in}^2}{1} \times \left(\frac{6.4516 \text{ cm}^2}{1 \text{ in}^2}\right) \times \left(\frac{1 \text{ m}^2}{10,000 \text{ cm}^2}\right) = 0.330 \text{ m}^2$$

> **Review Video: Measurement Conversions**
> Visit mometrix.com/academy and enter code: 316703

COMMON UNITS AND EQUIVALENTS

METRIC EQUIVALENTS

1000 µg (microgram)	1 mg
1000 mg (milligram)	1 g
1000 g (gram)	1 kg
1000 kg (kilogram)	1 metric ton
1000 mL (milliliter)	1 L
1000 µm (micrometer)	1 mm
1000 mm (millimeter)	1 m
100 cm (centimeter)	1 m
1000 m (meter)	1 km

DISTANCE AND AREA MEASUREMENT

Unit	Abbreviation	US equivalent	Metric equivalent
Inch	in	1 inch	2.54 centimeters
Foot	ft	12 inches	0.305 meters
Yard	yd	3 feet	0.914 meters
Mile	mi	5280 feet	1.609 kilometers
Acre	ac	4840 square yards	0.405 hectares
Square Mile	sq. mi. or mi.^{2}	640 acres	2.590 square kilometers

CAPACITY MEASUREMENTS

Unit	Abbreviation	US equivalent	Metric equivalent
Fluid Ounce	fl oz	8 fluid drams	29.573 milliliters
Cup	c	8 fluid ounces	0.237 liter
Pint	pt.	16 fluid ounces	0.473 liter
Quart	qt.	2 pints	0.946 liter
Gallon	gal.	4 quarts	3.785 liters
Teaspoon	t or tsp.	1 fluid dram	5 milliliters
Tablespoon	T or tbsp.	4 fluid drams	15 or 16 milliliters
Cubic Centimeter	cc or cm^3	0.271 drams	1 milliliter

WEIGHT MEASUREMENTS

Unit	Abbreviation	US equivalent	Metric equivalent
Ounce	oz	16 drams	28.35 grams
Pound	lb	16 ounces	453.6 grams
Ton	tn.	2,000 pounds	907.2 kilograms

VOLUME AND WEIGHT MEASUREMENT CLARIFICATIONS

Always be careful when using ounces and fluid ounces. They are not equivalent.

1 pint = 16 fluid ounces	1 fluid ounce ≠ 1 ounce
1 pound = 16 ounces	1 pint ≠ 1 pound

Having one pint of something does not mean you have one pound of it. In the same way, just because something weighs one pound does not mean that its volume is one pint.

In the United States, the word "ton" by itself refers to a short ton or a net ton. Do not confuse this with a long ton (also called a gross ton) or a metric ton (also spelled *tonne*), which have different measurement equivalents.

$$1 \text{ US ton} = 2000 \text{ pounds} \qquad \neq \qquad 1 \text{ metric ton} = 1000 \text{ kilograms}$$

Points, Lines, and Planes

POINTS AND LINES

A **point** is a fixed location in space, has no size or dimensions, and is commonly represented by a dot. A **line** is a set of points that extends infinitely in two opposite directions. It has length, but no width or depth. A line can be defined by any two distinct points that it contains. A **line segment** is a portion of a line that has definite endpoints. A **ray** is a portion of a line that extends from a single point on that line in one direction along the line. It has a definite beginning, but no ending.

INTERACTIONS BETWEEN LINES

Intersecting lines are lines that have exactly one point in common. **Concurrent lines** are multiple lines that intersect at a single point. **Perpendicular lines** are lines that intersect at right angles. They are represented by the symbol ⊥. The shortest distance from a line to a point not on the line is a perpendicular segment from the point to the line. **Parallel lines** are lines in the same plane that have no points in common and never meet. It is possible for lines to be in different planes, have no points in common, and never meet, but they are not parallel because they are in different planes.

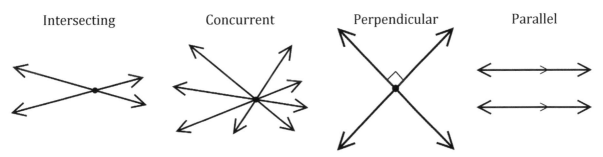

Review Video: Parallel and Perpendicular Lines
Visit mometrix.com/academy and enter code: 815923

A **transversal** is a line that intersects at least two other lines, which may or may not be parallel to one another. A transversal that intersects parallel lines is a common occurrence in geometry. A

bisector is a line or line segment that divides another line segment into two equal lengths. A **perpendicular bisector** of a line segment is composed of points that are equidistant from the endpoints of the segment it is dividing.

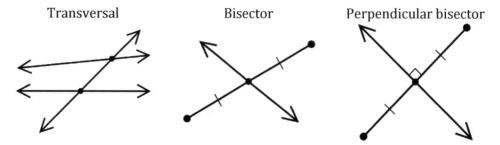

Transversal   Bisector   Perpendicular bisector

The **projection of a point on a line** is the point at which a perpendicular line drawn from the given point to the given line intersects the line. This is also the shortest distance from the given point to the line. The **projection of a segment on a line** is a segment whose endpoints are the points formed when perpendicular lines are drawn from the endpoints of the given segment to the given line. This is similar to the length a diagonal line appears to be when viewed from above.

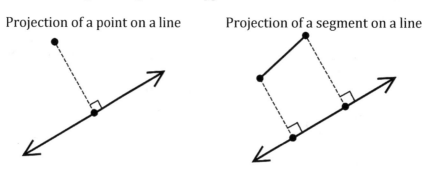

Projection of a point on a line   Projection of a segment on a line

PLANES

A **plane** is a two-dimensional flat surface defined by three non-collinear points. A plane extends an infinite distance in all directions in those two dimensions. It contains an infinite number of points, parallel lines and segments, intersecting lines and segments, as well as parallel or intersecting rays. A plane will never contain a three-dimensional figure or skew lines, which are lines that don't intersect and are not parallel. Two given planes are either parallel or they intersect at a line. A plane may intersect a circular conic surface to form **conic sections**, such as a parabola, hyperbola, circle or ellipse.

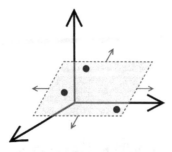

Review Video: Lines and Planes
Visit mometrix.com/academy and enter code: 554267

106

Angles

ANGLES AND VERTICES

An **angle** is formed when two lines or line segments meet at a common point. It may be a common starting point for a pair of segments or rays, or it may be the intersection of lines. Angles are represented by the symbol ∠.

The **vertex** is the point at which two segments or rays meet to form an angle. If the angle is formed by intersecting rays, lines, and/or line segments, the vertex is the point at which four angles are formed. The pairs of angles opposite one another are called vertical angles, and their measures are equal.

- An **acute** angle is an angle with a degree measure less than 90°.
- A **right** angle is an angle with a degree measure of exactly 90°.
- An **obtuse** angle is an angle with a degree measure greater than 90° but less than 180°.
- A **straight angle** is an angle with a degree measure of exactly 180°. This is also a semicircle.
- A **reflex angle** is an angle with a degree measure greater than 180° but less than 360°.
- A **full angle** is an angle with a degree measure of exactly 360°. This is also a circle.

> **Review Video: Angles**
> Visit mometrix.com/academy and enter code: 264624

RELATIONSHIPS BETWEEN ANGLES

Two angles whose sum is exactly 90° are said to be **complementary**. The two angles may or may not be adjacent. In a right triangle, the two acute angles are complementary.

Two angles whose sum is exactly 180° are said to be **supplementary**. The two angles may or may not be adjacent. Two intersecting lines always form two pairs of supplementary angles. Adjacent supplementary angles will always form a straight line.

Two angles that have the same vertex and share a side are said to be **adjacent**. Vertical angles are not adjacent because they share a vertex but no common side.

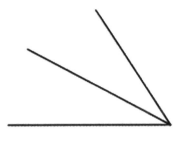 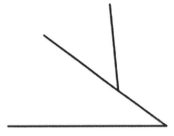

| **Adjacent** | **Not adjacent** |
| Share vertex and side | Share part of a side, but not vertex |

When two parallel lines are cut by a transversal, the angles that are between the two parallel lines are **interior angles**. In the diagram below, angles 3, 4, 5, and 6 are interior angles.

When two parallel lines are cut by a transversal, the angles that are outside the parallel lines are **exterior angles**. In the diagram below, angles 1, 2, 7, and 8 are exterior angles.

When two parallel lines are cut by a transversal, the angles that are in the same position relative to the transversal and a parallel line are **corresponding angles**. The diagram below has four pairs of corresponding angles: angles 1 and 5, angles 2 and 6, angles 3 and 7, and angles 4 and 8. Corresponding angles formed by parallel lines are congruent.

When two parallel lines are cut by a transversal, the two interior angles that are on opposite sides of the transversal are called **alternate interior angles**. In the diagram below, there are two pairs of alternate interior angles: angles 3 and 6, and angles 4 and 5. Alternate interior angles formed by parallel lines are congruent.

When two parallel lines are cut by a transversal, the two exterior angles that are on opposite sides of the transversal are called **alternate exterior angles**.

In the diagram below, there are two pairs of alternate exterior angles: angles 1 and 8, and angles 2 and 7. Alternate exterior angles formed by parallel lines are congruent.

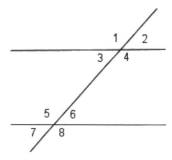

When two lines intersect, four angles are formed. The non-adjacent angles at this vertex are called vertical angles. Vertical angles are congruent. In the diagram, $\angle ABD \cong \angle CBE$ and $\angle ABC \cong \angle DBE$. The other pairs of angles, $(\angle ABC, \angle CBE)$ and $(\angle ABD, \angle DBE)$, are supplementary, meaning the pairs sum to 180°.

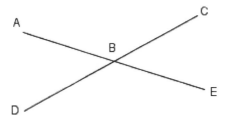

Polygons

POLYGONS

A **polygon** is a closed, two-dimensional figure with three or more straight line segments called **sides**. The point at which two sides of a polygon intersect is called the **vertex**. In a polygon, the number of sides is always equal to the number of vertices. A polygon with all sides congruent and all angles equal is called a **regular polygon**. Common polygons are:

$$\text{Triangle} = 3 \text{ sides}$$
$$\text{Quadrilateral} = 4 \text{ sides}$$
$$\text{Pentagon} = 5 \text{ sides}$$
$$\text{Hexagon} = 6 \text{ sides}$$
$$\text{Heptagon} = 7 \text{ sides}$$
$$\text{Octagon} = 8 \text{ sides}$$
$$\text{Nonagon} = 9 \text{ sides}$$
$$\text{Decagon} = 10 \text{ sides}$$
$$\text{Dodecagon} = 12 \text{ sides}$$

More generally, an n-gon is a polygon that has n angles and n sides.

Review Video: <u>Intro to Polygons</u>
Visit mometrix.com/academy and enter code: 271869

The sum of the interior angles of an n-sided polygon is $(n - 2) \times 180°$. For example, in a triangle $n = 3$. So the sum of the interior angles is $(3 - 2) \times 180° = 180°$. In a quadrilateral, $n = 4$, and the sum of the angles is $(4 - 2) \times 180° = 360°$.

Review Video: <u>Sum of Interior Angles</u>
Visit mometrix.com/academy and enter code: 984991

CONVEX AND CONCAVE POLYGONS

A **convex polygon** is a polygon whose diagonals all lie within the interior of the polygon. A **concave polygon** is a polygon with a least one diagonal that is outside the polygon. In the diagram below, quadrilateral $ABCD$ is concave because diagonal $\overline{AC}$ lies outside the polygon and quadrilateral $EFGH$ is convex because both diagonals lie inside the polygon.

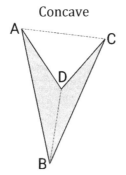
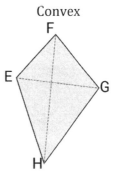

Apothem and Radius

APOTHEM AND RADIUS

A line segment from the center of a polygon that is perpendicular to a side of the polygon is called the **apothem**. A line segment from the center of a polygon to a vertex of the polygon is called a

radius. In a regular polygon, the apothem can be used to find the area of the polygon using the formula $A = \frac{1}{2}ap$, where a is the apothem, and p is the perimeter.

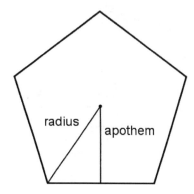

A **diagonal** is a line segment that joins two non-adjacent vertices of a polygon. The number of diagonals a polygon has can be found by using the formula:

$$\text{number of diagonals} = \frac{n(n-3)}{2}$$

Note that n is the number of sides in the polygon. This formula works for all polygons, not just regular polygons.

Congruence and Similarity

CONGRUENCE AND SIMILARITY

Congruent figures are geometric figures that have the same size and shape. All corresponding angles are equal, and all corresponding sides are equal. Congruence is indicated by the symbol ≅.

Congruent polygons

Similar figures are geometric figures that have the same shape, but do not necessarily have the same size. All corresponding angles are equal, and all corresponding sides are proportional, but they do not have to be equal. It is indicated by the symbol ∼.

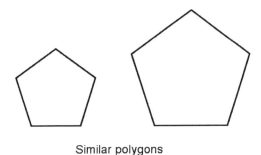

Similar polygons

Note that all congruent figures are also similar, but not all similar figures are congruent.

Line of Symmetry

LINE OF SYMMETRY

A line that divides a figure or object into congruent parts is called a **line of symmetry**. An object may have no lines of symmetry, one line of symmetry, or multiple (i.e., more than one) lines of symmetry.

None   One   Multiple

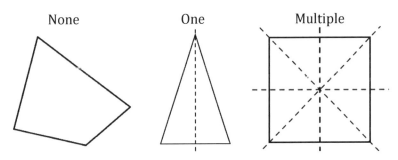

Triangles

TRIANGLES

A triangle is a three-sided figure with the sum of its interior angles being 180°. The **perimeter of any triangle** is found by summing the three side lengths; $P = a + b + c$. For an equilateral triangle, this is the same as $P = 3a$, where a is any side length, since all three sides are the same length.

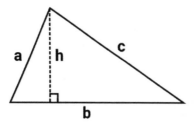

Review Video: **Proof that a Triangle is 180 Degrees**
Visit mometrix.com/academy and enter code: 687591
Review Video: **Area and Perimeter of a Triangle**
Visit mometrix.com/academy and enter code: 853779

The **area of any triangle** can be found by taking half the product of one side length referred to as the base, often given the variable b and the perpendicular distance from that side to the opposite vertex called the altitude or height and given the variable h. In equation form that is $A = \frac{1}{2}bh$. Another formula that works for any triangle is $A = \sqrt{s(s-a)(s-b)(s-c)}$, where s is the semiperimeter: $\frac{a+b+c}{2}$, and a, b, and c are the lengths of the three sides. Special cases include isosceles triangles, $A = \frac{1}{2}b\sqrt{a^2 - \frac{b^2}{4}}$, where b is the unique side and a is the length of one of the two congruent sides, and equilateral triangles, $A = \frac{\sqrt{3}}{4}a^2$, where a is the length of a side.

Review Video: **Area of Any Triangle**
Visit mometrix.com/academy and enter code: 138510

PARTS OF A TRIANGLE

An **altitude** of a triangle is a line segment drawn from one vertex perpendicular to the opposite side. In the diagram that follows, $\overline{BE}$, $\overline{AD}$, and $\overline{CF}$ are altitudes. The length of an altitude is also called the height of the triangle. The three altitudes in a triangle are always concurrent. The point of concurrency of the altitudes of a triangle, O, is called the **orthocenter**. Note that in an obtuse triangle, the orthocenter will be outside the triangle, and in a right triangle, the orthocenter is the vertex of the right angle.

A **median** of a triangle is a line segment drawn from one vertex to the midpoint of the opposite side. In the diagram that follows, $\overline{BH}$, $\overline{AG}$, and $\overline{CI}$ are medians. This is not the same as the altitude, except the altitude to the base of an isosceles triangle and all three altitudes of an equilateral triangle. The point of concurrency of the medians of a triangle, T, is called the **centroid**. This is the same point as the orthocenter only in an equilateral triangle. Unlike the orthocenter, the centroid is always inside the triangle. The centroid can also be considered the exact center of the triangle. Any

112

shape triangle can be perfectly balanced on a tip placed at the centroid. The centroid is also the point that is two-thirds the distance from the vertex to the opposite side.

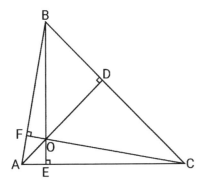 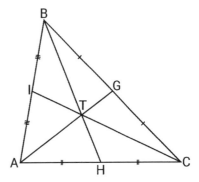

Review Video: <u>Centroid, Incenter, Circumcenter, and Orthocenter</u>
Visit mometrix.com/academy and enter code: 598260

Triangle Properties

CLASSIFICATIONS OF TRIANGLES

A **scalene triangle** is a triangle with no congruent sides. A scalene triangle will also have three angles of different measures. The angle with the largest measure is opposite the longest side, and the angle with the smallest measure is opposite the shortest side. An **acute triangle** is a triangle whose three angles are all less than 90°. If two of the angles are equal, the acute triangle is also an **isosceles triangle**. An isosceles triangle will also have two congruent angles opposite the two congruent sides. If the three angles are all equal, the acute triangle is also an **equilateral triangle**. An equilateral triangle will also have three congruent angles, each 60°. All equilateral triangles are also acute triangles. An **obtuse triangle** is a triangle with exactly one angle greater than 90°. The other two angles may or may not be equal. If the two remaining angles are equal, the obtuse triangle is also an isosceles triangle. A **right triangle** is a triangle with exactly one angle equal to 90°. All right triangles follow the Pythagorean theorem. A right triangle can never be acute or obtuse.

The table below illustrates how each descriptor places a different restriction on the triangle:

Sides \ Angles	Acute: All angles < 90°	Obtuse: One angle > 90°	Right: One angle = 90°
Scalene: No equal side lengths	$90° > \angle a > \angle b > \angle c$ $x > y > z$	$\angle a > 90° > \angle b > \angle c$ $x > y > z$	$90° = \angle a > \angle b > \angle c$ $x > y > z$
Isosceles: Two equal side lengths	$90° > \angle a, \angle b, or \angle c$ $\angle b = \angle c, \quad y = z$	$\angle a > 90° > \angle b = \angle c$ $x > y = z$	$\angle a = 90°$ $\angle b = \angle c = 45°$ $x > y = z$
Equilateral: Three equal side lengths	$60° = \angle a = \angle b = \angle c$ $x = y = z$		

> **Review Video: Introduction to Types of Triangles**
> Visit mometrix.com/academy and enter code: 511711

GENERAL RULES FOR TRIANGLES

The **triangle inequality theorem** states that the sum of the measures of any two sides of a triangle is always greater than the measure of the third side. If the sum of the measures of two sides were equal to the third side, a triangle would be impossible because the two sides would lie flat across the third side and there would be no vertex. If the sum of the measures of two of the sides was less than the third side, a closed figure would be impossible because the two shortest sides would never meet. In other words, for a triangle with sides lengths A, B, and C: $A + B > C$, $B + C > A$, and $A + C > B$.

The sum of the measures of the interior angles of a triangle is always 180°. Therefore, a triangle can never have more than one angle greater than or equal to 90°.

In any triangle, the angles opposite congruent sides are congruent, and the sides opposite congruent angles are congruent. The largest angle is always opposite the longest side, and the smallest angle is always opposite the shortest side.

The line segment that joins the midpoints of any two sides of a triangle is always parallel to the third side and exactly half the length of the third side.

> **Review Video: General Rules (Triangle Inequality Theorem)**
> Visit mometrix.com/academy and enter code: 166488

SIMILARITY AND CONGRUENCE RULES

Similar triangles are triangles whose corresponding angles are equal and whose corresponding sides are proportional. Represented by AAA. Similar triangles whose corresponding sides are congruent are also congruent triangles.

Triangles can be shown to be **congruent** in 5 ways:

- **SSS**: Three sides of one triangle are congruent to the three corresponding sides of the second triangle.
- **SAS**: Two sides and the included angle (the angle formed by those two sides) of one triangle are congruent to the corresponding two sides and included angle of the second triangle.
- **ASA**: Two angles and the included side (the side that joins the two angles) of one triangle are congruent to the corresponding two angles and included side of the second triangle.
- **AAS**: Two angles and a non-included side of one triangle are congruent to the corresponding two angles and non-included side of the second triangle.
- **HL**: The hypotenuse and leg of one right triangle are congruent to the corresponding hypotenuse and leg of the second right triangle.

> **Review Video: Similar Triangles**
> Visit mometrix.com/academy and enter code: 398538

Transformations

ROTATION

A **rotation** is a transformation that turns a figure around a point called the **center of rotation**, which can lie anywhere in the plane. If a line is drawn from a point on a figure to the center of rotation, and another line is drawn from the center to the rotated image of that point, the angle between the two lines is the **angle of rotation**. The vertex of the angle of rotation is the center of rotation.

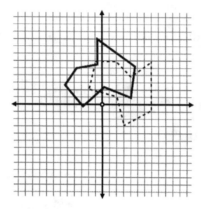

Review Video: <u>Rotation</u>
Visit mometrix.com/academy and enter code: 602600

TRANSLATION AND DILATION

A **translation** is a transformation which slides a figure from one position in the plane to another position in the plane. The original figure and the translated figure have the same size, shape, and orientation. A **dilation** is a transformation which proportionally stretches or shrinks a figure by a **scale factor**. The dilated image is the same shape and orientation as the original image but a different size. A polygon and its dilated image are similar.

Translation

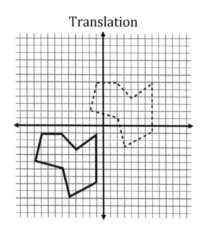

Dilation

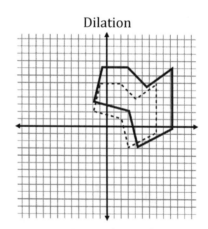

Review Video: <u>Translation</u>
Visit mometrix.com/academy and enter code: 718628
Review Video: <u>Dilation</u>
Visit mometrix.com/academy and enter code: 471630

A **reflection of a figure over a line** (a "flip") creates a congruent image that is the same distance from the line as the original figure but on the opposite side. The **line of reflection** is the perpendicular bisector of any line segment drawn from a point on the original figure to its reflected image (unless the point and its reflected image happen to be the same point, which happens when a figure is reflected over one of its own sides). A **reflection of a figure over a point** (an inversion) in two dimensions is the same as the rotation of the figure 180° about that point. The image of the

116

figure is congruent to the original figure. The **point of reflection** is the midpoint of a line segment which connects a point in the figure to its image (unless the point and its reflected image happen to be the same point, which happens when a figure is reflected in one of its own points).

Reflection of a figure over a line

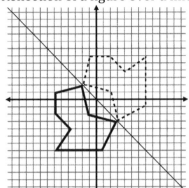

Reflection of a figure over a point

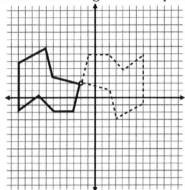

Pythagorean Theorem

PYTHAGOREAN THEOREM

The side of a triangle opposite the right angle is called the **hypotenuse**. The other two sides are called the legs. The Pythagorean theorem states a relationship among the legs and hypotenuse of a right triangle: $(a^2 + b^2 = c^2)$, where a and b are the lengths of the legs of a right triangle, and c is the length of the hypotenuse. Note that this formula will only work with right triangles.

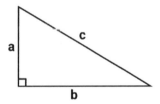

Trigonometric Formulas

TRIGONOMETRIC FORMULAS

In the diagram below, angle C is the right angle, and side c is the hypotenuse. Side a is the side opposite to angle A and side b is the side opposite to angle B. Using ratios of side lengths as a means to calculate the sine, cosine, and tangent of an acute angle only works for right triangles.

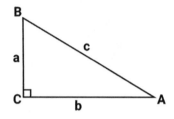

$$\sin A = \frac{\text{opposite side}}{\text{hypotenuse}} = \frac{a}{c} \qquad \csc A = \frac{1}{\sin A} = \frac{\text{hypotenuse}}{\text{opposite side}} = \frac{c}{a}$$

$$\cos A = \frac{\text{adjacent side}}{\text{hypotenuse}} = \frac{b}{c} \qquad \sec A = \frac{1}{\cos A} = \frac{\text{hypotenuse}}{\text{adjacent side}} = \frac{c}{b}$$

$$\tan A = \frac{\text{opposite side}}{\text{adjacent side}} = \frac{a}{b} \qquad \cot A = \frac{1}{\tan A} = \frac{\text{adjacent side}}{\text{opposite side}} = \frac{b}{a}$$

LAWS OF SINES AND COSINES

The **law of sines** states that $\frac{\sin A}{a} = \frac{\sin B}{b} = \frac{\sin C}{c}$, where A, B, and C are the angles of a triangle, and a, b, and c are the sides opposite their respective angles. This formula will work with all triangles, not just right triangles.

The **law of cosines** is given by the formula $c^2 = a^2 + b^2 - 2ab(\cos C)$, where a, b, and c are the sides of a triangle, and C is the angle opposite side c. This is a generalized form of the Pythagorean theorem that can be used on any triangle.

> **Review Video: Law of Sines**
> Visit mometrix.com/academy and enter code: 206844
>
> **Review Video: Law of Cosines**
> Visit mometrix.com/academy and enter code: 158911

Quadrilaterals

QUADRILATERALS

A **quadrilateral** is a closed two-dimensional geometric figure that has four straight sides. The sum of the interior angles of any quadrilateral is 360°.

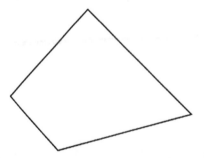

> **Review Video: Diagonals of Parallelograms, Rectangles, and Rhombi**
> Visit mometrix.com/academy and enter code: 320040

KITE

A **kite** is a quadrilateral with two pairs of adjacent sides that are congruent. A result of this is perpendicular diagonals. A kite can be concave or convex and has one line of symmetry.

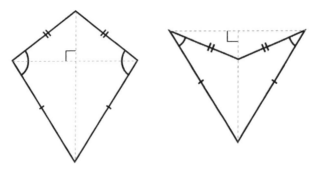

TRAPEZOID

Trapezoid: A trapezoid is defined as a quadrilateral that has at least one pair of parallel sides. There are no rules for the second pair of sides. So, there are no rules for the diagonals and no lines of symmetry for a trapezoid.

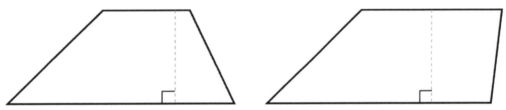

The **area of a trapezoid** is found by the formula $A = \frac{1}{2}h(b_1 + b_2)$, where h is the height (segment joining and perpendicular to the parallel bases), and b_1 and b_2 are the two parallel sides (bases). Do not use one of the other two sides as the height unless that side is also perpendicular to the parallel bases.

The **perimeter of a trapezoid** is found by the formula $P = a + b_1 + c + b_2$, where $a, b_1, c,$ and b_2 are the four sides of the trapezoid.

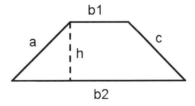

Review Video: Area and Perimeter of a Trapezoid
Visit mometrix.com/academy and enter code: 587523

Isosceles trapezoid: A trapezoid with equal base angles. This gives rise to other properties including: the two nonparallel sides have the same length, the two non-base angles are also equal, and there is one line of symmetry through the midpoints of the parallel sides.

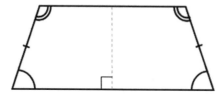

PARALLELOGRAM

A **parallelogram** is a quadrilateral that has two pairs of opposite parallel sides. As such it is a special type of trapezoid. The sides that are parallel are also congruent. The opposite interior angles are always congruent, and the consecutive interior angles are supplementary. The diagonals of a parallelogram divide each other. Each diagonal divides the parallelogram into two congruent triangles. A parallelogram has no line of symmetry, but does have 180-degree rotational symmetry about the midpoint.

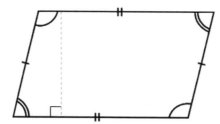

The **area of a parallelogram** is found by the formula $A = bh$, where b is the length of the base, and h is the height. Note that the base and height correspond to the length and width in a rectangle, so this formula would apply to rectangles as well. Do not confuse the height of a parallelogram with the length of the second side. The two are only the same measure in the case of a rectangle.

The **perimeter of a parallelogram** is found by the formula $P = 2a + 2b$ or $P = 2(a + b)$, where a and b are the lengths of the two sides.

> **Review Video: How to Find the Area and Perimeter of a Parallelogram**
> Visit mometrix.com/academy and enter code: 718313

RECTANGLE

A **rectangle** is a quadrilateral with four right angles. All rectangles are parallelograms and trapezoids, but not all parallelograms or trapezoids are rectangles. The diagonals of a rectangle are congruent. Rectangles have two lines of symmetry (through each pair of opposing midpoints) and 180-degree rotational symmetry about the midpoint.

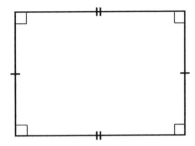

The **area of a rectangle** is found by the formula $A = lw$, where A is the area of the rectangle, l is the length (usually considered to be the longer side) and w is the width (usually considered to be the shorter side). The numbers for l and w are interchangeable.

The **perimeter of a rectangle** is found by the formula $P = 2l + 2w$ or $P = 2(l + w)$, where l is the length, and w is the width. It may be easier to add the length and width first and then double the result, as in the second formula.

RHOMBUS

A **rhombus** is a quadrilateral with four congruent sides. All rhombuses are parallelograms and kites; thus, they inherit all the properties of both types of quadrilaterals. The diagonals of a rhombus are perpendicular to each other. Rhombi have two lines of symmetry (along each of the diagonals) and 180° rotational symmetry. The **area of a rhombus** is half the product of the diagonals: $A = \frac{d_1 d_2}{2}$ and the perimeter of a rhombus is: $P = 2\sqrt{(d_1)^2 + (d_2)^2}$.

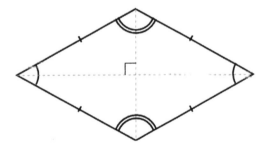

SQUARE

A **square** is a quadrilateral with four right angles and four congruent sides. Squares satisfy the criteria of all other types of quadrilaterals. The diagonals of a square are congruent and perpendicular to each other. Squares have four lines of symmetry (through each pair of opposing midpoints and along each of the diagonals) as well as 90° rotational symmetry about the midpoint.

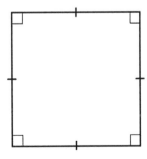

The **area of a square** is found by using the formula $A = s^2$, where s is the length of one side. The **perimeter of a square** is found by using the formula $P = 4s$, where s is the length of one side. Because all four sides are equal in a square, it is faster to multiply the length of one side by 4 than to add the same number four times. You could use the formulas for rectangles and get the same answer.

> **Review Video: Area and Perimeter of Rectangles and Squares**
> Visit mometrix.com/academy and enter code: 428109

HIERARCHY OF QUADRILATERALS

The hierarchy of quadrilaterals is as follows:

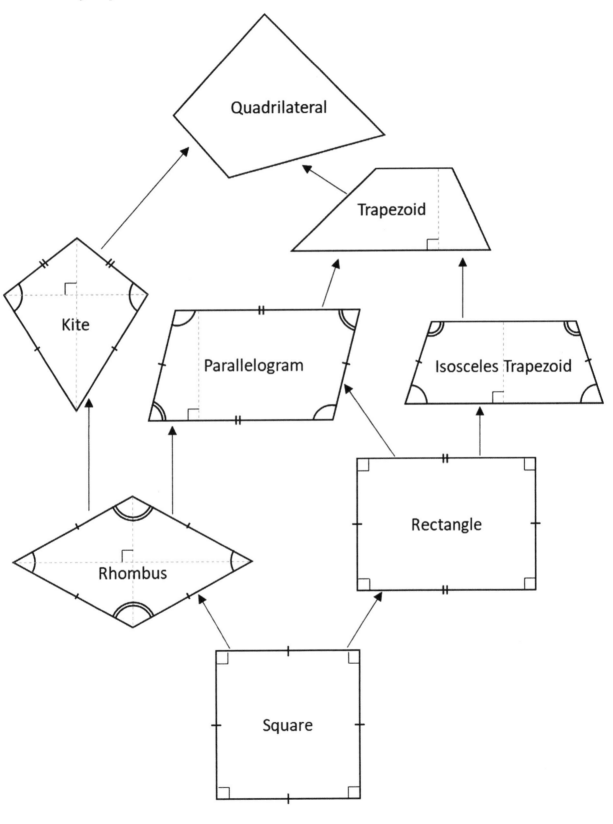

Circles

CIRCLES

The **center** of a circle is the single point from which every point on the circle is **equidistant**. The **radius** is a line segment that joins the center of the circle and any one point on the circle. All radii of a circle are equal. Circles that have the same center but not the same length of radii are **concentric**. The **diameter** is a line segment that passes through the center of the circle and has both endpoints on the circle. The length of the diameter is exactly twice the length of the radius. Point O in the diagram below is the center of the circle, segments $\overline{OX}$, $\overline{OY}$, and $\overline{OZ}$ are radii; and segment $\overline{XZ}$ is a diameter.

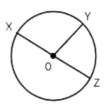

> **Review Video: Points of a Circle**
> Visit mometrix.com/academy and enter code: 420746
>
> **Review Video: The Diameter, Radius, and Circumference of Circles**
> Visit mometrix.com/academy and enter code: 448988

The **area of a circle** is found by the formula $A = \pi r^2$, where r is the length of the radius. If the diameter of the circle is given, remember to divide it in half to get the length of the radius before proceeding.

The **circumference** of a circle is found by the formula $C = 2\pi r$, where r is the radius. Again, remember to convert the diameter if you are given that measure rather than the radius.

> **Review Video: Area and Circumference of a Circle**
> Visit mometrix.com/academy and enter code: 243015

INSCRIBED AND CIRCUMSCRIBED FIGURES

These terms can both be used to describe a given arrangement of figures, depending on perspective. If each of the vertices of figure A lie on figure B, then it can be said that figure A is **inscribed** in figure B, but it can also be said that figure B is **circumscribed** about figure A. The following table and examples help to illustrate the concept. Note that the figures cannot both be circles, as they would be completely overlapping and neither would be inscribed or circumscribed.

Given	Description	Equivalent Description	Figures
Each of the sides of a pentagon is tangent to a circle	The circle is inscribed in the pentagon	The pentagon is circumscribed about the circle	
Each of the vertices of a pentagon lie on a circle	The pentagon is inscribed in the circle	The circle is circumscribed about the pentagon	

Circle Properties

ARCS

An **arc** is a portion of a circle. Specifically, an arc is the set of points between and including two points on a circle. An arc does not contain any points inside the circle. When a segment is drawn from the endpoints of an arc to the center of the circle, a sector is formed. A **minor arc** is an arc that has a measure less than 180°. A **major arc** is an arc that has a measure of at least 180°. Every minor arc has a corresponding major arc that can be found by subtracting the measure of the minor arc from 360°. A **semicircle** is an arc whose endpoints are the endpoints of the diameter of a circle. A semicircle is exactly half of a circle.

Arc length is the length of that portion of the circumference between two points on the circle. The formula for arc length is $s = \frac{\pi r \theta}{180°}$, where s is the arc length, r is the length of the radius, and θ is the angular measure of the arc in degrees, or $s = r\theta$, where θ is the angular measure of the arc in radians (2π radians = 360 degrees).

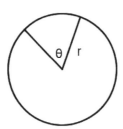

ANGLES OF CIRCLES

A **central angle** is an angle whose vertex is the center of a circle and whose legs intercept an arc of the circle. The measure of a central angle is equal to the measure of the minor arc it intercepts.

An **inscribed angle** is an angle whose vertex lies on a circle and whose legs contain chords of that circle. The portion of the circle intercepted by the legs of the angle is called the intercepted arc. The measure of the intercepted arc is exactly twice the measure of the inscribed angle. In the following diagram, angle ABC is an inscribed angle. $\widehat{AC} = 2(\mathrm{m}\angle ABC)$.

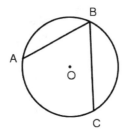

Any angle inscribed in a semicircle is a right angle. The intercepted arc is 180°, making the inscribed angle half that, or 90°. In the diagram below, angle ABC is inscribed in semicircle ABC, making angle ABC equal to 90°.

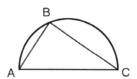

> **Review Video: Arcs and Angles of Circles**
> Visit mometrix.com/academy and enter code: 652838

SECANTS, CHORDS, AND TANGENTS

A **secant** is a line that intersects a circle in two points. The segment of a secant line that is contained within the circle is called a **chord**. Two secants may intersect inside the circle, on the circle, or outside the circle. When the two secants intersect on the circle, an inscribed angle is formed. When two secants intersect inside a circle, the measure of each of two vertical angles is equal to half the sum of the two intercepted arcs. Consider the following diagram where $\mathrm{m}\angle AEB = \frac{1}{2}(\widehat{AB} + \widehat{CD})$ and $\mathrm{m}\angle BEC = \frac{1}{2}(\widehat{BC} + \widehat{AD})$.

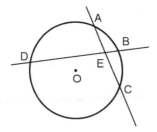

When two secants intersect outside a circle, the measure of the angle formed is equal to half the difference of the two arcs that lie between the two secants. In the diagram below, $m\angle AEB = \frac{1}{2}(\widehat{AB} - \widehat{CD})$.

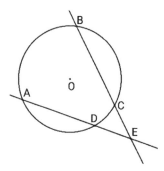

A **tangent** is a line in the same plane as a circle that touches the circle in exactly one point. The point at which a tangent touches a circle is called the **point of tangency**. While a line segment can be tangent to a circle as part of a line that is tangent, it is improper to say a tangent can be simply a line segment that touches the circle in exactly one point.

In the diagram below, $\overleftrightarrow{EB}$ is a secant and contains chord $\overline{EB}$, and $\overleftrightarrow{CD}$ is tangent to circle A. Notice that $\overline{FB}$ is not tangent to the circle. $\overline{FB}$ is a line segment that touches the circle in exactly one point, but if the segment were extended, it would touch the circle in a second point. In the diagram below, point B is the point of tangency.

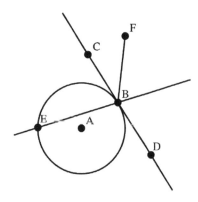

Review Video: <u>Secants, Chords, and Tangents</u>
Visit mometrix.com/academy and enter code: 258360

Review Video: <u>Tangent Lines of a Circle</u>
Visit mometrix.com/academy and enter code: 780167

SECTORS

A **sector** is the portion of a circle formed by two radii and their intercepted arc. While the arc length is exclusively the points that are also on the circumference of the circle, the sector is the entire area bounded by the arc and the two radii.

The **area of a sector** of a circle is found by the formula, $A = \frac{\theta r^2}{2}$, where A is the area, θ is the measure of the central angle in radians, and r is the radius. To find the area with the central angle in degrees, use the formula, $A = \frac{\theta \pi r^2}{360}$, where θ is the measure of the central angle and r is the radius.

3D Shapes

SOLIDS

The **surface area of a solid object** is the area of all sides or exterior surfaces. For objects such as prisms and pyramids, a further distinction is made between base surface area (B) and lateral surface area (LA). For a prism, the total surface area (SA) is $SA = LA + 2B$. For a pyramid or cone, the total surface area is $SA = LA + B$.

The **surface area of a sphere** can be found by the formula $A = 4\pi r^2$, where r is the radius. The volume is given by the formula $V = \frac{4}{3}\pi r^3$, where r is the radius. Both quantities are generally given in terms of π.

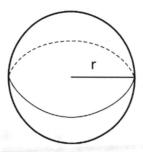

> **Review Video: Volume and Surface Area of a Sphere**
> Visit mometrix.com/academy and enter code: 786928

The **volume of any prism** is found by the formula $V = Bh$, where B is the area of the base, and h is the height (perpendicular distance between the bases). The surface area of any prism is the sum of the areas of both bases and all sides. It can be calculated as $SA = 2B + Ph$, where P is the perimeter of the base.

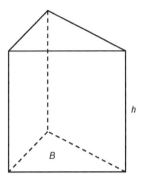

For a **rectangular prism**, the volume can be found by the formula $V = lwh$, where V is the volume, l is the length, w is the width, and h is the height. The surface area can be calculated as $SA = 2lw + 2hl + 2wh$ or $SA = 2(lw + hl + wh)$.

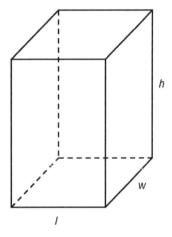

The **volume of a cube** can be found by the formula $V = s^3$, where s is the length of a side. The surface area of a cube is calculated as $SA = 6s^2$, where SA is the total surface area and s is the length of a side. These formulas are the same as the ones used for the volume and surface area of a rectangular prism, but simplified since all three quantities (length, width, and height) are the same.

The **volume of a cylinder** can be calculated by the formula $V = \pi r^2 h$, where r is the radius, and h is the height. The surface area of a cylinder can be found by the formula $SA = 2\pi r^2 + 2\pi rh$. The first term is the base area multiplied by two, and the second term is the perimeter of the base multiplied by the height.

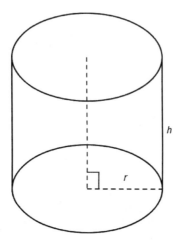

Review Video: <u>Finding the Volume and Surface Area of a Right Circular Cylinder</u>
Visit mometrix.com/academy and enter code: 226463

The **volume of a pyramid** is found by the formula $V = \frac{1}{3}Bh$, where B is the area of the base, and h is the height (perpendicular distance from the vertex to the base). Notice this formula is the same as $\frac{1}{3}$ times the volume of a prism. Like a prism, the base of a pyramid can be any shape.

Finding the **surface area of a pyramid** is not as simple as the other shapes we've looked at thus far. If the pyramid is a right pyramid, meaning the base is a regular polygon and the vertex is directly over the center of that polygon, the surface area can be calculated as $SA = B + \frac{1}{2}Ph_s$, where P is the perimeter of the base, and h_s is the slant height (distance from the vertex to the midpoint of one side of the base). If the pyramid is irregular, the area of each triangle side must be calculated individually and then summed, along with the base.

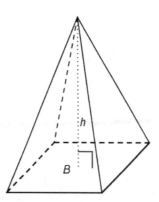

Review Video: <u>Finding the Volume and Surface Area of a Pyramid</u>
Visit mometrix.com/academy and enter code: 621932

The **volume of a cone** is found by the formula $V = \frac{1}{3}\pi r^2 h$, where r is the radius, and h is the height. Notice this is the same as $\frac{1}{3}$ times the volume of a cylinder. The surface area can be calculated as $SA = \pi r^2 + \pi rs$, where s is the slant height. The slant height can be calculated using the Pythagorean theorem to be $\sqrt{r^2 + h^2}$, so the surface area formula can also be written as $SA = \pi r^2 + \pi r\sqrt{r^2 + h^2}$.

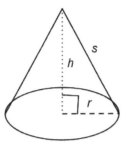

> **Review Video: <u>Volume and Surface Area of a Right Circular Cone</u>**
> Visit mometrix.com/academy and enter code: 573574

Conic Sections

CONIC SECTIONS

Conic sections are a family of shapes that can be thought of as cross sections of a pair of infinite right cones stacked vertex to vertex. This is easiest to see with a visual representation:

A three-dimensional look at representative conic sections. (Note that a hyperbola intersects both cones.)

A side-on look at representative conic sections. (Note that the parabola is parallel to the slant of the cones.)

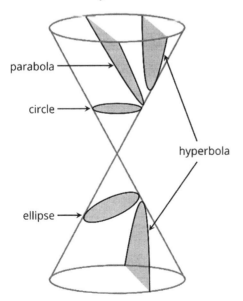

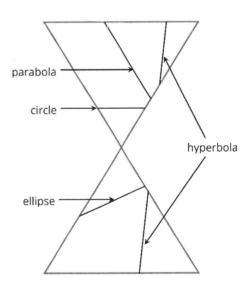

In short, a circle is a horizontal cross section, a parabola is a cross section parallel to the slant of the cone, an ellipse is a cross section at an angle *less than* the slant of the cone, and a hyperbola is a cross section at an angle *greater than* the slant of the cone.

Ellipses and Hyperbolas

ELLIPSE

An **ellipse** is the set of all points in a plane whose total distance from two fixed points called the **foci** (singular: focus) is constant, and whose center is the midpoint between the foci.

The standard equation of an ellipse that is taller than it is wide is $\frac{(x-h)^2}{a^2} + \frac{(y-k)^2}{b^2} = 1$, where a and b are coefficients. The center is the point (h, k) and the foci are the points $(h, k + c)$ and $(h, k - c)$, where $c^2 = a^2 - b^2$ and $a^2 > b^2$.

The major axis has length $2a$, and the minor axis has length $2b$.

Eccentricity (e) is a measure of how elongated an ellipse is, and is the ratio of the distance between the foci to the length of the major axis. Eccentricity will have a value between 0 and 1. The closer to 1 the eccentricity is, the closer the ellipse is to being a circle. The formula for eccentricity is $e = \frac{c}{a}$.

> **Review Video: Ellipse**
> Visit mometrix.com/academy and enter code: 703899

HYPERBOLA

A **hyperbola** is the set of all points in a plane, whose distance from two fixed points, called foci, has a constant difference.

The standard equation of a horizontal hyperbola is $\frac{(x-h)^2}{a^2} - \frac{(y-k)^2}{b^2} = 1$, where a, b, h, and k are real numbers. The center is the point (h, k), the vertices are the points $(h + a, k)$ and $(h - a, k)$, and the foci are the points that every point on one of the parabolic curves is equidistant from. The foci are found using the formulas $(h + c, k)$ and $(h - c, k)$, where $c^2 = a^2 + b^2$. The asymptotes are two lines the graph of the hyperbola approaches but never reaches, and are given by the equations $y = \left(\frac{b}{a}\right)(x - h) + k$ and $y = -\left(\frac{b}{a}\right)(x - h) + k$.

The standard equation of a vertical hyperbola is $\frac{(y-k)^2}{a^2} - \frac{(x-h)^2}{b^2} = 1$, where a, b, k, and h are real numbers. The center is the point (h, k), the vertices are the points $(h, k + a)$ and $(h, k - a)$, and the foci are the points that every point on one of the hyperbolic curves is equidistant from and are found using the formulas $(h, k + c)$ and $(h, k - c)$, where $c^2 = a^2 + b^2$. The asymptotes are two lines the graph of the hyperbola approaches but never reaches, and are given by the equations $y = \left(\frac{a}{b}\right)(x - h) + k$ and $y = -\left(\frac{a}{b}\right)(x - h) + k$.

> **Review Video: Hyperbolas**
> Visit mometrix.com/academy and enter code: 509429

Statistics and Probability

Introduction to Statistics

STATISTICS

Statistics is the branch of mathematics that deals with collecting, recording, interpreting, illustrating, and analyzing large amounts of **data**. The following terms are often used in the discussion of data and **statistics**:

- **Data** – the collective name for pieces of information (singular is datum)
- **Quantitative data** – measurements (such as length, mass, and speed) that provide information about quantities in numbers
- **Qualitative data** – information (such as colors, scents, tastes, and shapes) that cannot be measured using numbers
- **Discrete data** – information that can be expressed only by a specific value, such as whole or half numbers. (e.g., since people can be counted only in whole numbers, a population count would be discrete data.)
- **Continuous data** – information (such as time and temperature) that can be expressed by any value within a given range
- **Primary data** – information that has been collected directly from a survey, investigation, or experiment, such as a questionnaire or the recording of daily temperatures. (Primary data that has not yet been organized or analyzed is called **raw data**.)
- **Secondary data** – information that has been collected, sorted, and processed by the researcher
- **Ordinal data** – information that can be placed in numerical order, such as age or weight
- **Nominal data** – information that *cannot* be placed in numerical order, such as names or places

DATA COLLECTION

POPULATION

In statistics, the **population** is the entire collection of people, plants, etc., that data can be collected from. For example, a study to determine how well students in local schools perform on a standardized test would have a population of all the students enrolled in those schools, although a study may include just a small sample of students from each school. A **parameter** is a numerical value that gives information about the population, such as the mean, median, mode, or standard deviation. Remember that the symbol for the mean of a population is μ and the symbol for the standard deviation of a population is σ.

SAMPLE

A **sample** is a portion of the entire population. Whereas a parameter helped describe the population, a **statistic** is a numerical value that gives information about the sample, such as mean, median, mode, or standard deviation. Keep in mind that the symbols for mean and standard deviation are different when they are referring to a sample rather than the entire population. For a sample, the symbol for mean is $\bar{x}$ and the symbol for standard deviation is s. The mean and standard deviation of a sample may or may not be identical to that of the entire population due to a sample only being a subset of the population. However, if the sample is random and large enough, statistically significant values can be attained. Samples are generally used when the population is

133

too large to justify including every element or when acquiring data for the entire population is impossible.

INFERENTIAL STATISTICS

Inferential statistics is the branch of statistics that uses samples to make predictions about an entire population. This type of statistic is often seen in political polls, where a sample of the population is questioned about a particular topic or politician to gain an understanding of the attitudes of the entire population of the country. Often, exit polls are conducted on election days using this method. Inferential statistics can have a large margin of error if you do not have a valid sample.

SAMPLING DISTRIBUTION

Statistical values calculated from various samples of the same size make up the **sampling distribution**. For example, if several samples of identical size are randomly selected from a large population and then the mean of each sample is calculated, the distribution of values of the means would be a sampling distribution.

The **sampling distribution of the mean** is the distribution of the sample mean, $\bar{x}$, derived from random samples of a given size. It has three important characteristics. First, the mean of the sampling distribution of the mean is equal to the mean of the population that was sampled. Second, assuming the standard deviation is non-zero, the standard deviation of the sampling distribution of the mean equals the standard deviation of the sampled population divided by the square root of the sample size. This is sometimes called the standard error. Finally, as the sample size gets larger, the sampling distribution of the mean gets closer to a normal distribution via the central limit theorem.

SURVEY STUDY

A **survey study** is a method of gathering information from a small group in an attempt to gain enough information to make accurate general assumptions about the population. Once a survey study is completed, the results are then put into a summary report.

Survey studies are generally in the format of surveys, interviews, or questionnaires as part of an effort to find opinions of a particular group or to find facts about a group.

It is important to note that the findings from a survey study are only as accurate as the sample chosen from the population.

CORRELATIONAL STUDIES

Correlational studies seek to determine how much one variable is affected by changes in a second variable. For example, correlational studies may look for a relationship between the amount of time a student spends studying for a test and the grade that student earned on the test or between student scores on college admissions tests and student grades in college.

It is important to note that correlational studies cannot show a cause and effect, but rather can show only that two variables are or are not potentially correlated.

EXPERIMENTAL STUDIES

Experimental studies take correlational studies one step farther, in that they attempt to prove or disprove a cause-and-effect relationship. These studies are performed by conducting a series of experiments to test the hypothesis. For a study to be scientifically accurate, it must have both an experimental group that receives the specified treatment and a control group that does not get the treatment. This is the type of study pharmaceutical companies do as part of drug trials for new

medications. Experimental studies are only valid when the proper scientific method has been followed. In other words, the experiment must be well-planned and executed without bias in the testing process, all subjects must be selected at random, and the process of determining which subject is in which of the two groups must also be completely random.

OBSERVATIONAL STUDIES

Observational studies are the opposite of experimental studies. In observational studies, the tester cannot change or in any way control all of the variables in the test. For example, a study to determine which gender does better in math classes in school is strictly observational. You cannot change a person's gender, and you cannot change the subject being studied. The big downfall of observational studies is that you have no way of proving a cause-and-effect relationship because you cannot control outside influences. Events outside of school can influence a student's performance in school, and observational studies cannot take that into consideration.

RANDOM SAMPLES

For most studies, a **random sample** is necessary to produce valid results. Random samples should not have any particular influence to cause sampled subjects to behave one way or another. The goal is for the random sample to be a **representative sample**, or a sample whose characteristics give an accurate picture of the characteristics of the entire population. To accomplish this, you must make sure you have a proper **sample size**, or an appropriate number of elements in the sample.

BIASES

In statistical studies, biases must be avoided. **Bias** is an error that causes the study to favor one set of results over another. For example, if a survey to determine how the country views the president's job performance only speaks to registered voters in the president's party, the results will be skewed because a disproportionately large number of responders would tend to show approval, while a disproportionately large number of people in the opposite party would tend to express disapproval. **Extraneous variables** are, as the name implies, outside influences that can affect the outcome of a study. They are not always avoidable but could trigger bias in the result.

Data Analysis

DISPERSION

A **measure of dispersion** is a single value that helps to "interpret" the measure of central tendency by providing more information about how the data values in the set are distributed about the measure of central tendency. The measure of dispersion helps to eliminate or reduce the disadvantages of using the mean, median, or mode as a single measure of central tendency, and give a more accurate picture of the dataset as a whole. To have a measure of dispersion, you must know or calculate the range, standard deviation, or variance of the data set.

RANGE

The **range** of a set of data is the difference between the greatest and lowest values of the data in the set. To calculate the range, you must first make sure the units for all data values are the same, and then identify the greatest and lowest values. If there are multiple data values that are equal for the highest or lowest, just use one of the values in the formula. Write the answer with the same units as the data values you used to do the calculations.

> **Review Video: <u>Statistical Range</u>**
> Visit mometrix.com/academy and enter code: 778541

SAMPLE STANDARD DEVIATION

Standard deviation is a measure of dispersion that compares all the data values in the set to the mean of the set to give a more accurate picture. To find the **standard deviation of a sample**, use the formula

$$s = \sqrt{\frac{\sum_{i=1}^{n}(x_i - \bar{x})^2}{n - 1}}$$

Note that s is the standard deviation of a sample, x_i represents the individual values in the data set, $\bar{x}$ is the mean of the data values in the set, and n is the number of data values in the set. The higher the value of the standard deviation is, the greater the variance of the data values from the mean. The units associated with the standard deviation are the same as the units of the data values.

> **Review Video: Standard Deviation**
> Visit mometrix.com/academy and enter code: 419469

SAMPLE VARIANCE

The **variance of a sample** is the square of the sample standard deviation (denoted s^2). While the mean of a set of data gives the average of the set and gives information about where a specific data value lies in relation to the average, the variance of the sample gives information about the degree to which the data values are spread out and tells you how close an individual value is to the average compared to the other values. The units associated with variance are the same as the units of the data values squared.

PERCENTILE

Percentiles and quartiles are other methods of describing data within a set. **Percentiles** tell what percentage of the data in the set fall below a specific point. For example, achievement test scores are often given in percentiles. A score at the 80th percentile is one which is equal to or higher than 80 percent of the scores in the set. In other words, 80 percent of the scores were lower than that score.

Quartiles are percentile groups that make up quarter sections of the data set. The first quartile is the 25th percentile. The second quartile is the 50th percentile; this is also the median of the dataset. The third quartile is the 75th percentile.

SKEWNESS

Skewness is a way to describe the symmetry or asymmetry of the distribution of values in a dataset. If the distribution of values is symmetrical, there is no skew. In general the closer the mean of a data set is to the median of the data set, the less skew there is. Generally, if the mean is to the right of the median, the data set is *positively skewed*, or right-skewed, and if the mean is to the left of the median, the data set is *negatively skewed*, or left-skewed. However, this rule of thumb is not infallible. When the data values are graphed on a curve, a set with no skew will be a perfect bell curve.

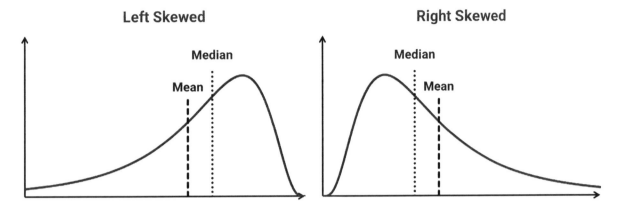

Left Skewed	Right Skewed

To estimate skew, use the formula:

$$\text{skew} = \frac{\sqrt{n(n-1)}}{n-2} \left(\frac{\frac{1}{n}\sum_{i=1}^{n}(x_i - \bar{x})^3}{\left(\frac{1}{n}\sum_{i=1}^{n}(x_i - \bar{x})^2\right)^{\frac{3}{2}}} \right)$$

Note that n is the datapoints in the set, x_i is the ith value in the set, and $\bar{x}$ is the mean of the set.

> **Review Video: Skew**
> Visit mometrix.com/academy and enter code: 661486

UNIMODAL VS. BIMODAL

If a distribution has a single peak, it would be considered **unimodal**. If it has two discernible peaks it would be considered **bimodal**. Bimodal distributions may be an indication that the set of data being considered is actually the combination of two sets of data with significant differences. A **uniform distribution** is a distribution in which there is *no distinct peak or variation* in the data. No values or ranges are particularly more common than any other values or ranges.

OUTLIER

An outlier is an extremely high or extremely low value in the data set. It may be the result of measurement error, in which case, the outlier is not a valid member of the data set. However, it may also be a valid member of the distribution. Unless a measurement error is identified, the experimenter cannot know for certain if an outlier is or is not a member of the distribution. There are arbitrary methods that can be employed to designate an extreme value as an outlier. One method designates an outlier (or possible outlier) to be any value less than $Q_1 - 1.5(IQR)$ or any value greater than $Q_3 + 1.5(IQR)$.

DATA ANALYSIS

SIMPLE REGRESSION

In statistics, **simple regression** is using an equation to represent a relation between independent and dependent variables. The independent variable is also referred to as the explanatory variable or the predictor and is generally represented by the variable x in the equation. The dependent variable, usually represented by the variable y, is also referred to as the response variable. The equation may be any type of function – linear, quadratic, exponential, etc. The best way to handle this task is to use the regression feature of your graphing calculator. This will easily give you the curve of best fit and provide you with the coefficients and other information you need to derive an equation.

LINE OF BEST FIT

In a scatter plot, the **line of best fit** is the line that best shows the trends of the data. The line of best fit is given by the equation $\hat{y} = ax + b$, where a and b are the regression coefficients. The regression coefficient a is also the slope of the line of best fit, and b is also the y-coordinate of the point at which the line of best fit crosses the y-axis. Not every point on the scatter plot will be on the line of best fit. The differences between the y-values of the points in the scatter plot and the corresponding y-values according to the equation of the line of best fit are the residuals. The line of best fit is also called the least-squares regression line because it is also the line that has the lowest sum of the squares of the residuals.

CORRELATION COEFFICIENT

The **correlation coefficient** is the numerical value that indicates how strong the relationship is between the two variables of a linear regression equation. A correlation coefficient of –1 is a perfect negative correlation. A correlation coefficient of +1 is a perfect positive correlation. Correlation coefficients close to –1 or +1 are very strong correlations. A correlation coefficient equal to zero indicates there is no correlation between the two variables. This test is a good indicator of whether or not the equation for the line of best fit is accurate. The formula for the correlation coefficient is

$$r = \frac{\sum_{i=1}^{n}(x_i - \bar{x})(y_i - \bar{y})}{\sqrt{\sum_{i=1}^{n}(x_i - \bar{x})^2}\sqrt{\sum_{i=1}^{n}(y_i - \bar{y})^2}}$$

where r is the correlation coefficient, n is the number of data values in the set, (x_i, y_i) is a point in the set, and $\bar{x}$ and $\bar{y}$ are the means.

Z-SCORE

A **z-score** is an indication of how many standard deviations a given value falls from the sample mean. To calculate a z-score, use the formula:

$$\frac{x - \bar{x}}{\sigma}$$

In this formula x is the data value, $\bar{x}$ is the mean of the sample data, and σ is the standard deviation of the population. If the z-score is positive, the data value lies above the mean. If the z-score is negative, the data value falls below the mean. These scores are useful in interpreting data such as standardized test scores, where every piece of data in the set has been counted, rather than just a small random sample. In cases where standard deviations are calculated from a random sample of the set, the z-scores will not be as accurate.

CENTRAL LIMIT THEOREM

According to the **central limit theorem**, regardless of what the original distribution of a sample is, the distribution of the means tends to get closer and closer to a normal distribution as the sample size gets larger and larger (this is necessary because the sample is becoming more all-encompassing of the elements of the population). As the sample size gets larger, the distribution of the sample mean will approach a normal distribution with a mean of the population mean and a variance of the population variance divided by the sample size.

Measures of Central Tendency

MEASURES OF CENTRAL TENDENCY

A **measure of central tendency** is a statistical value that gives a reasonable estimate for the center of a group of data. There are several different ways of describing the measure of central tendency. Each one has a unique way it is calculated, and each one gives a slightly different perspective on the data set. Whenever you give a measure of central tendency, always make sure the units are the same. If the data has different units, such as hours, minutes, and seconds, convert all the data to the same unit, and use the same unit in the measure of central tendency. If no units are given in the data, do not give units for the measure of central tendency.

MEAN

The **statistical mean** of a group of data is the same as the arithmetic average of that group. To find the mean of a set of data, first convert each value to the same units, if necessary. Then find the sum of all the values, and count the total number of data values, making sure you take into consideration each individual value. If a value appears more than once, count it more than once. Divide the sum of the values by the total number of values and apply the units, if any. Note that the mean does not have to be one of the data values in the set, and may not divide evenly.

$$\text{mean} = \frac{\text{sum of the data values}}{\text{quantity of data values}}$$

For instance, the mean of the data set {88, 72, 61, 90, 97, 68, 88, 79, 86, 93, 97, 71, 80, 84, 89} would be the sum of the fifteen numbers divided by 15:

$$\frac{88 + 72 + 61 + 90 + 97 + 68 + 88 + 79 + 86 + 93 + 97 + 71 + 80 + 84 + 88}{15} = \frac{1242}{15}$$
$$= 82.8$$

While the mean is relatively easy to calculate and averages are understood by most people, the mean can be very misleading if It is used as the sole measure of central tendency. If the data set has outliers (data values that are unusually high or unusually low compared to the rest of the data values), the mean can be very distorted, especially if the data set has a small number of values. If unusually high values are countered with unusually low values, the mean is not affected as much. For example, if five of twenty students in a class get a 100 on a test, but the other 15 students have an average of 60 on the same test, the class average would appear as 70. Whenever the mean is skewed by outliers, it is always a good idea to include the median as an alternate measure of central tendency.

A **weighted mean**, or weighted average, is a mean that uses "weighted" values. The formula is weighted mean $= \frac{w_1 x_1 + w_2 x_2 + w_3 x_3 \dots + w_n x_n}{w_1 + w_2 + w_3 + \dots + w_n}$. Weighted values, such as $w_1, w_2, w_3, \dots w_n$ are assigned to each member of the set $x_1, x_2, x_3, \dots x_n$. When calculating the weighted mean, make sure a weight value for each member of the set is used.

> **Review Video: All About Averages**
> Visit mometrix.com/academy and enter code: 176521

MEDIAN

The **statistical median** is the value in the middle of the set of data. To find the median, list all data values in order from smallest to largest or from largest to smallest. Any value that is repeated in the set must be listed the number of times it appears. If there are an odd number of data values, the median is the value in the middle of the list. If there is an even number of data values, the median is the arithmetic mean of the two middle values.

For example, the median of the data set {88, 72, 61, 90, 97, 68, 88, 79, 86, 93, 97, 71, 80, 84, 88} is 86 since the ordered set is {61, 68, 71, 72, 79, 80, 84, **86**, 88, 88, 88, 90, 93, 97, 97}.

The big disadvantage of using the median as a measure of central tendency is that is relies solely on a value's relative size as compared to the other values in the set. When the individual values in a set of data are evenly dispersed, the median can be an accurate tool. However, if there is a group of rather large values or a group of rather small values that are not offset by a different group of values, the information that can be inferred from the median may not be accurate because the distribution of values is skewed.

MODE

The **statistical mode** is the data value that occurs the greatest number of times in the data set. It is possible to have exactly one mode, more than one mode, or no mode. To find the mode of a set of data, arrange the data like you do to find the median (all values in order, listing all multiples of data values). Count the number of times each value appears in the data set. If all values appear an equal number of times, there is no mode. If one value appears more than any other value, that value is the mode. If two or more values appear the same number of times, but there are other values that appear fewer times and no values that appear more times, all of those values are the modes.

For example, the mode of the data set {**88**, 72, 61, 90, 97, 68, **88**, 79, 86, 93, 97, 71, 80, 84, **88**} is 88.

The main disadvantage of the mode is that the values of the other data in the set have no bearing on the mode. The mode may be the largest value, the smallest value, or a value anywhere in between in the set. The mode only tells which value or values, if any, occurred the greatest number of times. It does not give any suggestions about the remaining values in the set.

> **Review Video: Mean, Median, and Mode**
> Visit mometrix.com/academy and enter code: 286207

Displaying Information

FREQUENCY TABLES

Frequency tables show how frequently each unique value appears in a set. A **relative frequency table** is one that shows the proportions of each unique value compared to the entire set. Relative frequencies are given as percentages; however, the total percent for a relative frequency table will not necessarily equal 100 percent due to rounding. An example of a frequency table with relative frequencies is below.

Favorite Color	Frequency	Relative Frequency
Blue	4	13%
Red	7	22%
Green	3	9%
Purple	6	19%
Cyan	12	38%

Review Video: Data Interpretation of Graphs
Visit mometrix.com/academy and enter code: 200439

CIRCLE GRAPHS

Circle graphs, also known as *pie charts*, provide a visual depiction of the relationship of each type of data compared to the whole set of data. The circle graph is divided into sections by drawing radii to create central angles whose percentage of the circle is equal to the individual data's percentage of the whole set. Each 1% of data is equal to 3.6° in the circle graph. Therefore, data represented by a 90° section of the circle graph makes up 25% of the whole. When complete, a circle graph often looks like a pie cut into uneven wedges. The pie chart below shows the data from the frequency table referenced earlier where people were asked their favorite color.

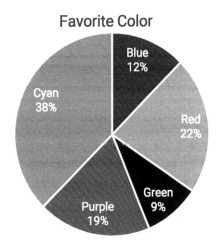

Favorite Color

PICTOGRAPHS

A **pictograph** is a graph, generally in the horizontal orientation, that uses pictures or symbols to represent the data. Each pictograph must have a key that defines the picture or symbol and gives the quantity each picture or symbol represents. Pictures or symbols on a pictograph are not always shown as whole elements. In this case, the fraction of the picture or symbol shown represents the same fraction of the quantity a whole picture or symbol stands for. For example, a row with $3\frac{1}{2}$ ears of corn, where each ear of corn represents 100 stalks of corn in a field, would equal $3\frac{1}{2} \times 100 = 350$ stalks of corn in the field.

Review Video: Pictographs
Visit mometrix.com/academy and enter code: 147860

LINE GRAPHS

Line graphs have one or more lines of varying styles (solid or broken) to show the different values for a set of data. The individual data are represented as ordered pairs, much like on a Cartesian plane. In this case, the x- and y-axes are defined in terms of their units, such as dollars or time. The individual plotted points are joined by line segments to show whether the value of the data is increasing (line sloping upward), decreasing (line sloping downward), or staying the same (horizontal line). Multiple sets of data can be graphed on the same line graph to give an easy visual comparison. An example of this would be graphing achievement test scores for different groups of students over the same time period to see which group had the greatest increase or decrease in performance from year to year (as shown below).

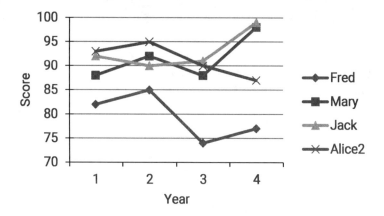

| Review Video: **How to Create a Line Graph** |
| Visit mometrix.com/academy and enter code: 480147 |

LINE PLOTS

A **line plot**, also known as a *dot plot*, has plotted points that are not connected by line segments. In this graph, the horizontal axis lists the different possible values for the data, and the vertical axis lists the number of times the individual value occurs. A single dot is graphed for each value to show the number of times it occurs. This graph is more closely related to a bar graph than a line graph. Do not connect the dots in a line plot or it will misrepresent the data.

| Review Video: **Line Plot** |
| Visit mometrix.com/academy and enter code: 754610 |

STEM AND LEAF PLOTS

A **stem and leaf plot** is useful for depicting groups of data that fall into a range of values. Each piece of data is separated into two parts: the first, or left, part is called the stem; the second, or right, part is called the leaf. Each stem is listed in a column from smallest to largest. Each leaf that has the common stem is listed in that stem's row from smallest to largest. For example, in a set of two-digit numbers, the digit in the tens place is the stem, and the digit in the ones place is the leaf. With a stem and leaf plot, you can easily see which subset of numbers (10s, 20s, 30s, etc.) is the largest. This information is also readily available by looking at a histogram, but a stem and leaf plot also allows you to look closer and see exactly which values fall in that range. Using a sample set of test

scores (82, 88, 92, 93, 85, 90, 92, 95, 74, 88, 90, 91, 78, 87, 98, 99), we can assemble a stem and leaf plot like the one below.

Test Scores

7	4	8						
8	2	5	7	8	8			
9	0	0	1	2	2	3	5	8	9

Review Video: Stem and Leaf Plots
Visit mometrix.com/academy and enter code: 302339

BAR GRAPHS

A **bar graph** is one of the few graphs that can be drawn correctly in two different configurations – both horizontally and vertically. A bar graph is similar to a line plot in the way the data is organized on the graph. Both axes must have their categories defined for the graph to be useful. Rather than placing a single dot to mark the point of the data's value, a bar, or thick line, is drawn from zero to the exact value of the data, whether it is a number, percentage, or other numerical value. Longer bar lengths correspond to greater data values. To read a bar graph, read the labels for the axes to find the units being reported. Then, look where the bars end in relation to the scale given on the corresponding axis and determine the associated value.

The bar chart below represents the responses from our favorite-color survey.

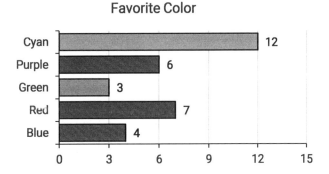

HISTOGRAMS

At first glance, a **histogram** looks like a vertical bar graph. The difference is that a bar graph has a separate bar for each piece of data and a histogram has one continuous bar for each *range* of data. For example, a histogram may have one bar for the range 0–9, one bar for 10–19, etc. While a bar graph has numerical values on one axis, a histogram has numerical values on both axes. Each range is of equal size, and they are ordered left to right from lowest to highest. The height of each column on a histogram represents the number of data values within that range. Like a stem and leaf plot, a

143

histogram makes it easy to glance at the graph and quickly determine which range has the greatest quantity of values. A simple example of a histogram is below.

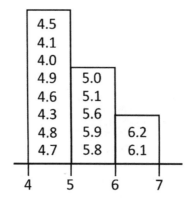

5-NUMBER SUMMARY

The **5-number summary** of a set of data gives a very informative picture of the set. The five numbers in the summary include the minimum value, maximum value, and the three quartiles. This information gives the reader the range and median of the set, as well as an indication of how the data is spread about the median.

BOX AND WHISKER PLOTS

A **box-and-whiskers plot** is a graphical representation of the 5-number summary. To draw a box-and-whiskers plot, plot the points of the 5-number summary on a number line. Draw a box whose ends are through the points for the first and third quartiles. Draw a vertical line in the box through the median to divide the box in half. Draw a line segment from the first quartile point to the minimum value, and from the third quartile point to the maximum value.

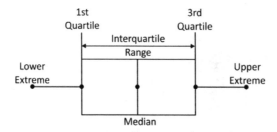

> **Review Video: Box and Whisker Plots**
> Visit mometrix.com/academy and enter code: 810817

EXAMPLE

Given the following data (32, 28, 29, 26, 35, 27, 30, 31, 27, 32), we first sort it into numerical order: 26, 27, 27, 28, 29, 30, 31, 32, 32, 35. We can then find the median. Since there are ten values, we take the average of the 5th and 6th values to get 29.5. We find the lower quartile by taking the median of the data smaller than the median. Since there are five values, we take the 3rd value, which is 27. We find the upper quartile by taking the median of the data larger than the overall median, which is 32. Finally, we note our minimum and maximum, which are simply the smallest and largest values in the set: 26 and 35, respectively. Now we can create our box plot:

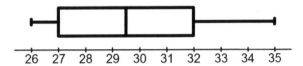

This plot is fairly "long" on the right whisker, showing one or more unusually high values (but not quite outliers). The other quartiles are similar in length, showing a fairly even distribution of data.

INTERQUARTILE RANGE

The **interquartile range, or IQR**, is the difference between the upper and lower quartiles. It measures how the data is dispersed: a high IQR means that the data is more spread out, while a low IQR means that the data is clustered more tightly around the median. To find the IQR, subtract the lower quartile value (Q_1) from the upper quartile value (Q_3).

EXAMPLE

To find the upper and lower quartiles, we first find the median and then take the median of all values above it and all values below it. In the following data set (16, 18, 13, 24, 16, 51, 32, 21, 27, 39), we first rearrange the values in numerical order: 13, 16, 16, 18, 21, 24, 27, 32, 39, 51. There are 10 values, so the median is the average of the 5th and 6th: $\frac{21+24}{2} = \frac{45}{2} = 22.5$. We do not actually need this value to find the upper and lower quartiles. We look at the set of numbers below the median: 13, 16, 16, 18, 21. There are five values, so the 3rd is the median (16), or the value of the lower quartile (Q_1). Then we look at the numbers above the median: 24, 27, 32, 39, 51. Again there are five values, so the 3rd is the median (32), or the value of the upper quartile (Q_3). We find the IQR by subtracting Q_1 from Q_3: $32 - 16 = 16$.

68-95-99.7 RULE

The **68–95–99.7 rule** describes how a normal distribution of data should appear when compared to the mean. This is also a description of a normal bell curve. According to this rule, 68 percent of the data values in a normally distributed set should fall within one standard deviation of the mean (34 percent above and 34 percent below the mean), 95 percent of the data values should fall within two standard deviations of the mean (47.5 percent above and 47.5 percent below the mean), and 99.7 percent of the data values should fall within three standard deviations of the mean, again, equally distributed on either side of the mean. This means that only 0.3 percent of all data values should fall more than three standard deviations from the mean. On the graph below, the normal

145

curve is centered on the *y*-axis. The *x*-axis labels are how many standard deviations away from the center you are. Therefore, it is easy to see how the 68-95-99.7 rule can apply.

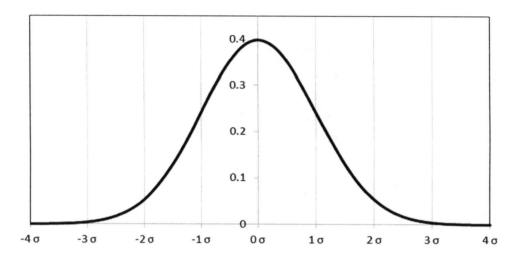

Scatter Plots

BIVARIATE DATA

Bivariate data is simply data from two different variables. (The prefix *bi-* means *two*.) In a *scatter plot*, each value in the set of data is plotted on a grid similar to a Cartesian plane, where each axis represents one of the two variables. By looking at the pattern formed by the points on the grid, you can often determine whether or not there is a relationship between the two variables, and what that relationship is, if it exists. The variables may be directly proportionate, inversely proportionate, or show no proportion at all. It may also be possible to determine if the data is linear, and if so, to find an equation to relate the two variables. The following scatter plot shows the relationship between preference for brand "A" and the age of the consumers surveyed.

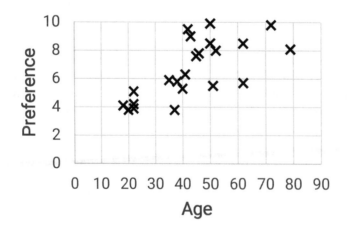

SCATTER PLOTS

Scatter plots are also useful in determining the type of function represented by the data and finding the simple regression. Linear scatter plots may be positive or negative. Nonlinear scatter plots are generally exponential or quadratic. Below are some common types of scatter plots:

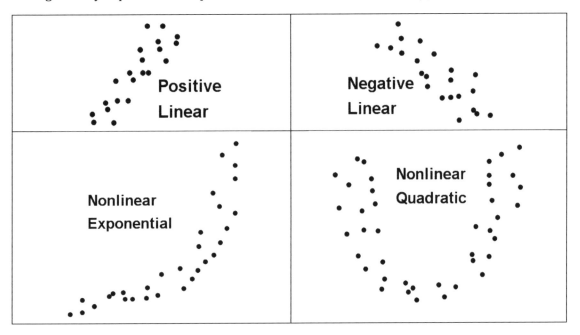

Positive Linear | Negative Linear | Nonlinear Exponential | Nonlinear Quadratic

Review Video: **What is a Scatter Plot?**
Visit mometrix.com/academy and enter code: 596526

Probability

PROBABILITY

Probability is the likelihood of a certain outcome occurring for a given event. An **event** is any situation that produces a result. It could be something as simple as flipping a coin or as complex as launching a rocket. Determining the probability of an outcome for an event can be equally simple or complex. As such, there are specific terms used in the study of probability that need to be understood:

- **Compound event**—an event that involves two or more independent events (rolling a pair of dice and taking the sum)
- **Desired outcome** (or success)—an outcome that meets a particular set of criteria (a roll of 1 or 2 if we are looking for numbers less than 3)
- **Independent events**—two or more events whose outcomes do not affect one another (two coins tossed at the same time)
- **Dependent events**—two or more events whose outcomes affect one another (two cards drawn consecutively from the same deck)
- **Certain outcome**—probability of outcome is 100% or 1
- **Impossible outcome**—probability of outcome is 0% or 0

147

- **Mutually exclusive outcomes**—two or more outcomes whose criteria cannot all be satisfied in a single event (a coin coming up heads and tails on the same toss)
- **Random variable**—refers to all possible outcomes of a single event which may be discrete or continuous.

> **Review Video: Intro to Probability**
> Visit mometrix.com/academy and enter code: 212374

SAMPLE SPACE

The total set of all possible results of a test or experiment is called a **sample space**, or sometimes a universal sample space. The sample space, represented by one of the variables S, Ω, or U (for universal sample space) has individual elements called outcomes. Other terms for outcome that may be used interchangeably include elementary outcome, simple event, or sample point. The number of outcomes in a given sample space could be infinite or finite, and some tests may yield multiple unique sample sets. For example, tests conducted by drawing playing cards from a standard deck would have one sample space of the card values, another sample space of the card suits, and a third sample space of suit-denomination combinations. For most tests, the sample spaces considered will be finite.

An **event**, represented by the variable E, is a portion of a sample space. It may be one outcome or a group of outcomes from the same sample space. If an event occurs, then the test or experiment will generate an outcome that satisfies the requirement of that event. For example, given a standard deck of 52 playing cards as the sample space, and defining the event as the collection of face cards, then the event will occur if the card drawn is a J, Q, or K. If any other card is drawn, the event is said to have not occurred.

For every sample space, each possible outcome has a specific likelihood, or probability, that it will occur. The probability measure, also called the **distribution**, is a function that assigns a real number probability, from zero to one, to each outcome. For a probability measure to be accurate, every outcome must have a real number probability measure that is greater than or equal to zero and less than or equal to one. Also, the probability measure of the sample space must equal one, and the probability measure of the union of multiple outcomes must equal the sum of the individual probability measures.

Probabilities of events are expressed as real numbers from zero to one. They give a numerical value to the chance that a particular event will occur. The probability of an event occurring is the sum of the probabilities of the individual elements of that event. For example, in a standard deck of 52 playing cards as the sample space and the collection of face cards as the event, the probability of drawing a specific face card is $\frac{1}{52} = 0.019$, but the probability of drawing any one of the twelve face cards is $12(0.019) = 0.228$. Note that rounding of numbers can generate different results. If you multiplied 12 by the fraction $\frac{1}{52}$ before converting to a decimal, you would get the answer $\frac{12}{52} = 0.231$.

THEORETICAL AND EXPERIMENTAL PROBABILITY

Theoretical probability can usually be determined without actually performing the event. The likelihood of an outcome occurring, or the probability of an outcome occurring, is given by the formula:

$$P(A) = \frac{\text{Number of acceptable outcomes}}{\text{Number of possible outcomes}}$$

Note that $P(A)$ is the probability of an outcome A occurring, and each outcome is just as likely to occur as any other outcome. If each outcome has the same probability of occurring as every other possible outcome, the outcomes are said to be equally likely to occur. The total number of acceptable outcomes must be less than or equal to the total number of possible outcomes. If the two are equal, then the outcome is certain to occur and the probability is 1. If the number of acceptable outcomes is zero, then the outcome is impossible and the probability is 0. For example, if there are 20 marbles in a bag and 5 are red, then the theoretical probability of randomly selecting a red marble is 5 out of 20, $\left(\frac{5}{20} = \frac{1}{4}, 0.25, \text{ or } 25\%\right)$.

If the theoretical probability is unknown or too complicated to calculate, it can be estimated by an experimental probability. **Experimental probability**, also called empirical probability, is an estimate of the likelihood of a certain outcome based on repeated experiments or collected data. In other words, while theoretical probability is based on what *should* happen, experimental probability is based on what *has* happened. Experimental probability is calculated in the same way as theoretical probability, except that actual outcomes are used instead of possible outcomes. The more experiments performed or datapoints gathered, the better the estimate should be.

Theoretical and experimental probability do not always line up with one another. Theoretical probability says that out of 20 coin-tosses, 10 should be heads. However, if we were actually to toss 20 coins, we might record just 5 heads. This doesn't mean that our theoretical probability is incorrect; it just means that this particular experiment had results that were different from what was predicted. A practical application of empirical probability is the insurance industry. There are no set functions that define lifespan, health, or safety. Insurance companies look at factors from hundreds of thousands of individuals to find patterns that they then use to set the formulas for insurance premiums.

> **Review Video: Empirical Probability**
> Visit mometrix.com/academy and enter code: 513468

OBJECTIVE AND SUBJECTIVE PROBABILITY

Objective probability is based on mathematical formulas and documented evidence. Examples of objective probability include raffles or lottery drawings where there is a pre-determined number of possible outcomes and a predetermined number of outcomes that correspond to an event. Other cases of objective probability include probabilities of rolling dice, flipping coins, or drawing cards. Most gambling games are based on objective probability.

In contrast, **subjective probability** is based on personal or professional feelings and judgments. Often, there is a lot of guesswork following extensive research. Areas where subjective probability is applicable include sales trends and business expenses. Attractions set admission prices based on subjective probabilities of attendance based on varying admission rates in an effort to maximize their profit.

COMPLEMENT OF AN EVENT

Sometimes it may be easier to calculate the possibility of something not happening, or the **complement of an event**. Represented by the symbol $\bar{A}$, the complement of A is the probability that event A does not happen. When you know the probability of event A occurring, you can use the formula $P(\bar{A}) = 1 - P(A)$, where $P(\bar{A})$ is the probability of event A not occurring, and $P(A)$ is the probability of event A occurring.

ADDITION RULE

The **addition rule** for probability is used for finding the probability of a compound event. Use the formula $P(A \cup B) = P(A) + P(B) - P(A \cap B)$, where $P(A \cap B)$ is the probability of both events occurring to find the probability of a compound event. The probability of both events occurring at the same time must be subtracted to eliminate any overlap in the first two probabilities.

CONDITIONAL PROBABILITY

Given two events A and B, the **conditional probability** $P(A|B)$ is the probability that event A will occur, given that event B has occurred. The conditional probability cannot be calculated simply from $P(A)$ and $P(B)$; these probabilities alone do not give sufficient information to determine the conditional probability. It can, however, be determined if you are also given the probability of the intersection of events A and B, $P(A \cap B)$, the probability that events A and B both occur.

Specifically, $P(A|B) = \frac{P(A \cap B)}{P(B)}$. For instance, suppose you have a jar containing two red marbles and two blue marbles, and you draw two marbles at random. Consider event A being the event that the first marble drawn is red, and event B being the event that the second marble drawn is blue. If we want to find the probability that B occurs given that A occurred, $P(B|A)$, then we can compute it using the fact that $P(A)$ is $\frac{1}{2}$, and $P(A \cap B)$ is $\frac{1}{3}$. (The latter may not be obvious, but may be determined by finding the product of $\frac{1}{2}$ and $\frac{2}{3}$). Therefore $P(B|A) = \frac{P(A \cap B)}{P(A)} = \frac{1/3}{1/2} = \frac{2}{3}$.

CONDITIONAL PROBABILITY IN EVERYDAY SITUATIONS

Conditional probability often arises in everyday situations in, for example, estimating the risk or benefit of certain activities. The conditional probability of having a heart attack given that you exercise daily may be smaller than the overall probability of having a heart attack. The conditional probability of having lung cancer given that you are a smoker is larger than the overall probability of having lung cancer. Note that changing the order of the conditional probability changes the meaning: the conditional probability of having lung cancer given that you are a smoker is a very different thing from the probability of being a smoker given that you have lung cancer. In an extreme case, suppose that a certain rare disease is caused only by eating a certain food, but even then, it is unlikely. Then the conditional probability of having that disease given that you eat the dangerous food is nonzero but low, but the conditional probability of having eaten that food given that you have the disease is 100%!

Review Video: Conditional Probability
Visit mometrix.com/academy and enter code: 397924

INDEPENDENCE

The conditional probability $P(A|B)$ is the probability that event A will occur given that event B occurs. If the two events are independent, we do not expect that whether or not event B occurs should have any effect on whether or not event A occurs. In other words, we expect $P(A|B) = P(A)$.

This can be proven using the usual equations for conditional probability and the joint probability of independent events. The conditional probability $P(A|B) = \frac{P(A \cap B)}{P(B)}$. If A and B are independent, then $P(A \cap B) = P(A)P(B)$. So $P(A|B) = \frac{P(A)P(B)}{P(B)} = P(A)$. By similar reasoning, if A and B are independent then $P(B|A) = P(B)$.

MULTIPLICATION RULE

The **multiplication rule** can be used to find the probability of two independent events occurring using the formula $P(A \cap B) = P(A) \times P(B)$, where $P(A \cap B)$ is the probability of two independent events occurring, $P(A)$ is the probability of the first event occurring, and $P(B)$ is the probability of the second event occurring.

The multiplication rule can also be used to find the probability of two dependent events occurring using the formula $P(A \cap B) = P(A) \times P(B|A)$, where $P(A \cap B)$ is the probability of two dependent events occurring and $P(B|A)$ is the probability of the second event occurring after the first event has already occurred.

Use a **combination of the multiplication** rule and the rule of complements to find the probability that at least one outcome of the element will occur. This is given by the general formula $P(\text{at least one event occurring}) = 1 - P(\text{no outcomes occurring})$. For example, to find the probability that at least one even number will show when a pair of dice is rolled, find the probability that two odd numbers will be rolled (no even numbers) and subtract from one. You can always use a tree diagram or make a chart to list the possible outcomes when the sample space is small, such as in the dice-rolling example, but in most cases it will be much faster to use the multiplication and complement formulas.

> **Review Video: Multiplication Rule**
> Visit mometrix.com/academy and enter code: 782598

UNION AND INTERSECTION OF TWO SETS OF OUTCOMES

If A and B are each a set of elements or outcomes from an experiment, then the **union** (symbol ∪) of the two sets is the set of elements found in set A or set B. For example, if $A = \{2, 3, 4\}$ and $B = \{3, 4, 5\}$, $A \cup B = \{2, 3, 4, 5\}$. Note that the outcomes 3 and 4 appear only once in the union. For statistical events, the union is equivalent to "or"; $P(A \cup B)$ is the same thing as $P(A \text{ or } B)$. The **intersection** (symbol ∩) of two sets is the set of outcomes common to both sets. For the above sets A and B, $A \cap B = \{3, 4\}$. For statistical events, the intersection is equivalent to "and"; $P(A \cap B)$ is the same thing as $P(A \text{ and } B)$. It is important to note that union and intersection operations commute. That is:

$$A \cup B = B \cup A \text{ and } A \cap B = B \cap A$$

Permutations and Combinations in Probability

PERMUTATIONS AND COMBINATIONS

When trying to calculate the probability of an event using the $\frac{\text{desired outcomes}}{\text{total outcomes}}$ formula, you may frequently find that there are too many outcomes to individually count them. **Permutation** and **combination formulas** offer a shortcut to counting outcomes. A permutation is an arrangement of a specific number of a set of objects in a specific order. The number of **permutations** of r items given a set of n items can be calculated as $_nP_r = \frac{n!}{(n-r)!}$. Combinations are similar to permutations, except there are no restrictions regarding the order of the elements. While ABC is considered a different permutation than BCA, ABC and BCA are considered the same combination. The number of **combinations** of r items given a set of n items can be calculated as $_nC_r = \frac{n!}{r!(n-r)!}$ or $_nC_r = \frac{_nP_r}{r!}$.

Suppose you want to calculate how many different 5-card hands can be drawn from a deck of 52 cards. This is a combination since the order of the cards in a hand does not matter. There are 52 cards available, and 5 to be selected. Thus, the number of different hands is $_{52}C_5 = \frac{52!}{5! \times 47!} = 2,598,960$.

> **Review Video: Probability - Permutation and Combination**
> Visit mometrix.com/academy and enter code: 907664

Tree Diagrams

TREE DIAGRAM

For a simple sample space, possible outcomes may be determined by using a **tree diagram** or an organized chart. In either case, you can easily draw or list out the possible outcomes. For example, to determine all the possible ways three objects can be ordered, you can draw a tree diagram:

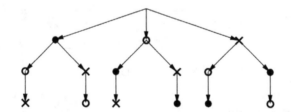

> **Review Video: Tree Diagrams**
> Visit mometrix.com/academy and enter code: 829158

You can also make a chart to list all the possibilities:

First object	Second object	Third object
●	X	O
●	O	X
O	●	X
O	X	●
X	●	O

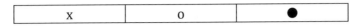

X	O	●

Either way, you can easily see there are six possible ways the three objects can be ordered.

If two events have no outcomes in common, they are said to be **mutually exclusive**. For example, in a standard deck of 52 playing cards, the event of all card suits is mutually exclusive to the event of all card values. If two events have no bearing on each other so that one event occurring has no influence on the probability of another event occurring, the two events are said to be independent. For example, rolling a standard six-sided die multiple times does not change that probability that a particular number will be rolled from one roll to the next. If the outcome of one event does affect the probability of the second event, the two events are said to be dependent. For example, if cards are drawn from a deck, the probability of drawing an ace after an ace has been drawn is different than the probability of drawing an ace if no ace (or no other card, for that matter) has been drawn.

In probability, the **odds in favor of an event** are the number of times the event will occur compared to the number of times the event will not occur. To calculate the odds in favor of an event, use the formula $\frac{P(A)}{1-P(A)}$, where $P(A)$ is the probability that the event will occur. Many times, odds in favor is given as a ratio in the form $\frac{a}{b}$ or $a:b$, where a is the probability of the event occurring and b is the complement of the event, the probability of the event not occurring. If the odds in favor are given as 2:5, that means that you can expect the event to occur two times for every 5 times that it does not occur. In other words, the probability that the event will occur is $\frac{2}{2+5} = \frac{2}{7}$.

In probability, the **odds against an event** are the number of times the event will not occur compared to the number of times the event will occur. To calculate the odds against an event, use the formula $\frac{1-P(A)}{P(A)}$, where $P(A)$ is the probability that the event will occur. Many times, odds against is given as a ratio in the form $\frac{b}{a}$ or $b: a$, where b is the probability the event will not occur (the complement of the event) and a is the probability the event will occur. If the odds against an event are given as 3:1, that means that you can expect the event to not occur 3 times for every one time it does occur. In other words, 3 out of every 4 trials will fail.

Two-Way Frequency Tables

TWO-WAY FREQUENCY TABLES

If we have a two-way frequency table, it is generally a straightforward matter to read off the probabilities of any two events A and B, as well as the joint probability of both events occurring, $P(A \cap B)$. We can then find the conditional probability $P(A|B)$ by calculating $P(A|B) = \frac{P(A \cap B)}{P(B)}$. We could also check whether or not events are independent by verifying whether $P(A)P(B) = P(A \cap B)$.

For example, a certain store's recent T-shirt sales:

	Small	Medium	Large	Total
Blue	25	40	35	100
White	27	25	22	74
Black	8	23	15	46
Total	60	88	72	220

Suppose we want to find the conditional probability that a customer buys a black shirt (event A), given that the shirt he buys is size small (event B). From the table, the probability $P(B)$ that a customer buys a small shirt is $\frac{60}{220} = \frac{3}{11}$. The probability $P(A \cap B)$ that he buys a small, black shirt is $\frac{8}{220} = \frac{2}{55}$. The conditional probability $P(A|B)$ that he buys a black shirt, given that he buys a small shirt, is therefore $P(A|B) = \frac{2/55}{3/11} = \frac{2}{15}$.

Similarly, if we want to check whether the event a customer buys a blue shirt, A, is independent of the event that a customer buys a medium shirt, B. From the table, $P(A) = \frac{100}{220} = \frac{5}{11}$ and $P(B) = \frac{88}{220} = \frac{4}{10}$. Also, $P(A \cap B) = \frac{40}{220} = \frac{2}{11}$. Since $\left(\frac{5}{11}\right)\left(\frac{4}{10}\right) = \frac{20}{110} = \frac{2}{11}$, $P(A)P(B) = P(A \cap B)$ and these two events are indeed independent.

Expected Value

EXPECTED VALUE

Expected value is a method of determining the expected outcome in a random situation. It is a sum of the weighted probabilities of the possible outcomes. Multiply the probability of an event occurring by the weight assigned to that probability (such as the amount of money won or lost). A practical application of the expected value is to determine whether a game of chance is really fair. If the sum of the weighted probabilities is equal to zero, the game is generally considered fair because the player has a fair chance to at least break even. If the expected value is less than zero, then players are expected to lose more than they win. For example, a lottery drawing might allow the player to choose any three-digit number, 000–999. The probability of choosing the winning number is 1:1000. If it costs \$1 to play, and a winning number receives \$500, the expected value is $\left(-\$1 \times \frac{999}{1,000}\right) + \left(\$499 \times \frac{1}{1,000}\right) = -\$0.50$. You can expect to lose on average 50 cents for every dollar you spend.

Review Video: Expected Value
Visit mometrix.com/academy and enter code: 643554

EXPECTED VALUE AND SIMULATORS

A die roll simulator will show the results of n rolls of a die. The result of each die roll may be recorded. For example, suppose a die is rolled 100 times. All results may be recorded. The numbers of 1s, 2s, 3s, 4s, 5s, and 6s, may be counted. The experimental probability of rolling each number will equal the ratio of the frequency of the rolled number to the total number of rolls. As the number of rolls increases, or approaches infinity, the experimental probability will approach the theoretical probability of $\frac{1}{6}$. Thus, the expected value for the roll of a die is shown to be $\left(1 \times \frac{1}{6}\right) +$ $\left(2 \times \frac{1}{6}\right) + \left(3 \times \frac{1}{6}\right) + \left(4 \times \frac{1}{6}\right) + \left(5 \times \frac{1}{6}\right) + \left(6 \times \frac{1}{6}\right)$, or 3.5.

Teaching Mathematics

Statements

PREMISE AND ARGUMENT

A premise is a statement that precedes a conclusion, in an argument. It is the proposition, or assumption, of an argument. An argument will have two or more premises.

Example:

> If it is hot, then I will go swimming. (Premise)
> It is hot. (Premise)
> Therefore, I will go swimming. (Conclusion)

SIMPLE AND COMPOUND STATEMENTS

A **statement** in propositional logic is any sentence or expression that has a truth value—that is, that may in principle be considered true or false. "Hello!", for example, is not a statement; there's no sense in which it could be considered true or false. On the other hand, "$2 = 3$" *is* a statement, albeit a clearly false one. A **compound statement** is a statement that contains one or more other statements, combined or modified in some way. A **simple statement**, or a **proposition**, is a statement that cannot be broken down further into smaller statements.

For example, consider the statement, "If it rains tomorrow, then the streets will be flooded and traffic will be slow." This is a compound statement, because two smaller statements are embedded within it: "it rains tomorrow" and "the streets will be flooded and traffic will be slow." the former cannot be broken down further, and is therefore a simple statement, but the latter is another compound statement, because it includes two simple statements: "the streets will be flooded" and "traffic will be slow."

Common operations used to combine and modify simple statements into compound statements include conjunction, disjunction, negation, and implication.

Logical Reasoning

CONJUNCTION

Conjunction is an operation that combines two or more statements into a compound statement that is true if and only if all of the component statements are true. When the statements are written out, conjunction is marked by the word "and." For example, the statement "Roses are red and violets are blue" is a compound statement that is a conjunction of the two simple statements "roses are red" and "violets are blue."

Conjunction is represented by the operator ∧. In the previous example, if proposition P is "roses are red" and proposition Q is "violets are blue," then the compound statement "roses are red and violets are blue" would be written as "$P \land Q$."

DISJUNCTION

Disjunction is an operation that combines two or more statements into a compound statement that is true if and only if at least one of the component statements is true. When the statements are

156

written out, conjunction is marked by the word "or." For example, the statement "I'll clean the closet today, or you'll clean it tomorrow" is a compound statement that is a disjunction of the simple statements "I'll clean the closet today" and "you'll clean the closet tomorrow."

Disjunction is represented by the operator ∨. In the previous example, if proposition P is "I'll clean the closet today" and proposition Q is "you'll clean the closet tomorrow," then the compound statement "I'll clean the closet today, or you'll clean it tomorrow" would be written as "$P \lor Q$."

Note that while in everyday language "or" implies exclusivity, as one or the other option but not both, in formal logic disjunction includes the possibility of both propositions being true. If I clean the closet today *and* you clean it tomorrow, then the sample statement "I'll clean the closet today, or you'll clean it tomorrow" is true.

Conditional and Biconditional Statements

A conditional statement, or **implication**, is a compound statement of the form "if P, then Q." for instance, the statement "if a snake has rattles, then it's venomous" is a conditional statement. It can also be written "P implies Q" ("that a snake has rattles implies that it's venomous") or "P only if Q" ("a snake has rattles only if it's venomous"). the conditional statement is true when both P and Q are true, and even when P is false, regardless of Q. In other words, the conditional statement is false only when P is true and Q is false. the conditional statement is written as "$P \rightarrow Q$." P is called the **premise** of the statement, and Q the **conclusion**.

A **biconditional statement** is a combination of two conditional statements: both "if P, then Q" and "if Q, then P." To state it more concisely, "P if and only if Q." an example is "A number is even if and only if it is divisible by 2." the biconditional statement is true when P and Q are either both true or both false; it is false if P is true and Q is false or vice versa. the biconditional statement is written "$P \leftrightarrow Q$."

Existential and Universal Quantifiers

Existential and Universal Quantifiers

A **quantifier** is a logical construct used in a compound statement to give information on the number of subjects for which a statement is true. The **existential quantifier** specifies that the statement is true for at least one subject. It is usually introduced as "there exists," such as "there exists a real number that is equal to its own square." The symbol ∃ is used to signify the existential quantifier. For example, the preceding statement could be written as "$\exists x \in \mathbb{R}\ x = x^2$." The **universal quantifier** specifies that the statement is true for *every* subject. It is usually said as "all" or "for all", such as "all real numbers are less than their own squares plus one." The symbol ∀ is used to signify the universal quantifier. For example, the preceding statement could be written as

$$\forall x \in \mathbb{R}\ x < x^2 + 1$$

Sometimes it is useful to specify that there exists *exactly* one subject that meets a given criterion. In other words, there exists a *unique* such subject. This can be signified by adding an exclamation mark after the existential quantifier: "$\exists!\ x \in \mathbb{R}\ |x| = 0$" means "there exists a unique real number that has an absolute value of zero."

Truth Tables

TRUTH TABLES

A truth table shows the truth value of one or more compound statements for each possible combination of truth values of the propositions within it. The truth table contains one column for each **proposition**, and one column for each of the **compound statements** to be analyzed. It has one row for each combination of **truth values** of the propositions. Since each proposition has two possible truth values, the number of possible combinations for N propositions is 2^N, so the truth table will have 2^N rows.

The table below is a simple truth table for some common compound statements involving two propositions.

P	Q	$P \wedge Q$	$P \vee Q$	$\neg P$	$\neg Q$	$P \to Q$	$Q \to P$	$P \leftrightarrow Q$
T	T	T	T	F	F	T	T	T
T	F	F	T	F	T	F	T	F
F	T	F	T	T	F	T	F	F
F	F	F	F	T	T	T	T	T

Truth tables are useful for comparing two compound statements to see if they are equivalent. They are also useful for analyzing whether complicated compound statements are true or false. A table can have a column for each of the increasingly complex compound statements that combine to form the total statement.

> **Review Video: Truth Tables**
> Visit mometrix.com/academy and enter code: 293095

TRUTH TABLE TO VALIDATE THE RULE OF DETACHMENT

The Rule of Detachment states that given the premises, $P \to Q$ and P, the valid conclusion is Q.

In other words, for every case where $(P \to Q) \wedge P$ is true, Q will also be true. The truth table below illustrates this fact:

P	Q	$P \to Q$	$(P \to Q) \wedge P$
T	T	T	T
T	F	F	F
F	T	T	F
F	F	T	F

Notice the first cell under $(P \to Q) \wedge P$ is true, while the first cell under Q is also true. Thus, for every case where $(P \to Q) \wedge P$ was true, Q was also true.

Truth Table to Validate the Chain Rule

The Chain Rule states that given the premises, $P \rightarrow Q$ and $Q \rightarrow R$, the valid conclusion is $P \rightarrow R$.

In other words, for every case where $(P \rightarrow Q) \wedge (Q \rightarrow R)$ is true, $P \rightarrow R$ will also be true. The truth table below illustrates this fact:

P	Q	R	$P \rightarrow Q$	$Q \rightarrow R$	$(P \rightarrow Q) \wedge (Q \rightarrow R)$	$P \rightarrow R$
T	T	T	T	T	T	T
T	T	F	T	F	F	F
T	F	T	F	T	F	T
T	F	F	F	T	F	F
F	T	T	T	T	T	T
F	T	F	T	F	F	T
F	F	T	T	T	T	T
F	F	F	T	T	T	T

Notice that for every case where $(P \rightarrow Q) \wedge (Q \rightarrow R)$ was true, $P \rightarrow R$ was also true.

For example, consider the premises below:

If I hike a mountain, I will not eat a sandwich.
If I do not eat a sandwich, I will drink some water.
I will not drink some water.

Write a valid conclusive statement. Explain how you arrived at your answer. Be specific in your explanation.

Valid conclusive statement: I will not hike a mountain.

Application of the chain rule and rule of contraposition give the valid conclusion of $\neg P$. According to the chain rule, given $P \rightarrow \neg Q$ and $\neg Q \rightarrow R$, then $P \rightarrow R$. According to the rule of contraposition, $P \rightarrow R$ and $\neg R$ yields $\neg P$. On a truth table, for every place where $(P \rightarrow R) \wedge \neg R$ is true, $\neg P$ is also true. Thus, this is a valid conclusive statement.

Converse, Inverse, and Contrapositive

Converse, Inverse, and Contrapositive of a Conditional Statement

The converse of a conditional statement is a conditional statement with the premise and conclusion interchanged. the converse of $P \rightarrow Q$ is $Q \rightarrow P$. The **inverse** has the premise and conclusion both negated. The inverse of $P \rightarrow Q$ is $\neg P \rightarrow \neg Q$. The **contrapositive** has the premise and conclusion both negated *and* interchanged. The contrapositive of $P \rightarrow Q$ is $\neg Q \rightarrow \neg P$.

For example, given the **conditional statement**, "If there is a key in the lock, then someone is home," the **converse** is "if someone is home, then there is a key in the lock," the **inverse** is "if there is not a key in the lock, then no one is home," and the **contrapositive** is "if no one is home, then there is not a key in the lock."

Note that the converse and inverse of a statement are *not* logically equivalent to the original statement. For instance, the statement "if $x = 4$, then $x > 2$" is true, but its converse "if $x > 2$, then $x = 4$" is not, because there are many numbers greater than 2, not just 4. A statement *is*, however, logically equivalent to its contrapositive—and the converse and inverse, while not equivalent to the

159

original statement, are equivalent to each other. The following truth table summarizes the relationships:

P	Q	$\neg P$	$\neg Q$	$P \rightarrow Q$ (statement)	$Q \rightarrow P$ (converse)	$\neg P \rightarrow \neg Q$ (inverse)	$\neg Q \rightarrow \neg P$ (contrapositive)
T	T	F	F	T	T	T	T
T	F	F	T	F	T	T	F
F	T	T	F	T	F	F	T
F	F	T	T	T	T	T	T

Review Video: <u>Converse, Inverse, and Contrapositive</u>
Visit mometrix.com/academy and enter code: 822844

Negation

NEGATION

In propositional logic, negation refers to the inversion of the truth value of a statement. The **negation** of a statement is true if the original statement is false, and false if the original statement is true. Negation can be signified by the word "not." For instance, the negation of the statement "Bob's cat is black" is "Bob's cat is not black." the symbol for negation is ¬. So, if the proposition P is "Bob's cat is black," then $\neg P$ would be "Bob's cat is not black." Two negations cancel each other out: $\neg\neg P = P$, or "not not P equals P."

It's important to be careful when combining negation with **quantifiers**. The negation of "there exists a cow that has a blue horn" is not "there exists a cow that does not have a blue horn." Rather, the negation is "there does not exist a cow that has a blue horn." the statements $\neg\exists x\, P(x)$ and $\exists x\, \neg P(x)$ are not equivalent. The same is true for the universal quantifier: $\neg\forall x\, P(x)$ and $\forall x\, \neg P(x)$ do not mean the same thing. There is, however, a connection between the negated quantifiers: $\neg\exists x\, P(x)$ is equivalent to $\forall x\, \neg P(x)$, and $\exists x\, \neg P(x)$ is equivalent to $\neg\forall x\, P(x)$.

Review Video: <u>Negation</u>
Visit mometrix.com/academy and enter code: 429150

DE MORGAN'S LAWS

De Morgan's Laws are a set of useful relations connecting negation, conjunction, and disjunction. They can be stated briefly as "the negation of a conjunction is the disjunction of the negations" and "the negation of a disjunction is the conjunction of the negations." This can be written as:

$$\neg(P \wedge Q) \leftrightarrow (\neg P) \vee (\neg Q) \text{ and } \neg(P \vee Q) \leftrightarrow (\neg P) \wedge (\neg Q)$$

For instance, if proposition P is "$x > 3$" and proposition Q is "$y > 3$", then De Morgan's Laws state that "it is not true that both x and y are greater than 3" is equivalent to "either x is not greater than 3, or y is not greater than 3."

The validity of **De Morgan's Laws** can be shown with truth tables. Note that the columns highlighted in the same color match:

P	Q	$\neg P$	$\neg Q$	$(\neg P) \wedge (\neg Q)$	$(\neg P) \vee (\neg Q)$	$P \wedge Q$	$P \vee Q$	$\neg(P \wedge Q)$	$\neg(P \vee Q)$
T	T	F	F	F	F	T	T	F	F
T	F	F	T	F	T	F	T	T	F
F	T	T	F	F	T	F	T	T	F
F	F	T	T	T	T	F	F	T	T

Types of Reasoning

INDUCTIVE REASONING

Inductive reasoning is a method used to make a conjecture, based on patterns and observations. The conclusion of an inductive argument may be true or false.

Mathematical Example:

A cube has 6 faces, 8 vertices, and 12 edges. A square pyramid has 5 faces, 5 vertices, and 8 edges. A triangular prism has 5 faces, 6 vertices, and 9 edges. Thus, the sum of the numbers of faces and vertices, minus the number of edges, will always equal 2, for any solid.

Non-Mathematical Example:

Almost all summer days in Tucson are hot. It is a summer day in Tucson. Therefore, it will probably be hot.

DEDUCTIVE REASONING

Deductive reasoning is a method that proves a hypothesis or set of premises. The conclusion of a valid deductive argument will be true, given that the premises are true. Deductive reasoning utilizes logic to determine a conclusion. For instance, consider the following application of the chain rule:

If a ding is a dong, then a ping is a pong.	$p \rightarrow q$
If a ping is a pong, then a ring is a ting.	$q \rightarrow r$
A ding is a dong.	p
Therefore, a ring is a ting.	$\therefore r$

FORMAL REASONING

Formal reasoning, in mathematics, involves justification using formal steps and processes to arrive at a conclusion. Formal reasoning is utilized when writing proofs and using logic. For example, when applying logic, validity of a conclusion is determined by truth tables. A set of premises will yield a given conclusion. This type of thinking is formal reasoning. Writing a geometric proof also employs formal reasoning. Example:

If a quadrilateral has four congruent sides, it is a rhombus.

If a shape is a rhombus, then the diagonals are perpendicular.

A quadrilateral has four congruent sides.

Therefore, the diagonals are perpendicular.

INFORMAL REASONING

Informal reasoning, in mathematics, uses patterns and observations to make conjectures. The conjecture may be true or false. Several, or even many, examples may show a certain pattern, shedding light on a possible conclusion. However, informal reasoning does not provide a justifiable conclusion. A conjecture may certainly be deemed as likely or probable. However, informal reasoning will not reveal a certain conclusion. Consider the following example:

Mathematical Idea – Given a sequence that starts with 1 and each term decreases by a factor of $\frac{1}{2}$, the limit of the sum of the sequence will be 2.

Informal Reasoning – The sum of 1 and $\frac{1}{2}$ is $1\frac{1}{2}$. The sum of 1, $\frac{1}{2}$, and $\frac{1}{4}$ is $1\frac{3}{4}$. The sum of 1, $\frac{1}{2}$, $\frac{1}{4}$, and $\frac{1}{8}$ is $1\frac{7}{8}$. Thus, it appears that as the sequence approaches infinity, the sum of the sequence approaches 2.

Proofs

PROOFS

A **proof** serves to show the deductive or inductive process that relates the steps leading from a hypothesis to a conclusion. A proof may be direct ($p \rightarrow q$), meaning that a conclusion is shown to be true, given a hypothesis. There are also proofs by contradiction ($p \wedge \sim q$), whereby the hypothesis is assumed to be true, and the negation of the conclusion is assumed to be true. (In other words, the statement is assumed to be false.) Proofs by contraposition ($\sim q \rightarrow \sim p$) show that the negation of the conclusion leads to the negation of the hypothesis. (In other words, the negation of the conclusion is assumed to be true, and it must be shown that the negation of the hypothesis is also true.) A mathematical induction proof seeks to show that $P(1)$ is true and that $P(k + 1)$ is true, given that $P(k)$ is true. Direct proofs, proofs by contradiction, and proofs by contraposition use deductive methods, while a mathematical induction proof uses an inductive method.

Direct proofs are those that assume a statement to be true. The purpose of such a proof is to show that the conclusion is true, given that the hypothesis is true. A sample of a direct proof is shown below:

Prove "If m divides a and m divides b, then m divides $a + b$."

Proof:

- Assume m divides a and m divides b.
- Thus, a equals the product of m and some integer factor, p, by the definition of division, and b equals the product of m and some integer factor, q, by the definition of division. According to substitution, $a + b$ may be rewritten as $(m \times p) + (m \times q)$. Factoring out the m gives $m(p + q)$. Since m divides $p + q$, and $p + q$ is an integer, according to the closure property, we have shown that m divides $a + b$, by the definition of division.

Indirect proofs (or proofs by contradiction) are those that assume a statement to be false. The purpose of such a proof is to show that a hypothesis is false, given the negation of the conclusion, indicating that the conclusion must be true. A sample of an indirect proof is shown below:

Prove "If $3x + 7$ is odd, then x is even."

Proof:

- Assume $3x + 7$ is odd and x is odd.
- According to the definition of odd, $x = 2a + 1$, where a is an element of the integers.
- Thus, by substitution, $3x + 7 = 3(2a + 1) + 7$, which simplifies as $6a + 3 + 7$, or $6a + 10$, which may be rewritten as $2(3a + 5)$. Any even integer may be written as the product of 2 and some integer, k. Thus, we have shown the hypothesis to be false, meaning that the conditional statement must be true.

A **proof by contraposition** is one written in the form, $\sim Q \to \sim P$. In other words, a proof by contraposition seeks to show that the negation of Q will yield the negation of P. A sample of a proof by contraposition is shown below:

Prove "If $5x + 7$ is even, then x is odd."

Proof:

- Assume that if x is even, then $5x + 7$ is odd.
- Assume x is even.
- Thus, by the definition of an even integer, $x = 2a$.

By substitution, $5x + 7$ may be rewritten as $5(2a) + 7$, which simplifies as $10a + 7$. This expression cannot be written as the product of 2 and some factor, k. Thus, $5x + 7$ is odd, by definition of an odd integer. So, when $5x + 7$ is even, x is odd, according to contraposition.

A **proof by contradiction** is one written in the form, $p \wedge \sim q$. In other words, a proof by contradiction seeks to show the negation of q will result in a false hypothesis, indicating that the conclusion of the statement, as written, must be true. In other words, the conditional statement of $p \to q$ is true.

MATHEMATICAL INDUCTION PROOF UTILIZING INDUCTIVE REASONING

A mathematical induction proof utilizes inductive reasoning in its assumption that if $P(k)$ is true, then $P(k + 1)$ is also true. The induction hypothesis is $P(k)$. This step utilizes inductive reasoning because an observation is used to make the conjecture that $P(k + 1)$ is also true.

Example:

For all natural numbers, n, the sum is equal to $(n + 1)\left(\frac{n}{2}\right)$.

Show that $P(1)$ is true.

$1 = (1 + 1)\left(\frac{1}{2}\right)$.

Assume $P(k)$ is true.

$1 + 2 + 3 + 4 + \cdots + k = (k + 1)\left(\frac{k}{2}\right)$.

This previous step is the inductive hypothesis. This hypothesis may be used to write the conjecture that $P(k + 1)$ is also true: $(1 + 2 + 3 + 4 + \cdots + k) + (k + 1) = [(k + 1) + 1]\left(\frac{k+1}{2}\right)$

$$(k + 1)\left(\frac{k}{2}\right) + (k + 1) = [(k + 1) + 1]\left(\frac{k}{2} + \frac{1}{2}\right)$$

$$(k + 1)\left(\frac{k}{2}\right) + (k + 1) = \left(\frac{k}{2}(k + 1) + \frac{k}{2}\right) + \left(\frac{1}{2}(k + 1) + \frac{1}{2}(1)\right)$$

$$(k + 1)\left(\frac{k}{2}\right) + (k + 1) = \frac{k}{2}(k + 1) + \frac{k}{2} + \frac{k + 1}{2} + \frac{1}{2}$$

$$(k + 1)\left(\frac{k}{2}\right) + (k + 1) = \frac{k}{2}(k + 1) + \frac{2k + 2}{2}$$

$$(k + 1)\left(\frac{k}{2}\right) + (k + 1) = \frac{k}{2}(k + 1) + (k + 1)$$

Instruction and Assessment

INSTRUCTION

MATHEMATICAL JARGON

Mathematical language is hard for beginners. Words such as "or" and "only" have more precise meanings than in everyday speech. Also confusing to beginners are words such as "open" and "field" that have been given specific mathematical meanings. Mathematical jargon includes technical terms such as homeomorphism and integrable. But there is a reason for special notation and technical jargon. Mathematics requires more precision than everyday speech. Mathematicians refer to this precision of language and logic as rigor.

RIGOR

Rigor is fundamentally a matter of mathematical proof. Mathematicians want their theorems to follow from axioms by means of systematic reasoning. This is to avoid mistaken "theorems", based upon fallible intuitions, of which many instances have occurred in the history of the subject. The level of rigor expected in mathematics has varied over time; the Greeks expected detailed arguments, but at the time of Isaac Newton the methods employed were less rigorous. Problems inherent in the definitions used by Newton would lead to a resurgence of careful analysis and formal proof in the 19th century. Today, mathematicians continue to argue amongst themselves about computer-assisted proofs. Because large computations are hard to verify, such proofs may not be sufficiently rigorous. Axioms in traditional thought were "self-evident truths," but that conception is problematic. At a formal level, an axiom is just a string of symbols which has an intrinsic meaning only in the context of all derivable formulas of an axiomatic system. It was the goal of Hilbert's program to put all of mathematics on a firm axiomatic basis, but according to Gödel's incompleteness theorem every (sufficiently powerful) axiomatic system has undecidable formulas; and thus, a final axiomatization of mathematics is impossible. Nonetheless mathematics is often imagined to be (as far as its formal content) nothing but set theory in some axiomatization, in the sense that every mathematical statement or proof could be cast into formulas within set theory.

NUMERALS AND NAMING SYSTEMS

Some of the systems for representing numbers in previous and present cultures are well known. Roman numerals use a few letters of the alphabet to represent numbers up to the thousands, but are not intended for arbitrarily large numbers and can only represent positive integers. Arabic numerals are a family of systems originating in India, passing to medieval Islamic civilization and then to Europe, and now are the standard in global culture. They have undergone many curious changes with time and geography, but can represent arbitrarily large numbers and have been adapted to negative numbers, fractions, and other real numbers.

Less-well-known systems include some that are written and can be read today, such as the Hebrew and Greek method of using the letters of the alphabet, in order, for digits 1–9, tens 10–90, and hundreds 100–900.

A completely different system is that of the quipu, which the Inca used to record numbers on knotted strings.

FINGER COUNTING

Many systems of finger counting have been, and still are, used in various parts of the world. Most are not as obvious as holding up a number of fingers. The position of fingers may be most important. One continuing use for finger counting is for people who speak different languages to communicate prices in the marketplace.

COGNITIVE THEORISTS AND CONSTRUCTIVISTS

Constructivists believe that students may construct knowledge by themselves. In other words, students are actively engaged in the construction of their own knowledge. Students will assimilate and accommodate in order to build new knowledge, based on previous knowledge. Thus, in planning instruction based on constructivism, a teacher would focus on grouping designs, environment, problem-solving tasks, and inclusion of multiple representations. The goal in such a classroom would be for students to construct knowledge on their own. There are different levels of constructivism, including weak constructivism and radical constructivism.

Cognitivists differ from constructivists in that they believe that active exploration is important in helping students make sense of observations and experiences. However, the students are not expected to invent or construct knowledge by themselves. They are only expected to make sense of the mathematics. In planning instruction based on cognitivism, a teacher would employ similar methods to those discussed above, with the focus on active exploration. Students would do a lot of comparisons of mathematical methods in making sense of ideas.

CONSTRUCTIVISM

Three types of constructivism are weak constructivism, social constructivism, and radical constructivism. **Weak constructivists** believe that students construct their own knowledge, but also accept certain preconceived notions or facts. **Social constructivists** believe that students construct knowledge by interacting with one another and holding discussions and conversations. **Radical constructivists** believe that all interpretations of knowledge are subjective, based on the individual learner. In other words, there is no real truth; it is all subjective. Classroom instructional planning based on a weak constructivist viewpoint might involve incorporation of some accepted theorems and definitions, while continuing to plan active explorations and discussions. Planning based on a social constructivist viewpoint might involve group activities, debates, discussion forums, etc. Planning based on a radical constructivist viewpoint would involve activities that are open-ended, where there is more than one correct answer. The problems would invite more than one correct answer.

PROJECT-BASED LEARNING

Project-based learning is learning that centers on the solving of a problem. Students learn many different ideas by solving one "big" problem. For example, for a unit on sine and cosine functions, a teacher may design a problem whereby the students are asked to model a real-world phenomenon using both types of functions. Students must investigate the effects of changes in amplitude, period, shifts, etc., on the graphs of the functions. Students will also be able to make connections between the types of functions when modeling the same phenomenon. Such a problem will induce high-level thinking.

Project-based learning is derived from constructivist theory, which contends that students learn by doing and constructing their own knowledge.

COOPERATIVE LEARNING

Cooperative learning simply means that students will learn by cooperating with one another. Students will be placed into groups of a size determined by the teacher. With such an approach, students work together to succeed in learning. Students may work together to learn a topic, complete an assignment, or compete with other groups.

Examples of cooperative learning include Think-Pair-Share and Jigsaw. **Think-Pair-Share** is a cooperative learning strategy that involves thinking about some given topic, sharing ideas, thoughts, or questions with a partner, and then sharing the partner discussion with the whole group. For example, in the mathematics classroom, a teacher may ask the class to think about the meaning of a proportional relationship. Each student would think for a set period of time, share ideas with a partner, and then each partner group would share their ideas regarding the meaning of proportionality. **Jigsaw** is another cooperative learning strategy that involves dividing among each group member reading material or ideas to be learned. Each student will then read his or her information, summarize it, and share the findings or ideas with the group. In mathematics, students might be given information on modeling with cosine and sine functions. Students could then share what they learned about real-world phenomena modeled by each. Different students may also be assigned to read in-depth material on amplitude, period, shifts, etc.

CONTROL STRATEGIES

"**Control strategies**" is another name for "metacognitive learning strategies," which indicate any strategy that promotes a learner's awareness of his or her level of learning. With such strategies, the student will work to determine what he or she knows and does not know regarding a subject. Possible control strategies are thinking, self-regulation, and discussing ideas with peers.

Example:

> A student may discover his or her level of "knowing" about functions by keeping a journal of any questions he or she might have regarding the topic. The student may list everything that he or she understands, as well as aspects not understood. As the student progresses through the course, he or she may go back and reconfirm any correct knowledge and monitor progress on any previous misconceptions.

MEMORIZATION AND ELABORATION STRATEGIES

Memorization is simply a technique whereby rote repetition is used to learn information. **Elaboration** strategies involve the connection of new information to some previously learned information. In mathematics, for example, students may use elaboration strategies when learning how to calculate the volume of a cone, based on their understood approach for calculating the volume of a cylinder. The student would be making connections in his or her mind between this new skill and other previously acquired skills. A memorization technique would simply involve memorization of the volume of a cone formula, as well as ways to evaluate the formula.

PRIOR KNOWLEDGE

Three ways of activating students' prior knowledge are concept mapping, visual imagery, and comparing and contrasting. With **concept mapping**, a student would detail and connect all known aspects of a mathematics topic. Ideas would be grouped into subgroups. Such an approach would allow a student to see what he or she does not know, prompting the activation of any prior knowledge on the subject. **Visual imagery** is simply the use of any pictures or diagrams to promote activation of prior knowledge. For example, giving a picture of Pascal's triangle would likely activate students' prior knowledge regarding the binomial theorem. **Comparing and contrasting** means that the student will compare and contrast ideas or approaches. For example, a student might be given a mapping of an inverse function. He or she could then compare and contrast this mapping to a known mapping of a function, in order to decide how they are the same and different. This would activate a student's prior understanding of functions and the definition thereof.

Three methods for ascertaining, or assessing, students' prior knowledge are portfolios, pre-tests, and self-inventories. **Portfolios** are simply a compilation of prior student activity related to mathematics topics. For example, a portfolio might show a student's work with transforming functions. **Pre-tests** are designed to measure a student's understanding of mathematics topics that will be taught in the course during the year. **Self-inventories** are just what the name implies: inventories that ask the students to name, list, describe, and explain information understood about various mathematics topics.

Once a teacher has assessed students' level of prior knowledge regarding some mathematics topic, he or she may use that information to scaffold the instruction. In other words, the teacher may decide to further break down the mathematics material into more integral parts. Exact processes or steps may be shown, including justification for using certain properties or theorems. More examples may be shown, while including examples of many different variations of problems, in order to ensure that students are not simply memorizing one approach that will be incorrectly applied to any problem of that sort. The teacher may also decide that more group work, peer cooperation, and discussion are needed.

For example, suppose a teacher determines that students have very little understanding of logic and valid arguments. The teacher may decide to re-teach the creation of truth tables, including truth values for intersections and "if p, then q" statements. The teacher may also decide to re-teach how a truth table may be used to show if an argument is valid. Students may be placed into groups and asked to determine the validity of several simple arguments. Once students understand the concept, they may move on to more rigorous arguments, including equivalence relations.

CONCEPT WHEREBY USAGE OF MANIPULATIVES WOULD INCREASE CONCEPTUAL UNDERSTANDING

Understanding of how to solve one-variable equations would certainly be enhanced by using rods and counters. With this manipulative, the rod would represent the variable, or x, while the counters would represent the constants on each side of the equation. A sample diagram of the equation, $x + 4 = 8$, is shown below. Note that the vertical line represents the equals sign.

In order to solve the equation (and isolate x), four counters may be removed from each side of the mat. This process is shown below:

Now, the final illustration is:

Thus, the solution is $x = 4$. The manipulative helps students understand the meaning of the subtraction property of equality in action, without simply memorizing its meaning.

PIAGET'S COGNITIVE DEVELOPMENT THEORY

Piaget's cognitive development theory is aligned with **constructivism**. In fact, constructivism is built on his ideas. Piaget's cognitive development theory indicates that students actively participate in the construction of their own knowledge via assimilation and accommodation. Current cognitive theorists do not believe that students have to construct their own knowledge, but instead that they only have to make sense of what they are observing.

The four stages of learning, as developed by Piaget, are sensorimotor, preoperational, concrete operational, and formal operational. The defined stages show the progression from concrete thinking to abstract thinking. In other words, a child would need an object to understand properties, in the first stage. By the fourth stage, the child would be able to think abstractly, without some concrete form. In mathematics, this idea might be illustrated by first working with diagrams and manipulatives of numbers and then later writing symbolic forms of the numbers, including the numerals. This would illustrate the progression from 0 to 7 years. In the years of 11 to adulthood, much deeper abstraction is utilized. For example, people would be able to discuss functions and general properties, without looking at any concrete graphs or representations.

PROGRESSION THAT A STUDENT UNDERGOES AS HE OR SHE LEARNS MATHEMATICS

When learning mathematics, students begin with concrete representations and ideas. Later, students are able to abstract meaning and make generalizations. Students will also be asked to apply abstract ideas from one topic to another mathematics topic. In other words, students would move from concrete representations, ideas, and facts to symbolic representations and generalizations. Piaget outlined such a progression in his general four stages of cognitive learning. For example, a student may first learn about solving equations by using a balance scale. After the student understands the process, he or she can solve alone, using the symbolic equations. He or she would also be able to describe the process for solving any equation.

DIRECT INSTRUCTION VERSUS STUDENT-CENTERED INSTRUCTION

Direct instruction is instruction whereby the teacher delivers all content knowledge to be learned, and students, more or less, passively listen. The teacher employs a step-by-step instruction method for learning content. Student-centered instruction is learning whereby the teacher serves as a facilitator of learning and students actively participate in their own learning. Research has shown that students show a higher level of procedural and conceptual understanding when learning in a student-centered approach. Direct instruction might be more appropriate when teaching basic or

fundamental theorems. Student-centered learning might be more appropriate when helping students make connections or develop higher-level thinking regarding a topic.

COOPERATIVE LEARNING TASK VERSUS TRADITIONAL TASK

Think-Pair-Share is an activity whereby a topic is first given for consideration on an individual basis. Next, the students are arranged in pairs and asked to discuss the topic (e.g., any questions, comments, generalizations, etc.). Finally, each pair will contribute to a whole-class discussion on the topic.

In mathematics, students would likely develop a higher level of understanding by using such an activity as Think-Pair-Share when learning about trigonometric functions. For example, students might be asked to consider different real-world situations that may be modeled with sine and cosine functions. Students could individually make a list and then share with a partner. Each partner group could then contribute to a whole class list. This list could be used as a reference sheet.

IMPLEMENTING TECHNOLOGY IN CLASSROOM INSTRUCTION

Technology may be implemented in the mathematics classroom in many ways. For example, Excel may be used to perform regressions, calculate lines of best fit, calculate correlation coefficients, plot residuals, show convergence or divergence of a sequence, etc. Calculators may be used to evaluate and graph functions, find area under the normal curve, calculate combinations and permutations, perform statistical tests, etc. Graphing software, such as GeoGebra, may be used to graph and explore many shapes and functions. Students may also use it to graph reflections, rotations, translations, and dilations.

MODIFYING INSTRUCTION TO ACCOMMODATE ENGLISH-LANGUAGE LEARNERS

In mathematics specifically, instruction may be modified to include illustrations of ideas, in addition to given words. Audio may also be included for problem tasks. English-language learners may also be grouped with other fluent English-speaking students in order to assist with learning of the mathematics topic. Students will be able to hear the conversation, in addition to seeing the topic in print. In addition, problems may be broken down into smaller pieces, which can help the student focus on one step at a time. Further, additional one-on-one time with the teacher may be needed, whereby the teacher reads aloud and illustrates examples to be learned.

EFFECTIVE LEARNING ENVIRONMENT FOR ELL STUDENTS

Characteristics of an effective learning environment for ELL students include creation of a low threshold for anxiety, use of pictures to teach vocabulary and mathematics ideas, implementation of graphic organizers, explicit teaching of vocabulary words, and use of active learning strategies. The latter two are extremely important, since ELL students need to learn exact terms and exact definitions while also engaging with fellow students, as opposed to sitting alone at a desk. Research completed by professors at the University of Houston and University of California list collaborative learning, use of multiple representations, and technology integration as important facets of an effective learning environment for ELL students (Waxman & Tellez, 2002).

MATHEMATICS QUESTION THAT IS CLOSED-ENDED AND THEN REWRITTEN IN AN OPEN-ENDED MANNER

Closed-Ended:

- Look at the graph of $y = x^2 + 2$. Decide if the graph represents a function.

Open-Ended:

- Provide an example of an equation that represents a function. Provide an example of an equation that does not represent a function. Explain how the graphs of the two equations compare to one another.

The first question will elicit a simple, straightforward response, or "Yes, it is a function."

The second question prompts the student to come up with two equations and then describe how the graphs of the two equations would compare. There is more than one possible answer, and the student has to make a comparison as well.

GOOD QUESTIONING RESPONSE TECHNIQUES

A few good questioning response techniques are:

- Make sure the wait time is sufficient;
- Do not include leading prompts within questions;
- Ask more questions based on student answers;
- Confirm or restate correct student comments.

The key to good questioning response techniques is to show the student that his or her comments are important and to connect those comments to other student comments. The student should feel that he or she has made a contribution to the community of learners. A teacher should always ask a meaningful, thought-provoking question and provide sufficient time for the student to provide a meaningful and well-thought-out response. Student answers should lead to more questions and ideas and not serve as an endpoint.

NCTM CATEGORIES OF QUESTIONS THAT TEACHERS SHOULD ASK

The professional standards describe five categories of questions that teachers should ask. These categories are: 1) working together to make sense of problems; 2) individually making sense of problems; 3) reasoning about mathematics; 4) providing conjectures about mathematics; and 5) making connections within and outside of mathematics. Sample questions include "What does this mean?," "How can you prove that?," and "What does this relate to?". Categories 4 and 5 are high level and include questions that prompt students to invent ideas and make meaningful connections.

ACCOUNTANTS AND MATHEMATICAL MODELING

Accountants use mathematical modeling in a variety of ways. For example, an accountant models the future value of a certificate of deposit (CD) using the compound interest formula. An accountant also may fit a regression line to a client's overall savings over x years. An accountant may model tax payments with residual plots. Accountants may use past income tax returns to predict future tax expenses. Accountants may compare rates of return when investing in different mutual funds, by fitting and comparing regression lines.

SCIENTISTS AND FUNCTIONS

Scientists use functions to model real-world phenomena. For example, scientists use quadratic functions to model the height of an object tossed into the air or dropped from a certain height. Scientists use sine and cosine functions to model real-world occurrences such as the depth of water at various times of the day, the movement of a pendulum, etc. Scientists use exponential functions to analyze and predict the number of bacteria present after x amount of time. Scientists also use functions when analyzing the time it takes a rocket to reach a destination.

MAKING MATHEMATICS RELEVANT TO STUDENTS' LIVES

Teachers can make mathematics relevant to students, using a variety of strategies. Teachers may include items relevant and pertinent to students within question stems, such as including "iPad," "apps," and video game names. Teachers should pose questions that are similar to what students may have asked themselves, such as, "If I invest this much money in an account and save for x years, after how many years will I have y dollars?" Teachers should include real-world problems to solve, and not simply include rote solving of equations. Students should know what sorts of scenarios may be modeled with rational expressions. Many researchers believe that curricula should be centered on the "real world," with all facets of mathematics learning spawning from that center. In other words, students often know how to convert a decimal to a percentage, but when reading *The Wall Street Journal*, they may not be able to interpret a percentage yield.

ASSESSMENT

ASSESSMENT TOOL

A **mathematics assessment tool** is used to assess a student's prior knowledge, current knowledge, skill set, procedural knowledge, conceptual understanding, depth of understanding, and ability to make abstractions and generalizations. Perhaps the most important purpose of such a tool is to help the student develop and modify instruction. A teacher may determine that students are ready to surpass the current lesson or need it to be much more scaffolded. A teacher may also use the assessment to track students' progress. For example, a portfolio might show students' initial understanding of functions and end with their work with function modeling.

When a teacher needs to decide on an appropriate assessment tool, he or she needs to consider the purpose of the assessment. For example, if the purpose of an assessment is to direct the instruction, a pre-test may be a good assessment to use. If the purpose of the assessment is to determine the level of student understanding, then a whole-class discussion may be desired. If the purpose of an assessment is to assess student understanding of a unit of material, then an exam would be appropriate. If a teacher wishes to analyze student understanding and ability to abstract knowledge, then a performance assessment may be used. If a teacher wishes to check off skills mastered by students, then a checklist would be appropriate.

VALID TEST

A test is valid if it tests what it is supposed to test. In other words, a test is valid if it appropriately covers the material it is supposed to cover. For example, a topic not taught in class should not be included on a valid test. In order to construct a valid test, a teacher should make a list of all standards covered during that time period. The teacher should also closely mirror the design of problems examined in class, for homework, and in group discussions. Finally, the teacher should make sure that there is an even balance of questions to cover all of the material.

VALID EXAM

In order to select a **valid exam**, a teacher should make sure that the test aligns with the objectives and standards covered in the unit. The teacher should also make sure that the test problems are similar to those covered during class time. The teacher should make sure the percentages of questions devoted to each objective are balanced. In order for a test to be valid, it must be reliable, meaning that it produces similar results with different groups. A teacher may wish to check the validity and reliability results of an exam.

In general, an exam is considered **invalid** if it does not measure what it is supposed to measure. The exam may include questions from another unit. It may include questions with different wording techniques, making it much more difficult. The exam may include representations different from

171

those covered in class. An invalid exam would not be reliable, meaning the results would not be consistent with different administrations of the exam. Biased questions and wording may also make an exam invalid.

Assessing Students' Understanding of What Has Been Taught

In order to assess thought processes, **open-ended questions** are needed. The teacher may wish to have students write an essay, write entries in a mathematics journal, undergo a performance task, or participate in a debate or discussion. The teacher may also design a pre-test that includes all constructed response questions. In particular, a performance task requires students to justify solutions, which provide the teacher with insight into students' understanding and reasoning. In general, the assessment should include questions that ask students to make abstractions and justify their thinking.

Testing Issue

Example: A student claims that an exam is more difficult and includes more content than what was presented in class. How might a teacher determine if the student's claim is true?

The teacher would need to make a list of all objectives and standards covered during the time period. The teacher would also need to compile all problems and examples covered in class and as homework. Finally, the teacher would need to do a careful analysis of the wording of the problems covered in class and as homework. If any of these items are not aligned to the exam, the teacher would need to go back and re-teach the material, using the created test as a guide for instruction.

Performance Task

A **performance task** allows the teacher to assess process as well as product, meaning that a teacher can assess students' thought processes as well as their final answer. The level of student learning will be much clearer when reviewing a performance task. A performance task goes beyond a multiple-choice format, allowing for oral and tactile-kinesthetic performances. Furthermore, a performance task may combine several mathematics concepts into one assessment instrument. This type of assessment often includes real-world problems, which helps the student connect mathematics to the outside world.

Formative and Summative Assessments

Formative assessments are those given during the learning process. Formative assessments provide the teacher with information related to a student's progress at various stages throughout a time period. Formative assessments are used to modify instruction as needed. In other words, formative assessments inform instruction. Summative assessments are those given at the end of a learning period. Summative assessments serve to measure the cumulative knowledge gained. Examples of formative assessments include quizzes, checklists, observations, and discussion. Examples of summative assessments include exams, portfolios, performance tasks, and standardized tests.

Four formative assessments include quizzes, checklists, observations, and discussion. **Quizzes** are often short assessments that may include multiple-choice items, short response items, or essay items. Quizzes are often administered following presentation of a portion of a mathematics unit. **Checklists** include a list of skills or concepts that should be mastered or understood. A teacher will check off all items mastered by a student. **Observations** are informal means of assessing students' understanding of a topic. A teacher may observe students' questions, engagement, and performance on projects. **Discussion** is another informal formative assessment. Discussions, both in groups and whole-class formats, allow the teacher to analyze students' thinking.

Four summative assessments include exams, portfolios, performance tasks, and standardized tests. **Exams** may include closed-ended or open-ended questions. Exams may be administered after each unit, semester, or at the end of the year. **Portfolios** include tasks created by a student and may include writing pieces and other large projects. Although the portfolio contains formative work, the tool itself may be used as a summative assessment piece. **Performance tasks** are large-scale problems that include many different components that relate to some big idea. For example, a student may be asked to formulate a plan for modeling a real-world phenomenon with a sine function. The student may be asked to explain how the function would change, given changes to the amplitude, period, shifts, etc. The student may then explain how these components would need to change to fit a new function. **Standardized tests** are tests that compare a student's performance to that of other students. They are often given at the end of the school year.

> **Review Video: Formative and Summative Assessments**
> Visit mometrix.com/academy and enter code: 804991

SCORING RUBRIC

A **strong rubric** will include unique performance criteria for each bullet. In other words, a portion of one criteria statement should not be included in a portion of another criteria statement. Each criteria statement should be clearly delineated, describing exactly what the student must be able to do. Furthermore, a strong rubric will often have scoring options, ranging from 0 to 4. When designing the rubric, it is helpful to create a model student response that will warrant each rubric score. It is also helpful to provide a space to provide feedback to students.

ENHANCING STUDENT UNDERSTANDING

In order for an assessment to enhance student understanding, it should provide an opportunity for the student to learn something. The assessment should be a learning opportunity for the student. It should prompt the student to think deeper about a mathematics topic. In other words, the student should think, "Okay. I understand this. I wonder how the process/solution would change if I did this." The assessment might prompt the student to ask deeper questions in the next class session or complete research on a certain topic. In order to create such an assessment, open-ended and challenging questions should be included on the exam. The exam should not consist of simple, lower-level, one-answer questions.

TESTING MATHEMATICAL MISCONCEPTIONS

In order to design such an assessment, the teacher should include mathematical error-type problems, whereby the student must look at a solution process or conjecture and determine if he or she agrees, of if and where an error occurred. The student would need to identify the error, correct it, and explain why it was erroneous. The assessment should include a variety of mathematical misconceptions. One solution process may include more than one error. A teacher may also simply ask students to participate in a collaborative learning activity, whereby the students must share ideas and thoughts regarding a new mathematical topic.

ASSESSING PRIOR KNOWLEDGE

Such a pre-test must not include any leading prompts. It should include open-ended and constructed-response items as well. A pre-test with solely multiple-choice items will not be sufficient, since a student has the option of guessing. The test should include higher-level questions that require connections within the field of mathematics. In other words, the questions should not all be mutually exclusive. They should build on one another. Finally, the test might include student error problems as well.

ASSESSING BOTH PROCEDURAL KNOWLEDGE AND CONCEPTUAL UNDERSTANDING

The assessment should include rote, algorithmic-type problems, as well as those that ask the student to utilize higher-level thinking, abstractions, and generalizations. The test should include open-ended, constructed-response-type problems. A performance task is an excellent assessment for assessing a student's ability to solve a problem, while also examining the student's thought processes, rationales, etc. In order to assess both types of understanding, the assessment will need to ask students to justify and explain solutions. In other words, the assessments should include questions at both ends of Bloom's Taxonomy.

PRE-TEST AND POST-TEST

A **post-test** should be exactly the same as an administered pre-test. If the teacher is to compare the results of a post-test to a pre-test, then the test and testing conditions should be identical. The **pre-test** assesses students' prior knowledge, while a post-test assesses students post knowledge. Comparing the results, side by side, allows the teacher to track student progress. The teacher may wish to add additional questions to the post-test, but the original questions should remain.

ASSESSMENT THAT WILL SHOW WHAT STUDENTS DO AND DO NOT KNOW

The teacher should include questions that are straightforward, involve errors, require justification, and require shown work. A student self-assessment is one such tool that would show misconceptions, understood material, and advanced knowledge. The assessment should include more than multiple-choice questions. Designing a performance assessment with scaffolded questions, whereby only one solution may be found based on a previous answer, will also show students' exact level of understanding. A debate format is one type of assessment whereby the teacher will be able to see a student's level of understanding, as he or she seeks to respond with a rebuttal.

ASSESSMENT TO HONE IN ON ANY ERROR PATTERNS EVIDENT IN STUDENTS' WORK

A **portfolio** would be an excellent assessment for monitoring any student error patterns. The teacher would be able to track student errors as the course progressed. The teacher would be given insight into how, and if, errors improved, or if some knowledge was acquired but other knowledge was still incorrect. The portfolio might include a series of similar questions related to a certain topic. For example, a portfolio may include function transformation questions. A student's ability to transform functions may be tracked, starting with simple linear functions and ending with complex sine functions.

COMPONENTS THAT MUST BE PRESENT IN AN ASSESSMENT THAT SUPPORTS STUDENT LEARNING

The assessment must require students to **think deeper** than what they have covered in class. It should prompt them to make connections between topics. It should invite different ways of thinking about problem solving. In other words, the student may think, "Okay. I have seen a similar version in class. This problem is slightly different, in that the parabola is shifted left. This is the opposite of shifting right, so I will add the constant to the x-term." The assessment will thus solidify the student's understanding of how to shift any function.

USING ASSESSMENT RESULTS OF ASSESSMENTS GIVEN TO ELL LEARNERS IN ORDER TO MODIFY INSTRUCTION

The teacher would be able to see if language itself is a barrier in learning. In other words, if the group of ELL students, as a whole, show difficulty with a mathematics topic, the teacher may deduce that the content was not clear due to minimal supporting pictures, diagrams, and auditory support. The teacher may decide to reteach the lesson, using more visual cues, verbal pronunciations, explicit vocabulary usage, and peer-group placement. Collaborative learning may be employed.

QUESTIONS THAT A TEACHER MAY ASK AFTER REVIEWING THE RESULTS OF AN ADMINISTERED EXAM

The teacher may ask the following:

- Did I cover the content in an explicit manner?
- Did I show plenty of examples?
- Did I use multiple representations when teaching the concepts?
- Did I design instruction such as to accommodate all modes of learning?
- Was the test valid?
- Did students have an adequate amount of time to complete the test?
- Why did some groups of students score lower or higher?
- Did any biased questions affect the results?

HOW FOCUS ON CAREER AND COLLEGE READINESS AFFECTS ASSESSMENT AND INSTRUCTIONAL DESIGN

The focus on college and career-readiness standards prompts publishers and teachers to utilize more real-world problems in instruction and assessments. The focus in mathematics classrooms is shifting to more real-world, cumulative problems that require understanding of many different mathematics concepts in order to solve. Problems are related to science, finance, medicine, etc. The focus includes the ability to apply the algorithms to many different career situations. In summary, the recent focus shifts the instructional design to an application-based status.

ROLE OF ASSESSMENT IN A CLASSROOM FOCUSED ON COGNITIVE INSTRUCTION

A cognitively guided classroom would be similar to a constructivist classroom, in that **active participation** would be present. However, in a cognitive classroom (as advocated by current cognitive theorists), students are not required to invent their own knowledge. Instead, they must simply make sense of what they are observing and experiencing. They may be assisted by the teacher. Thus, the role of an assessment in such a classroom is to ascertain student thought processes. Such an assessment would ask students to describe thinking and perhaps make connections to other mathematics topics. The assessment must ascertain students' reasoning abilities.

INSTRUCTIONAL CYCLE DESCRIBED BY A LEARNING THEORIST

The **5E Learning Model** is based on the thinking of Jean Piaget. It is a constructivist learning model. Piaget believed that students construct their own knowledge via active participation and experiences. Problem solving is integral to student learning. The cycle is listed as engagement, exploration, explanation, elaboration, and evaluation. Thus, with active engagement and exploration, the student is able to develop his or her own explanation, use assimilation and accommodation to make sense of the information, and then evaluate the material and make conjectures, etc.

Praxis Practice Test #1

√ **1. Ava and Jack packed a picnic lunch and went for a hike. The graph below shows their distance from the start of the trail at times throughout the hike. If the *x*-axis represents the number of hours they spent and the *y*-axis represents their distance from the beginning of the trail in miles, which of the following statements is (are) true?**

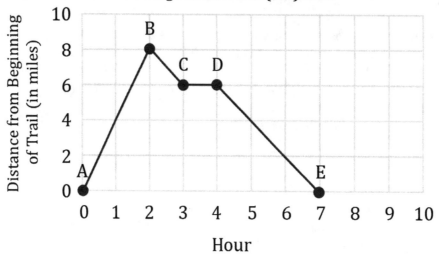

I. Their average speed was 4 mph.
II. Their speed from point B to point C was the same as from point D to E.
III. They walked a total distance of sixteen miles.

   a. I only
   b. II only
   c. II and III
   d. I, II, and III

2. Consider the function f, whose graph appears here, and the function g, defined by $g(x) = -x^2 + 8x - 15$. Which of the following statements correctly describes properties these two functions have in common?

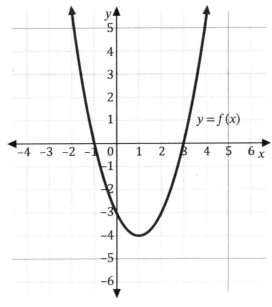

a. They have the same vertex.

b. They have the same two roots.

c. They have the same y-intercept.

d. They have exactly one common root.

3. Which of these does NOT simulate randomly selecting a person from a group of 11?

a. Assigning each student a unique card value of A, 2, 3, 4, 5, 6, 7, 8, 9, 10, or J and drawing a single card from a deck of cards, redrawing if an invalid card is selected.

b. Assigning each student a unique number 2–12 and rolling a pair of dice to determine which student is selected.

c. Assigning each student a unique letter A–K, labeling 11 index cards A–K, and blindly drawing one.

d. Assigning each student a unique numeric value of 1–11 and spinning a spinner mounted on a 11-section wheel.

4. Graph the following piecewise function and use your graph to determine which of the following statements about discontinuities and extrema is correct.

$$f(x) = \begin{cases} 4 - x^2, & \text{if } x < 0 \\ 4 - 2x, & \text{if } 0 \le x < 2 \\ 7 - x, & \text{if } x \ge 2 \end{cases}$$

a. The function has 2 discontinuities and a maximum value of 7.

b. The function has 1 discontinuity and a maximum of 5.

c. The function has 2 discontinuities and no extrema.

d. The function has no discontinuities and a maximum of 4.

5. Find the area between the curves $f(x) = \frac{1}{2}x^2$ and $g(x) = \sqrt{x} - \frac{1}{x^2}$ over the interval $[1, 4]$.
Hint: The graphs of these two functions never cross.

    a. $6\frac{7}{12}$

    b. $5\frac{1}{12}$

    c. $14\frac{5}{12}$

    d. $15\frac{9}{14}$

6. A cube inscribed in a sphere has a volume of 125 cubic units. What is the volume of the sphere in cubic units?

    a. $25\pi\sqrt{3}$

    b. $\frac{125\pi\sqrt{3}}{2}$

    c. $\frac{25\pi\sqrt{3}}{6}$

    d. $\frac{5\pi\sqrt{3}}{12}$

7. A target is made of concentric circles, as shown below. The width of each band is $2m$ and the center is a circle with radius of $2m$.

Which of the following gives the area of the two white rings as a function of m?

    a. $A = 16\pi m^2$
    b. $A = 24\pi m^2$
    c. $A = 40\pi m^2$
    d. $A = 64\pi m^2$

8. A bird looks down from a tree at a 30° angle of depression and sees a beetle in the grass. When he turns his gaze downward to a 60° angle of depression, he sees a worm. If the beetle is 30 feet from the worm, how far from the tree is the worm?

    a. 15.0 feet
    b. 22.7 feet
    c. 24.8 feet
    d. 27.6 feet

Refer to the following for question 9:

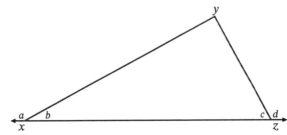

Given: $\angle a \cong \angle d$
Prove: $\triangle XYZ$ is isosceles

Statement	Reason
1. $\angle a \cong \angle d$	Given
2. $m\angle a + m\angle b = 180°$; $m\angle c + m\angle d = 180°$	Linear pair angles are supplementary
3. $m\angle a + m\angle b = m\angle c + m\angle d$	Substitution
4. $m\angle a = m\angle d$	Congruent angles have equal measures
5. $m\angle b = m\angle c$	_____
6. $\angle b \cong \angle c$	Congruent angles have equal measures
7. _____	If two angles of a triangle are congruent, the sides opposite them are congruent
8. $\triangle XYZ$ is isosceles	An isosceles triangle has two congruent sides

∎

9. Which of the following justifies step 5 in the proof?
   a. Linear pair angles are supplementary
   b. Subtraction property of equality
   c. Definition of supplementary angles
   d. An isosceles triangle has two congruent angles

10. If $f(x) = 4x^3 - x^2 - 4x + 2$, which of the following statements is (are) true of its graph?

   I. The point $\left(-\frac{1}{2}, 3\frac{1}{4}\right)$ is a relative maximum.

   II. The graph of f is concave upward on the interval $\left(-\infty, \frac{1}{12}\right)$.

   a. I
   b. II
   c. I and II
   d. Neither I nor II

11. Zeke drove from his house to a furniture store in Atlanta and then back home along the same route. It took Zeke three hours to drive to the store. By driving an average of 20 mph faster on his return trip, Zeke was able to save an hour of driving time. What was Zeke's average driving speed on his round trip?

12. Which of these graphs is NOT representative of the data set shown below?

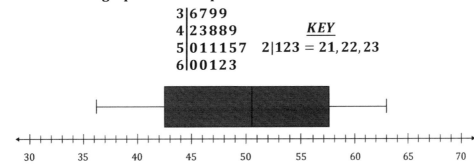

```
3|6799
4|23889          KEY
5|011157   2|123 = 21, 22, 23
6|00123
```

a.

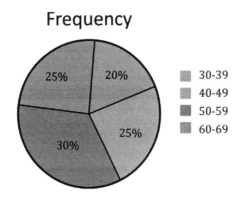

Frequency

- 30-39
- 40-49
- 50-59
- 60-69

b.

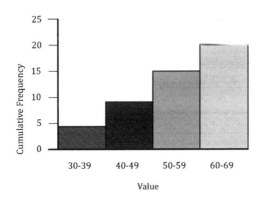

c.

d. All of these graphs represent the data set.

13. Last year, Jenny tutored students in math, in chemistry, and for the ACT. She tutored ten students in math, eight students in chemistry, and seven students for the ACT. She tutored five students in both math and chemistry, and she tutored four students both in chemistry and for the ACT, and five students both in math and for the ACT. She tutored three students in all three subjects. How many students did Jenny tutor last year?

14. This question may have more than one correct answer. Select all correct answers.

You ask your students to reduce the fraction $\frac{72}{120}$ to lowest terms in a single step by canceling the greatest common factor of the numerator and denominator. Three students take different approaches to finding the greatest common factor. Which of their approaches are mathematically correct? Select all correct approaches.

a.

Student A concludes that the greatest common factor is 24 based on the following calculation.
$$120 - 72 = 48$$
$$72 - 48 = 24$$
$$48 = 2 \cdot 24$$

b.

Student B finds the prime factorizations of 72 and 120.
$$72 = 8 \cdot 9 = 2^3 \cdot 3^2$$
$$120 = 10 \cdot 12 = 2 \cdot 5 \cdot 3 \cdot 4 = 2^3 \cdot 3 \cdot 5$$

Student B then forms a product of the common primes raised to the lower power to which they appear.
$$2^3 \cdot 3 = 24$$

c.

Student C works out that the factors of 72 are 1, 2, 3, 4, 6, 8, 9, 12, 18, 24, 36, and 72. Then finds the factors of 120 are 1, 2, 3, 4, 5, 6, 8, 10, 12, 15, 20, 24, 30, 40, 60, and 120. After some examination, the student finds that the greatest number common to the two lists is 24.

15. The heights of 200 high school males are normally distributed with a mean height of 67.5 inches and a standard deviation of 3.5 inches. In a normal distribution, approximately 68% of values are within one standard deviation of the mean. About how many individuals from the selected group are shorter than 5′11″?

    a.   125
    b.   142
    c.   168
    d.   184

16. Solve: $7x^2 + 6x = -2$.

    a. $x = \dfrac{-3 \pm \sqrt{23}}{7}$
    b. $x = \pm i\sqrt{5}$
    c. $x = \pm \dfrac{2i\sqrt{2}}{7}$
    d. $x = \dfrac{-3 \pm i\sqrt{5}}{7}$

17. Calculate $\int \left(6x^2 + \frac{1}{2}x - 3\right) dx$.

    a. $x^3 + x^2 - 3x + C$
    b. $12x^3 + x^2 - 3x + C$
    c. $2x^3 + \frac{1}{4}x^2 - 3x + C$
    d. $12x^2 + x + C$

18. Which of these is the least biased sampling technique?

    a. A politician interviews every 8th grade student in the district to get the opinion of youth on a new policy.
    b. A business directs users to leave anonymous reviews online.
    c. A principal goes through the school directory and calls every 5th family to request opinions on a policy change.
    d. A political commercial asks voters to call in with ideas for reform so that he can get a better understanding of what his constituents want.

Refer to the following for question 19:

The box-and-whisker plot displays student test scores assessed throughout a semester to see if students were improving.

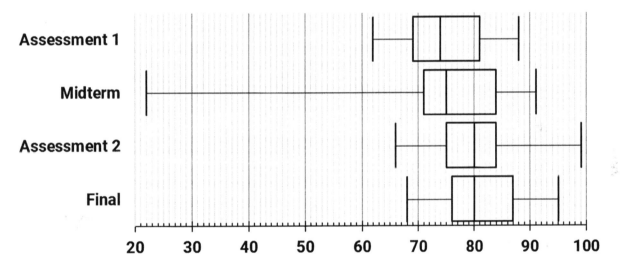

19. What is the probability that a test score chosen at random from the Final is less than 87?

    a. 0.25
    b. 0.5
    c. 0.6
    d. 0.75

20. This question may have more than one correct answer. Select all correct answers.

You give your students a test on which they are supposed to find the range of the function $f(x) = 3x^2 - 18x + 30$. Three of your students get the correct answer but show different work explaining their answers. Which of your students arrived at their answers in mathematically correct ways? Select all correct approaches.

a. Student A writes, "The leading coefficient is positive, so the parabola opens upward. The GCF of the coefficients of the function is gcf(3,18,30) = 3. The range consists of all values greater than or equal to this GCF. In other words, the range is $[3, \infty)$."

b. Student B writes, "I complete the square to put the function in vertex form. This gives me $f(x) = 3x^2 - 18x + 30 = 3(x^2 - 6x) + 30 = 3(x^2 - 6x + 9) + 30 - 27 = 3(x - 3)^2 + 3$. The vertex of the parabola is at the point (3,3). Since the leading coefficient is positive, the range consists of all real numbers greater than or equal to the y-value of the vertex. Thus, the range of the function is $[3, \infty)$."

c. Student C writes, "The graph of $f(x) = ax^2 + bx + c$ is a parabola with axis of symmetry $-\frac{b}{2a}$. For the given parabola, $a = 3$ and $b = -18$, so the axis of symmetry is $-\frac{-18}{2 \cdot 3} = 3$. The range consists of all values greater than or equal to the axis of symmetry since the leading coefficient is positive. That is, the range is $[3, \infty)$."

21. This question may have more than one correct answer. Select all correct answers.

Three students attempt to solve the equation $5^{3x-1} = 96$. Which of their answers are correct? Select all correct answers.

a.

Student A

$$5^{3x-1} = 96$$
$$\log_2 5^{3x-1} = \log_2 96$$
$$(3x - 1)\log_2 5 = \log_2(32 \cdot 3)$$
$$3x - 1 = \frac{\log_2 32 + \log_2 3}{\log_2 5}$$
$$3x = \frac{5 + \log_2 3}{\log_2 5} + 1$$
$$x = \frac{5 + \log_2 3}{3\log_2 5} + \frac{1}{3}$$

b.

Student B

$$5^{3x-1} = 96$$
$$\log 5^{3x-1} = \log 96$$
$$(3x - 1)\log 5 = \log 96$$
$$3x - 1 = \frac{\log 96}{\log 5}$$

$$3x = \log 96 - \log 5 + 1$$
$$x = \frac{\log 96 - \log 5 + 1}{3}$$

c.

Student C

$$5^{3x-1} = 96$$
$$\ln 5^{3x-1} = \ln 96$$
$$(3x - 1)\ln 5 = \ln 96$$
$$3x - 1 = \frac{\ln 96}{\ln 5}$$
$$3x = \frac{96}{5} + 1$$
$$x = \frac{96}{15} + \frac{1}{3} = \frac{101}{15}$$

Refer to the following for question 22:

The box-and-whisker plot displays student test scores assessed throughout a semester to see if students were improving.

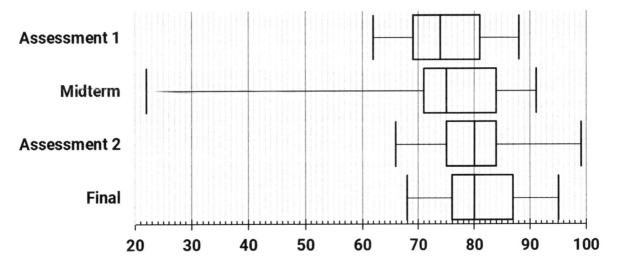

22. Which assessment has the greatest range of test scores?
a. Assessment 1
b. Midterm
c. Assessment 2
d. Final

23. If 1 inch on a map represents 10 feet, how many yards apart are two points if the distance between the points on the map is 24 inches?

    a. 240 yards
    b. 80 yards
    c. 24 yards
    d. 12 yards

24. Which of these equations is represented by the graph below?

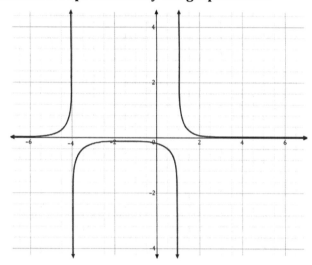

    a. $y = \dfrac{2x-2}{x^2+3x-4}$

    b. $y = \dfrac{1}{x^2+3x-4}$

    c. $y = \dfrac{1}{x+4} + \dfrac{1}{x-1}$

    d. $y = \dfrac{2}{3x^2+9x-12}$

25. Identify the cross-section polygon formed by a plane containing the given points on the cube.

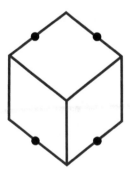

    a. Rectangle
    b. Trapezoid
    c. Pentagon
    d. Hexagon

26. Find $(g \circ f)(x)$ when $f(x) = 2x + 4$ and $g(x) = x^2 - 3x + 2$.

 a. $4x^2 + 10x + 6$
 b. $2x^2 - 6x + 8$
 c. $4x^2 + 13x + 18$
 d. $2x^2 - 3x + 6$

27. Which of these defines the recursive sequence $a_1 = 2$, $a_{n+1} = a_n - 3$ explicitly?

 a. $a_n = 2n - 3$
 b. $a_n = -3n + 5$
 c. $a_n = n - 1$
 d. $a_n = -2n + 2$

28. Find $f''(x)$ if $f(x) = -3x^3 - x^2 + 2x - 4$.

 a. $-9x^2 - 2x + 2$
 b. $-18x - 2$
 c. $-27x^2 - 2x$
 d. $-9x^3 - 2x^2 - 2x$

29. A student begins solving the linear inequality $3x - 7 < 20$ as follows.

$$3x - 7 < 20$$
$$x - 7 < \frac{20}{3}$$

When asked to justify this first step, the student replies, "I divided both sides by 3." How would you evaluate this step and the student's justification?

 a. Dividing both sides of the inequality by 3 is a correct first step, but the student carried it out incorrectly by failing to apply the distributive property on the left side of the inequality.
 b. Dividing both sides of the inequality by 3 is a correct first step, and the student carried it out correctly
 c. Dividing both sides of the inequality by 3 is an incorrect first step. The correct first step is to add 7 to both sides of the inequality.
 d. Dividing both sides of the inequality by 3 is an incorrect first step. The correct first step is to add 7 to both sides of the inequality and reverse the direction of the inequality.

30. A student devises a method for constructing the center of a circle and asks you to evaluate it. The method involves drawing two secants of the circle and constructing their perpendicular bisectors. The point at which the perpendicular bisectors intersect is the center of the circle. How do you evaluate this method?

 a. You congratulate the student on finding a clever construction that always works.
 b. You congratulate the student on finding a clever construction that works in general, but you explain that it fails in a special case.
 c. You explain that the method fails in general, though it often produces a point deceptively close to the center, but works in a special case.
 d. You explain that the method always fails though it often produces a point deceptively close to the center.

31. Three teachers from a county are chosen at random to attend a conference for high school science educators. What is the approximate probability that two women from the same department will be chosen?

	Biology	Chemistry	Physics
Women	26	31	20
Men	16	11	25

a. 8.6%
b. 10.7%
c. 11.9%
d. 13.8%

32. Solve $\sec^2\theta = 2\tan\theta$ for $0 < \theta \le 2\pi$.

a. $\theta = \dfrac{\pi}{6}$ or $\dfrac{7\pi}{6}$
b. $\theta = \dfrac{\pi}{4}$ or $\dfrac{5\pi}{4}$
c. $\theta = \dfrac{3\pi}{4}$ or $\dfrac{7\pi}{4}$
d. There is no solution to the equation.

33. Three students attempt to put the equation $4x^2 - 8x + 9 = 20$ into the form $(x - p)^2 = q$ by completing the square. Which approach is correct?

a.

Student A

$$4x^2 - 8x + 9 = 20$$
$$4x^2 - 8x + 16 = 27$$
$$4(x^2 - 2x + 4) = 27$$
$$(x - 2)^2 = \frac{27}{4}$$

b.

Student B

$$4x^2 - 8x + 9 = 20$$
$$4(x^2 - 2x) = 11$$
$$4(x^2 - 2x + 1) = 15$$
$$(x - 1)^2 = \frac{15}{4}$$

c.

Student C

$$4x^2 - 8x + 9 = 20$$
$$4(x^2 - 2x) = 11$$
$$4(x^2 - 2x + 1) = 12$$

$$(x-1)^2 = 3$$

d. More than one student has a correct approach.

34. The vertices of a polygon are $(-2, 3)$, $(1, -1)$, $(3, 6)$, and $(5, 1)$. Which of the following describes the polygon most specifically?

a. Parallelogram
b. Rhombus
c. Rectangle
d. Square

35. A teacher recorded the dates that students turned in projects in two different classes to compare trends and noticed that a large number of students were submitting their work late. She plotted charts to see how many students in each class were turning in late work, and how late they were.

Which of the following is a true statement for these data?

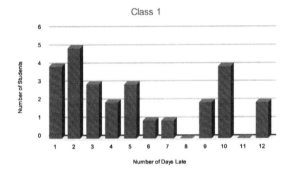
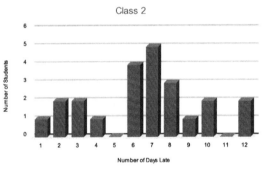

a. The median number of days late in Class 1 is 2 days less than in Class 2.
b. On average, students turned in work 4 days later in Class 2 than in Class 1 (round to nearest whole number).
c. The mode late time is higher for Class 2 than for Class 1.
d. The median late time for Class 1 is greater than the mean for Class 1.

36. A crane, 80 feet tall, moves a 200 lb. bucket suspended from a cable that weighs 3 lbs. per linear foot. You need to construct a function, F, that models the combined downward force (weight) of the bucket and the cable as the bucket rises and falls (changing the amount of cable hanging down). Ignore the height of the bucket itself. Which of the following functions constitute correct models? Select all correct solutions.

    a. $F(y) = 320 - 3(y - 40)$, where y is the height (in feet) of the bucket above the ground.

    b. $F(y) = 200 - 3(80 - y)$, where y is the height (in feet) of the bucket above the ground.

    c. $F(y) = 200 - 3y$, where y is distance (in feet) of the bucket from the top of the crane.

37. You play a game as follows: you flip a fair coin up to five times, stopping the first time you flip tails. You win one dollar for every time you flip heads. Let X be the number of dollars you win, making X a random variable. Calculate $E(X)$, the expected value of this random variable (that is, your expected winnings from playing the game). Hint: If H represents flipping heads and T represents flipping tails, the sample space for this game is $\{T, HT, HHT, HHHT, HHHHT, HHHHH\}$.

    a. $\frac{57}{64}$ dollars

    b. $\frac{31}{32}$ dollars

    c. 3 dollars

    d. $\frac{5}{2}$ dollars

38. Solve: $\frac{x+2}{x+1} = \frac{x+9}{x+7} + \frac{2}{x+1}$.

    a. $x = -3$

    b. $x = -1$

    c. $x = 1$

    d. $x = 5$

39. If a, b, and c are multiples of 6 and $3a^2 + 2b^3 = c$, of the following integers, which is the largest integer that must be factor of c?

    a. 6

    b. 36

    c. 72

    d. 108

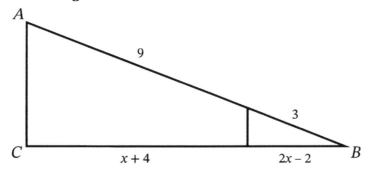

40. For ΔABC, what is the length of $\overline{BC}$?

41. Given the partial table of values for $f(x)$ and $g(x)$, find $f(g(-4))$. (Assume that $f(x)$ and $g(x)$ are the simplest polynomials that fit the data.)

x	f(x)	g(x)
−2	8	1
−1	2	3
0	0	5
1	2	7
2	8	9

42. Three students solve the equation $y = a + 3ax$ for the variable x. They are not required to simplify their solutions. Which solutions are correct? Select all correct solutions.

a. $y = a + 3ax$

$y = 4ax$

$\dfrac{y}{4a} = x$

b. $y = a + 3ax$

$y - a = 3ax$

$\dfrac{y - a}{3a} = x$

c. $y = a + 3ax$

$y = a(1 + 3x)$

$\dfrac{y}{a} = 1 + 3x$

$\dfrac{y}{a} - 1 = 3x$

$\dfrac{\dfrac{y}{a} - 1}{3} = x$

43. For the right triangle below, where $a \neq b$, which of the following is a true statement of equality?

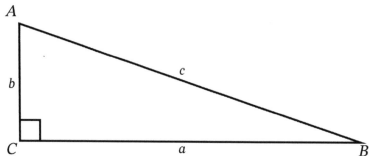

a. $\tan B = \dfrac{\sqrt{c^2 - a^2}}{a}$

b. $\cos B = \dfrac{a\sqrt{a^2 + b^2}}{a^2 + b^2}$

c. $\sec B = \dfrac{\sqrt{a^2 + b^2}}{b}$

d. $\csc B = \dfrac{a^2 + b^2}{b}$

44. Solve the system of equations.

$$3x + 4y = 2$$
$$2x + 6y = -2$$

a. $\left(0, \frac{1}{2}\right)$

b. $\left(\frac{2}{5}, \frac{1}{5}\right)$

c. $(2, -1)$

d. $\left(-1, \frac{5}{4}\right)$

45. A colony of *Escherichia coli* is inoculated from a Petri dish into a test tube containing 50 mL of nutrient broth. The test tube is placed in a 37 °C incubator and agitator. After one hour, the number of bacteria in the test tube is determined to be 8×10^6. Given that the doubling time of *Escherichia coli* is 20 minutes with agitation at 37 °C, approximately how many bacteria should the test tube contain after eight hours of growth?

a. 2.56×10^8

b. 2.05×10^9

c. 1.7×10^{14}

d. 1.7×10^{13}

Refer to the following for question 46:

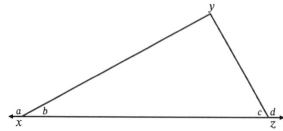

Given: $\angle a \cong \angle d$
Prove: $\triangle XYZ$ is isosceles

Statement	Reason
1. $\angle a \cong \angle d$	Given
2. $m\angle a + m\angle b = 180°$; $m\angle c + m\angle d = 180°$	Linear pair angles are supplementary
3. $m\angle a + m\angle b = m\angle c + m\angle d$	Substitution
4. $m\angle a = m\angle d$	Congruent angles have equal measures
5. $m\angle b = m\angle c$	_____
6. $\angle b \cong \angle c$	Congruent angles have equal measures
7. _____	If two angles of a triangle are congruent, the sides opposite them are congruent
8. $\triangle XYZ$ is isosceles	An isosceles triangle has two congruent sides

■

46. Step 7 in the proof should contain which of the following statements?
   a. $XY \cong YZ$
   b. $XZ \cong XZ$
   c. $XY \cong XZ$
   d. $\angle YXZ \cong \angle YZX$

47. A private tutor works with 11 five-year-olds, 8 six-year-olds, 9 seven-year-olds, 14 eight-year-olds, 11 nine-year-olds, and 13 ten-year-olds. If a student is randomly selected for a free session, what is the probability that he or she is no more than eight years old?
   a. $\frac{7}{11}$
   b. $\frac{14}{33}$
   c. $\frac{4}{11}$
   d. $\frac{3}{7}$

48. Which of the following is a subset of the set of rational numbers?

   a. Integers
   b. Real numbers
   c. Imaginary numbers
   d. Complex numbers

49. This question may have more than one correct answer. Select all correct answers.

Three students attempt to solve the equation $6x^2 + 13x = 5$. All three get the correct answer that $x = \frac{1}{3}$ or $x = -\frac{5}{2}$, but they take three different approaches. Which of their approaches are mathematically correct? Select all correct approaches.

   a.

Student A calculates the following.

$$6x^2 + 13x - 5 = 0$$

$$x = \frac{-13 \pm \sqrt{13^2 - 4(6)(-5)}}{2 \cdot 6} = \frac{-13 \pm \sqrt{289}}{12} = -\frac{13}{12} \pm \frac{17}{12}$$

$$x = -\frac{13}{12} + \frac{17}{12} = \frac{4}{12} = \frac{1}{3} \text{ or } x = -\frac{13}{12} - \frac{17}{12} = -\frac{30}{12} = -\frac{5}{2}$$

   b.

Student B calculates the following.

$$6\left(x^2 + \frac{13}{6}x + \frac{169}{144}\right) = 5 + \frac{169}{24}$$

$$6\left(x + \frac{13}{12}\right)^2 = \frac{289}{24}$$

$$\left(x + \frac{13}{12}\right)^2 - \frac{289}{144}$$

$$x + \frac{13}{12} = \pm\sqrt{\frac{289}{144}}$$

$$x = -\frac{13}{12} \pm \frac{17}{12}$$

$$x = -\frac{13}{12} - \frac{17}{12} = -\frac{30}{12} = -\frac{5}{2} \text{ or } x = -\frac{13}{12} + \frac{17}{12} = \frac{4}{12} = \frac{1}{3}$$

   c.

Student C calculates the following.

$$6x^2 + 13x - 5 = 0$$
$$(3x - 1)(2x + 5) = 0$$
$$3x - 1 = 0 \text{ or } 2x + 5 = 0$$
$$x = \frac{1}{3} \text{ or } x = -\frac{5}{2}$$

50. You tell your students that in $\triangle ABC$, segment $\overline{AD}$ is a median. Further, the measure of $\angle BAD$ is 54° and the measure of segment $\overline{AD}$ is half the measure of side $\overline{BC}$. That is, $m\overline{AD} = \frac{1}{2} \cdot m\overline{BC}$. Based on this information, you ask your students to deduce the measure of $\angle CAD$.

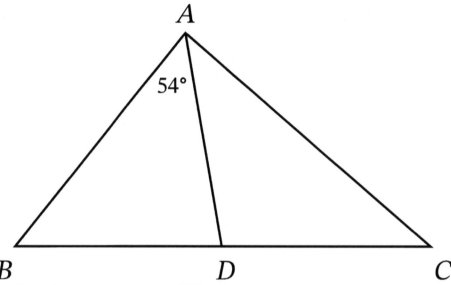

A

54°

B D C

One student offers this argument: Since $\overline{AD}$ is a median, point D is the midpoint of side $\overline{BC}$. So $BD = AD = CD = \frac{1}{2} \cdot BC$, which makes $\triangle BAD$ and $\triangle CAD$ isosceles. Angles opposite equal sides are equal, so $m\angle B = 54°$. Then $m\angle ADC = m\angle B + m\angle BAD = 54° + 54° = 108°$, since an exterior angle equals the sum of the remote interior angles. Now $m\angle CAD = m\angle ACD$, which makes each of them half of $180° - m\angle ADC = 180° - 108° = 72°$. Hence, $m\angle CAD = \frac{1}{2} \cdot 72° = 36°$.

How do you evaluate this student's argument?

     a.   The argument is correct and reasonably simple.

     b.   The argument is correct but unnecessarily complicated. It is simpler to observe that $\angle BAC$ appears to be a right angle. Thus, $\angle CAD$ is the complement of $\angle BAD$ and has a measure of $90° - 54° = 36°$.

     c.   The argument is incorrect because a median bisects the angle it belongs to but not necessarily the opposite side. So $m\angle CAD = 54°$.

     d.   The argument is incorrect because a median is perpendicular to the opposite side of the triangle but does not necessarily bisect it. This makes $\triangle ABD$ and $\triangle ACD$ right triangles, but this provides inadequate information to determine the value of $m\angle CAD$.

51. This question may have more than one correct answer. Select all correct answers.

You give your students the following problem: On a computer system, users are assigned random usernames consisting of strings of six uppercase letters with repetitions allowed (e.g., RGMAQZ, TTOPTG). Administrators receive usernames that include the letter A at least once in the username. Under this scheme, how many administrator usernames are possible?

Three students take different approaches to answering this question. Which of their approaches are correct? Select all correct approaches.

a. Student A: Since we choose any letter of the alphabet for each of six positions, there are 26^6 usernames without restriction. Of these, 25^6 have no A's (put a non-A in each of 6 positions). Subtract these out to get that the number of usernames with at least one A is the difference $26^6 - 25^6$.

b. Student B: We need to place letters in all six positions in the username. First, guarantee there will be an A by choosing one of the six positions to receive an A (6 possibilities). Then, fill in the remaining five positions with any letter of the alphabet (26^5 possibilities). So, the number of possible administrator usernames is $6 \cdot 26^5$.

c. Student C: We can count the administrator usernames according to the number of A's in them. To count usernames with exactly one A, first choose one of the six positions in the word to get the A ($C(6,1)$ possibilities, where $C(n,r) = \frac{n!}{r!(n-r)!}$ is a binomial coefficient). Then choose letters besides A for the remaining five positions (25^5 possibilities). To get usernames with exactly two A's, choose two of the six positions to receive A's ($C(6,2)$ possibilities) and then choose letters besides A for the remaining four positions (25^4 possibilities). Continuing in this manner, we get a total of $C(6,1) \times 25^5 + C(6,2) \times 25^4 + C(6,3) \times 25^3 + C(6,4) \times 25^2 + C(6,5) \times 25^1 + C(6,6) \times 25^0$ administrator usernames.

52. Lisa is selling brownies and cupcakes at a bake sale. Brownies cost \$2 each and cupcakes cost \$3 each. Lisa must sell at least \$150 worth of baked goods to break even on baking costs and the cost of renting the booth. If the x-axis represents the number of brownies sold and the y-axis represents the number of cupcakes sold, which of the following graphs shows the amount of baked goods Lisa must sell to break even or make a profit?

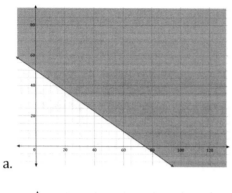

a.

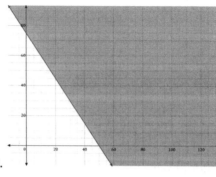

c.

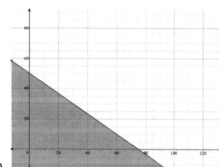

b.

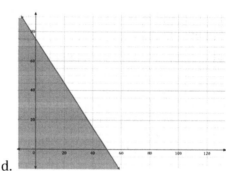

d.

53. Given the relation $y - 2 = \pm\sqrt{x - 3}$, find the inverse relation and determine whether it is a function. If it is a function, express it in the form $y = f(x)$.

   a. The inverse relation is not a function and is given by the equation $(y - 2)^2 = \pm(x - 3)$.

   b. The inverse relation is the function $y = 2 \pm \sqrt{x - 3}$.

   c. The inverse relation is the function $y = (x - 2)^2 + 3$.

   d. The inverse relation is the function $y = x^2 + 7$.

54. You are writing a multiple-choice quiz with four questions. Each question has five answer choices, identified by letters a, b, c, d, and e. Each question has only one correct answer. Suppose you choose the letter for the correct answer to each question at random (i.e., each letter has an equal chance of being chosen). Use the fundamental counting principle to find the probability that none of the questions is assigned answer c as the correct answer.

   a. 0.4096

   b. 0.8

   c. 0.2

   d. 0.0384

55. The ratio of Jon's monthly expenses to his savings is $7 : 1$. If he is able to save \$725 per month, what are his monthly expenses?

56. If $\sin \theta = \frac{\sqrt{3}}{2}$ when $\frac{\pi}{2} < \theta < \pi$, what is the value of θ?

   a. $\frac{\pi}{6}$

   b. $\frac{3\pi}{4}$

   c. $\frac{2\pi}{3}$

   d. $\frac{5\pi}{6}$

57. If the square of three times the sum of a and six is fourteen more than a, which of these is a possible value of a?

   a. $\sqrt{2}$

   b. $\frac{3}{2}$

   c. 1

   d. -5

58. A teacher asks students how many seconds are in a common year (a non-leap year). Three students set their solutions up in three different ways. Which, if any, will produce correct answers? Select all that apply.

   a. Emily: $\frac{1\text{ year}}{365\text{ days}} \times \frac{24\text{ hours}}{1\text{ day}} \times \frac{60\text{ minutes}}{1\text{ hour}} \times \frac{60\text{ seconds}}{1\text{ minute}}$

   b. Jonathon: $\frac{1\text{ year}}{1} \times \frac{365\text{ days}}{1\text{ year}} \times \frac{24\text{ hours}}{1\text{ day}} \times \frac{60\text{ minutes}}{1\text{ hour}} \times \frac{60\text{ seconds}}{1\text{ minute}}$

   c. Sarah: $1\text{ year} \times \frac{60\text{ seconds}}{1\text{ minute}} \times \frac{1{,}440\text{ minutes}}{1\text{ day}} \times \frac{365\text{ days}}{1\text{ year}}$

59. Solve: $2 - \sqrt{x} = \sqrt{x - 20}$.

   a. $x = 6$

   b. $x = 36$

   c. $x = 144$

   d. No solution

60. The homework assignment says, "Find an equation of the line through the points $(12, 3)$ and $(0, -6)$. You do not need to simplify your answer." A student thinks of three possible approaches. Which produce correct equations? Select all correct approaches.

a. The slope of the line is $m = \frac{3-(-6)}{12-0} = \frac{9}{12} = \frac{3}{4}$. I can substitute the slope and the point $(12, 3)$ into the equation $y - y_1 = m(x - x_1)$. So, the line has the equation $y - 3 = \frac{3}{4}(x - 12)$.

b. The slope of the line is $m = \frac{-6-3}{0-12} = \frac{-9}{-12} = \frac{3}{4}$. Since the point $(0, -6)$ lies on the y-axis, I can substitute the slope and the value $b = -6$ into the equation $y = mx + b$. So, the line has the equation $y = \frac{3}{4}x - 6$.

c. The slope of the line is $m = \frac{-6-3}{0-12} = \frac{-9}{-12} = \frac{3}{4}$. I can substitute the slope and the point $(0, -6)$ into the equation $y - y_1 = m(x - x_1)$. So, the line has the equation $y + 6 = \frac{3}{4}(x - 0)$.

61. Find the area A of the finite region between the graphs of $y = x - 3$ and $y = x^2 - 2x - 7$.

    a. 7

    b. $\frac{56}{3}$

    c. $\frac{125}{6}$

    d. 12

62. Roxana walks x meters west and $x + 20$ meters south to get to her friend's house. On a neighborhood map which has a scale of 1 cm: 10 m, the direct distance between Roxana's house and her friend's house is 10 cm. How far did Roxana walk to her friend's house?

63. You draw a hexagon with a perimeter of 60 mm and an area of 250 mm². Then you make a photocopy of your drawing on a photocopier set to enlarge the image by 20%. That is, it produces a similar image with all lengths increased by 20%. What are the perimeter and area of the enlarged hexagon?

    a. The perimeter is 72 mm, and the area is 300 mm².

    b. The perimeter is 72 mm, and the area is 360 mm².

    c. The perimeter is 67.2 mm, and the area is 300 mm².

    d. The perimeter is 72 mm, and the area cannot be determined from the given information.

64. The velocity of a car which starts at position 0 at time 0 is given by the equation $v(t) = -t^2 + 8t$ for $0 \leq t \leq 8$. Find the position of the car when its acceleration is 0.

    a. 64

    b. $\frac{128}{3}$

    c. 16

    d. $\frac{56}{3}$

65. A pair of jeans is marked down 30% and placed on a clearance rack, on which is posted a sign reading, "Take an extra 15% off already reduced merchandise." What fraction of the original price is the final sale price of the jeans?

a. $\dfrac{61}{100}$

b. $\dfrac{119}{200}$

c. $\dfrac{4}{7}$

d. $\dfrac{3}{5}$

66. Evaluate $\lim\limits_{x \to -3} \dfrac{x^3+3x^2-x-3}{x^2-9}$.

a. 0

b. $\dfrac{1}{3}$

c. $-\dfrac{4}{3}$

d. ∞

Answer Key and Explanations

1. C: Ava and Jack hiked 8 miles from home and then back again, so they traveled a total of 16 miles. Therefore, statement III is true. They traveled these 16 miles in 7 hours, so their average speed was $\frac{16}{7}$ mph or approximately 2.3 mph. Therefore, statement I is false. Ava and Jack hiked 2 miles from point B to C in 1 hour, so they were hiking at a speed of 2 mph. They hiked 6 miles from D to E in 3 hours, so they hiked $\frac{6 \text{ miles}}{3 \text{ hours}} = \frac{2 \text{ miles}}{1 \text{ hour}} = 2$ mph. Therefore, their speed was the same during both these times, and statement II is also true.

2. D: By inspection of the graph, the function f has roots $x = -1$ and $x = 3$. We can factor g as $g(x) = -x^2 + 8x - 15 = -(x^2 - 8x + 15) = -(x - 3)(x - 5)$. To find the roots, set each factor equal to 0 and solve for x. The roots are $x = 3$ and $x = 5$. Thus functions f and g share the root $x = 3$ but not a second root. The y-intercept of f can be found by determining the point where the graph crosses the y-axis, which is at the point $(0, -3)$. The y-intercept of g can be found by determining $g(0)$, which is –15, so the y-intercept is at the point $(0, 15)$. Therefore, the functions f and g have different y-intercepts.

3. B: Choice B does not simulate random selection because the probability of different outcomes is not equal. For instance, there is only one combination of dice outcomes that can produce the value 2 or 12, whereas there are several combinations that produce the value of 7.

4. B: To graph a piecewise function, graph each part of the function for the given domain values. In this case, graph the function $4 - x^2$ for the x-values $x < 0$, graph the function $4 - 2x$ for the values $0 \leq x < 2$, and graph the function $7 - x$ for the values $x \geq 2$. By inspection of the graph, we see that there is no discontinuity at $x = 0$, because the two functions on either side of $x = 0$ meet at 4. There is a discontinuity at $x = 2$, because the function to the left of $x = 2$ approaches 0, while the function to the right of $x = 2$ is equal to 5 at the point $x = 2$. Also, the maximum value of the function is $f(2) = 5$.

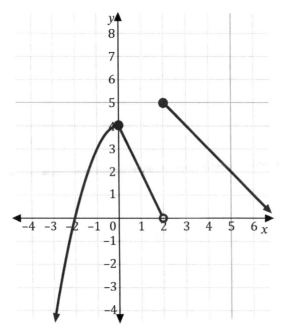

202

5. A: Since $f(1) = \frac{1}{2}$, $g(1) = 0$, $\frac{1}{2} > 0$, and the graphs never cross, we know that $f(x) > g(x)$ throughout the interval $[1,4]$. Thus, the area between the curves over this interval is the definite integral from $x = 1$ to $x = 4$ of $f(x) - g(x)$, the difference of the larger curve and the smaller curve. This gives us:

$$A = \int_1^4 \frac{1}{2}x^2 - \left(\sqrt{x} - \frac{1}{x^2}\right) dx$$

$$= \int_1^4 \left(\frac{1}{2}x^2 - x^{\frac{1}{2}} + x^{-2}\right) dx = \frac{1}{6}x^3 - \frac{2}{3}x^{\frac{3}{2}} - x^{-1}\Big|_1^4$$

$$= \left(\frac{1}{6}(4)^3 - \frac{2}{3}(4)^{\frac{3}{2}} - (4)^{-1}\right) - \left(\frac{1}{6}(1)^3 - \frac{2}{3}(1)^{\frac{3}{2}} - (1)^{-1}\right)$$

$$= \frac{1}{6} \cdot 64 - \frac{2}{3} \cdot 8 - \frac{1}{4} - \frac{1}{6} + \frac{2}{3} + 1$$

$$= \frac{32}{3} - \frac{16}{3} - \frac{1}{4} - \frac{1}{6} + \frac{2}{3} + 1$$

$$= \frac{16}{3} - \frac{3}{12} - \frac{2}{12} + \frac{2}{3} + 1$$

$$= \frac{18}{3} - \frac{5}{12} + 1$$

$$= 7 - \frac{5}{12}$$

$$= 6\frac{7}{12}$$

6. C: The center of the sphere is shared by the center of the cube, and each of the corners of the cube touches the surface of the sphere. Therefore, the diameter of the sphere is the line that passes through the center of the cube and connects one corner of the cube to the opposite corner on the opposite face. Notice in the illustration below that the diameter d of the sphere can be represented as the hypotenuse of a right triangle with a short leg measuring 5 units. Since the volume of the cube is 125 cubic units, each of its sides measure $\sqrt[3]{125} = 5$ units. The long leg of the triangle is the diagonal of the base of the cube. Its length can be found using the Pythagorean theorem:

$$5^2 + 5^2 = x^2$$

$$x = \sqrt{50} = 5\sqrt{2}$$

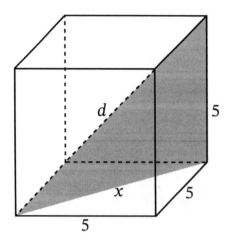

Use the Pythagorean theorem again to find d, the diameter of the sphere: $d^2 = \left(5\sqrt{2}\right)^2 + 5^2$, which then becomes $d = \sqrt{75} = 5\sqrt{3}$.

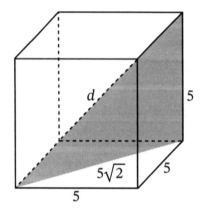

To find the volume of the sphere, use the formula $V = \frac{4}{3}\pi r^3$. Since the radius r of the sphere is half the diameter, $r = \frac{5\sqrt{3}}{2}$, and $V = \frac{4}{3}\pi\left(\frac{5\sqrt{3}}{2}\right)^3 = \frac{4}{3}\pi\left(\frac{125\sqrt{3}}{8}\right) = \frac{125\pi\sqrt{3}}{6}$ cubic units.

7. C: We can find the area of the white part by viewing the target as five separate circles of various sizes, one inside the other. We ignore the outer circle since we are only interested in the white parts, and add the areas of the two white circles and subtract the areas of the two interior shaded circles. The formula for area of a circle is πr^2, so the area of the largest white circle is $\pi(8m)^2$. We subtract the shaded circle inside it, add the white circle inside that one, and then subtract the smallest shaded circle.

$$A = \pi(8m)^2 - \pi(6m)^2 + \pi(4m)^2 - \pi(2m)^2$$
$$= 64\pi m^2 - 36\pi m^2 + 16\pi m^2 - 4\pi m^2$$
$$= (64 - 36 + 16 - 4)\pi m^2$$
$$= 40\pi m^2$$

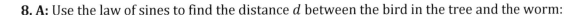
8. A: Use the law of sines to find the distance d between the bird in the tree and the worm:

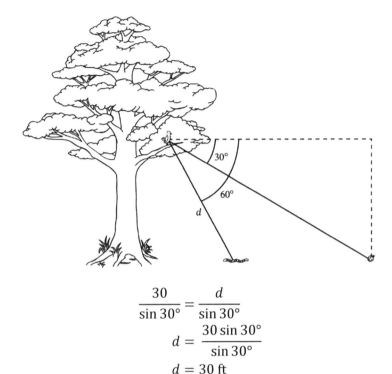

$$\frac{30}{\sin 30°} = \frac{d}{\sin 30°}$$
$$d = \frac{30 \sin 30°}{\sin 30°}$$
$$d = 30 \text{ ft}$$

Use this number in a sine or cosine function to find the distance between the worm and the base of the tree:

$$\sin 30° = \frac{w}{30}$$
$$w = 30 \sin 30°$$
$$w = 15$$

Therefore, the worm is 15 feet from the tree.

9. B: Since it has been established that $m\angle a + m\angle b = m\angle c + m\angle d$ and $m\angle a = m\angle d$, we can conclude that $m\angle b = m\angle c$ because of the subtraction property of equality, which states that subtracting equal amounts from each side of a balanced equation will keep it balanced.

10. A: The critical points of the graph occur when $f'(x) = 0$.

$$f(x) = 4x^3 - x^2 - 4x + 2$$
$$f'(x) = 12x^2 - 2x - 4$$
$$f'(x) = 2(6x^2 - x - 2)$$
$$f'(x) = 2(3x - 2)(2x + 1)$$
$$0 = 2(3x - 2)(2x + 1)$$
$$3x - 2 = 0$$
$$x = \frac{2}{3}$$
$$2x + 1 = 0$$
$$x = -\frac{1}{2}$$

Take the derivative of $f(x)$.
Factor a 2 out of each term in $f'(x)$.
Factor the new polynomial in $f'(x)$.
Set $f'(x)$ equal to 0.

Solve the first factor to find the value of x that makes it 0.

Solve the second factor to find the value of x that makes it 0.

The critical points of the graph are at $x = \frac{2}{3}$ and $x = -\frac{1}{2}$.

To determine if these points are relative maximums or minimums, test points on each end of the intervals surrounding them. Start by testing a point less than $-\frac{1}{2}$. For example, solve for the value of $f'(x)$ when $x = -1$.

$$f'(-1) = 12(-1)^2 - 2(-1) - 4 = 12 + 2 - 4 = 10$$

Now, test a point greater than $-\frac{1}{2}$ and less than $\frac{2}{3}$, like 0.

$$f'(0) = 12(0)^2 - 2(0) - 4 = 0 - 0 - 4 = -4$$

Therefore, when $x < -\frac{1}{2}$, $f'(x) > 0$, and when $-\frac{1}{2} < x < \frac{2}{3}$, $f'(x) < 0$, so the point where $x = -\frac{1}{2}$ is a relative maximum of the function. Now, test a point greater than $\frac{2}{3}$, like 1.

$$f'(1) = 12(1)^2 - 2(1) - 4 = 12 - 2 - 4 = 6$$

When $x > \frac{2}{3}$, $f'(x) > 0$, so the point where $x = \frac{2}{3}$ is a relative minimum. To find the corresponding y-values for these points, substitute each value of x into the original function and solve for y.

If $f''(x) > 0$ for all x in an interval, the graph of the function is concave upward on that interval, and if $f''(x) < 0$ for all x in an interval, the graph of the function is concave downward on that interval. Find the second derivative of the function and determine the intervals in which $f''(x)$ is less than zero and greater than zero.

$$f''(x) = 24x - 2$$

$$24x - 2 < 0 \qquad 24x - 2 > 0$$
$$x < \frac{1}{12} \qquad x > \frac{1}{12}$$

The graph of f is concave downward on the interval $\left(-\infty, \frac{1}{12}\right)$ and concave upward on the interval $\left(\frac{1}{12}, \infty\right)$.

11. 48: Rate in miles per hour can be expressed as, mph $= \frac{\text{distance in miles}}{\text{time in hours}}$. So, Zeke's driving speed on the way to Atlanta and home from Atlanta in mph can be expressed as $\frac{d}{3}$ and $\frac{d}{2}$, respectively, where d is the distance between Zeke's house and his destination. Since Zeke drove 20 mph faster on his way home, (speed home) $-$ (speed to store) $= 20$. Substitute Zeke's speeds and solve for d.

$$\frac{d}{2} - \frac{d}{3} = 20$$

$$6\left(\frac{d}{2} - \frac{d}{3} = 20\right)$$
$$3d - 2d = 120$$
$$d = 120$$

Since the distance between Zeke's house and the store in Atlanta is 120 miles, Zeke drove a total distance of 240 miles in five hours. Therefore, his average speed was $\frac{240 \text{ miles}}{5 \text{ hours}} = 48$ mph.

12. D: To draw a box-and-whisker plot from the data, find the median, quartiles, and upper and lower limits.

```
3 | 6 7 9 9
4 | 2|3 8 8 9                Key
5 | 0|1 1 1 5|7            3 | 6 = 36
6 | 0 0 1 2 3
```

The median is $\frac{50+51}{2} = 50.5$, the lower quartile is $\frac{22+23}{2} = 22.5$, and the upper quartile is $\frac{57+60}{2} = 58.5$. The box of the box-and-whisker plot goes through the quartiles, and a line through the box represents the median of the data. The whiskers extend from the box to the lower and upper limits, unless there are any outliers in the set. In this case, there are no outliers, so the box-and-whisker plot in choice A correctly represents the data set.

To draw a pie chart, find the percentage of data contained in each of the ranges shown. There are four out of twenty numbers between 30 and 39, inclusive, so the percentage shown in the pie chart for that range of data is $\frac{4}{20} \times 100\% = 20\%$; there are five values between 40 to 49, inclusive, so the percentage of data for that sector is $\frac{5}{20} \times 100\% = 25\%$; $\frac{6}{20} \times 100\% = 30\%$ of the data is within the range of 50-59, and $\frac{5}{20} \times 100\% = 25\%$ is within the range of 60-69. The pie chart shows the correct percentage of data in each category.

To draw a cumulative frequency histogram, find the cumulative frequency of the data.

Range	Frequency	Cumulative frequency
30-39	4	4
40-49	5	9
50-59	6	15
60-69	5	20

The histogram shows the correct cumulative frequencies.

Therefore, all of the graphs represent the data set.

13. 14: Use a Venn diagram to help organize the given information. Start by filling in the space where the three circles intersect: Jenny tutored three students in all three areas. Use that information to fill in the spaces where two circles intersect. For example, she tutored four students in chemistry and for the ACT, and three of those were students she tutored in all three areas, so one student was tutored in chemistry and for the ACT but not for math. Once the diagram is completed, add the number of students who were tutored in all areas to the number of students tutored in only two of the three areas to the number of students tutored in only one area. The total number of students tutored was $3 + 2 + 2 + 1 + 3 + 2 + 1 = 14$.

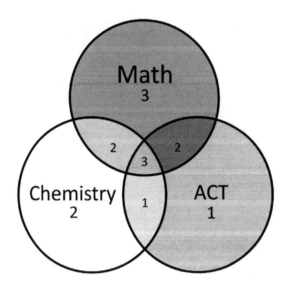

14. A, B, C: Student A uses a form of the Euclidean Algorithm for finding the greatest common factor of two numbers. Student B uses the fact that the greatest common factor of numbers is the product of their common prime factors, each raised to the lowest power it appears to. Student C uses the definition of greatest common factor, by listing the factors of both numbers and finding the largest factor they have in common.

15. C: A height of 5'11", or 71 inches, is one standard deviation above the mean. Since approximately 68% of the data is within one standard deviation of the mean, about 32% (100% − 68%) of the data is outside of one standard deviation within the mean. Normally distributed data is symmetric about the mean, which means that about 16% of the data lies below one standard deviation below the mean and about 16% of data lies above one standard deviation above the mean. Therefore, approximately 16% of individuals are 5'11" or taller, while approximately 84% of the population is shorter than 5'11". Multiply to find 84% of 200, $0.84 \times 200 = 168$. So, about 168 people from the selected group are shorter than 5'11".

16. D: There are many ways to solve quadratic equations in the form $ax^2 + bx + c = 0$. However, some methods, such as graphing and factoring, are not useful for equations with irrational or complex roots. Solve this equation by using the quadratic formula, $x = \frac{-b \pm \sqrt{b^2 - 4ac}}{2a}$. Set the given equation equal to zero, so $7x^2 + 6x + 2 = 0$. Substitute the values $a = 7$, $b = 6$, and $c = 2$ into the quadratic formula.

$$x = \frac{-b \pm \sqrt{b^2 - 4ac}}{2a}$$

$$x = \frac{-6 \pm \sqrt{6^2 - 4(7)(2)}}{2(7)}$$

$$x = \frac{-6 \pm \sqrt{36 - 56}}{14}$$

$$x = \frac{-6 \pm \sqrt{-20}}{14}$$

$$x = \frac{-6 \pm 2i\sqrt{5}}{14}$$

$$x = \frac{-3 \pm i\sqrt{5}}{7}$$

17. C: Evaluate the integral by adding 1 to the exponent of each term and dividing the coefficient by the new exponent. Don't forget to add the constant of integration to the end.

$$\int 6x^2 + \frac{1}{2}x - 3 \, dx = \frac{6}{2+1}x^{(2+1)} + \frac{\frac{1}{2}}{1+1}x^{(1+1)} - \frac{3}{0+1}x^{(0+1)} + C$$

$$= 2x^3 + \frac{1}{4}x^2 - 3x + C$$

18. C: Choice A represents convenience sampling since it is limited to one age. The pool of 8th grade students may not represent the opinions of all youth in the district. Choice B is biased because participants are self-selected rather than randomly selected. It may be that customers who have a strong opinion are more likely to respond than those who are more neutral, and this would give a skewed perspective of opinions. In choice C, families are randomly selected, so the sampling technique is not biased. Choice D, like choice B, is biased because participants are self-selected rather than randomly selected.

19. D: For the Final, the third quartile is 87. Since 75% of the data in a set is below the third quartile, there is a 75% chance, or a probability of 0.75, that a test score chosen at random from the Final scored below 87.

20. B: Student A is wrong because the GCF of the coefficients of a quadratic function does not determine the range. For instance, the function $f(x) = x^2 + 5$ has coefficients with a GCF of 1 but a range of $[5, \infty)$.

Student B is correct because the y-value of the vertex of parabola that opens upward is the minimum value of the function.

Student C is wrong because the axis of symmetry is the x-value of the vertex, not the y-value.

21. A: Student A correctly uses the rule $\log_a x^y = y \log_a x$ to convert $\log_2 5^{3x-1}$ into $(3x-1)\log_2 5$ and combines this rule with the rules $\log_a xy = \log_a x + \log_a y$ and $\log_a a^x = x$ to calculate $\log_2(32 \cdot 3) = \log_2 32 + \log_2 3 = \log_2 2^5 + \log_2 3 = 5 + \log_2 3$.

Student B tries to apply the rule $\log\left(\frac{a}{b}\right) = \log a - \log b$ but confuses $\log\left(\frac{a}{b}\right)$ with $\frac{\log a}{\log b}$, incorrectly rewriting $\frac{\log 96}{\log 5}$ as $\log 96 - \log 5$.

Student C incorrectly "cancels the logarithms" turning $\frac{\ln 96}{\ln 5}$ into $\frac{96}{5}$.

22. B: The range is the spread of the data. It can be calculated for each test by subtracting the lowest test score from the highest, or it can be determined visually from the graph. The difference between the highest and lowest test scores on the Midterm is $91 - 22 = 69$ points. The range for each of the other classes is much smaller.

23. B: This problem can be solved using proportions. Determine the number of feet between the two points by setting up the proportion:

$$\frac{1 \text{ in}}{10 \text{ ft}} = \frac{24 \text{ in}}{x \text{ ft}}$$

Cross multiply to solve for x.

$$1 \times x = 24 \times 10$$
$$x = 240$$

Therefore, the two points are 240 feet apart. From here, convert 240 feet to a distance in yards. To do so, multiply by the conversion factor $\frac{1 \text{ yd}}{3 \text{ ft}}$.

$$240 \text{ ft} \times \frac{1 \text{ yd}}{3 \text{ ft}} = 80 \text{ yd}$$

The two points are 80 yards apart.

24. B: A simple test of each option at $x = -5$, $x = 0$, and $x = 2$ demonstrates that only choice B works:

x	Observed	y_a	y_b	y_c	y_d
-5	$\sim\frac{1}{4}$	-2	$\frac{1}{6}$	$-\frac{7}{6}$	$\frac{1}{9}$
0	$\sim-\frac{1}{4}$	$\frac{1}{2}$	$-\frac{1}{4}$	$\frac{3}{4}$	$-\frac{1}{6}$
2	$\sim\frac{1}{4}$	$\frac{1}{3}$	$\frac{1}{6}$	$\frac{7}{6}$	$\frac{1}{9}$

25. D: The cross-section is a hexagon.

26. A: The composition function $(g \circ f)(x)$ can be rewritten as $g(f(x))$. This means that anywhere there is an x in the function $g(x)$, it should be replaced with $2x + 4$. After substituting, simplify the expression.

$$g(2x + 4) = (2x + 4)^2 - 3(2x + 4) + 2$$
$$= 4x^2 + 16x + 16 - 6x - 12 + 2$$
$$= 4x^2 + 10x + 6$$

27. B: The recursive definition of the sequence gives the first term of the series, $a_1 = 2$. The definition also defines each term in the series as the sum of the previous term and –3. Therefore, the second term in the series is $2 + (-3) = -1$, the third term in the series is $-1 + (-3) = -4$, and so on.

n	a_n
1	2
2	–1
3	–4

The relationship between n and a_n is linear, so the equation of the sequence can be found using the explicit formula for an arithmetic sequence, $a_n = a_1 + d(n - 1)$, where a_n is the value of any term n, a_1 is the value of the first term, and d is the common difference between each term. The value of a_n decreases by 3 each time the value of n increases by 1, so the common difference (d) is –3.

Substitute all the known values into the equation for the explicit formula for an arithmetic sequence, and simplify the formula.

$$a_n = 2 + (-3)(n - 1)$$
$$a_n = 2 - 3n + 3$$
$$a_n = -3n + 5$$

28. B: To find the second derivative of the function, take the derivative of the first derivative of the function. Remember, to take a derivative, multiply the exponent of each term by the term's coefficient and then decrease the exponent by 1.

$$f(x) = -3x^3 - x^2 + 2x - 4$$
$$f'(x) = -9x^2 - 2x + 2$$
$$f''(x) = -18x - 2$$

29. A: Beginning by adding 7 to both sides of the inequality is an easier approach, but dividing both sides by 3 is also mathematically correct because it produces an equivalent inequality and makes progress in isolating the variable. Dividing by 3, however, requires application of the distributive property on the left side to get the inequality $x - \frac{7}{3} < \frac{20}{3}$. This yields the solution $x < \frac{27}{3}$, or $x < 9$.

30. B: A standard result from high school geometry states that the perpendicular bisector of a secant passes through the center of the circle. Thus, two distinct perpendicular bisectors of secants intersect at the center of the circle. Therefore, this construction works except in the case that both secants share the same perpendicular bisector, which happens precisely when the secants are parallel, the special case in which the student's construction fails.

31. C: There are three ways in which two women from the same department can be selected: two women can be selected from Biology, two women can be selected from Chemistry, or two women can be selected from Physics. Since the events of choosing one woman and then another are both independent events, multiply the two probabilities together to get the probability of choosing two women from the same department.

Biology	**Chemistry**	**Physics**
$\frac{26}{129} \times \frac{25}{128} = \frac{650}{16,512}$	$\frac{31}{129} \times \frac{30}{128} = \frac{930}{16,512}$	$\frac{20}{129} \times \frac{19}{128} = \frac{380}{16,512}$

Since any of these is a distinct possible outcome, the probability that two women will be selected from the same department is the sum of these outcomes.

$$\frac{650}{16,512} + \frac{930}{16,512} + \frac{380}{16,512} = \frac{1,960}{16,512} \approx 0.119 = 11.9\%$$

32. B: The trigonometric identity $\sec^2\theta = \tan^2\theta + 1$ can be used to rewrite the equation $\sec^2\theta = 2\tan\theta$ as $\tan^2\theta + 1 = 2\tan\theta$, which can then be rearranged into the form $\tan^2\theta - 2\tan\theta + 1 = 0$. Solve by factoring and using the zero-product property.

$$\tan^2\theta - 2\tan\theta + 1 = 0$$
$$(\tan\theta - 1)^2 = 0$$
$$\tan\theta - 1 = 0$$
$$\tan\theta = 1$$

Since $\tan\theta = 1$ when $\sin\theta = \cos\theta$, for $0 < \theta \leq 2\pi$, $\theta = \frac{\pi}{4}$ or $\frac{5\pi}{4}$.

33. B: Student A goes wrong by incorrectly treating $x^2 - 2x + 4$ as the perfect square $(x - 2)^2$.

Student B's approach is correct. First, we subtract 9 from both sides of the equation and factor 4 out of the terms on the lefthand side to get $4(x^2 - 2x) = 11$. Then we add 1 inside the parentheses to complete the square. Because of the leading factor of 4, this has the effect of adding 4 on the left side of the equation. So we also add 4 to the right side of the equation, getting $4(x^2 - 2x + 1) = 15$. Now we divide by 4 on both sides to get $(x - 1)^2 = \frac{15}{4}$.

Student C goes wrong by adding 4 to the left side of the equation $4(x^2 - 2x) = 11$ when he or she adds 1 inside the parentheses, but only adds 1 to the right side of the equation.

34. D: Since all of the answer choices are parallelograms, determine whether the parallelogram is also a rhombus or a rectangle, or both. One way to do this is by examining the parallelogram's diagonals. If the parallelogram's diagonals are perpendicular, then the parallelogram is a rhombus.

If the parallelogram's diagonals are congruent, then the parallelogram is a rectangle. If a parallelogram is both a rhombus and a rectangle, then it is a square. To determine whether the diagonals are perpendicular, find the slopes of the diagonals of the quadrilateral.

Diagonal 1: $(-2, 3)$ and $(5, 1)$
$$m = \frac{y_2 - y_1}{x_2 - x_1} = \frac{1 - 3}{5 - (-2)} = \frac{-2}{7} = -\frac{2}{7}$$

Diagonal 2: $(1, -1)$ and $(3, 6)$
$$m = \frac{y_2 - y_1}{x_2 - x_1} = \frac{6 - (-1)}{3 - 1} = \frac{7}{2}$$

The diagonals have opposite inverse slopes and are therefore perpendicular. Thus, the parallelogram is a rhombus. To determine whether the diagonals are congruent, find the lengths of the diagonals of the quadrilateral using the distance formula.

Diagonal 1: $(-2, 3)$ and $(5, 1)$
$$d = \sqrt{(x_2 - x_1)^2 + (y_2 - y_1)^2}$$
$$d = \sqrt{(5 - (-2))^2 + (1 - 3)^2}$$
$$d = \sqrt{(7)^2 + (-2)^2}$$
$$d = \sqrt{49 + 4}$$
$$d = \sqrt{53}$$

Diagonal 2: $(1, -1)$ and $(3, 6)$
$$d = \sqrt{(x_2 - x_1)^2 + (y_2 - y_1)^2}$$
$$d = \sqrt{(3 - 1)^2 + (6 - (-1))^2}$$
$$d = \sqrt{(2)^2 + (7)^2}$$
$$d = \sqrt{4 + 49}$$
$$d = \sqrt{53}$$

The diagonals are congruent, so the parallelogram is a rectangle. Since the parallelogram is a rhombus and a rectangle, it is also a square.

35. C: In Class 1, 26 students submitted late work, so the median is between the 13th and 14th piece of homework. Both the 13th and 14th fall on Day 4, so the median for Class 1 is 4. In Class 2, 23 students submitted late work, so the median is at the 12th piece of homework. This falls on Day 7. So, because $7 - 4 = 3$, the median number of days late in Class 1 is 3 less than the median number of days late in Class 2.

To find the mean late time for each class, find the sum of the late times and divide by the number of students turning in late work in each class. If the frequency of a one-day late time is 4, the number 1 is added four times (1×4), if frequency of a two-day late time is 5, the number 2 is added five times (2×5), and so on. So, to find the average turn-in time, divide the sum of the products of each late time and its corresponding frequency by the number of late turn-ins in each class. For Class 1, the mean late time is 4.96 days, which rounds to approximately 5 days.

$$\text{Mean} = \frac{4(1) + 5(2) + 3(3) + 2(4) + 3(5) + 1(6) + 1(7) + 2(9) + 4(10) + 1(12)}{4 + 5 + 3 + 2 + 3 + 1 + 1 + 2 + 4 + 1} = \frac{129}{26} \approx 4.96$$

For Class 2, the mean late time is 6.57, which rounds to approximately 7 days.

$$\text{Mean} = \frac{1(1) + 2(2) + 2(3) + 1(4) + 4(6) + 5(7) + 3(8) + 1(9) + 2(10) + 2(12)}{1 + 2 + 2 + 1 + 4 + 5 + 3 + 1 + 2 + 2} = \frac{151}{23} \approx 6.57$$

So, because $7 - 5 = 2$, the students in Class 2 turned in work 2 days later than in Class 1.

The mode late time is the date for which the frequency is the highest. For Class 1, the mode late time is 2 days, and for Class 2, the mode late time is 7 days.

The median late time for Class 1 is 4 and the mean is 4.96, so the median late time is less than the mean.

36. A: In correct answer choice A, the variable y is the height of the bucket above the ground, making $y - 40$ the position (negative if $y < 40$) of the bucket above the point halfway to the top of the crane. At this halfway point, the cable weighs $3 \cdot 40 = 120$ lbs. which, added to the weight of the bucket, gives a total weight of 320 lbs. Each foot above halfway means one foot less of cable hanging down and thus subtracts 3 lbs. from this weight so that at position y, the total is $320 - 3(y - 40)$ lbs.

In incorrect answer choice B, the variable y is the height of the bucket above the ground, making $80 - y$ the length of cable hanging down to support the bucket. The weight of this cable is $3(80 - y)$ lbs., which must be added to, not subtracted from, the weight of the bucket, giving a total weight of $200 + 3(80 - y)$ lbs. instead of the $200 - 3(80 - y)$ lbs. in choice B. When the bucket is at ground level ($y = 0$), this incorrect function makes the total weight $F(0) = 200 - 3(80 - 0) = -40$ lbs., which is wrong.

In incorrect answer choice C, the variable y is the distance of the bucket from the top of the crane. In other words, y is the length of cable hanging down to support the bucket. The weight of this cable is $3y$ lbs., which must be added to, not subtracted from, the weight of the bucket, giving a total weight of $200 + 3y$ lbs. instead of the $200 - 3y$ lbs. in choice C. When the bucket is at ground level ($y = 80$), this incorrect function makes the total weight $F(80) = 200 - 3 \cdot 80 = -40$ lbs., which is wrong.

37. B: The range of random variable X is $\{0, 1, 2, 3, 4, 5\}$. To calculate the probability of getting the possible values of X keep in mind the coin flips are independent with the probability of getting heads (and, similarly, tails) being $\frac{1}{2}$. Thus, $P(0) = P(\{T\}) = \frac{1}{2}, P(1) = P(\{HT\}) = \left(\frac{1}{2}\right)^2 = \frac{1}{4}, P(2) = P(\{HHT\}) = \left(\frac{1}{2}\right)^3 = \frac{1}{8}, P(3) = P(\{HHHT\}) = \left(\frac{1}{2}\right)^4 = \frac{1}{16}, P(4) = P(\{HHHHT\}) = \left(\frac{1}{2}\right)^5 = \frac{1}{32}$, and $P(5) = P(\{HHHHH\}) = \left(\frac{1}{2}\right)^5 = \frac{1}{32}$. So, using the definition of expected value, we get:

$$E(X) = \sum_{x=0}^{5} xP(x) = 0 \cdot P(0) + 1 \cdot P(1) + 2 \cdot P(2) + 3 \cdot P(3) + 4 \cdot P(4) + 5 \cdot P(5)$$

$$= 0 \cdot \frac{1}{2} + 1 \cdot \frac{1}{4} + 2 \cdot \frac{1}{8} + 3 \cdot \frac{1}{16} + 4 \cdot \frac{1}{32} + 5 \cdot \frac{1}{32}$$

$$= 0 + \frac{1}{4} + \frac{1}{4} + \frac{3}{16} + \frac{1}{8} + \frac{5}{32}$$

$$= \frac{8}{32} + \frac{8}{32} + \frac{6}{32} + \frac{4}{32} + \frac{5}{32} = \frac{31}{32}$$

38. A: Start by determining which values of x are not possible solutions. For this equation, x cannot equal –1 or –7 because these would result in denominator values of 0.

Then, solve the equation as normal.

$$\frac{x+2}{x+1} = \frac{x+9}{x+7} + \frac{2}{x+1}$$

$\dfrac{x}{x+1} = \dfrac{x+9}{x+7}$	Subtract $\frac{2}{x+1}$ from both sides of the equation.
$(x)(x+7) = (x+9)(x+1)$	Cross multiply to eliminate the fractions.
$x^2 + 7x = x^2 + 10x + 9$	Multiply the polynomials.
$7x = 10x + 9$	Subtract x^2 from both sides of the equation
$-3x = 9$	Subtract $10x$ from both sides of the equation.
$x = -3$	Divide both sides of the equation by –3.

Since –3 is not one of the values x cannot be equal to, our answer is $x = -3$.

39. D: Since a and b are multiples of 6, each can be expressed as the product of 6 and an integer. So, if we write $a = 6x$ and $b = 6y$ then, $3(6x)^2 + 2(6y)^3 = c$. Simplify and factor.

$$3(6x)^2 + 2(6y)^3 = c$$
$$108x^2 + 432y^3 = c$$
$$108(x^2 + 4y^3) = c$$

Since c is the product of 108 and some other integer, 108 must be a factor of c.

40. 8: $\triangle ABC$ is similar to the smaller triangle with which it shares vertex B.

$$\overline{BC} = (2x - 2) + (x + 4) = 3x + 2$$

$$\overline{AB} = 3 + 9 = 12$$

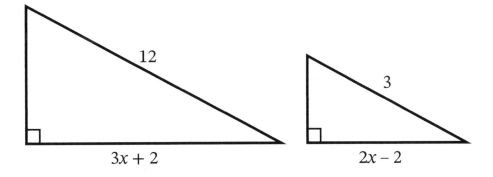

Set up a proportion and solve for x:

$$\frac{3x + 2}{12} = \frac{2x - 2}{3}$$
$$9x + 6 = 24x - 24$$
$$30 = 15x$$
$$x = 2$$

So, $BC = 3x + 2 = 3(2) + 2 = 8$.

41. 18: Use the table of values to first write equations for $f(x)$ and $g(x)$: $f(x) = 2x^2$ and $g(x) = 2x + 5$. Then, use those equations to find $f(g(-4))$. Start by finding $g(-4)$.

$$g(-4) = 2(-4) + 5 = -3$$

From here, substitute $g(-4)$ into the function $f(x)$ to find $f(g(-4))$. Since $g(-4) = -3$, plug in –3 anywhere an x is found in $f(x)$.

$$f(-3) = 2(-3)^2 = 18$$

So, $f(g(-4)) = 18$.

42. B, C: Student A makes a mistake at the first step, violating order of operations by adding the a to $3a$ which is joined to x by multiplication (or, alternatively, by trying to combine unlike terms as though they were like terms). The correct way to combine these terms is by factoring out the a, getting $a + 3ax = a(1 + 3x)$ as student C does.

Student B takes a correct approach, first subtracting a from both sides of the equation and then dividing both sides of the equation by the coefficient $3a$ to isolate the x.

Student C also takes a correct approach, first factoring out the common factor of a on the right-hand side of the equation, then dividing both sides of the equation by the factor a. Next, they subtract 1 from both sides of the equation, and finally divide both sides of the equation by the coefficient 3 to isolate the x

43. A: Determine the veracity of each option given that the hypotenuse of a right triangle is equal to the square root of the sum of the squares of the legs or $c = \sqrt{a^2 + b^2}$:

A $\quad \tan B = ? \dfrac{\sqrt{c^2 - a^2}}{a} \qquad \tan B = \dfrac{\text{opposite}}{\text{adjacent}} = \dfrac{b}{a} = \dfrac{\sqrt{c^2 - a^2}}{a}$

B $\quad \cos B = ? \dfrac{b\sqrt{a^2 + b^2}}{a^2 + b^2}$

$\cos B = \dfrac{\text{adjacent}}{\text{hypotenuse}} = \dfrac{a}{\sqrt{a^2 + b^2}} = \dfrac{a}{\sqrt{a^2 + b^2}} \times \dfrac{\sqrt{a^2 + b^2}}{\sqrt{a^2 + b^2}} = \dfrac{a\sqrt{a^2 + b^2}}{a^2 + b^2}$

$\neq \dfrac{b\sqrt{a^2 + b^2}}{a^2 + b^2}$

C $\quad \sec B = ? \dfrac{\sqrt{a^2 + b^2}}{b} \qquad \sec B = \dfrac{\text{hypotenuse}}{\text{adjacent}} = \dfrac{\sqrt{a^2 + b^2}}{a} \neq \dfrac{\sqrt{a^2 + b^2}}{b}$

D $\quad \csc B = ? \dfrac{a^2 + b^2}{b} \qquad \csc B = \dfrac{\text{hypotenuse}}{\text{opposite}} = \dfrac{\sqrt{a^2 + b^2}}{b} \neq \dfrac{a^2 + b^2}{b}$

44. C: A system of linear equations can be solved by using matrices or by using the graphing, substitution, or elimination (also called linear combination) method. The elimination method is shown here:

$$3x + 4y = 2$$
$$2x + 6y = -2$$

In order to eliminate x by linear combination, multiply the top equation by 2 and the bottom equation by -3 so that the coefficients of the x-terms will be additive inverses.

$$2(3x + 4y = 2)$$
$$-3(2x + 6y = -2)$$

Then, add the two equations and solve for y.

$$6x + 8y = 4$$
$$\underline{-6x - 18y = 6}$$
$$-10y = 10$$
$$y = -1$$

Substitute -1 for y in either of the given equations and solve for x.

$$3x + 4y = 2$$
$$3x + 4(-1) = 2$$
$$3x - 4 = 2$$
$$3x = 6$$
$$x = 2$$

The solution to the system of equations is $(2, -1)$.

45. D: Bacterial growth is exponential. Let x be the number of times the population doubles, a be the number of bacteria in the colony originally transferred into the broth, and y be the number of bacteria in the broth after x doubling times. After 1 hour, the population would have doubled three times:

$$a(2)^x = y$$
$$a(2^3) = 8 \times 10^6$$
$$8a = 8 \times 10^6$$
$$a = 10^6$$

So, the number of bacteria originally transferred into the petri dish was 10^6. The equation for determining the number of bacteria is $y = (2^x) \times 10^6$. Since the bacteria double every twenty minutes, they go through three doubling times every hour. So, when the bacteria are allowed to grow for eight hours, they will have gone through $8 \times 3 = 24$ doubling times. When $x = 24$, $y = (2^{24}) \times 10^6 = 16{,}777{,}216 \times 10^6$, which is approximately 1.7×10^{13}.

46. A: Because Step 6 established that $\angle b \cong \angle c$, we can conclude that the sides opposite these congruent angles are congruent, or $XY \cong ZY$.

47. A: The probability of an event is the number of possible occurrences of that event divided by the number of all possible outcomes. A student who is eight years old or less can be five, six, seven, or eight years old, so the probability is:

$$\frac{\text{number of 5-, 6-, 7-, and 8-year-old students}}{\text{total number of students}} = \frac{11+8+9+14}{11+8+9+14+11+13} = \frac{42}{66} = \frac{7}{11}$$

48. A: The set of integers is a subset of the set of rational numbers, which is a subset of the set real numbers, which is a subset of the set of complex numbers.

49. A, B, C: Student A uses the quadratic formula. Student B uses the completing the square method. Student C uses factoring. These are the three common ways to find the exact solution of a quadratic equation.

50. A: Choice B is incorrect because we are not given that $\angle BAC$ is a right angle and we cannot assume it is right because it looks like a right angle. It is possible to prove that it is right, but this requires an argument very much like the one the student makes. Choices C and D are incorrect because the definition of median is a line segment joining a vertex of a triangle to the midpoint of the opposite side. The student gave an argument that is correct and reasonably simple, so choice A is correct.

51. A, C: Student A recognizes that the set of all usernames is the disjoint union of usernames with A and those without A, and from this correctly derives the equation "usernames with A" $+ 25^6 = 26^6$ and concludes "usernames with A" $= 26^6 - 25^6$.

Student B's plan looks promising but overcounts administrator usernames with more than one A. For instance, a username that begins with two A's gets counted twice—once when the first position is chosen as the "guaranteed" A and then A happens to be chosen as the second letter, and once when the second position is chosen as the "guaranteed" A and then A happens to be chosen as the first letter.

Student C recognizes that the set of usernames with A's is the disjoint union of the subset of usernames with exactly one A, the subset of those with exactly two A's, etc. Thus, we can get the total by adding up the sizes of these six subsets, which Student C calculates correctly.

52. A: The equation for this scenario is $2b + 3c \geq 150$, where b is the number of brownies that must be sold and c is the number of cupcakes that must be sold. Solve for the intercepts of the inequality by momentarily changing the inequality sign to an equal sign, substituting 0 for b and solving for c, and then substituting 0 for c and solving for b. The intercepts of this linear inequality are $b = 75$ and $c = 50$. The x-axis represents the number of brownies sold, so the x-intercept is $(75, 0)$. The y-axis represents the number of cupcakes sold, so the y-intercept is $(0, 50)$. The solid line through the two intercepts, $(75,0)$ and $(0,50)$, represents the minimum number of each type of baked good that must be sold to offset production costs. Since you are breaking even or making a profit, shade above the line.

53. C: To get the inverse relation, we swap the variables, replacing y with x and vice versa. This gives us the equation $x - 2 = \pm\sqrt{y-3}$, which we solve for y:

$$\pm\sqrt{y-3} = x - 2$$
$$\left(\pm\sqrt{y-3}\right)^2 = (x-2)^2$$
$$y - 3 = (x-2)^2$$
$$y = (x-2)^2 + 3$$

The variable x in this final equation can take on any real value, and each choice of x will produce a single value of y. Thus, this relation is a function, written in the form $y = f(x)$. Alternatively, we might note that the quadratic equation $y = (x-2)^2 + 3$ is in vertex form, indicating that its graph is a parabola opening upward with a vertex of (2,3). It passes the vertical line test and is, thus, a function. To verify our work, we can graph this function and the original equation $y - 2 = \pm\sqrt{x - 3}$, which is a parabola opening to the right with a vertex of (3,2), to find that they are—as they should be—mirror images of each other across the line $y = x$.

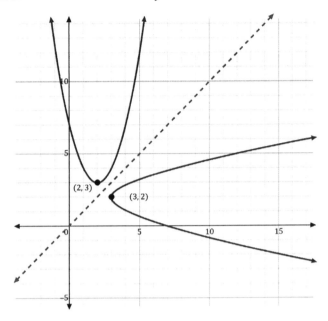

54. A: Since there are five possible choices for the correct answer to the first problem, five for the second, five for the third, and five for the fourth, by the Fundamental Counting Principle, the total number of possible ways to assign the letters of the correct answers is $5 \cdot 5 \cdot 5 \cdot 5 = 5^4$. But if we exclude the letter c from consideration, there are four choices for the correct answer to the first problem, four for the second, etc. Thus, there are $4 \cdot 4 \cdot 4 \cdot 4 = 4^4$ ways to assign the letters with c never being correct. Thus, the probability of randomly assigning the letters so that c is never correct is:

$$\frac{\text{\# of assignments without } c}{\text{\# of unrestricted assignments}} = \frac{4^4}{5^4} = \frac{256}{625} = 0.4096$$

55. 5,075: The ratio of expenses to income is $7 : 1$. Since we know he saves \$725 per month, we need to multiply this value by 7 to find out how much he spends on expenses each month. $\$725 \times 7 = \$5,075$. So, Jon spends \$5,075 on expenses each month.

56. C: On the unit circle, $\sin\theta = \frac{\sqrt{3}}{2}$ when $\theta = \frac{\pi}{3}$ and when $\theta = \frac{2\pi}{3}$. Since only $\frac{2\pi}{3}$ is in the given range of $\frac{\pi}{2} < \theta < \pi$, $\theta = \frac{2\pi}{3}$.

57. D: "The square of three times the sum of a and six is fourteen more than a" is represented by the equation $[3(a + 6)]^2 = a + 14$. Solve for a.

$$[3a + 18]^2 = a + 14$$
$$9a^2 + 108a + 324 = a + 14$$
$$9a^2 + 107a + 310 = 0$$
$$(a + 5)(9a + 62) = 0$$
$$a = -5, -\frac{62}{9}$$

So, −5 is a possible value of a.

58. B, C: To convert a quantity with units (in this case, 1 year), we multiply it by conversion factors (namely, fractions that equal 1) in such a fashion that all units cancel except those we want in our answer (in this case, seconds). From the time facts, 1 (common) year = 365 days, 1 day = 24 hours, 1 hour = 60 minutes, and 1 minute = 60 seconds, we get the conversion factors $\frac{365 \text{ days}}{1 \text{ year}}$, $\frac{24 \text{ hours}}{1 \text{ day}}$, $\frac{60 \text{ minutes}}{1 \text{ hour}}$, and $\frac{60 \text{ seconds}}{1 \text{ minute}}$.

Emily sets the problem up incorrectly. She multiplies only conversion factors without including the actual quantity, 1 year, that needs conversion. She also combines the factors in such a fashion that the units do not cancel correctly, leaving years and seconds in the numerator and two factors of days in the denominator.

Jonathon sets the problem up correctly, beginning with the quantity 1 year (written as the fraction $\frac{1 \text{ year}}{1}$) and multiplying by conversion factors in order from longer times to shorter times (years to days, days to hours, etc.). He does this in such a fashion that all units cancel except for seconds.

Sarah sets the problem up correctly, beginning with the quantity 1 year and multiplying by conversion factors in order from shorter times to longer ones in such a fashion that all units cancel except for seconds. This student converts minutes directly to days, bypassing hours, by using the time fact 1,440 minutes = 1 day.

59. D: To solve this equation, start by squaring both sides, then isolate the variable.

$$2 - \sqrt{x} = \sqrt{x - 20}$$
$$\left(2 - \sqrt{x}\right)^2 = \left(\sqrt{x - 20}\right)^2$$
$$\left(2 - \sqrt{x}\right)\left(2 - \sqrt{x}\right) = x - 20$$
$$4 - 4\sqrt{x} + x = x - 20$$
$$-4\sqrt{x} = -24$$
$$\sqrt{x} = 6$$
$$x = 36$$

When solving radical equations, check for extraneous solutions by substituting the found value into the original equation.

$$2 - \sqrt{x} = \sqrt{x - 20}$$

$$2 - \sqrt{36} = \sqrt{36 - 20}$$
$$2 - 6 = \sqrt{16}$$
$$-4 \neq 4$$

Since the solution results in an untrue statement, there is no solution. Alternatively, consider the graphs of the left and right side of the given equation. Notice the graphs $y = 2 - \sqrt{x}$ and $y = \sqrt{x - 20}$ do not intersect, which confirms there is no solution.

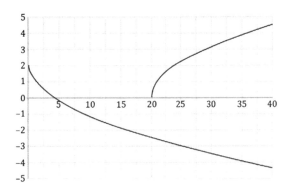

60. A, B, C: In the slope formula, $m = \frac{y_2 - y_1}{x_2 - x_1}$, the ordering of the points—that is, which is (x_1, y_1) and which is (x_2, y_2)—is irrelevant. So, all three approaches correctly calculate the slope as $m = \frac{3}{4}$.

Approach A correctly substitutes the slope of the line, $m = \frac{3}{4}$, and the coordinates of a point on the line, $(x_1, y_1) = (12, 3)$, into point-slope form of a linear equation, $y - y_1 = m(x - x_1)$, to get an equation of the line.

Approach B correctly substitutes the slope of the line, $m = \frac{3}{4}$, and the y-intercept of the line, $b = -6$, into the slope-intercept form of a linear equation, $y = mx + b$.

Approach C is the same as approach A, except that it substitutes the coordinates of the other point on the line, $(0, -6)$, into point-slope form. Since the choice of points on the line is irrelevant, this produces a different correct equation of the same line.

61. C: Find the points of intersection of the two graphs:

$$x^2 - 2x - 7 = x - 3$$
$$x^2 - 3x - 4 = 0$$
$$(x + 1)(x - 4) = 0$$
$$x = -1 \qquad x = 4$$

So, the area is between the graphs on the interval $[-1,4]$. To determine which of the graphs is the upper or lower bound, pick a test point in the interval. Using $x = 0$ as the test point.

$$y = x^2 - 2x - 7 \quad y = x - 3$$
$$y = 0^2 - 2(0) - 7 \quad y = 0 - 3$$
$$y = -7 \quad\quad y = -3$$

The finite region is bound at the top by the line $y = x - 3$ and at the bottom by $y = x^2 - 2x - 7$. The height of the region at point x is defined by $[(x - 3) - (x^2 - 2x - 7)]$, so the area is:

$$A = \int_{-1}^{4} [(x - 3) - (x^2 - 2x - 7)]dx$$
$$= \int_{-1}^{4} (-x^2 + 3x + 4) \, dx$$
$$= \left[-\frac{1}{3}x^3 + \frac{3}{2}x^2 + 4x\right]_{-1}^{4}$$
$$= \left[-\frac{1}{3}(4)^3 + \frac{3}{2}(4)^2 + 4(4)\right] - \left[-\frac{1}{3}(-1)^3 + \frac{3}{2}(-1)^2 + 4(-1)\right]$$
$$= \left[-\frac{64}{3} + 24 + 16\right] - \left[\frac{1}{3} + \frac{3}{2} - 4\right]$$
$$= \frac{56}{3} - \left(-\frac{13}{6}\right)$$
$$= \frac{125}{6}$$

62. 140: If the distance between the two houses is 10 cm on the map, then the actual distance between the houses is 100 m. To find x, use the Pythagorean theorem:

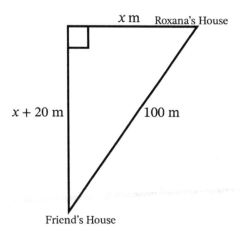

$$x^2 + (x + 20)^2 = (100)^2$$
$$x^2 + x^2 + 40x + 400 = 10,000$$
$$2x^2 + 40x - 9,600 = 0$$
$$2(x^2 + 20x - 4,800) = 0$$
$$2(x - 60)(x + 80) = 0$$
$$x = 60 \quad x = -80$$

Since x represents a distance, it cannot equal –80. Since $x = 60$, $x + 20 = 80$. Roxana walks a total of 140 m to get to her friend's house.

63. B: To increase a value by 20%, multiply the value by 1.2. Multiplying the lengths in a closed figure by a given factor (to produce a similar figure) multiplies the perimeter of the figure by the same factor. So, multiplying all lengths by 1.2 (increasing them 20%) increases the perimeter by a factor of 1.2. The new perimeter is $1.2 \cdot 60$ mm $= 72$ mm. On the other hand, multiplying the lengths in a closed figure by a given factor multiplies the area of the figure by the square of that factor. So, multiplying all lengths by 1.2 increases the area by a factor of 1.2^2. Thus, the new area is $1.2^2 \cdot 250$ mm$^2 = 360$ mm^2.

64. B: The acceleration a of an object at time t is the derivative of the velocity v of the object with respect to time t. Velocity of the object is the derivative of the position s of the object with respect to time t. So, given the velocity of an object at time t, $s(t)$ can be found by taking the integral of the $v(t)$, and $a(t)$ can be found by taking the derivative of $v(t)$.

$$s(t) = \int v(t)dt$$
$$= \int (-t^2 + 8t)dt$$
$$= -\frac{1}{3}t^3 + 4t^2 + C$$

Since the position of the car at time 0 is 0:

$$0 = s(0)$$
$$0 = 4(0)^2 - \frac{1}{3}(0)^3 + C$$
$$0 = 0 - 0 + C$$
$$0 = C$$

Therefore, $s(t) = -\frac{1}{3}t^3 + 4t^2$.

The acceleration at time t is: $a(t) = v'(t) = -2t + 8$.

Find the time at which the acceleration is equal to 0.

$$0 = 8 - 2t$$
$$t = 4$$

Then, find $s(4)$ to find the position of the car when the velocity is 0.

$$s(t) = -\frac{1}{3}t^3 + 4t^2$$
$$s(4) = -\frac{1}{3}(4)^3 + 4(4)^2$$
$$s(4) = -\frac{64}{3} + 64$$
$$s(4) = \frac{128}{3}$$

Therefore, the position of the car when its acceleration is 0 is $\frac{128}{3}$.

65. B: When the jeans are marked down by 30%, the cost is 70% of its original price. Thus, the reduced price of the dress can be written as $\frac{70}{100}x$, or $\frac{7}{10}x$, where x is the original price. When discounted an extra 15%, the jeans cost 85% of the reduced price, or $\frac{85}{100}\left(\frac{7}{10}x\right)$. This can be simplified to $\frac{17}{20}\left(\frac{7}{10}x\right)$. Multiply the fractions to get $\frac{119}{200}x$. So, the final price is $\frac{119}{200}$ of the original price.

66. C: Evaluate $\frac{x^3+3x^2-x-3}{x^2-9}$ at $x = 3$.

$$\frac{(3)^3 + 3(3)^2 - (3) - 3}{(3)^2 - 9} = \frac{27 + 3(9) - 3 - 3}{9 - 9} = \frac{27 + 27 - 3 - 3}{9 - 9} = \frac{48}{0}$$

Since evaluating $\frac{x^3+3x^2-x-3}{x^2-9}$ at $x = -3$ produces a fraction with a zero denominator, simplify the polynomial expression before evaluating the limit.

Simplify the polynomial expression:

$$\frac{x^3 + 3x^2 - x - 3}{x^2 - 9}$$

$$\frac{x^2(x + 3) - 1(x + 3)}{(x + 3)(x - 3)}$$
Factor out $(x + 3)$ from the first two terms and the 3rd and 4th terms in the numerator, and factor the denominator.

$$\frac{(x + 3)(x^2 - 1)}{(x + 3)(x - 3)}$$
Factor out $(x + 3)$ completely in the numerator.

$$\frac{(x + 1)(x - 1)}{x - 3}$$
Cancel the common $(x + 3)$ terms in the numerator and denominator.

Now, evaluate the limit.

$$\lim_{x \to -3} \frac{(x + 1)(x - 1)}{x - 3}$$

$$\frac{(-3 + 1)(-3 - 1)}{-3 - 3}$$
Substitute –3 into the expression for x.

$$\frac{8}{-6}$$
Simplify the numerator and denominator.

$$-\frac{4}{3}$$
Simplify the fraction.

Praxis Practice Test #2

Number and Quantity

1. The ratio of employee wages and benefits to all other operational costs of a business is 2:3. If a business's total operating expenses are $130,000 per month, how much money does the company spend on employee wages and benefits?

    a. $43,333.33
    b. $86,666.67
    c. $52,000.00
    d. $78,000.00

2. Identical rugs are offered for sale at two local shops and one online retailer, designated Stores A, B, and C, respectively. The rug's regular sales price is $296 at Store A, $220 at Store B, and $198.00 at Store C. Stores A and B collect 8% in sales tax on any after-discount price, while Store C collects no tax but charges a $35 shipping fee. A buyer has a 30% off coupon for Store A and a $10 off coupon for Store B. Which of these lists the stores in order of lowest to highest final sales price after all discounts, taxes, and fees are applied?

    a. Store A, Store B, Store C
    b. Store B, Store C, Store A
    c. Store C, Store A, Store B
    d. Store C, Store B, Store A

3. Which of these demonstrates the relationship between the sets of prime numbers, real numbers, natural numbers, complex numbers, rational numbers, and integers?

$$\mathbb{P}\text{–Prime; } \mathbb{R}\text{–Real; } \mathbb{N}\text{–Natural; } \mathbb{C}\text{–Complex; } \mathbb{Q}\text{–Rational; } \mathbb{Z}\text{–Integer}$$

    a. $\mathbb{P} \subseteq \mathbb{Q} \subseteq \mathbb{R} \subseteq \mathbb{Z} \subseteq \mathbb{C} \subseteq \mathbb{N}$
    b. $\mathbb{P} \subseteq \mathbb{N} \subseteq \mathbb{Z} \subseteq \mathbb{Q} \subseteq \mathbb{R} \subseteq \mathbb{C}$
    c. $\mathbb{C} \subseteq \mathbb{R} \subseteq \mathbb{Q} \subseteq \mathbb{Z} \subseteq \mathbb{N} \subseteq \mathbb{P}$
    d. None of these

4. Simplify $\left| (2 - 3i)^2 - (1 - 4i) \right|$.

    a. $\sqrt{61}$
    b. $-6 - 8i$
    c. $6 + 8i$
    d. 10

Refer to the following for question 5:

This data shows the number of students at a high school who are enrolled in various electives.

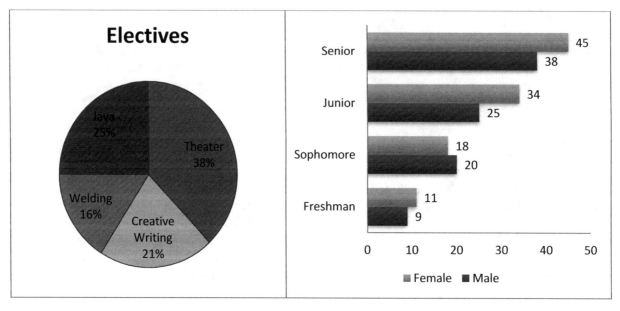

5. Compare the two quantities.

Quantity A
The percentage of students taking Java or Creative Writing

Quantity B
The percentage of male students

a. Quantity A is greater.
b. Quantity B is greater.
c. The two quantities are the same.
d. The relationship cannot be determined from the given information.

6. Given that x is a positive, even integer and that the greatest common factor of x and y is greater than 1, which of the following are possibly true for Quantity A and Quantity B?

Quantity A
y

Quantity B
the least common multiple of x and y

I. Quantity A is greater
II. Quantity B is greater
III. The two quantities are the same

a. I
b. II
c. I and III
d. II and III

7. Simplify $\dfrac{(x^2y^{-3})(4xy)^2}{16x^4y^4} + \dfrac{3}{2xy}$

a. $\dfrac{3x+24y^6}{8xy^7}$

b. $\dfrac{2x+6y^6}{2xy^4}$

c. $\dfrac{x+24y^5}{8xy^6}$

d. $\dfrac{2x+3y^4}{2xy^5}$

Algebra

8. Aaron goes on a run every morning down the straight country road that he lives on. The graph below shows Aaron's distance from home at times throughout his morning run. Which of the following statements is (are) true?

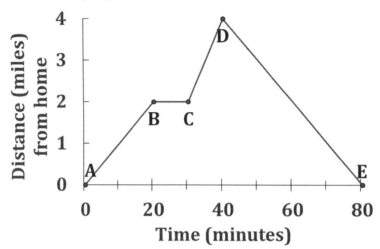

     I. Aaron's average running speed was 6 mph.
     II. Aaron's running speed from A to B was the same as from D to E.
     III. Aaron ran a total distance of four miles.

  a. I only
  b. II only
  c. I and II
  d. I, II, and III

9. If a, b, and c are even integers and $3a^2 + 9b^3 = c$, which of these is the largest number which must be factor of c?

  a. 2
  b. 3
  c. 6
  d. 12

10. Solve $3x^3y^2 - 45x^2y = 15x^3y - 9x^2y^2$ for x and y.

  a. $x = \{0, -3\}, y = \{0, 5\}$
  b. $x = \{0\}, y = \{0\}$
  c. $x = \{0, -3\}, y = \{0\}$
  d. $x = \{0\}, y = \{0, 5\}$

11. Solve $\sqrt{2x} - 3 = \sqrt{2x - 15}$.

  a. $x = 0$
  b. $x = 4$
  c. $x = 8$
  d. $x = 10$

12. Solve $\frac{x-1}{x+2} = \frac{6}{x+2} - \frac{x-3}{x-2}$.

    a. $x = 0,2$
    b. $x = 1,4$
    c. $x = -3,1$
    d. $x = 1,-3$

13. Ben is purchasing notebooks and boxes of pencils for a class he is teaching. Notebooks cost \$1 each and pencils cost \$3 per box. If the y-axis represents notebooks and the x-axis represents boxes of pencils, and Ben can spend a maximum of \$30, which of the following graphs shows the amount of notebooks and pencils Ben can purchase?

a.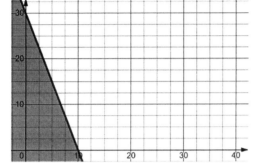

c.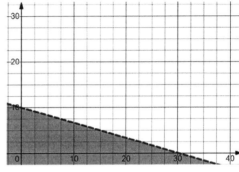

b.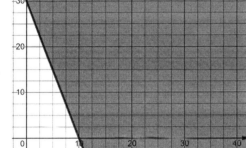

d.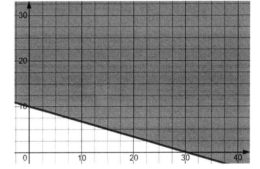

14. Solve $x^4 + 9 = 10x^2$.

    a. $x = \{1, 3\}$
    b. $x = \{-3i, -i, i, 3i\}$
    c. $x = \{i, 3i\}$
    d. $x = \{-3, -1, 1, 3\}$

15. Which of these does NOT have a solution set of $\{x: -1 \le x \le 1\}$?

    a. $9 \ge 1 + 2(x + 3) \ge 5$
    b. $-x^2 + 4 + 3x^2 \le 3x^2 + 3$
    c. $\frac{12 - |6x|}{2} \ge 3$
    d. $2|2x| + 4 \le 8$

16. **Which system of linear inequalities has no solution?**

   a. $\begin{cases} x - 2y > 7 \\ 3x \le -3 + 6y \end{cases}$

   b. $\begin{cases} y \le 6 - 3x \\ \frac{1}{3}y + x \ge 1 \end{cases}$

   c. $\begin{cases} 3x + 2y \le 9 \\ 3x \ge 7 - y \end{cases}$

   d. $\begin{cases} \frac{1}{4}x + 4y \le -8 \\ y + 4x > -8 \end{cases}$

17. **Solve the system of equations:** $\begin{array}{l} -4x + 3y = 8 \\ 6x - 2y = -7 \end{array}$

   a. $\left(\frac{1}{2}, \frac{10}{3}\right)$

   b. $\left(-1, \frac{3}{2}\right)$

   c. $\left(2, -\frac{5}{2}\right)$

   d. $\left(-\frac{1}{2}, 2\right)$

18. **Which of these is the equation graphed below?**

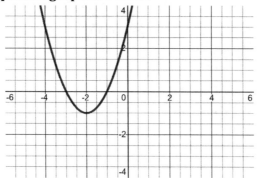

   a. $y = x^2 + 4x + 3$
   b. $y = x^2 - 2x - 1$
   c. $y = 2x^2 + 4x + 1$
   d. $y = \frac{1}{2}x^2 - 2x + \frac{5}{2}$

19. Simplify $\sqrt{\dfrac{-54x^5}{80y^6}}$.

   a. $\dfrac{3x^2\sqrt{6x}i}{20y^3}$

   b. $\dfrac{3x^2\sqrt{6x}i}{4y^3}$

   c. $\dfrac{-3x^2\sqrt{30x}i}{8y^3}$

   d. $\dfrac{3x^2\sqrt{30x}i}{20y^3}$

20. Gillian is deciding between two data plans for her cell. Plan A provides 2.5 GB of data for a flat rate of \$20/month and charges \$15 per GB for any extra use. Plan B provides unlimited data for \$50/month. Both plans would cost the same if Gillian used:

   a.   2.75 GB

   b.   3.25 GB

   c.   3.75 GB

   d.   4.5 GB

Functions

21. Which of the following piecewise functions can describe the graph below?

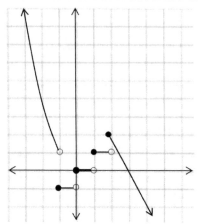

a. $f(x) = \begin{cases} x^2 & x < -1 \\ [\![x]\!] & -1 \le x < 2 \\ -2x + 6 & x \ge 2 \end{cases}$

c. $f(x) = \begin{cases} (x+1)^2 & x < -1 \\ [\![x]\!] + 1 & -1 \le x < 2 \\ -2x + 6 & x \ge 2 \end{cases}$

b. $f(x) = \begin{cases} x^2 & x \le -1 \\ [\![x]\!] & -1 \le x \le 2 \\ -2x + 6 & x > 2 \end{cases}$

d. $f(x) = \begin{cases} (x+1)^2 & x < -1 \\ [\![x-1]\!] & -1 \le x < 2 \\ -2x + 6 & x \ge 2 \end{cases}$

22. Which of the graphs shown represents $f(x) = -2|-x + 4| - 1$?

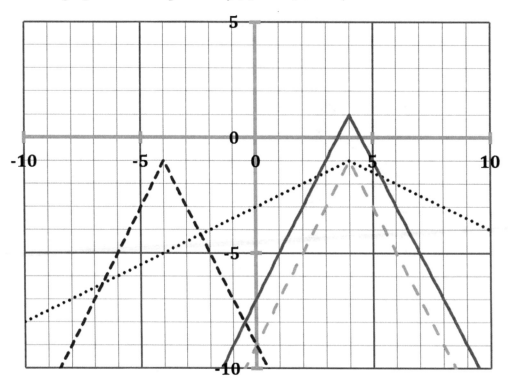

a. ⚊ ⚊
b. ▬ ▬ ▬
c. ▬▬▬▬
d. ••••••

23. Which of the following expressions is equal to $\cos\theta\cot\theta$?

a. $\sin\theta$
b. $\sec\theta\tan\theta$
c. $\csc\theta - \sin\theta$
d. $\sec\theta - \sin\theta$

24. Which of the graphs below represents $f(x) = -3|-x + 2| + 1$?

a.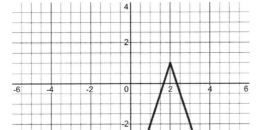

c.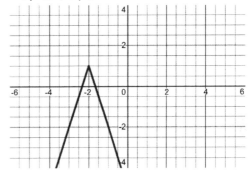

b.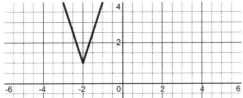

d.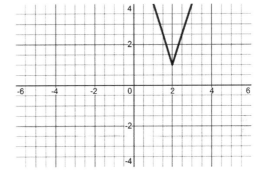

25. Use the operation table to determine $(w * y) * (x * x)$.

*	w	x	y	z
w	w	x	y	z
x	z	w	x	y
y	y	z	w	x
z	x	y	z	w

a. w
b. x
c. y
d. z

26. Which of these statements is (are) true for function $g(x)$?

$$g(x) = \begin{cases} -\dfrac{1}{2}x + 3 & x \geq 2 \\ x & x < 2 \end{cases}$$

I. $g(1) = 1$
II. The domain of $g(x)$ is all real numbers.
III. The range of $g(x)$ is $y \geq 2$.

a. II
b. III
c. I, II
d. I, II, III

27. If $f(x)$ and $g(x)$ are inverse functions, which of these is the value of x when $f(g(x)) = \frac{1}{8}$?

a. -8
b. $\dfrac{1}{8}$
c. 8
d. $-\dfrac{1}{8}$

28. Complete the analogy: $\dfrac{1}{x}$ is to $\dfrac{1}{y}$ as ...

a. x^2 is to y^3.
b. e^x is to $\log y, y > 0$.
c. x is to $\sqrt{y}, x, y \neq 0$.
d. x^2 is to $\sqrt{y}, y > 0$.

29. Which of these relationships represents y as a function of x?

a. $x = y^4$ c. $y = |x - 2|$

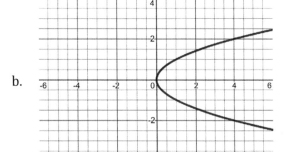

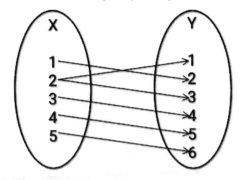

b.   d.

30. Which of the following statements is (are) true when $f(x) = \dfrac{x^2 - x - 2}{x^3 - 7x + 6}$?

I. The graph $f(x)$ has vertical asymptotes at $x = -3$, $x = 1$, and $x = 2$.
II. The x- and y-intercepts of the graph of $f(x)$ are both $-\dfrac{1}{3}$.

a. I
b. II
c. I and II
d. Neither statement is true.

31. Which of these statements is NOT necessarily true when $f(x) = \log_b x$ and $b > 1$?

    a.   The x-intercept of the graph of $f(x)$ is 1.
    b.   The graph of $f(x)$ passes through $(b, 1)$
    c. $f(x) < 0$ when $0 < x < 1$
    d.   If $g(x) = x^b$, the graph of $f(x)$ is symmetric to the graph of $g(x)$ with respect to $y = x$.

32. Which of these defines the recursive sequence $a_1 = -2$, $a_{n+1} = a_n + \frac{1}{2}$ explicitly?

    a. $a_n = \frac{1}{2}n - 2$
    b. $a_n = -2n + \frac{1}{2}$
    c. $a_n = \frac{1}{2}n - \frac{5}{2}$
    d. $a_n = -2n + \frac{5}{2}$

33. What is the value of b when $f\big(g(b)\big) = -6$, if $f(x)$ and $g(x)$ are inverse functions?

    a. -6
    b. $\frac{1}{6}$
    c. 6
    d. $-\frac{1}{6}$

Calculus

34. If $f(x) = \frac{1}{4}x^2 - 3$, find the slope of the line tangent to graph of $f(x)$ at $x = 2$.

    a. −2
    b. 0
    c. 1
    d. 4

35. For functions $f(x)$, $g(x)$, and $h(x)$, determine the limit of the function as x approaches 2 and the continuity of the function at $x = 2$ given:

$$\lim_{x \to 2+} f(x) = 4 \qquad \lim_{x \to 2+} g(x) = 2 \qquad \lim_{x \to 2+} h(x) = 2$$
$$\lim_{x \to 2-} f(x) = 2 \qquad \lim_{x \to 2-} g(x) = 2 \qquad \lim_{x \to 2-} h(x) = 2$$
$$f(2) = 2 \qquad\qquad g(2) = 4 \qquad\qquad h(2) = 2$$

a. $\begin{cases} \lim_{x \to 2} f(x)\ DNE & \text{The function } f(x) \text{ is discontinuous at 2} \\ \lim_{x \to 2} g(x) = 2 & \text{The function } g(x) \text{ is discontinuous at 2} \\ \lim_{x \to 2} h(x) = 2 & \text{The function } h(x) \text{ is continuous at 2} \end{cases}$

b. $\begin{cases} \lim_{x \to 2} f(x)\ DNE & \text{The function } f(x) \text{ is continuous at 2} \\ \lim_{x \to 2} g(x)\ DNE & \text{The function } g(x) \text{ is continuous at 2} \\ \lim_{x \to 2} h(x) = 2 & \text{The function } h(x) \text{ is continuous at 2} \end{cases}$

c. $\begin{cases} \lim_{x \to 2} f(x) = 2 & \text{The function } f(x) \text{ is continuous at 2} \\ \lim_{x \to 2} g(x) = 2 & \text{The function } g(x) \text{ is discontinuous at 2} \\ \lim_{x \to 2} h(x) = 2 & \text{The function } h(x) \text{ is continuous at 2} \end{cases}$

d. $\begin{cases} \lim_{x \to 2} f(x) = 2 & \text{The function } f(x) \text{ is discontinuous at 2} \\ \lim_{x \to 2} g(x) = 2 & \text{The function } g(x) \text{ is discontinuous at 2} \\ \lim_{x \to 2} h(x) = 2 & \text{The function } h(x) \text{ is continuous at 2} \end{cases}$

36. Suppose the path of a baseball hit straight up from three feet above the ground is modeled by the first quadrant graph of the function $h = -16t^2 + 50t + 3$, where t is the flight time of the ball in seconds and h is the height of the ball in feet. What is the velocity of the ball two seconds after it is hit?

    a. 39 ft/s upward
    b. 19.5 ft/s upward
    c. 19.5 ft/s downward
    d. 14 ft/s downward

37. To the nearest hundredth, what is the area in square units under the curve $f(x) = \frac{1}{x}$ on $[1, 2]$?

    a. 0.50
    b. 0.69
    c. 1.30
    d. 1.50

38. Calculate $\int 3x^2 + 2x - 1 \, dx$.

   a. $x^3 + x^2 - x + C$
   b. $6x^2 + 2$
   c. $\frac{3}{2}x^3 + 2x^2 - x + C$
   d. $6x^2 + 2 + C$

39. Find the area A of the finite region between the graphs of $y = -x + 2$ and $y = x^2 - 4$.

   a. 18
   b. $\frac{125}{6}$
   c. $\frac{45}{2}$
   d. 25

40. Evaluate $\lim\limits_{x \to \infty} \frac{x^2 - x + 3}{3x^2 + 1}$.

   a. 0
   b. 3
   c. $\frac{1}{3}$
   d. ∞

Geometry

41. Determine the number of diagonals of a dodecagon.

  a. 12
  b. 24
  c. 54
  d. 108

42. As shown below, four congruent isosceles trapezoids are positioned such that they form an arch. Find x for the indicated angle.

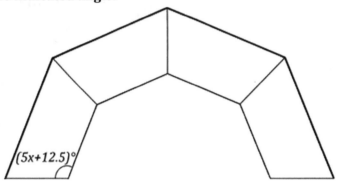

  a. $x = 11$
  b. $x = 20$
  c. $x = 24.5$
  d. The value of x cannot be determined from the information given.

Refer to the following for question 43:

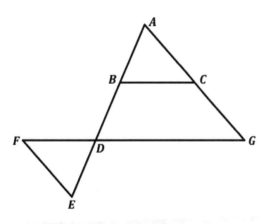

Statement	Reason
1. $\overline{BC} \parallel \overline{FG}$	Given
2.	
3. $\overline{FD} \cong \overline{BC}$	Given
4. $\overline{AB} \cong \overline{DE}$	Given
5. $\triangle ABC \cong \triangle EDF$	_____
6. _____	
7. $\overline{FE} \parallel \overline{AG}$	

Given: $\overline{BC} \parallel \overline{FG}$; $\overline{FD} \cong \overline{BC}$; $\overline{AB} \cong \overline{DE}$

Prove: $\overline{FE} \parallel \overline{AG}$

43. Which of the following justifies step 5 in the proof?

  a. AAS
  b. SSS
  c. ASA
  d. SAS

44. A triangle with vertices $A(-4, 2)$, $B(-1, 3)$, and $C(-5, 7)$ is reflected across $y = x + 2$ to give $\Delta A'B'C'$, which is subsequently reflected across the y-axis to give $\Delta A''B''C''$. Which of these statements is true?

    a.   A 90° rotation of ΔABC about $(-2,0)$ gives $\Delta A''B''C''$.
    b.   A reflection of ΔABC about the x-axis gives $\Delta A''B''C''$.
    c.   A 270° rotation of ΔABC about $(0,2)$ gives $\Delta A''B''C''$.
    d.   A translation of ΔABC two units down gives $\Delta A''B''C''$.

45. For the right triangle below, where $a \neq b$, which of the following is a true statement of equality?

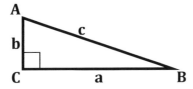

    a. $\tan B = \dfrac{a}{b}$
    b. $\cos B = \dfrac{b\sqrt{a^2+b^2}}{a^2+b^2}$
    c. $\sec B = \dfrac{\sqrt{a^2+b^2}}{a}$
    d. $\csc B = \dfrac{a^2+b^2}{b}$

46. Line segment $\overline{PQ}$ has endpoints $(-2, 1)$ and $(6, 1)$. If $\overline{P'Q'}$ is the translation of $\overline{PQ}$ along a diagonal line such that P' is located at point $(6, 3)$, what is the area of quadrilateral $PP'Q'Q$ in square units?

    a.   12
    b.   16
    c.   24
    d.   32

47. Given the figure and the following information, find DE to the nearest tenth.

    $\overline{AD}$ is an altitude of ΔABC
    $\overline{DE}$ is an altitude of triangle ΔADC
    $\overline{BD} \cong \overline{DC}$
    $\overline{AB} = 17; \overline{AD} = 8$

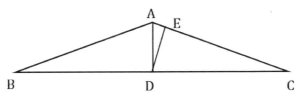

    a.   5.8
    b.   6.2
    c.   6.9
    d.   7.1

48. A target is made of concentric circles as shown below. The width of each band is a and the center is a circle with radius a. Which of the following gives the area A of the shaded region as a function of a?

    a. $A = 12\pi a^2$
    b. $A = 15\pi a^2$
    c. $A = 18\pi a^2$
    d. $A = 25\pi a^2$

49. A greenhouse is built in the shape of a square pyramid. Each of the sides of the square base measures x ft, and the height is y feet. If the height were increased by 4 ft, how much more interior space would the greenhouse have?

    a. $\frac{x^2y+4x^2}{3}$ ft^3
    b. $\frac{y(x^2+4)}{3}$ ft^3
    c. $\frac{4x^2}{3}$ ft^3
    d. 64 ft^3

Refer to the following for question 50:

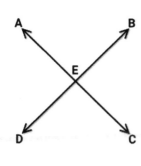

Statement	Reason
1. $\angle BEA \cong \angle DEA$	Given
2. $\angle BEA + \angle DEA = 180°$	Linear pair angles add up to 180°
3. _____	Substitution
4. $\angle BEA = 90°$	Algebra
5. $\overleftrightarrow{BD} \perp \overleftrightarrow{AC}$	_____

Given: $\angle BEA \cong \angle DEA$
Prove: $\overleftrightarrow{BD} \perp \overleftrightarrow{AC}$

50. Step 3 in the proof should contain which of the following statements?

a. $\angle BEA - \angle DEA = 0°$
b. $\angle BEA + \angle DEA = 2(90°)$
c. $2\angle BEA = 180°$
d. $\angle BEA = 180° - 90°$

51. What is the radius of the circle defined by the equation $x^2 + y^2 + 2x - 10y + 18 = 0$?

a. $2\sqrt{2}$
b. $2\sqrt{5}$
c. 4
d. $3\sqrt{2}$

52. If the midpoint of a line segment graphed on the xy-coordinate plane is $(1, -4)$ and the slope of the line segment is 3, which of these is a possible endpoint of the line segment?

a. $(-3, -16)$
b. $(2, -7)$
c. $(-1, 4)$
d. $(5, 9)$

53. Marcus is putting chicken wire around his rectangular garden. He decides to add cantaloupes to his garden so he needs to expand the size of the garden. He finds that by moving the boundary line back x feet on each of the four sides, he fences a rectangular space 34 yd^2 larger than the original plan and spends an extra \$36 on fencing, which costs \$1.50 per linear foot. How much does he spend?

a. \$145.50
b. \$171
c. \$352
d. \$223.50

Statistics and Probability

54. Which of these would best illustrate the percentage of a budget allocated to various departments?

    a. Pie chart
    b. Line graph
    c. Box-and-whisker plot
    d. Venn diagram

55. A random sample of 90 students at an elementary school were asked these three questions:

Do you like carrots?
Do you like broccoli?
Do you like cauliflower?

The results of the survey are shown below. If these data are representative of the population of students at the school, which of these is most probable?

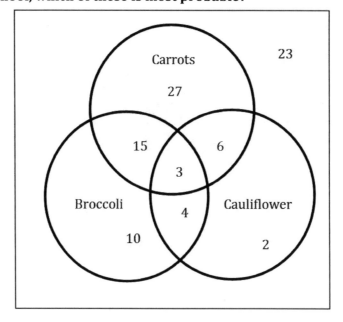

    a. A student chosen at random likes broccoli.
    b. If a student chosen at random likes carrots, they will also like at least one other vegetable.
    c. If a student chosen at random likes cauliflower and broccoli, they will also like carrots.
    d. A student chosen at random does not like carrots, broccoli, or cauliflower.

56. How many different seven-digit telephone numbers can be created in which no digit repeats and in which zero cannot be the first digit?

    a. 5,040
    b. 35,280
    c. 544,320
    d. 3,265,920

57. Which of these graphs is representative of the data set shown below?

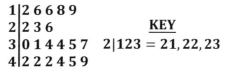

```
1|2 6 6 8 9
2|2 3 6              KEY
3|0 1 4 4 5 7    2|123 = 21, 22, 23
4|2 2 2 4 5 9
```

a.

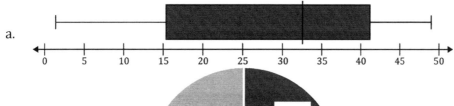

b.

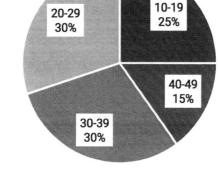

c.

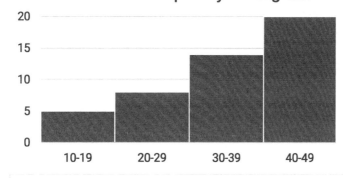

d.

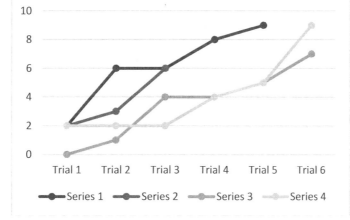

58. Which of these is the least biased sampling technique?

a. A PE teacher records the height of the entire girls' volleyball team to show that the average height of high school girls today is greater than it was 50 years ago.

b. A woman surveys her entire neighborhood for opinions on the new business coming to town.

c. A news website requests feedback via an anonymous online form.

d. A journalist calls the first 50 names on a randomly generated list of all voters in the county to request opinions on a politician.

Refer to the following for question 59:

This data shows the number of students at a high school who are enrolled in various electives.

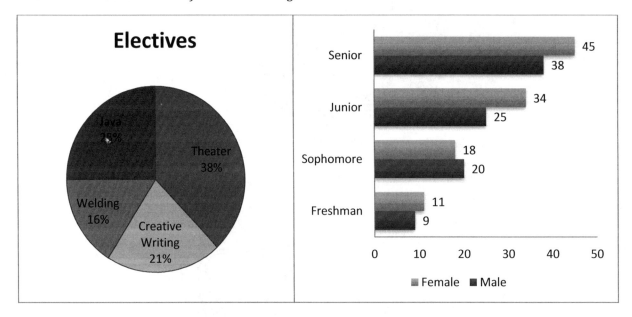

59. Which of these is the greatest quantity?

a. The number of students taking welding

b. The number of male sophomores taking an elective

c. The difference in the number of male and female students taking an elective

d. The difference in the number of 11th and 12th graders taking an elective

60. The high school honors program is offering three special electives: Biophysics, Intro to Law, and Latin. Seventeen students enrolled in Biophysics, twenty-two in Intro to Law, and nineteen in Latin. Two students are taking both Biophysics and Intro to Law, seven are taking both Intro to Law and Latin, and four are taking both Biophysics and Latin. One student enrolled in all three electives. How many students are taking special electives?

a. 46

b. 49

c. 55

d. 58

Refer to the following for question 61:

The box-and-whisker plot displays student test scores assessed throughout a semester to see if students were improving.

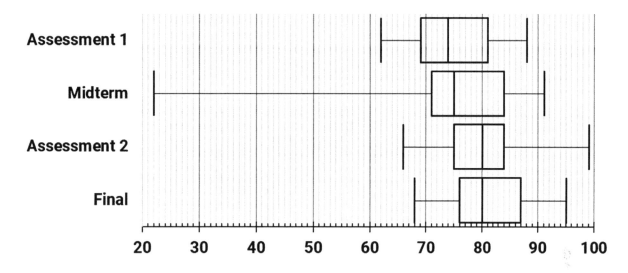

61. Which of the following statements is necessarily true of the data?
   a. The mean better reflects student performance at the Midterm than the median.
   b. The mean test score for assessment 2 and the final is the same.
   c. Assessment 1 had the highest median grade.
   d. The median test score is below the mean for Assessment 2.

Refer to the following for question 62:

For a science fair project, Paul wanted to find the probability of rolling an even number with a weighted die versus a fair die. He did fifty tests, rolling the die three times for each test and recording the number of even numbers that came up. The chart below shows his results.

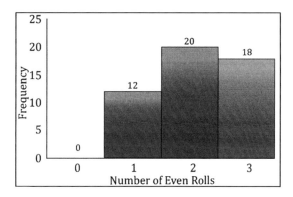

62. Given these experimental data, which of these approximates $P(\text{even})$ for a single roll of this die?
   a. 0.468
   b. 0.5
   c. 0.625
   d. 0.707

63. A random sample of 241 children ages 5 to 10 were asked these three questions:

Do you like baseball?
Do you like basketball?
Do you like football?

The results of the survey are shown below. If these data are representative of the population of students at the school, which of these is least probable?

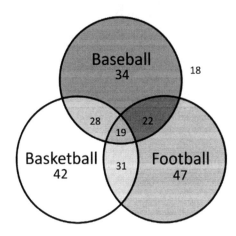

 a. A child chosen at random likes football.
 b. If a child chosen at random likes baseball, he also likes at least one other sport.
 c. If a child chosen at random likes baseball and basketball, he also likes football.
 d. A student chosen at random does not like baseball, basketball, or football.

64. Which of these would best illustrate the distribution of data across a range?

 a. Pie chart
 b. Line graph
 c. Box-and-whisker plot
 d. Venn diagram

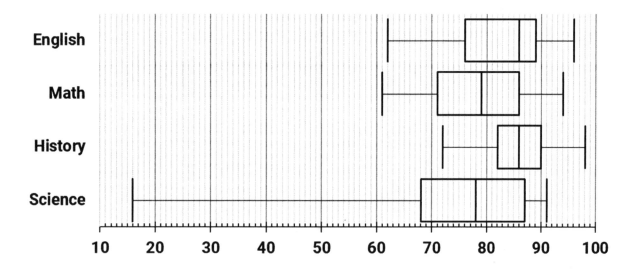

Refer to the following for questions 65 - 66:

The box-and-whisker plot displays a district's standardized test scores by subject.

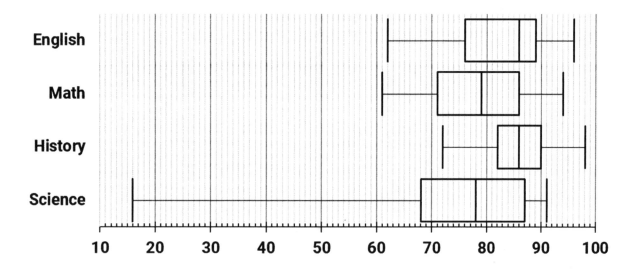

65. Which subject has the smallest range of test scores?

    a. English
    b. Math
    c. History
    d. Science

66. Which of the following statements is NOT true of the data?

    a. The median better reflects student performance in Science than the mean.
    b. The mean test score for English and history is the same.
    c. The median of the History scores is the same as the 3rd quartile score for Math.
    d. The median test score is above the mean for English.

Copyright © Mometrix Media. You have been licensed one copy of this document for personal use only. Any other reproduction or redistribution is strictly prohibited. All rights reserved.
This content is provided for test preparation purposes only and does not imply an endorsement by Mometrix of any particular political, scientific, or religious point of view.

Answer Key and Explanations

Number and Quantity

1. C: When you have a ratio, you can find the fraction that each part of the ratio is of the whole by putting it over the sum of the parts. In other words, since the ratio of wages and benefits to other costs is $2:3$, the amount of money spent on wages and benefits is $\frac{2}{2+3} = \frac{2}{5}$ of total expenditures.

$$\frac{2}{5} \times \$130,000 = \$52,000$$

2. A: The final sales price of the rug is:

$$1.08(0.7 \times \$296) = \$223.78 \text{ at Store A}$$
$$1.08(\$220 - \$10) = \$226.80 \text{ at Store B}$$
$$\$198 + \$35 = \$233 \text{ at Store C}$$

3. B: The notation $\mathbb{P} \subseteq \mathbb{N} \subseteq \mathbb{Z} \subseteq \mathbb{Q} \subseteq \mathbb{R} \subseteq \mathbb{C}$ means that the set of prime numbers is a subset of the set natural numbers, which is a subset of the set of integers, which is a subset of the set of rational numbers, which is a subset of the set real numbers, which is a subset of the set of complex numbers.

4. D: First, simplify the expression within the absolute value symbol.

$$|(2 - 3i)^2 - (1 - 4i)| = |4 - 12i + 9i^2 - 1 + 4i|$$
$$= |4 - 12i - 9 - 1 + 4i|$$
$$= |-6 - 8i|$$

The absolute value of a complex number is its distance from 0 on the complex plane. Use the Pythagorean theorem to find the distance of $-6 - 8i$ from the origin. Since the distance from the origin to the point $-6 - 8i$ is 10, $|-6 - 8i| = 10$.

5. C: The percentage of students taking java or creative writing is $25\% + 21\% = 46\%$. The percentage of male students taking an elective is $\frac{92}{200} \times 100\% = 46\%$. So the two quantities are equal.

6. D: If x is a positive, even integer and the greatest common factor of x and y is greater than 1, the greatest common factor of x and y must be at least as great as y. For example, if x is 2 and y is 4, the greatest common factor is 2 and the least common multiple is 4, which is equal to y. Or if x is 6 and y is 9, the greatest common factor is 3 and the least common multiple is 18, which is greater than y.

248

7. D: First, apply the laws of exponents to simplify the expression on the left. Then, add the two fractions:

$$\frac{(x^2y^{-3})(4xy)^2}{16x^4y^4} + \frac{3}{2xy} = \frac{(x^2y^{-3})(16x^2y^2)}{16x^4y^4} + \frac{3}{2xy}$$

$$= \frac{16x^4y^{-1}}{16x^4y^4} + \frac{3}{2xy}$$

$$= \frac{1}{y^5} + \frac{3}{2xy}$$

$$= \frac{1}{y^5} \times \frac{2x}{2x} + \frac{3}{2xy} \times \frac{y^4}{y^4}$$

$$= \frac{2x}{2xy^5} + \frac{3y^4}{2xy^5}$$

$$= \frac{2x + 3y^4}{2xy^5}$$

Algebra

8. C: Aaron ran four miles from home and then back again, so he ran a total of eight miles. Therefore, statement III is false. Statements I and II, however, are both true. Since Aaron ran eight miles in eighty minutes, he ran an average of one mile every ten minutes, or six miles per hour; he ran two miles from point A to B in 20 minutes and four miles from D to E in 40 minutes, so his running speed between both sets of points was the same.

9. D: Since a and b are even integers, each can be expressed as the product of 2 and an integer. So, if we write $a = 2x$ and $b = 2y$, $3(2x)^2 + 9(2y)^3 = c$.

$$3(4x^2) + 9(8y^3) = c$$
$$12x^2 + 72y^3 = c$$
$$12(x^2 + 6y^3) = c$$

Since c is the product of 12 and some other integer, 12 must be a factor of c. Incidentally, the numbers 2, 3, and 6 must also be factors of c since each is also a factor of 12.

10. A: First, set the equation equal to zero, then factor it.

$$3x^3y^2 - 45x^2y = 15x^3y - 9x^2y^2$$
$$3x^3y^2 - 15x^3y + 9x^2y^2 - 45x^2y = 0$$
$$3x^2y(xy - 5x + 3y - 15) = 0$$
$$3x^2y[x(y - 5) + 3(y - 5)] = 0$$
$$3x^2y[(y - 5)(x + 3)] = 0$$

Use the zero product property to find the solutions.

$$3x^2y = 0 \qquad y - 5 = 0 \qquad x + 3 = 0$$
$$x = 0 \qquad\qquad y = 5 \qquad\qquad x = -3$$
$$y = 0$$

So, the solutions are $x = \{0, -3\}$ and $y = \{0,5\}$.

11. C: When solving radical equations, check for extraneous solutions.

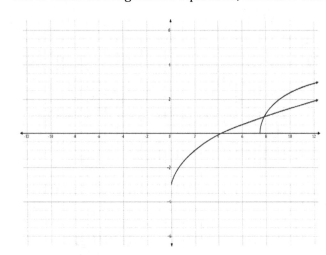

$$\sqrt{2x} - 3 = \sqrt{2x - 15}$$
$$\left(\sqrt{2x} - 3\right)^2 = \left(\sqrt{2x - 15}\right)^2$$
$$2x - 6\sqrt{2x} + 9 = 2x - 15$$
$$-6\sqrt{2x} = -24$$
$$\sqrt{2x} = 4$$
$$2x = 16$$
$$x = 8$$
$$\sqrt{16} - 3 = \sqrt{16 - 15}$$
$$4 - 3 = \sqrt{1}$$
$$1 = 1$$

Since the solution checks, it is a valid solution. Notice that the graphs $y = \sqrt{2x} - 3$ and $y = \sqrt{2x - 15}$ intersect, which confirms there is a solution.

12. B: Notice that choice A cannot be correct since $x \neq 2$. ($x = 2$ results in a zero in the denominator.)

$$\frac{x - 1}{x + 2} = \frac{6}{x + 2} - \frac{x - 3}{x - 2}$$
$$\frac{x - 7}{x + 2} = -\frac{x - 3}{x - 2}$$
$$(x - 7)(x - 2) = -(x - 3)(x + 2)$$
$$x^2 - 9x + 14 = -x^2 + x + 6$$
$$2x^2 - 10x + 8 = 0$$
$$2(x^2 - 5x + 4) = 0$$
$$2(x - 1)(x - 4) = 0$$
$$x = 1, 4$$

13. A: $n + 3p \leq 30$ where n is the number of notebooks and p is the number of boxes of pencils. The intercepts of this linear inequality are $n = 30$ and $p = 10$. The solid line through the two intercepts represents the maximum number of each item that may be purchased. All first-quadrant points below the line are also possible purchase amounts within Ben's budget.

14. D: One way to solve the equation is to write $x^4 + 9 = 10x^2$ in the quadratic form:

$$(x^2)^2 - 10(x^2) + 9 = 0$$

This trinomial can be factored as $(x^2 - 1)(x^2 - 9) = 0$. In each set of parentheses is a difference of squares, which can be factored further: $(x + 1)(x - 1)(x + 3)(x - 3) = 0$. Use the zero product property to find the solutions to the equation.

$$
\begin{array}{cccc}
x + 1 = 0 & x - 1 = 0 & x + 3 = 0 & x - 3 = 0 \\
x = -1 & x = 1 & x = -3 & x = 3
\end{array}
$$

15. B: Test each of the options:

$$
\begin{array}{llll}
9 \geq 1 + 2(x + 3) \geq 5 & -x^2 + 4 + 3x^2 \leq 3x^2 + 3 & \dfrac{12 - |6x|}{2} \geq 3 & 2|2x| + 4 \leq 8 \\
8 \geq 2(x + 3) \geq 4 & 2x^2 + 4 \leq 3x^2 + 3 & 12 - |6x| \geq 6 & 2|2x| \leq 4 \\
4 \geq x + 3 \geq 2 & 1 \leq x^2 & -|6x| \geq -6 & |2x| \leq 2 \\
1 \geq x \geq -1 & x^2 \geq 1 & |6x| \leq 6 & -2 \leq 2x \leq 2 \\
-1 \leq x \leq 1 & x \geq 1, x \leq -1 & -6 \leq 6x \leq 6 & -1 \leq x \leq 1 \\
 & & -1 \leq x \leq 1 &
\end{array}
$$

16. A: The graph below shows that the lines are parallel and that the shaded regions do not overlap. There is no solution to the set of inequalities given in Choice A.

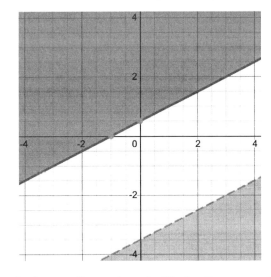

$$x - 2y > 7$$
$$-2y > -x + 7$$
$$y < \frac{1}{2}x - \frac{7}{2}$$
$$3x \leq -3 + 6y$$
$$6y \geq 3x + 3$$
$$y \geq \frac{1}{2}x + \frac{1}{2}$$

As in Choice A, the two lines given in Choice B are parallel; however, the shading overlaps between the lines, so that region represents the solution to the system of inequalities.

Choices C and D contains sets of inequalities that have intersecting shaded regions; the intersections represent the solutions to the systems of inequalities.

17. D: A system of linear equations can be solved by using matrices or by using the graphing, substitution, or elimination (also called linear combination) method. The elimination method is shown here:

$$-4x + 3y = 8$$
$$6x - 2y = -7$$

In order to eliminate y by linear combination, multiply the top equation by 2 and the bottom equation by 3 so that the coefficients of the y-terms will be additive inverses.

$$2(-4x + 3y) = (8)2 \qquad\qquad 3(6x - 2y) = (-7)(3)$$
$$-8x + 6y = 16 \qquad\qquad 18x - 6y = -21$$

Then, add the two equations and solve for x.

$$
\begin{array}{rrrr}
-8x & +6y & = & 16 \\
+ \quad 18x & -6y & = & -21 \\
\hline
10x & & = & -5 \\
x & & = & -\dfrac{1}{2}
\end{array}
$$

Substitute $-\frac{1}{2}$ for x in either of the given equations and solve for y.

$$-4\left(-\frac{1}{2}\right) + 3y = 8$$
$$2 + 3y = 8$$
$$3y = 6$$
$$y = 2$$

The solution to the system of equations is $\left(-\frac{1}{2}, 2\right)$.

18. A: The vertex form of a quadratic equation is $y = a(x - h)^2 + k$, where $x = h$ is the parabola's axis of symmetry and (h, k) is the parabola's vertex. The vertex of the graph is $(-2, -1)$, so the equation can be written as $y = a(x + 2)^2 - 1$. The parabola passes through point $(0,3)$, so $3 = a(0 + 2)^2 - 1$. Solve for a:

$$3 = a(0 + 2)^2 - 1$$
$$3 = a(2)^2 - 1$$
$$3 = 4a - 1$$
$$4 = 4a$$
$$1 = a$$

So, the vertex form of the parabola is $y = (x + 2)^2 - 1$. Write the equation in the form $y = ax^2 + bx + c$.

$$y = (x + 2)^2 - 1$$
$$y = (x^2 + 4x + 4) - 1$$
$$y = x^2 + 4x + 3$$

19. D: Get as many terms as possible out from the radical and any radicals out from the denominator:

$$\sqrt{\frac{-54x^5}{80y^6}} = \sqrt{\frac{-9x^4 \times (6x)}{16y^6 \times (5)}}$$

$$= \sqrt{\frac{-(3x^2)^2 \times (6x)}{(4y^3)^2 \times (5)}}$$

$$= \frac{3x^2\sqrt{6x}i}{4y^3\sqrt{5}} \times \frac{\sqrt{5}}{\sqrt{5}}$$

$$= \frac{3x^2\sqrt{30x}i}{20y^3}$$

20. D: The expression representing the monthly charge for Plan A is $\$20 + \$15(d - 2.5)$, where d is the data used. Set this expression equal to the monthly charge for Plan B, which is $50. Solve for d to find the number of GB for which the two plans charge the same amount:

$$\$20 + \$15(d - 2.5) = \$50$$
$$\$15(d - 2.5) = \$30$$
$$d - 2.5 = 2$$
$$d = 4.5$$

So the plans have the same cost when Gillian uses 4.5 GB of data.

Functions

21. A: In the range $(-\infty, -1)$, the graph represented is $y = x^2$. In the range $[-1, 2)$, the graph is the greatest integer function, $y = [\![x]\!]$. In the range $[2, \infty)$, the graph is $y = -2x + 6$.

22. A: An easy way to determine which is the graph of $f(x) = -2|-x + 4| - 1$ is to find $f(x)$ for a few values of x. For example, $f(0) = -2|0 + 4| - 1 = -9$. Graphs A and B pass through $(0, -9)$, but graphs C and D do not. $f(4) = -2|-4 + 4| - 1 = -1$. Graphs A and D pass through $(4, -1)$, but graphs B and C do not. Graph A is the correct graph.

23. C: Use trigonometric equalities and identities to simplify.

$$\cos\theta \cot\theta = \cos\theta \times \frac{\cos\theta}{\sin\theta} = \frac{\cos^2\theta}{\sin\theta} = \frac{1 - \sin^2\theta}{\sin\theta} = \frac{1}{\sin\theta} - \sin\theta = \csc\theta - \sin\theta$$

24. A: An easy way to determine which is the graph of $f(x) = -3|-x + 2| + 1$ is to find $f(x)$ for a few values of x. For example, $f(0) = -3|0 + 2| + 1 = -5$. Graphs A and C pass through $(0, -5)$, but graphs B and D do not. $f(2) = -3|-2 + 2| + 1 = 1$. Graphs A and D pass through $(2,1)$, but graphs B and C do not. Graph A is the correct graph.

25. C: First, use the table to determine the values of $(w * y)$ and $(x * x)$:

$*$	w	x	y	z
w	w	x	y	z
x	z	w	x	y
y	y	z	w	x
z	x	y	z	w

Since $(w * y) = y$ and $(x * x) = w$, that means $(w * y) * (x * x) = y * w$, which is equal to y.

26. C: The two functions that combine to form $g(x)$ meet at $x = 2$. The slope is positive to the left of $x = 2$, rising to the intersection point $(2,2)$. The slope is negative to the right of $x = 2$. Thus, while the domain of $g(x)$ is all real numbers (because there is a solution for every possible x-value), the range is $y \leq 2$. We can find the solution when $x = 1$ by plugging 1 into the bottom equation, since 1 is less than 2. If $g(x) = x$ and $x = 1$, then $g(x) = 1$. So statements I and II are true, while statement III is false.

27. B: By definition, when $f(x)$ and $g(x)$ are inverse functions, $f(g(x)) = g(f(x)) = x$. So, $f\left(g\left(\frac{1}{8}\right)\right) = x = \frac{1}{8}$.

28. D: When $y = \frac{1}{x}$, $x = \frac{1}{y}$. Similarly, when $y = x^2$, $x = \sqrt{y}$ for $y > 0$. On the other hand, when $y = x^2$, $x = \pm\sqrt{y}$; when $y = e^x$, $x = \ln y$ for $y > 0$; and when $y = x$, $x = y$.

29. C: Choice C is the absolute value function. A function is a relationship in which for every element of the domain (x), there is exactly one element of the range (y). Graphically, a relationship between x and y can be identified as a function if the graph passes the vertical line test.

The first relation is a parabola on its side, which fails the vertical line test for functions. Choice B also fails the vertical line test and is therefore not a function. The relation in Choice D pairs two elements of the range with one of the elements of the domain, so it is also not a function.

30. D: First, state the exclusions of the domain.

$$x^3 - 7x + 6 \neq 0$$
$$(x + 3)(x - 1)(x - 2) \neq 0$$
$$x + 3 \neq 0 \quad x - 1 \neq 0 \quad x - 2 \neq 0$$
$$x \neq -3 \quad x \neq 1 \quad x \neq 2$$

To determine whether there are asymptotes or holes at these values of x, simplify the expression:

$$\frac{x^2 - x - 2}{x^3 - 7x + 6} = \frac{(x - 2)(x + 1)}{(x + 3)(x - 1)(x - 2)} = \frac{x + 1}{(x + 3)(x - 1)}$$

There are asymptotes at $x = 1$ and at $x = -3$ and a hole at $x = 2$. Statement I is false.

To find the x-intercept of $f(x)$, solve $f(x) = 0$. $f(x) = 0$ when the numerator is equal to zero. The numerator equals zero when $x = 2$ and $x = -1$; however, 2 is excluded from the domain of $f(x)$, so the x-intercept is –1. To find the y-intercept of $f(x)$, find $f(0)$.

$$\frac{0^2 - 0 - 2}{0^3 - 7(0) + 6} = \frac{-2}{6} = -\frac{1}{3}$$

The y-intercept is $-\frac{1}{3}$, but the x-intercept is not $-\frac{1}{3}$. Statement II is false.

31. D: The x-intercept is the point at which $f(x) = 0$. When $0 = \log_b x$, $b^0 = x$; since $b^0 = 1$, the x-intercept of $f(x) = \log_b x$ is always 1. If $f(x) = \log_b x$ and $x = b$, then $f(x) = \log_b b$, which is, by definition, 1 ($b^1 = b$). The statement $f(x) < 0$ is true only for x values between 0 and 1 ($0 < x < 1$). If $g(x) = b^x$ (not x^b), then $f(x)$ and $g(x)$ are inverse functions and are therefore symmetric with respect to $y = x$.

32. C: The recursive definition of the sequence gives the first term of the series, $a_1 = -2$. The definition also defines each term in the series as the sum of the previous term and $\frac{1}{2}$. Therefore, the second term in the series is $-2 + \frac{1}{2} = -\frac{3}{2}$, the third term in the series is $-\frac{3}{2} + \frac{1}{2} = -1$, and so on.

n	a_n
1	-2
2	$-\frac{3}{2}$
3	-1

The relationship between n and a_n is linear, so the equation of the sequence can be found in the same way as the equation of a line. The value of a_n increases by $\frac{1}{2}$ each time the value of n increases by 1.

n	$\frac{n}{2}$	a_n
1	$\frac{1}{2}$	-2
2	1	$-\frac{3}{2}$
3	$\frac{3}{2}$	-1

Since the difference in $\frac{1}{2}n$ and a_n is $-\frac{5}{2}$, $a_n = \frac{1}{2}n - \frac{5}{2}$.

n	$\dfrac{n}{2} - \dfrac{5}{2}$	a_n
1	$\dfrac{1}{2} - \dfrac{5}{2}$	-2
2	$1 - \dfrac{5}{2}$	$-\dfrac{3}{2}$
3	$\dfrac{3}{2} - \dfrac{5}{2}$	-1

33. A: By definition, when $f(x)$ and $g(x)$ are inverse functions, $f(g(x)) = g(f(x)) = x$. So, $f\big(g(4)\big) = b = -6$.

Calculus

34. C: The slope of the line tangent to the graph of a function f at $x = a$ is $f'(a)$. Since $f(x) = \frac{1}{4}x^2 - 3$, $f'(x) = 2\left(\frac{1}{4}\right)x^{(2-1)} - 0 = \frac{1}{2}x$. So, the slope at $x = 2$ is $f'(2) = \frac{1}{2}(2) = 1$.

35. A: If $\lim\limits_{x \to a^+} f(x) = \lim\limits_{x \to a^-} f(x)$, then $\lim\limits_{x \to a^+} f(x) = \lim\limits_{x \to a^-} f(x) = \lim\limits_{x \to a} f(x)$. Otherwise, $\lim\limits_{x \to a} f(x)$ does not exist. If $\lim\limits_{x \to a} f(x)$ exists, and if $\lim\limits_{x \to a} f(x) = f(a)$, then the function is continuous at a. Otherwise, f is discontinuous at a.

36. D: The velocity v of the ball at any time t is the slope of the line tangent to the graph of h at time t. The slope of a line tangent to the curve $h = -16t^2 + 50t + 3$ is the same as h'.

$$h' = v = -32t + 50$$

When $t = 2$, the velocity of the ball is $-32(2) + 50 = -14$. The velocity is negative because the slope of the tangent line at $t = 2$ is negative; velocity has both magnitude and direction, so a velocity of -14 means that the velocity is 14 ft/s downward.

37. B: The area under curve $f(x)$ is $\int_1^2 \frac{1}{x} dx = [\ln x + C]_1^2 = [\ln(2) + C] - [\ln(1) + C] \approx 0.69$.

38. A: $\int 3x^2 + 2x - 1\, dx = \frac{3}{2+1}x^{(2+1)} + \frac{2}{1+1}x^{(1+1)} - x + C = x^3 + x^2 - x + C$

39. B: Find the points of intersection of the two graphs:

$$x^2 - 4 = -x + 2$$
$$x^2 + x - 6 = 0$$
$$(x + 3)(x - 2) = 0$$
$$x = -3, x = 2$$

So, the area is between the graphs on $[-3, 2]$. To determine which of the graphs is the upper or lower bound, pick a test point in the interval. Using $x = 0$ as the test point:

$$y = 0^2 - 4 \qquad y = -0 + 2$$
$$y = -4 \qquad\quad y = 2$$

The finite region is bound at the top by the line $y = -x + 2$ and at the bottom by $y = x^2 - 4$, and the height of the region at point x is defined by $[(-x + 2) - (x^2 - 4)]$, so the area of the region is:

$$A = \int_{-3}^{2} [(-x + 2) - (x^2 - 4)]dx$$

$$= \int_{-3}^{2} (-x^2 - x + 6)\, dx$$

$$= \left[-\frac{1}{3}x^3 - \frac{1}{2}x^2 + 6x + C \right]_{-3}^{2}$$

$$= \left[-\frac{1}{3}(2)^3 - \frac{1}{2}(2)^2 + 6(2) + C \right] - \left[-\frac{1}{3}(-3)^3 - \frac{1}{2}(-3)^2 + 6(-3) + C \right]$$

$$= \left[-\frac{8}{3} - 2 + 12 \right] - \left[9 - \frac{9}{2} - 18 \right]$$

$$= \frac{22}{3} - \left(-\frac{27}{2} \right)$$

$$= \frac{125}{6}$$

40. C: To evaluate the limit, divide the numerator and denominator by x^2 and use these properties of limits: $\lim\limits_{x \to \infty} \frac{1}{x} = 0$; the limit of a sum of terms is the sum of the limits of the terms; and the limit of a product of terms is the product of the limits of the terms.

$$\lim_{x \to \infty} \frac{x^2 - x + 3}{3x^2 + 1} = \lim_{x \to \infty} \frac{\frac{x^2}{x^2} - \frac{x}{x^2} + \frac{3}{x^2}}{\frac{3x^2}{x^2} + \frac{1}{x^2}} = \lim_{x \to \infty} \frac{1 - \frac{1}{x} + \frac{3}{x^2}}{3 + \frac{1}{x^2}} = \frac{1 + 0 - 0}{3 + 0} = \frac{1}{3}$$

Geometry

41. C: One strategy is to consider a progression of polygons with fewer sides and look for a pattern in the number of the polygons' diagonals.

Polygon	Sides	Diagonals	Additional Diagonals
(triangle)	3	0	-
(square)	4	2	2
(pentagon)	5	5	3
(hexagon)	6	9	4

A quadrilateral has two more diagonals than a triangle, a pentagon has three more diagonals than a quadrilateral, and a hexagon has four more diagonals than a pentagon. Continue this pattern to find that a dodecagon has 54 diagonals.

42. B: If the touching edges of the trapezoids are extended, they meet at a point on the horizontal. Using this information and the following geometric relationships, solve for x:

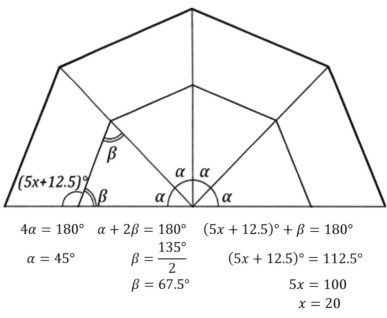

$$4\alpha = 180° \quad \alpha + 2\beta = 180° \quad (5x + 12.5)° + \beta = 180°$$
$$\alpha = 45° \quad \beta = \frac{135°}{2} \quad (5x + 12.5)° = 112.5°$$
$$\beta = 67.5° \quad 5x = 100$$
$$x = 20$$

43. D. Since it is given that $\overline{FD} \cong \overline{BC}$ and $\overline{AB} \cong \overline{DE}$, step 2 needs to establish either that $\overline{AC} \cong \overline{EF}$ or that $\Delta ABC \cong \Delta FDE$ in order for step 5 to show that $\Delta ABC \cong \Delta EDF$. The statement $\overline{AC} \cong \overline{EF}$ cannot be shown directly from the given information. On the other hand, $\Delta ABC \cong \Delta FDE$ can be determined: when two parallel lines $\overline{BC} \parallel \overline{FG}$ are cut by a transversal ($\overline{AE}$), alternate exterior angles ($\Delta ABC, \Delta FDE$) are congruent. Therefore, $\Delta ABC \cong \Delta EDF$ by the side-angle-side (SAS) theorem.

44. C: When a figure is reflected twice over non-parallel lines, the resulting transformation is a rotation about the point of intersection of the two lines of reflection. The two lines of reflection $y = x + 2$ and $x = 0$ intersect at $(0,2)$. So, $\Delta A''B''C''$ represents a rotation of ΔABC about the point $(0,2)$. The angle of rotation is equal to twice the angle between the two lines of reflection when measured in a clockwise direction from the first to the second line of reflection. Since the angle between the lines or reflection measures 135°, the angle of rotation which is the composition of the two reflections measures 270°. All of these properties can be visualized by drawing $\triangle ABC$, $\triangle A'B'C'$, and $\triangle A''B''C''$.

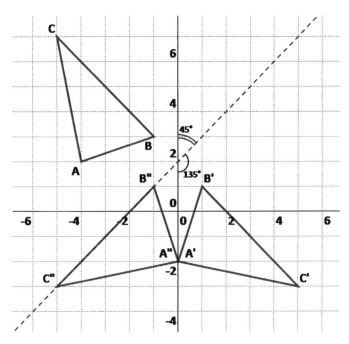

45. C: Determine the veracity of each option given that the hypotenuse of a right triangle is equal to the square root of the sum of the squares of the legs or $c = \sqrt{a^2 + b^2}$:

a. $\tan B = ? \dfrac{a}{b}$

$$\tan B = \frac{\text{opposite}}{\text{adjacent}} = \frac{b}{a} \neq \frac{a}{b}$$

b. $\cos B = ? \dfrac{b\sqrt{a^2+b^2}}{a^2+b^2} = \dfrac{bc}{c^2}$

$$\cos B = \frac{\text{adjacent}}{\text{hypotenuse}} = \frac{a}{\sqrt{a^2+b^2}} = \frac{a}{\sqrt{a^2+b^2}} \times \frac{\sqrt{a^2+b^2}}{\sqrt{a^2+b^2}}$$

$$= \frac{a\sqrt{a^2+b^2}}{a^2+b^2} \neq \frac{b\sqrt{a^2+b^2}}{a^2+b^2}$$

c. $\sec B = ? \dfrac{\sqrt{a^2+b^2}}{a} = \dfrac{c}{a}$

$$\sec B = \frac{\text{hypotenuse}}{\text{adjacent}} = \frac{\sqrt{a^2+b^2}}{a}$$

d. $\csc B = ? \dfrac{a^2+b^2}{b}$

$$\csc B = \frac{\text{hypotenuse}}{\text{opposite}} = \frac{\sqrt{a^2+b^2}}{b} \neq \frac{a^2+b^2}{b}$$

46. B: Since the y-coordinates of points P and Q are the same, line segment $\overline{PQ}$ is a horizontal line segment whose length is the difference in the x-coordinates; $PQ = |6 - (-2)| = 8$. Since the x-coordinates of Q and Q' are the same, line segment $\overline{P'Q}$ is a vertical line segment whose length is $|3 - 1| = 2$. The quadrilateral formed by the transformation of $\overline{PQ}$ to $\overline{P'Q'}$ is a parallelogram. If the base of the parallelogram is $\overline{PQ}$, then the height is $\overline{P'Q}$ since $\overline{PQ} \perp \overline{P'Q}$. For a parallelogram, $A = bh$, so $A = 8 \times 2 = 16$.

47. D: $\triangle ADC$ is a right triangle with legs measuring 8 and 15 and a hypotenuse of 17. (8–15–17 is a Pythagorean triple.) $\triangle ADC$ and $\triangle DEC$ are both right triangles which share vertex C. By the AA similarity theorem, $\triangle ADC \sim \triangle DEC$. Therefore, a proportion can be written and solved to find DE.

$$\frac{8}{DE} = \frac{17}{15}$$
$$DE \approx 7.1$$

48. B: We can find the area of the shaded part by viewing the target as five separate circles of various sizes, one inside the other. We add the areas of the three shaded circles and subtract the areas of the two white circles. The area of a circle is πr^2, so the area of the largest circle (the entire target) is $\pi(5a)^2$. We subtract the white circle inside it, add the shaded circle inside that one, and so on:

$$A = \pi(5a)^2 - \pi(4a)^2 + \pi(3a)^2 - \pi(2a)^2 + \pi(a)^2$$
$$= 25\pi a^2 - 16\pi a^2 + 9\pi a^2 - 4\pi a^2 + \pi a^2$$
$$= (25 - 16 + 9 - 4 + 1)\pi a^2$$
$$= 15\pi a^2$$

49. C: The volume of the greenhouse is $\frac{x^2 y}{3}$. If the height were increased by 4 ft, the volume would be $\frac{x^2(y+4)}{3} = \frac{x^2 y + 4x^2}{3}$. Notice this is the volume of the greenhouse, $\frac{x^2 y}{3}$, increased by $\frac{4x^2}{3}$.

50. C: Since it is established that $\angle BEA \cong \angle DEA$, we can substitute $\angle BEA$ for $\angle DEA$ in the equation from Step 2.

51. A: The equation of the circle is given in general form. When the equation is written in the standard form $(x - h)^2 + (y - k)^2 = r^2$, where (h, k) is the center of the circle and r is the radius of the circle, the radius is easy to determine. Putting the equation into standard form requires completing the square for x and y:

$$x^2 + y^2 + 2x - 10y = -18$$
$$(x^2 + 2x + 1) + (y^2 - 10y + 25) = -18 + 1 + 25$$
$$(x + 1)^2 + (y - 5)^2 = 8$$

Since $r^2 = 8$, and since r must be a positive number, $r = \sqrt{8} = 2\sqrt{2}$.

52. A: The point $(-3, -16)$ lies on the line that has a slope of 3 and that passes through $(1, -4)$. If $(-3, -16)$ is one of the endpoints of the line, the other would be $(5, 8)$.

53. B: If l and w represent the length and width of the enclosed area, its perimeter is equal to $2l + 2w$; since the fence is positioned x feet from the lot's edges on each side, the perimeter of the enlarged garden is $2(l + 2x) + 2(w + 2x)$. Since the extra amount of money spent by fencing the larger area is $36, and since the fencing material costs $1.50 per linear foot, 24 more feet of material are used to fence around the garden than would have been used for the original. This can be expressed as the equation:

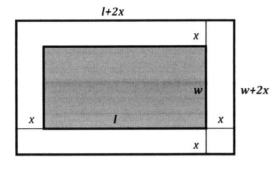

$$2(l + 2x) + 2(w + 2x) - (2l + 2w) = 24$$
$$2l + 4x + 2w + 4x - 2l - 2w = 24$$
$$8x = 24$$
$$x = 3 \text{ ft}$$

The difference in the area of the lot and the enclosed space is 34 yd², which is the same as 306 ft². So, $(l + 2x)(w + 2x) - lw = 306$. Substituting 3 for x,

$$(l + 6)(w + 6) - lw = 306$$
$$lw + 6l + 6w + 36 - lw = 306$$
$$6l + 6w = 270$$
$$6(l + w) = 270$$
$$l + w = 45 \text{ ft}$$

This is the original length and width, so we add 6 to each, or 12 total, for a new length and width of $l + w = 57$ ft. Therefore, the perimeter of the enclosed space, $2(l + w)$, is $2(57) = 114$ ft. The cost of 114 ft of chicken wire is $114 \times \$1.50 = \$171$.

Statistics and Probability

54. A: A pie chart shows the relationship of parts to a whole. A line graph is often used to show change over time. A box-and-whisker plot displays how numeric data are distributed throughout the range. A Venn diagram shows the relationships among sets.

55. B: Determine the probability of each option (if b = likes broccoli, c = likes carrots, and f = likes cauliflower).

For choice A, this is the total number of students in the broccoli circle of the Venn diagram divided by the total number of students surveyed:

$$P(b) = \frac{10 + 4 + 3 + 15}{90} = \frac{32}{90} \approx 35.6\%$$

For choice B, this is the total number of students in the carrots circle and also in at least one other circle divided by the total number in the carrots circle:

$$P(b \cup f | c) = \frac{15 + 3 + 6}{15 + 3 + 6 + 27} = \frac{24}{51} \approx 47.1\%$$

For choice C, this is the number of students in the intersection of all three circles divided by the total number in the overlap of the broccoli and cauliflower circles:

$$P(c | b \cap f) = \frac{3}{3 + 4} = \frac{3}{7} \approx 42.9\%$$

For choice D, this is the number of students outside of all the circles divided by the total number of students surveyed:

$$P([c \cup b \cup f]') = \frac{23}{90} \approx 25.6\%$$

56. C: There are nine ways to assign the first digit since it can be any of the numbers 1–9. There are nine ways to assign the second digit since it can be any digit 0–9 EXCEPT for the digit assigned in place 1. There are eight ways to assign the third number since there are ten digits, two of which have already been assigned. There are seven ways to assign the fourth number, six ways to assign the fifth, five ways to assign the sixth, and four ways to assign the seventh. So, the number of combinations is $9 \times 9 \times 8 \times 7 \times 6 \times 5 \times 4 = 544{,}320$.

Another way to approach the problem is to notice that the arrangement of nine digits in the last six places is a sequence without repetition, or a permutation. (Note: this may be called a partial permutation since all of the elements of the set need not be used.) The number of possible sequences of a fixed length r of elements taken from a given set of size n is permutation $_nP_r = \frac{n!}{(n-r)!}$. So, the number of ways to arrange the last six digits is $_9P_6 = \frac{9!}{(9-6)!} = \frac{9!}{3!} = 60{,}480$. Multiply this number by nine since there are nine possibilities for the first digit of the phone number. $_9P_6 \times 9 = 544{,}320$.

57. C: To draw a box-and-whisker plot from the data, find the median, quartiles, and upper and lower limits. The median is $\frac{31+34}{2} = 32.5$, the lower quartile is $\frac{19+22}{2} = 20.5$, and the upper quartile is $\frac{42+42}{2} = 42$. The box of the box-and-whisker plot goes through the quartiles, and a line through the box represents the median of the data. The whiskers extend from the box to the lower and upper limits, unless there are any outliers in the set. In the box-and-whisker plot in choice A, the lower limit and first quartile are much too low, so choice A is **not** representative of the data from the stem and leaf plot.

To draw a pie chart, find the percentage of data contained in each of the ranges shown. There are 5 out of 20 numbers between 10 and 19, inclusive, so the percentage shown in the pie chart for that range of data is $\frac{5}{20} \times 100\% = 25\%$; there are 3 values between 20 and 29, inclusive, so the percentage of data for that sector is $\frac{3}{20} \times 100\% = 15\%$; $\frac{6}{20} \times 100\% = 30\%$ of the data is within the range of 30–39, and $\frac{6}{20} \times 100\% = 30\%$ is within the range of 40–49. The pie chart in choice B reverses the percentages for the 20-29 and 40-49 age categories.

To draw a cumulative frequency histogram, find the cumulative frequency of the data.

Range	Frequency	Cumulative Frequency
10–19	5	5
20–29	3	8
30–39	6	14
40–49	6	20

The histogram shows the correct cumulative frequencies.

262

The data points in the line graph in choice D do not correspond to the data points given for the question.

58. D: In choice A, the teacher uses convenience sampling, which is a biased technique. A group of athletes is likely not representative of all high school girls. Choice B also represents convenience sampling, as all surveys were taken from the same neighborhood. While this likely included a variety of ages, career paths, etc., it most likely represented a narrow demographic since homes in a neighborhood tend to be similar in value. Choice C is biased because the participants are self-selected rather than randomly selected. It may be that people who have a strong opinion are more likely to respond than those who are more neutral, and this would give a skewed perspective of opinions. Choice D represents random selection since names are organized by computer generation rather than any particular demographic.

59. A: The total number of students taking electives is 200, as seen in the chart on the right, and 16% of these are taking welding, so the number of students taking welding is $0.16(200) = 32$. The number of male sophomores taking an elective is 20. The difference in the number of male and female students taking an elective is $108 - 92 = 16$, and the difference in the number of 11th and 12th grade students taking an elective is $83 - 59 = 24$. The greatest quantity of these is 32, the number of students taking welding.

60. A: Use a Venn diagram to help organize the given information. Start by filling in the space where the three circles intersect: one student enrolled in all three areas. Use that information to fill in the spaces where two circles intersect: for example, seven students are taking both Intro to Law and Latin, and one of those is also taking Biophysics, so six students are taking Intro to Law and Latin but not Biophysics. Once the diagram is completed, add the number of students from each portion of the diagram. The total number of students taking special electives is $12 + 14 + 9 + 3 + 1 + 6 + 1 = 46$.

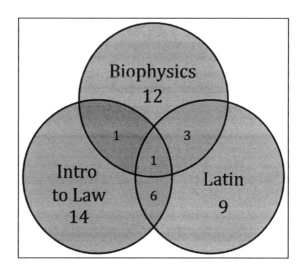

61. D: The box plot for Assessment 2 is skewed to the right, which means that the mean is above the median.

62. D: We count the number of evens that were rolled, divided by the number of total rolls, to find the probability: $\frac{0+12+20(2)+18(3)}{50(3)} = \frac{106}{150} = \frac{53}{75}$ or 0.707.

63. D: Determine the probability of each option (if s = likes baseball, b = likes basketball, and f = likes football).

For choice A, this is the total number of students in the football circle of the Venn diagram divided by the total number of students surveyed:

$$P(f) = \frac{47 + 22 + 19 + 31}{241} = \frac{119}{241} \approx 49.4\%$$

For choice B, this is the total number of students in the baseball circle and also in at least one other circle divided by the total number in the baseball circle:

$$P(s \cup f|b) = \frac{28 + 19 + 22}{28 + 19 + 22 + 34} = \frac{69}{103} \approx 67.0\%$$

For choice C, this is the number of students in the intersection of all three circles divided by the total number in the overlap of the baseball and basketball circles:

$$P(s|b \cap f) = \frac{19}{19 + 28} = \frac{19}{47} \approx 40.4\%$$

For choice D, this is the number of students outside of all the circles divided by the total number of students surveyed:

$$P([c \cup b \cup f]') = \frac{18}{241} \approx 7.5\%$$

Since Choice D has the lowest probability, it is the correct answer.

64. C: A pie chart shows the relationship of parts to a whole. A line graph is often used to show change over time. A box-and-whisker plot displays how numeric data are distributed throughout the range. A Venn diagram shows the relationships among sets.

65. C: The range is the spread of the data. It can be calculated for each subject by subtracting the lowest test score from the highest, or it can be determined visually from the graph. The difference between the highest and lowest test scores in History is $98 - 72 = 26$ points. The range for each of the other subjects is greater.

66. B: The line through the center of the box represents the median. The median test score for English and History is the same.

Note that for Science, the median is a better representation of the data than the mean. There is at least one outlier (a point that lies outside of two standard deviations from the mean), which brings down the average test score. In cases such as this, the mean is not the best measure of central tendency.

Praxis Practice Test #3

Number and Quantity

1. A dress is marked down by 20% and placed on a clearance rack, on which is posted a sign reading, "Take an extra 25% off already reduced merchandise." What fraction of the original price is the final sale price of the dress?

- a. $\frac{9}{20}$
- b. $\frac{11}{20}$
- c. $\frac{2}{5}$
- d. $\frac{3}{5}$

2. In a town of 35,638 people, about a quarter of the population is under the age of 35. Of those, just over a third attend local K-12 schools. If the number of students in each grade is about the same, how many fourth graders likely reside in the town?

- a. Fewer than 100
- b. Between 200 and 300
- c. Between 300 and 400
- d. More than 400

3. Which of the following expressions is equivalent to $\frac{2+3i}{4-2i}$?

- a. $\frac{1}{10} + \frac{4}{5}i$
- b. $\frac{1}{10}$
- c. $\frac{7}{6} + \frac{2}{3}i$
- d. $\frac{1}{10} + \frac{3}{10}i$

4. Simplify $\frac{(x^3y)(3x^{-1}y)^2}{6x^3y} - \frac{2}{xy}$.

- a. $\frac{9x^3y^2-2xy}{6x^3y}$
- b. $\frac{x+6y^6}{2x^2y}$
- c. $\frac{3y^3-4x}{2x^2y}$
- d. $\frac{x+6y^5}{2xy^6}$

5. The ratio of new car sales to used car sales at the car lot is $3:5$. If the total car sales were $287,400 last month, what was the total of the used car sales?

6. Jen sells honey from her beehive through two local grocery stores, as well as offering it online. The two local stores (Store A and Store B) charge $10.50 and $11.00 per pint, respectively. Jen receives 80% of the revenue from the local stores. She charges $6.75 per pint plus a $2.50 shipping fee for online shoppers (Store C). During a holiday, Store A offers a sale price of 25% off. Store B offers a coupon for $1.50 off. Jen offers a deal for free shipping. Which of the following lists the stores in order from lowest revenue to highest revenue that Jen receives during the holiday sale after all discounts and fees are applied?

    a. Store A, Store C, Store B
    b. Store B, Store C, Store A
    c. Store C, Store A, Store B
    d. Store C, Store B, Store A

Refer to the following for question 7:

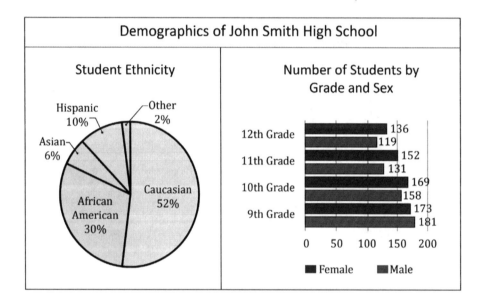

7. Compare the two quantities.

Quantity A	Quantity B
The percentage of Caucasian students	The percentage of female students, rounded to the nearest whole number

    a. Quantity A is greater.
    b. Quantity B is greater.
    c. The two quantities are the same.
    d. The relationship cannot be determined from the given information.

Algebra

8. Solve the following system of equations by substitution. Write your solutions as ordered pairs:

$$\begin{cases} 2x - 2y = 1 \\ x^2 - 8x - 2y = -20 \end{cases}$$

a. $\left(3, \frac{5}{2}\right)$ or $\left(7, \frac{13}{2}\right)$

b. $\left(\frac{5}{2}, 2\right)$ or $\left(7, \frac{13}{2}\right)$

c. $\left(\frac{5}{2}, 2\right)$ or $\left(6, \frac{11}{2}\right)$

d. $\left(3, \frac{5}{2}\right)$ or $\left(6, \frac{11}{2}\right)$

9. If the square of twice the sum of x and three is equal to the product of twenty-four and x, which of these is a possible value of x?

a. $6 + 3\sqrt{2}$

b. $\frac{3}{2}$

c. $-3i$

d. -3

10. A school is selling tickets to its production of *Annie Get Your Gun*. Student tickets cost $3 each, and non-student tickets are $5 each. To offset the costs of the production, the school must earn at least $300 in ticket sales. Which graph shows the number of tickets the school must sell to offset production costs?

c.

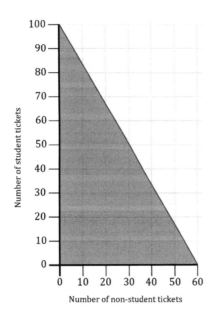

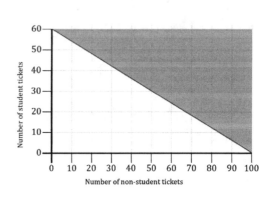

a.

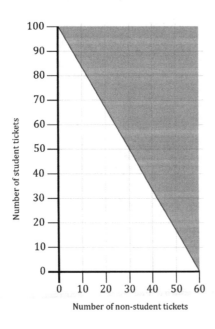

d.

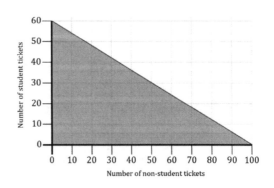

b.

11. Solve $x^4 + 64 = 20x^2$.

    a. $x = \{2, 4\}$
    b. $x = \{-4, -2, 2, 4\}$
    c. $x = \{2i, 4i\}$
    d. $x = \{-4i, -2i, 2i, 4i\}$

12. Which of the following expressions are equivalent to the following rational expression?

$$\frac{36x - 9x^2}{x^2 - 16}$$

Select all equivalent expressions, regardless of whether they are in simplest form.

   a. $\dfrac{18x^2 - 72x}{32 - 2x^2}$

   b. $\dfrac{-9x}{x+4}$, with $x \neq 4$

   c. $\dfrac{9x}{4-x}$, with $x \neq -4$

13. Given the cubic polynomial $f(x) = 2x^3 - 13x^2 + cx - 28$, where c is a real constant, use the remainder theorem to determine the value of c that makes the linear polynomial $x - 4$ a factor of $f(x)$.

   a. $c = 30$

   b. $c = -14$

   c. $c = 24$

   d. $c = 27$

14. If a, b, and c are multiples of 3 and $4a^2 + b^3 = c$, which of these is the largest number that must be factor of c?

   a. 3

   b. 6

   c. 9

   d. 12

15. Solve the system of equations: $\begin{cases} 3x + y = 1 \\ -4x + 3y = 29 \end{cases}$.

   a. $\left(0, \frac{1}{2}\right)$

   b. $(-2, 7)$

   c. $\left(2, -\frac{5}{2}\right)$

   d. $(-1, 3)$

16. Which of these statements is true for functions $f(x)$, $g(x)$, and $h(x)$?

$$f(x) = -2x + 1$$
$$g(x) = -2x^2 + 1$$
$$h(x) = -2x^3 + 1$$

   a. The degree of each polynomial function is –2.

   b. The leading coefficient of each function is –2.

   c. Each function has exactly one real zero.

   d. Each function has an x-intercept at $(1,0)$.

17. Tessa rode her bike to the lake in an hour and 15 minutes. On her way home, she rode 4 mph faster and arrived in 45 minutes. What was her average speed on her round trip?

    a. 3.5 mph
    b. 5.5 mph
    c. 7.5 mph
    d. 9.5 mph

18. Solve $3x^2 + 6x = -4$.

    a. $x = \dfrac{-3 \pm i\sqrt{3}}{3}$

    b. $x = -1 \pm i\sqrt{3}$

    c. $x = \pm \dfrac{i\sqrt{3}}{3}$

    d. $x = \dfrac{-3 \pm i\sqrt{3}}{6}$

19. Three students attempt to rewrite the quadratic equation $3x^2 + 42x - 33 = 0$ in the form $(x - p)^2 = q$ by completing the square. Which sequences of algebraic steps, if any, are correct? Select all correct approaches.

a.

$$3x^2 + 42x - 33 = 0$$
$$3(x^2 + 14x) = 33$$
$$3(x^2 + 14x + 49) = 33 + 49$$
$$3(x + 7)^2 = 82$$
$$(x + 7)^2 = \frac{82}{3}$$

b.

$$3x^2 + 42x - 33 = 0$$
$$3(x^2 + 14x) = 33$$
$$3(x^2 + 14x + 49) = 33 + 147$$
$$3(x + 7)^2 = 180$$
$$(x + 7)^2 = 60$$

c.

$$3x^2 + 42x - 33 = 0$$
$$3x^2 + 42x = 33$$
$$3x^2 + 42x + 441 = 33 + 441$$
$$3(x^2 + 42x + 441) = 474$$
$$(x + 21)^2 = 158$$

20. If a square root of twice the sum of x and six is equal to half of x, which of these is a possible value of x?

    a.   12
    b. $\frac{3}{2}$
    c. $-3i$
    d. -3

Functions

21. If $f(x)$ and $g(x)$ are inverse functions, which of these is the value of x when $f(g(x)) = 4$?

   a. -4

   b. $\dfrac{1}{4}$

   c. 2

   d. 4

22. Which of these statements is (are) true for the function $g(x)$?

$$g(x) = \begin{cases} -x + 3 & x < 2 \\ 2x - 1 & x \geq 2 \end{cases}$$

   I. $g(3) = 0$
   II. The graph of $g(x)$ is discontinuous at $x = 2$.
   III. The range of $g(x)$ is all real numbers.

   a. II only
   b. III only
   c. I and II
   d. II and III

23. Which of the following statements is (are) true when $f(x) = \dfrac{x^2 - x - 6}{x^3 + 2x^2 - x - 2}$?

   I. The graph $f(x)$ has vertical asymptotes at $x = -2$, $x = -1$, and $x = 1$.
   II. The x- and y-intercepts of the graph of $f(x)$ are both 3.

   a. I only
   b. II only
   c. I and II
   d. Neither statement is true.

24. To graph the function $f(x) = 2(2x^2 - 3x - 27)$, you put the formula into different forms, from which you read off important features of the graph. Select all the following procedures and conclusions that are correct.

    a. From the following calculation you conclude that the parabola opens upward and that the

       x-intercepts are $x = \dfrac{9}{2}$ and $x = -3$.

$$f(x) = 2(2x^2 - 3x - 27) = 2(2x - 9)(x + 3) = 4\left(x - \dfrac{9}{2}\right)(x + 3)$$

    b. From the following calculation you conclude that the parabola opens upward, that its vertex

       is the point $\left(\dfrac{3}{4}, -56\dfrac{1}{4}\right)$, and that its minimum value is $-56\dfrac{1}{4}$.

$$f(x) = 2(2x^2 - 3x - 27) = 4\left(x^2 - \dfrac{3}{2}x\right) - 54 = 4\left(x^2 - \dfrac{3}{2}x + \dfrac{9}{16}\right) - 54 - \dfrac{9}{4}$$

$$= 4\left(x - \dfrac{3}{4}\right)^2 - 56\dfrac{1}{4}$$

    c. From the following calculation you conclude that the parabola opens upward and that the

       y-intercept is $y = -54$.

$$f(x) = 2(2x^2 - 3x - 27) = 4x^2 - 6x - 54$$

25. Find $[g \circ f\,]x$ when $f(x) = x + 2$ and $g(x) = 2x^2 - 4x + 2$.

    a. $4x^2 + 10x + 6$
    b. $2x^2 - 4x + 8$
    c. $x^2 - 2$
    d. $2x^2 + 4x + 2$

26. The diagram shows the graphs of two related functions, with the graph of $f(x)$ dashed and the graph of $g(x)$ solid. Which of the following equations gives the algebraic relationship between functions f and g?

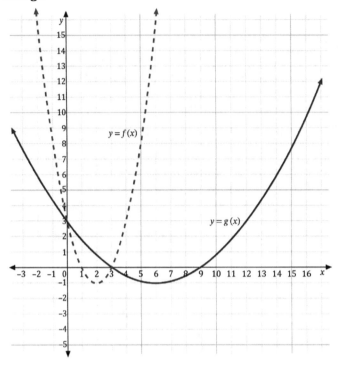

a. $g(x) = f\left(\frac{1}{3}x\right)$

b. $g(x) = f(3x)$

c. $g(x) = 3f(x)$

d. $g(x) = \frac{1}{3}f(x)$

27. Which of these is the equation of the function graphed below?

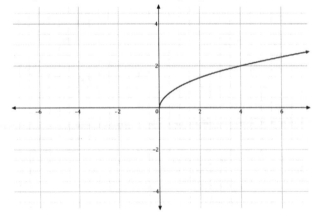

a. $f(x) = x^2$

b. $f(x) = \sqrt{x}$

c. $f(x) = 2^x$

d. $f(x) = \log_2 x$

28. What is the exact value of $\tan(-\frac{7\pi}{6})$?

   a. $\frac{1}{2}$

   b. $-\frac{\sqrt{3}}{2}$

   c. $-\frac{\sqrt{3}}{3}$

   d. -1

29. Given the partial table of values for $f(x)$ and $g(x)$, find $f(g(3))$. Assume that $f(x)$ and $g(x)$ are the simplest polynomials that fit the data.

x	$f(x)$	$g(x)$
−2	−16	−11
−1	−2	−8
0	0	−5
1	2	−2
2	16	1

30. Complete the analogy: $y = \frac{1}{\sqrt{x}}$ is to $x = y^{-2}$ as ...

   a. $y = 2x$ is to $x = y^2$.

   b. $y = e^x$ is to $x = \frac{1}{e^y}$, where $y > 0$.

   c. $y = \frac{1}{x^2}$ is to $x = y^2$, where $x, y \neq 0$.

   d. $y = \cos x$ is to $x = \cos^{-1} y$.

31. Which of these relationships represents y as a function of x?

a. $x^2 + y^2 = 16$

c. $y = \pm\sqrt{x}$

d.

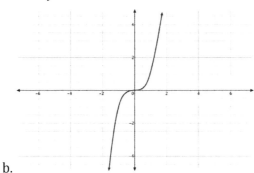

b.

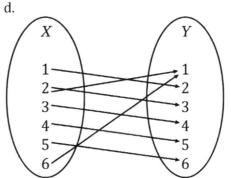

32. Given: $f(x) = 10^x$. If $f(x) = 1$, which of these approximates x?

   a.   10

   b.   1

   c.   0.1

   d.   0

33. Solve $\csc^2\theta = 2\cot\theta$ for $0 < \theta \leq 2\pi$.

   a. $\theta = \dfrac{\pi}{6}$ or $\dfrac{7\pi}{6}$

   b. $\theta = \dfrac{\pi}{4}$ or $\dfrac{5\pi}{4}$

   c. $\theta = \dfrac{3\pi}{4}$ or $\dfrac{7\pi}{4}$

   d. $\theta = \dfrac{3\pi}{4}$ or $\dfrac{\pi}{6}$

Calculus

34. Evaluate the two one-sided limits and the (two-sided) limit of the function $f(x) = \frac{|3x-15|}{10-2x}$ **as x approaches 5. Which of the following answers gives all three limits correctly? [Note: In this problem the notation $\lim\limits_{x \to a^-} x$ indicates the lefthand limit (the limit from below) and the notation $\lim\limits_{x \to a^+} x$ indicates the righthand limit (the limit from above).]**

a. $\lim\limits_{x \to 5^-} \frac{|3x-15|}{10-2x} = \frac{3}{2}$ and $\lim\limits_{x \to 5^+} \frac{|3x-15|}{10-2x} = -\frac{3}{2}$ and $\lim\limits_{x \to 5} \frac{|3x-15|}{10-2x}$ does not exist.

b. $\lim\limits_{x \to 5^-} \frac{|3x-15|}{10-2x} = -\frac{3}{2}$ and $\lim\limits_{x \to 5^+} \frac{|3x-15|}{10-2x} = \frac{3}{2}$ and $\lim\limits_{x \to 5} \frac{|3x-15|}{10-2x} = 0$.

c. All three limits, $\lim\limits_{x \to 5^-} \frac{|3x-15|}{10-2x}$, $\lim\limits_{x \to 5^+} \frac{|3x-15|}{10-2x}$, and $\lim\limits_{x \to 5} \frac{|3x-15|}{10-2x}$ do not exist.

d. $\lim\limits_{x \to 5^-} \frac{|3x-15|}{10-2x} = \frac{3}{2}$ and $\lim\limits_{x \to 5^+} \frac{|3x-15|}{10-2x} = \frac{3}{2}$ and $\lim\limits_{x \to 5} \frac{|3x-15|}{10-2x} = \frac{3}{2}$.

35. Find the derivative of $f(x) = e^{3x^2-1}$.

a. $6xe^{6x}$
b. e^{3x^2-1}
c. $(3x^2-1)e^{3x^2-2}$
d. $6xe^{3x^2-1}$

36. Calculate $\int 4xe^{2x^2}\, dx$.

a. $e^{2x^2} + C$
b. $e^{x^3} + C$
c. $3x^2 e^{3x^2} + C$
d. $\ln x^3 + C$

37. If $f(x) = 2x^3 + x^2 - 4x + 3$, which of the following statements is (are) true of its graph?

    I. The point $\left(\frac{2}{3}, \frac{37}{27}\right)$ is a relative maximum.

    II. The graph of f is concave upward on the interval $\left(-\infty, -\frac{1}{6}\right)$.

a. I
b. II
c. I and II
d. Neither I nor II

38. Suppose the path of a baseball hit straight up from 3.5 feet above the ground is modeled by the first quadrant graph of the function $h(t) = -15t^2 + 56t + 3.5$, where t is the flight time of the ball in seconds and h is the height of the ball in feet. What is the velocity of the ball 1.5 seconds after it is hit?

a. 11 ft/s upward
b. 56 ft/s upward
c. 11 ft/s downward
d. 56 ft/s downward

39. If $f(x) = 3x^3 - x^2 + \frac{1}{2}$, what is $\lim\limits_{h \to 0} \frac{f(1+h) - f(1)}{h}$?

a. $\frac{1}{2}$

b. 4

c. 7

d. 11

40. What is the area in square units under the curve $f(x) = 3x^2 + 1$ on $[0, 2]$?

Geometry

41. A circle is inscribed inside quadrilateral $ABCD$. $\overline{CD}$ is bisected by the point at which it is tangent to the circle. If $\overline{AB} = 14$, $\overline{BC} = 10$, $\overline{CD} = 8$, then which of the following statements is true?

    a. $\overline{AD} = 11$
    b. $\overline{AD} = 2\sqrt{34}$
    c. $\overline{AD} = 12$
    d. $\overline{AD} = 17.5$

42. What is the radius of the circle defined by the equation $x^2 + y^2 - 10x + 8y + 29 = 0$?

    a. $2\sqrt{3}$
    b. $2\sqrt{5}$
    c. $\sqrt{29}$
    d. 12

43. Line segment $\overline{PQ}$ has endpoints (a, b) and (c, b). If $\overline{P'Q'}$ is the translation of $\overline{PQ}$ along a diagonal line such that P' is located at point (c, d), what is the area of quadrilateral $PP'Q'Q$?

    a. $|a - c| \times |b - d|$
    b. $|a - b| \times |c - d|$
    c. $|a - d| \times |b - c|$
    d. $(a - c)^2$

44. A right triangle has legs of lengths 9 and 11. Which of the following expressions give the length, c, of the hypotenuse? Select all correct solutions.

    a. $c = \sqrt{9^2 + 11^2}$
    b. $c = 9\sec\left(\arctan\frac{11}{9}\right)$
    c. $c = \dfrac{11}{\cos\left(\tan^{-1}\frac{9}{11}\right)}$

45. Jan creates a mosaic with tiles in the shape of congruent isosceles triangles, as seen below. What is the value of x in the figure?

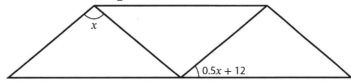

    a. $x = 56$
    b. $x = 78$
    c. $x = 89.5$
    d. The value of x cannot be determined from the information given.

46. Which of these is a net of a triangular pyramid?

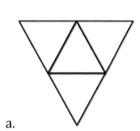

a.

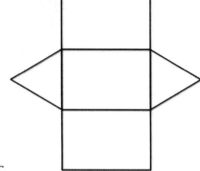

c.

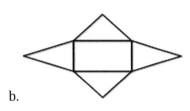

b.

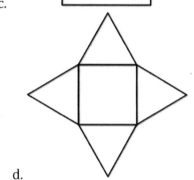

d.

47. For which of these does a rotation of 45° about the center of the polygon map the polygon onto itself?

a. Square
b. Regular hexagon
c. Regular octagon
d. Regular decagon

48. For ΔABC, what is the length of $\overline{AB}$?

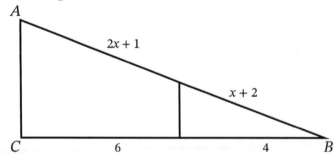

49. The vertices of a polygon are $(0, 3)$, $(1, -1)$, $(3, 3)$, and $(4, -1)$. Which of the following describes the polygon most specifically?

    a. Parallelogram
    b. Rhombus
    c. Rectangle
    d. Square

50. On a floor plan drawn at a scale of $1 : 150$, the area of a rectangular room is 20 cm^2. What is the actual area of the room?

    a. $4{,}500 \text{ cm}^2$
    b. $45{,}000 \text{ cm}^2$
    c. 45 m^2
    d. 450 m^2

51. You have two triangles, ΔABC and ΔDEF with $\angle A \cong \angle D$, $\angle B \cong \angle E$, $\angle C \cong \angle F$, $\overline{BC} \cong \overline{DE}$, and $\overline{CA} \cong \overline{EF}$. Which triangle congruence property, if any, allows you to conclude $\Delta ABC \cong \Delta DEF$?

    a. ASA
    b. AAS
    c. SAS
    d. The given information is not sufficient to prove that $\Delta ABC \cong \Delta DEF$.

52. Equilateral triangle ΔABC has sides 4 cm long. Which of the following statements is true? Select all true statements.

    a. The area of ΔABC is $4\sqrt{3} \text{ cm}^2$.

    b. The length of the altitude from vertex A is $\sqrt{3}$ cm.

    c. The length of the median from vertex A is $2\sqrt{3}$ cm.

53. Which of the following expressions gives the area A of the triangle below in terms of x? Note: The figure is not drawn to scale.

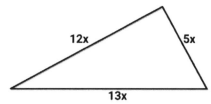

    a. $30x^2$

    b. $5\sqrt{3x^2 - 1}$

    c. $\dfrac{x\sqrt{5x^2}}{12}$

    d. $\dfrac{3x\sqrt{13x^2}}{25}$

Statistics and Probability

54. Which of these does NOT simulate randomly selecting a student from a group of 11 students?

   a. Assigning each student a unique card value of A, 2, 3, 4, 5, 6, 7, 8, 9, 10, or J, removing queens and kings from a standard deck of 52 cards, shuffling the remaining cards, and drawing a single card from the deck

   b. Assigning each student a unique number 0–10 and using a computer to randomly generate a number within that range

   c. Assigning each student a unique number from 2 to 12, rolling two dice, and finding the sum of the numbers on the dice

   d. All of these can be used as a simulation of the event.

55. In how many distinguishable ways can a family of five be seated at a circular table with five chairs if Tasha and Mac must be kept separated by at least one chair?

   a. 6
   b. 12
   c. 24
   d. 60

Refer to the following for question 56:

The box-and-whisker plot displays student test scores by class period.

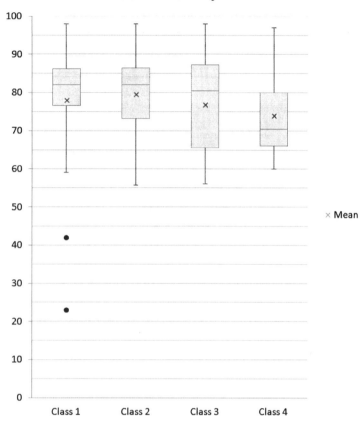

56. Which class has the greatest range of test scores?

    a. Class 1
    b. Class 2
    c. Class 3
    d. Class 4

57. A small company is divided into three departments, as shown. Two individuals are chosen at random to attend a conference. What is the approximate probability that two women from the same department will be chosen?

	Department 1	Department 2	Department 3
Women	12	28	16
Men	18	14	15

    a. 8.6%
    b. 10.7%
    c. 11.2%
    d. 13.8%

Refer to the following for question 58:

Each day for 100 days, a student tossed a single misshapen coin three times in succession and recorded the number of times the coin landed on heads. The results of his experiment are shown below.

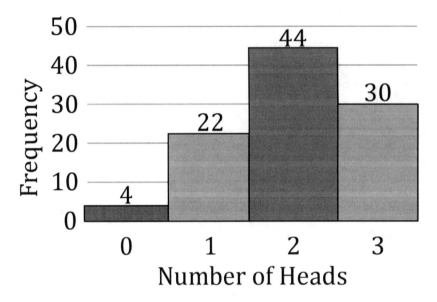

58. Which of these shows the graphs of the probability distributions from ten flips of this misshapen coin and ten flips of a fair coin?

Fair Coin Misshapen Coin

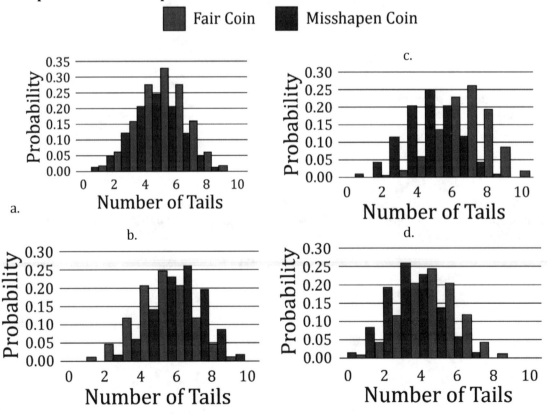

284

59. The intelligence quotients (IQs) of a randomly selected group of 300 people are normally distributed with a mean IQ of 100 and a standard deviation of 15. In a normal distribution, approximately 68% of values are within one standard deviation of the mean. About how many individuals from the selected group have IQs of at least 85?

   a. 96
   b. 200
   c. 216
   d. 252

60. A random sample of 250 students at a high school were asked these three questions:

   Do you drink coffee?
   Do you drink tea?
   Do you drink hot chocolate?

The results of the survey are shown below. If these data are representative of the population of students at the school, which of these is most probable?

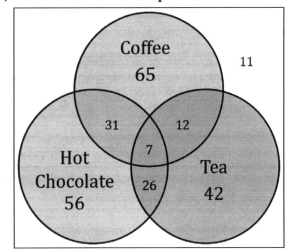

   a. A student chosen at random drinks tea.
   b. If a student chosen at random drinks hot chocolate, he also drinks at least one other beverage.
   c. If a student chosen at random drinks coffee and hot chocolate, he also drinks tea.
   d. A student chosen at random does not drink coffee, tea, or hot chocolate.

61. You have three colored boxes containing red and green beads. The blue box contains 6 red beads and 4 green beads. The red box contains 6 red beads and 2 green beads. The green box contains 2 red beads and 4 green beads. You play a game by drawing two beads as follows: You draw your first bead at random from the blue box. You draw your second bead at random from the box whose color matches the first bead (red box if the first bead is red, green box if the first bead is green). What is the probability that you end up with one red bead and one green bead, drawn in either order?

   a. $\frac{2}{15}$
   b. $\frac{1}{4}$
   c. $\frac{17}{60}$
   d. $\frac{3}{20}$

62. For the holidays, Luke's Bakery offered three seasonal items: pumpkin bread, cranberry muffins, and their famous eggnog pie. They received 57 orders for pumpkin bread, 37 orders for cranberry muffins, and 70 orders for eggnog pie. Fourteen customers ordered both pumpkin bread and cranberry muffins, ten customers ordered both cranberry muffins and eggnog pie, and fifteen customers ordered both pumpkin bread and eggnog pie. Six customers ordered all three items. How many customers placed an order for seasonal items?

Refer to the following for questions 63 - 64:

The diagrams below show the number of people in a small town who participate in various types of volunteer work.

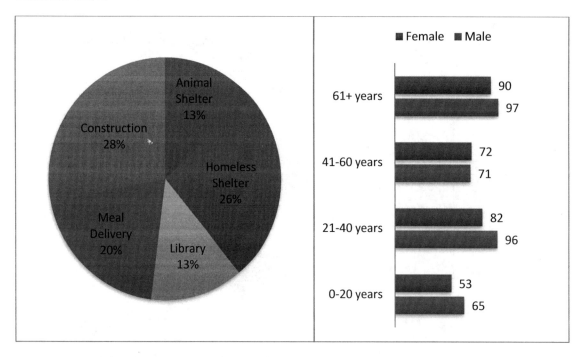

63. Which of these is the greatest quantity?
   a. The average number of females per age bracket
   b. The number of volunteers at the animal shelter
   c. The difference in the number of male and female volunteers
   d. The difference in the number of volunteers over age 60 and under age 21

64. A volunteer under age 21 is chosen at random for a scholarship. What is the approximate probability that the student is male?
   a. 0.47
   b. 0.51
   c. 0.55
   d. 0.58

65. A high school club divides into five small groups for a service project. Each group has four girls and four boys. How many possible groups are there?

    a. 748,650
    b. 1,225,000
    c. 9,126,350
    d. 23,474,025

66. The Probability Honor Society has 19 members, of whom 7 are juniors and 12 are seniors. The society decides to choose officers by randomly assigning four members to the offices of president, vice-president, secretary, and treasurer. No member may hold more than one office at the same time. You want to determine the probability that the junior and senior classes are both represented among the officers—in other words, the probability that the officers include at least one junior and at least one senior. Which of the following lines of reasoning lead to the correct probability? Select all that are correct.

[Recall that $C(n, r)$, also written $_nC_r$ or $\binom{n}{r}$, denotes the number of subsets (combinations) of size r from a set of n elements; and $P(n, r)$, also written $_nP_r$ or $n^{\underline{r}}$, denotes the number of permutations of n objects taken r at a time.]

    a. There are $C(19,4)$ unrestricted ways to choose which 4 members will be officers without assigning them to offices. To count the ways that include both classes, first choose one of the 7 juniors to be an officer. Then choose one of the 12 seniors to be an officer. Then choose 2 of the remaining 17 members (without restriction) to be the other two officers. This gives us $7 \cdot 12 \cdot C(17,2)$ ways to choose officers that represent both classes. Thus, the probability of such a choice occurring randomly is $\frac{7 \cdot 12 \cdot C(17,2)}{C(19,4)}$.

    b. There are $P(19,4)$ unrestricted ways to choose president, vice-president, secretary, and treasurer from the 19 members. Of these, $P(7,4)$ are chosen only from the juniors and $P(12,4)$ only from the seniors. If we eliminate those, we get the choices that include both classes. Thus, the probability of such a choice occurring randomly is $\frac{P(19,4) - P(7,4) - P(12,4)}{P(19,4)}$.

    c. There are $C(19,4)$ unrestricted ways to choose which 4 members will be officers without assigning them to offices. Of these, $C(7,4)$ are chosen only from the juniors and $C(12,4)$ only from the seniors. If we eliminate those, we get the choices that include both classes. The probability of such a choice occurring randomly is $\frac{C(19,4) - C(7,4) - C(12,4)}{C(19,4)}$.

Answer Key and Explanations

Number and Quantity

1. D: When the dress is marked down by 20%, the cost of the dress is 80% of its original price; thus, the reduced price of the dress can be written as $\frac{80}{100}x$, or $\frac{4}{5}x$, where x is the original price. When discounted an extra 25%, the dress costs 75% of the reduced price, or $\frac{75}{100}\left(\frac{4}{5}x\right)$, or $\frac{3}{4}\left(\frac{4}{5}x\right)$, which simplifies to $\frac{3}{5}x$. So, the final price of the dress is three-fifths of the original price.

2. B: The population is approximately 36,000, so one-quarter of the population consists of about 9,000 individuals under age 35. A third of 9,000 is 3,000, the approximate number of students in grades K-12. Since there are thirteen grades, divide 3,000 by 13. There are about 230 students in each grade. So, the number of fourth graders is between 200 and 300.

3. A: First, multiply the numerator and denominator by the denominator's conjugate, $4 + 2i$. Then, simplify the result and write the answer in the form $a + bi$. Remember, $i^2 = -1$.

$$\frac{2 + 3i}{4 - 2i} \times \frac{4 + 2i}{4 + 2i} = \frac{8 + 4i + 12i + 6i^2}{16 - 4i^2}$$
$$= \frac{8 + 16i - 6}{16 + 4}$$
$$= \frac{2 + 16i}{20}$$
$$= \frac{2}{20} + \frac{16i}{20}$$
$$= \frac{1}{10} + \frac{4}{5}i$$

4. C: First, apply the laws of exponents to simplify the expression on the left. Then, add the two fractions:

$\dfrac{(x^3y)(3x^{-1}y)^2}{6x^3y} - \dfrac{2}{xy}$	
$\dfrac{(x^3y)(9x^{-2}y^2)}{6x^3y} - \dfrac{2}{xy}$	Distribute the exponent to the parentheses in the numerator of the first term.
$\dfrac{9xy^3}{6x^3y} - \dfrac{2}{xy}$	Simplify the numerator of the first term using the exponent rule $a^m \times a^n = a^{m+n}$.
$\dfrac{3y^2}{2x^2} - \dfrac{2}{xy}$	Simplify the first term by dividing both the numerator and denominator by 3 and by using the exponent rule $\dfrac{a^m}{a^n} = a^{m-n}$.
$\dfrac{3y^2}{2x^2} \times \dfrac{y}{y} - \dfrac{2}{xy} \times \dfrac{2x}{2x}$	Multiply by factors equivalent to 1 that will create a common denominator between the two fractions.
$\dfrac{3y^3}{2x^2y} - \dfrac{4x}{2x^2y}$	Simplify the multiplication.

288

$$\frac{3y^3 - 4x}{2x^2y}$$ Combine the two fractions into one.

5. \$179,625: The ratio of new car sales to used car sales is $3:5$, so the used car sales total $\frac{5}{8}$ of the total sales.

$$\frac{5}{8} \times \$287,400 = \$179,625$$

6. A: The revenue Jen receives from each method of sale is:

$$0.8 \times 0.75 \times \$10.50 = \$6.30 \text{ from Store A}$$
$$0.8(\$11.00 - \$1.50) = \$7.60 \text{ from Store B}$$
$$\$6.75 + \$2.50 - \$2.50 = \$6.75 \text{ from Store C}$$

So, Store A will give the lowest revenue, Store C is next, and Store B brings the highest revenue during the sale.

7. C: 52% of the student population is white. There are 630 female students at the school out of 1,219 students, so the percentage of female students is $\frac{630}{1,219} \times 100\% \approx 52\%$. The percentages, rounded to the nearest whole number, are the same.

Algebra

8. A: To solve by substitution, we solve the first equation for $2y$, getting $2y = 2x - 1$. Then we substitute this value for $2y$ into the second equation.

$$x^2 - 8x - (2x - 1) = -20$$

$$x^2 - 10x + 1 = -20$$

$$x^2 - 10x + 21 = 0$$

We can continue to solve equation by factoring, getting $(x - 3)(x - 7) = 0$, which has solutions $x = 3$ or $x = 7$. Substituting $x = 3$ into the equation $2y = 2x - 1$, gives us $y = \frac{5}{2}$, and substituting $x = 7$ into it gives us $y = \frac{13}{2}$.

9. C: "The square of twice the sum of x and three is equal to the product of twenty-four and x" is represented by the equation $[2(x + 3)]^2 = 24x$. Solve for x.

$$[2x + 6]^2 = 24x$$
$$(2x + 6)(2x + 6) = 24x$$
$$4x^2 + 24x + 36 = 24x$$
$$4x^2 + 36 = 0$$
$$4x^2 = -36$$
$$x^2 = -9$$
$$x = \pm\sqrt{-9}$$
$$x = \pm 3i$$

So, $-3i$ is a possible value of x.

10. B: The inequality that represents this scenario is $5n + 3s \geq 300$, where n is the number of non-student tickets that must be sold, and s is the number of student tickets that must be sold. The intercepts of this linear inequality can be found by substituting 0 for s and solving for n and then by substituting 0 for n and solving for s. The intercepts are $n = 60$ and $s = 100$. The solid line through the two intercepts represents the minimum number of each type of ticket that must be sold to offset production costs. The shading above the line represents sales which result in a profit for the school.

11. B: To solve the equation, write $x^4 + 64 = 20x^2$ in the quadratic form, then factor.

$$(x^2)^2 - 20(x^2) + 64 = 0$$

This trinomial can be factored as $(x^2 - 4)(x^2 - 16) = 0$. Each set of parentheses contains a difference of squares, which can be factored further: $(x + 2)(x - 2)(x + 4)(x - 4) = 0$. Use the zero product property to find the solutions to the equation.

$$
\begin{array}{cccc}
x + 2 = 0 & x - 2 = 0 & x + 4 = 0 & x - 4 = 0 \\
x = -2 & x = 2 & x = -4 & x = 4
\end{array}
$$

12. A, B: To see the equivalence of choice A, we multiply the original expression by $\frac{-2}{-2}$.

$$\frac{36x - 9x^2}{x^2 - 16} \cdot \frac{-2}{-2} = \frac{-72x + 18x^2}{-2x^2 + 32} = \frac{18x^2 - 72x}{32 - 2x^2}$$

To see the equivalence of choice B, we factor the GCF, $-9x$, out of the numerator and factor the difference of squares in the denominator. Then we cancel the common factor of $x - 4$, noting the restriction that x cannot equal 4 in the new expression because it makes the original expression undefined:

$$\frac{36x - 9x^2}{x^2 - 16} = \frac{-9x(-4 + x)}{(x + 4)(x - 4)} = \frac{-9x(x - 4)}{(x + 4)(x - 4)} = \frac{-9x}{x + 4}, \text{with } x \neq 4$$

To see that choice C is not equivalent to the original expression, we may note that it is plainly not equivalent to choice B. More directly, we can substitute a value for x in choice C and then substitute the same value in the original expression. Consider $x = 1$, for example, then $\frac{9x}{4-x} = \frac{9(1)}{4-(1)} = \frac{9}{3} = 3$, but $\frac{36x-9x^2}{x^2-16} = \frac{36(1)-9(1)^2}{(1)^2-16} = \frac{27}{-15} = -\frac{9}{5}$.

Since equivalent expressions take the same value for *all* values of the variable, choice C is not equivalent to the original rational expression.

13. D: The remainder theorem says that when we divide a polynomial $p(x)$ by the linear polynomial $x - a$, the remainder is $p(a)$. Thus $x - a$ is a factor of $p(x)$ if and only if $p(a) = 0$. In the given problem, we want $x - 4$ to be a factor of $f(x)$, so we want $f(4)$ to be zero. Thus, we first calculate $f(4) = 2(4)^3 - 13(4)^2 + c(4) - 28 = 128 - 208 + 4c - 28 = 4c - 108$. Then set $f(4) = 0$ and solve for c. $f(4) = 4c - 108 = 0$, getting $c = 27$.

14. C: Since a and b are multiples of 3, each can be expressed as the product of 3 and an integer. So, if we write $a = 3x$ and $b = 3y$, then the equation becomes $4(3x)^2 + (3y)^3 = c$.

$$4(3x)^2 + (3y)^3 = c$$
$$36x^2 + 27y^3 = c$$
$$9(4x^2 + 3y^3) = c$$

Since c is the product of 9 and some other integer, 9 must be a factor of c.

15. B: A system of linear equations can be solved by using matrices or by using the graphing, substitution, or elimination (also called linear combination) method. The elimination method is shown here:

$$3x + y = 1$$
$$-4x + 3y = 29$$

To eliminate y by linear combination, multiply the top equation by –3 so that the coefficients of the y-terms will be additive inverses.

$$-3(3x + y) = (1)(-3)$$
$$-9x - 3y = -3$$

Then, add the two equations and solve for x.

$$\begin{array}{rcl} -9x\ -3y &=& -3 \\ +\ -4x\ +3y &=& 29 \\ \hline -13x &=& 26 \\ x &=& -2 \end{array}$$

Substitute –2 for x in either of the given equations and solve for y. Here $x = -2$ is substituted into the top equation.

$$3(-2) + y = 1$$
$$-6 + y = 1$$
$$y = 7$$

The solution to the system of equations is $(-2, 7)$.

16. B: The degree of a polynomial refers to the largest exponent. The degree of $f(x)$ is 1, the degree of $g(x)$ is 2, and the degree of $h(x)$ is 3. The leading coefficient for each function is –2. Functions $f(x)$ and $h(x)$ have exactly one real zero, while $g(x)$ has two real zeros:

$$\begin{array}{lll} f(x) = 0 & g(x) = 0 & h(x) = 0 \\ -2x + 1 = 0 & -2x^2 + 1 = 0 & -2x^3 + 1 = 0 \\ -2x = -1 & -2x^2 = -1 & -2x^3 = -1 \\ x = \dfrac{1}{2} & x^2 = \dfrac{1}{2} & x^3 = \dfrac{1}{2} \\ & x = \sqrt{\dfrac{1}{2}};\ x = -\sqrt{\dfrac{1}{2}} & x = \sqrt[3]{\dfrac{1}{2}} \end{array}$$

The zeros of the function are also the x-intercepts, so none of the functions have an x-intercept at $(1,0)$.

17. C: Since rate in mph $= \frac{\text{distance in miles}}{\text{time in hours}}$, Tessa's speed on the way to the lake and back home in mph can be expressed as $\frac{d}{1.25}$ and $\frac{d}{0.75}$, respectively, when d is the distance between Tessa's house and the lake. Since she rode 4 mph faster on her way home:

$$\frac{d}{0.75} - \frac{d}{1.25} = 4$$

$$\frac{d}{0.75} \times \frac{4}{4} - \frac{d}{1.25} \times \frac{4}{4} = 4$$

$$\frac{4d}{3} - \frac{4d}{5} = 4$$

$$15\left(\frac{4d}{3} - \frac{4d}{5}\right) = 4(15)$$

$$20d - 12d = 60$$

$$d = 7.5$$

Since the distance between Tessa's house and the lake is 7.5 miles, she rode a total distance of 15 miles in 2 hours (1 hour 15 minutes + 45 minutes = 2 hours). Therefore, her average speed was $\frac{15 \text{ miles}}{2 \text{ hours}} = 7.5$ mph.

18. A: There are many ways to solve quadratic equations in the form $ax^2 + bx + c = 0$. From the answer choices, the equation must have complex solutions. So, solve this equation by completing the square or by using the quadratic formula, $x = \frac{-b \pm \sqrt{b^2 - 4ac}}{2a}$. Here we will use the quadratic formula. Given $3x^2 + 6x + 4 = 0$; $a = 3$, $b = 6$, $c = 4$:

$$x = \frac{-(6) \pm \sqrt{(6)^2 - 4(3)(4)}}{2(3)}$$

$$x = \frac{-6 \pm \sqrt{36 - 48}}{6}$$

$$x = \frac{-6 \pm \sqrt{-12}}{6}$$

$$x = \frac{-6 \pm 2i\sqrt{3}}{6}$$

$$x = \frac{-3 \pm i\sqrt{3}}{3}$$

19. B: In choice A, the incorrect step is the equation $3(x^2 + 14x + 49) = 33 + 49$, which gives the illusion of adding the same number, 49, to both sides of the equation. On the left side, however, the 49 is inside the parentheses, being multiplied by 3. Thus, this step really adds 147 to the left side of the equation but 49 to the right side.

Choice B is correct. The first step correctly adds 33 to both sides of the equation and factors 3 (the leading coefficient) out of the quadratic and linear terms.

$$3x^2 + 42x - 33 = 0$$

$$3(x^2 + 14x) = 33$$

This is crucial because completing the square works only with a leading coefficient of 1. The next step correctly completes the square *inside* the parentheses (Half of 14 is 7. The square of 7 is 49.), adding 49 inside the parentheses. Since the parentheses are multiplied by 3, this adds $3 \cdot 49 = 147$ to the left side of the equation, which is balanced by adding 147 to the right side as well.

$$3(x^2 + 14x + 49) = 33 + 147$$

The next two steps find the sum on the right side of the equation and then divide both sides of the equation by 3 to reach the desired form.

$$3(x + 7)^2 = 180$$

$$(x + 7)^2 = 60$$

In choice C, the student goes wrong in the step $3x^2 + 42x + 441 = 33 + 441$, which is not false but is unhelpful. This step tries to complete the square (Half of 42 is 21. The square of 21 is 441.) with a leading coefficient of 3, but completing the square works only with a leading coefficient of 1. The next step, $3(x^2 + 42x + 441) = 474$, is the false one, in which the student tries to factor 3 out of the left side but fails to take it out of the linear and constant terms.

20. A: "A square root of twice the sum of x and six is equal to half of x" is represented by the equation $\sqrt{2(x + 6)} = \frac{1}{2}x$. Solve for x.

$$\sqrt{2(x + 6)} = \frac{1}{2}x$$
$$\sqrt{2x + 12} = \frac{1}{2}x$$
$$\left(\sqrt{2x + 12}\right)^2 = \left(\frac{1}{2}x\right)^2$$
$$2x + 12 = \frac{1}{4}x^2$$
$$4(2x + 12) = x^2$$
$$8x + 48 = x^2$$
$$x^2 - 8x - 48 = 0$$
$$(x + 4)(x - 12) = 0$$
$$x = -4, 12$$

There is not an answer choice of, "no solution." So, there is no need to check your answer in the original equation. 12 must be a possible value of x.

Functions

21. D: By definition, when $f(x)$ and $g(x)$ are inverse functions, $f(g(x)) = g(f(x)) = x$. So, $f(g(4)) = 4$.

22. A: Below is the graph of $g(x)$.

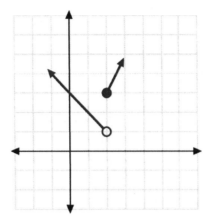

Statement II is true. The graph is discontinuous at $x = 2$. Statement I is false, because $g(3) = 2(3) - 1 = 5$. Statement II is also false because, from the graph, the range of the function is $y > 1$.

23. B: First, state the exclusions of the domain. This can be done by factoring the denominator, then finding where the denominator is equal to 0.

$$x^3 + 2x^2 - x - 2 \neq 0$$
$$x^2(x + 2) - (x + 2) \neq 0$$
$$(x + 2)(x^2 - 1) \neq 0$$
$$(x + 2)(x - 1)(x + 1) \neq 0$$
$$x + 2 \neq 0 \quad x - 1 \neq 0 \quad x + 1 \neq 0$$
$$x \neq -2 \qquad x \neq 1 \qquad x \neq -1$$

To determine whether there are vertical asymptotes or holes at these values of x, simplify the expression:

$$\frac{x^2 - x - 6}{x^3 + 2x^2 - x - 2} = \frac{(x - 3)(x + 2)}{(x + 2)(x - 1)(x + 1)} = \frac{x - 3}{(x - 1)(x + 1)}$$

There are vertical asymptotes at $x = 1$ and at $x = -1$ and a hole at $x = -2$. Statement I is false.

To find the x-intercept of $f(x)$, solve $f(x) = 0$. $f(x) = 0$ when the numerator is equal to zero.

$$x^2 - x - 6 = 0$$

$$(x + 2)(x - 3) = 0$$

$$x = -2, 3$$

The numerator equals zero when $x = -2$ and $x = 3$; however, -2 is excluded from the domain of $f(x)$, so the x-intercept is 3. To find the y-intercept of $f(x)$, find $f(0)$.

$$\frac{(0)^2 - (0) - 6}{(0)^3 + 2(0)^2 - (0) - 2} = \frac{-6}{-2} = 3$$

The y-intercept is 3. Statement II is true.

24. A, B, C: In choice A, you rewrite the function in factored form $f(x) = a(x - r)(x - s)$ and read off the direction the parabola opens from the value $a = 4$ and $4 > 0$. The x-intercepts are found from the roots $r = \frac{9}{2}$ and $s = -3$.

In choice B, you rewrite the function in vertex form $f(x) = a(x - h)^2 + k$ and read off the direction the parabola opens from the value $a = 4$ and $4 > 0$, the vertex (h, k) from $h = \frac{3}{4}$ and $k = -56\frac{1}{4}$, and the minimum (since the parabola opens upward) from $k = -56\frac{1}{4}$.

In choice C, you rewrite the function in general form $f(x) = ax^2 + bx + c$ and read off the direction the parabola opens from the value $a = 4$ and $4 > 0$. The y-intercept is found from the constant $c = -54$.

25. D: Substitute and simplify.

$$\begin{aligned}
[g \circ f]x &= g\big(f(x)\big) \\
&= g(x + 2) \\
&= 2(x + 2)^2 - 4(x + 2) + 2 \\
&= 2(x^2 + 4x + 4) - 4(x + 2) + 2 \\
&= 2x^2 + 8x + 8 - 4x - 8 + 2 \\
&= 2x^2 + 4x + 2
\end{aligned}$$

26. A: If f and g are functions with $g(x) = f(kx)$, with $k > 0$, then the graph of g is the graph of f expanded horizontally by a factor of $\frac{1}{k}$ (which is a horizontal *compression* if $k > 1$). That is, if the point (x, y) appears on the graph of f, then the point $\left(\frac{1}{k}x, y\right)$ appears on the graph of g since $g\left(\frac{1}{k}x\right) = f\left(k\left(\frac{1}{k}\right)x\right) = f(x) = y$. Careful examination of the diagram reveals that the graph of f has been expanded horizontally by a factor of 3 to produce the graph of g. For instance, the minimum at $(2, -1)$ on the graph of f has a corresponding minimum at $(6, -1)$ on the graph of g; and the point $(4,3)$ on the graph of f has a corresponding point $(12,3)$ on the graph of g. Horizontal expansion by a factor of $\frac{1}{k} = 3$, indicates that that $k = \frac{1}{3}$ (since $\frac{1}{\frac{1}{3}} = 3$). Thus $g(x) = f\left(\frac{1}{3}x\right)$.

27. B: The graph shown is the function $y = \sqrt{x}$. This is the graph of the parent function $y = \sqrt{x}$. Another way to determine the function is by testing points. Notice that the graph passes through the points $(0,0)$, and $(4,2)$. A quick check of each x-value shows that the only function that produces y-values of 0 and 2 is $y = \sqrt{x}$.

x	x^2	$\sqrt{x}$	2^x	$\log_2 x$
0	0	0	1	undefined
4	16	2	16	2

28. C: The coterminal angle for $-\frac{7\pi}{6}$ is $-\frac{7\pi}{6} + 2\pi = \frac{5\pi}{6}$. Also, remember that tangent of an angle can be found by dividing the sine of the angle by the cosine of the angle.

$$\tan\left(-\frac{7\pi}{6}\right) = \tan\left(\frac{5\pi}{6}\right) = \frac{\sin\left(\frac{5\pi}{6}\right)}{\cos\left(\frac{5\pi}{6}\right)}$$

From the unit circle, the values of $\sin\left(\frac{5\pi}{6}\right)$ and $\cos\left(\frac{5\pi}{6}\right)$ are $\frac{1}{2}$ and $-\frac{\sqrt{3}}{2}$, respectively. Substitute these values and simplify.

$$\tan\left(-\frac{7\pi}{6}\right) = \frac{\frac{1}{2}}{-\frac{\sqrt{3}}{2}} = -\frac{2}{2\sqrt{3}} = -\frac{\sqrt{3}}{3}$$

29. 128: Use the table of values to first write equations for $f(x)$ and $g(x)$: $f(x) = 2x^3$ and $g(x) = 3x - 5$. Then, use those equations to find $f(g(3))$.

$$g(3) = 3(3) - 5 = 4$$
$$f(4) = 2(4)^3 = 128$$

So, $f(g(3)) = f(4) = 128$.

30. D: Set the given expression equal to y, then solve for y. When $y = \frac{1}{\sqrt{x}}$, $x = \frac{1}{y^2}$ or y^{-2}. Similarly, when $y = \cos x$, $x = \cos^{-1} y$. On the other hand, when $y = 2x$, $x = \frac{y}{2}$; when $y = e^x$, $x = \ln y$ for $y > 0$; and when $y = \frac{1}{x^2}$, $x = \pm\sqrt{\frac{1}{y}}$.

31. B: Graphically, a relationship between x and y can be identified as a function if the graph passes the vertical line test. Choice B is the graph of $y = x^3$, which is a function because it passes the vertical line test. A function is a relationship in which for every element of the domain (x) produces exactly one element of the range (y).

The first relation is a circle, which fails the vertical line test for functions. Choice C is a parabola on its side, which also fails the vertical line test and is therefore not a function. The relation in choice D has an element of the domain (2) that maps to two different range values, so it is also not a function.

32. D: If $f(x) = 10^x$ and $f(x) = 1$, then $1 = 10^x$. To solve the equation for x, write the equation as a logarithm and simplify.

$$1 = 10^x$$
$$\log_{10} 1 = x$$
$$0 = x$$

33. B: The trigonometric identity $1+\cot^2\theta = \csc^2\theta$ can be used to rewrite the equation $\csc^2\theta = 2\cot\theta$ as $1+\cot^2\theta = 2\cot\theta$. Now, set the equation equal to 0 to get $\cot^2\theta - 2\cot\theta + 1 = 0$. Solve by factoring.

$$\cot^2\theta - 2\cot\theta + 1 = 0$$
$$(\cot\theta - 1)^2 = 0$$
$$\cot\theta - 1 = 0$$
$$\cot\theta = 1$$

Thus, from the unit circle, for $0 < \theta \le 2\pi$, $\cot\theta = 1$ when $\theta = \frac{\pi}{4}$ or $\frac{5\pi}{4}$.

Calculus

34. A: Recall that $|x| = x$ if $x \ge 0$ and $|x| = -x$ if $x < 0$. Consequently, $|x - 5| = x - 5$ if $x \ge 5$ and $|x - 5| = -(x - 5)$ if $x < 5$. The lefthand limit can be evaluating using $|x - 5| = -(x - 5)$.

$$\lim_{x\to 5^-}\frac{|3x - 15|}{10 - 2x} = \lim_{x\to 5^-}\frac{3|x - 5|}{-2(x - 5)} = \lim_{x\to 5^-}\frac{3\big(-(x - 5)\big)}{-2(x - 5)} = \lim_{x\to 5^-}\frac{-3}{-2} = \frac{3}{2}$$

The righthand limit can be evaluating using $|x - 5| = x - 5$.

$$\lim_{x\to 5^+}\frac{|3x - 15|}{10 - 2x} = \lim_{x\to 5^+}\frac{3|x - 5|}{-2(x - 5)} = \lim_{x\to 5^+}\frac{3(x - 5)}{-2(x - 5)} = \lim_{x\to 5^+}-\frac{3}{2} = -\frac{3}{2}$$

Finally, the limit (that is, the two-sided limit) exists if and only if the two one-sided limits exist and have the same value. Otherwise, as in this case, the limit does not exist.

35. D: To find the derivative, use the Chain Rule $\left(\frac{dy}{dx} = \frac{dy}{du} \times \frac{du}{dx}\right)$:

$$y = e^{3x^2-1}$$

$$\text{Let } u = 3x^2 - 1 \qquad \rightarrow \qquad \frac{du}{dx} = 6x$$

$$y = e^u \qquad \rightarrow \qquad \frac{dy}{du} = e^u$$

$$\frac{dy}{dx} = \frac{dy}{du} \times \frac{du}{dx}$$
$$= e^{3x^2-1} \times 6x$$
$$= 6xe^{3x^2-1}$$

36. A: To find the integral, use u-substitution:

$$\int 4xe^{2x^2}\,dx \qquad \text{Let } u = 2x^2;\ du = 4x\,dx$$

$$\int e^u\,du = e^u + C$$

$$= e^{2x^2} + C$$

37. D: The critical points of the graph occur when $f'(x) = 0$.

$$f(x) = 2x^3 + x^2 - 4x + 3$$
$$f'(x) = 6x^2 + 2x - 4$$
$$= 2(3x - 2)(x + 1)$$

$$0 = 2(3x - 2)(x + 1)$$

$$3x - 2 = 0 \qquad x + 1 = 0$$
$$x = \frac{2}{3} \qquad x = -1$$

To determine if a point is a maximum or minimum, test points around the critical points and determine if the slope is positive or negative. Start by choosing an x-value less than –1, like –2, and substitute it into the derivative function.

$$f'(-2) = 6(-2)^2 + 2(-2) - 4 = 6(4) + 2(-2) - 4 = 24 - 4 - 4 = 16$$

Since the derivative is positive, the slope is increasing when $x < -1$. Now test a point between –1 and $\frac{2}{3}$, like 0.

$$f'(0) = 6(0)^2 + 2(0) - 4 = 6(0) - 2(0) - 4 = 0 - 0 - 4 = -4$$

Since the derivative is negative, the slope is decreasing when $-1 < x < \frac{2}{3}$. Therefore, the critical point at $x = -1$ is a relative maximum. Now test a point greater than $\frac{2}{3}$, like 1.

$$f'(1) = 6(1)^2 + 2(1) - 4 = 6(1) + 2(1) - 4 = 6 + 2 - 4 = 8 - 4 = 4$$

Since the derivative is positive, the slope is increasing when $x > \frac{2}{3}$. Therefore, the critical point at $x = \frac{2}{3}$ is a relative minimum.

If $f''(x) > 0$ for all x in an interval, the graph of the function is concave upward on that interval, and if $f''(x) < 0$ for all x in an interval, the graph of the function is concave upward on that interval. Find the second derivative of the function and determine the intervals in which $f''(x)$ is less than zero and greater than zero:

$$f''(x) = 12x + 2$$

$$12x + 2 < 0 \qquad 12x + 2 > 0$$
$$x < -\frac{1}{6} \qquad x > -\frac{1}{6}$$

The graph of f is concave downward on the interval $\left(-\infty, -\frac{1}{6}\right)$ and concave upward on the interval $\left(-\frac{1}{6}, \infty\right)$. The inflection point of the graph is $\left(-\frac{1}{6}, f\left(-\frac{1}{6}\right)\right) = \left(-\frac{1}{6}, \frac{199}{54}\right)$. The point $\left(\frac{2}{3}, f\left(\frac{2}{3}\right)\right) = \left(\frac{2}{3}, \frac{37}{27}\right)$ is a relative minimum, and the point $(-1, f(-1)) = (-1, 6)$ is a relative maximum.

38. A: The velocity v of the ball at any time t is the slope of the line tangent to the graph of h at time t. The slope of a line tangent to the curve $h(t) = -15t^2 + 56t + 3.5$ is the same as h'.

$$h'(t) = v = -30t + 56$$

When $t = 1.5$, the velocity of the ball is $-30(1.5) + 56 = 11$. The velocity is positive because the slope of the tangent line at $t = 1.5$ is positive. Velocity has both magnitude and direction, so a velocity of 11 means that the velocity is 11 ft/s upward.

39. C: The definition of the derivative of f at 1, or $f'(1)$, is the limit of the difference quotient $\lim\limits_{h \to 0} \frac{f(1+h)-f(1)}{h}$. Rather than find the limit, evaluate the derivative of the function at $x = 1$.

$$f(x) = 3x^3 - x^2 + \frac{1}{2}$$
$$f'(x) = 9x^2 - 2x$$
$$f'(1) = 9(1)^2 - 2(1) = 9 - 2 = 7$$

40. 10: The area under curve $f(x)$ is:

$$\int_0^2 3x^2 + 1 \, dx = [x^3 + x]_0^2$$
$$= [(2)^3 + (2)] - [(0)^3 + (0)]$$
$$= 8 + 2$$
$$= 10$$

Geometry

41. C: Sketch a diagram (this one is not to scale) and label the known segments. Because $\overline{CD}$ is bisected, the point of tangency divides the segment into two pieces measuring 4 and 4. From here, use the property that two segments are congruent when they originate from the same point outside of a circle and are both tangent to the circle. The point of tangency of $\overline{BC}$ divides the segment into two pieces measuring 4 and 6; the point of tangency of $\overline{AB}$ divides the segment into two pieces measuring 6 and 8; the point of tangency of $\overline{AD}$ divides the segment into two pieces measuring 8 and 4. Therefore $\overline{AD} = 8 + 4 = 12$.

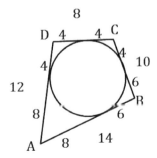

42. A: The equation of the circle is given in general form. When the equation is written in the standard form $(x - h)^2 + (y - k)^2 = r^2$, where (h, k) is the center of the circle and r is the radius of the circle, the radius is easy to determine. Write the equation in standard form by completing the square for x and y.

$$x^2 - 10x + y^2 + 8y = -29$$
$$(x^2 - 10x + 25) + (y^2 + 8y + 16) = -29 + 25 + 16$$
$$(x - 5)^2 + (y + 4)^2 = 12$$

Since $r^2 = 12$, and since r must be a positive number, $r = \sqrt{12} = 2\sqrt{3}$.

43. A: Since the y-coordinates of points P and Q are the same, line segment $\overline{PQ}$ is a horizontal line segment whose length is the difference in the x-coordinates a and c. Because the length of a line cannot be negative, and because it is unknown whether $a > c$ or $a < c$, $PQ = |a - c|$ or $|c - a|$. Since the x-coordinates of Q and P' are the same, line segment $\overline{P'Q}$ is a vertical line segment whose length is $|d - b|$ or $|b - d|$. The quadrilateral formed by the transformation of $\overline{PQ}$ to $\overline{P'Q'}$ is a parallelogram. If the base of the parallelogram is $\overline{PQ}$, then the height is $\overline{P'Q}$ since $\overline{PQ} \perp \overline{P'Q}$. For a parallelogram, $A = bh$, so $A = |a - c| \times |b - d|$.

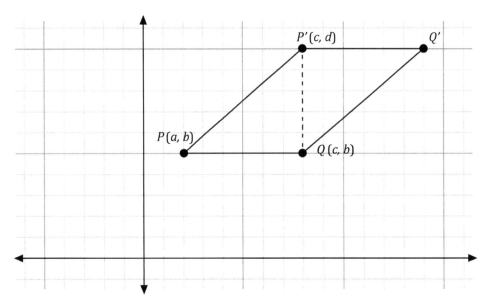

44. A, B, C: The diagram shows a right triangle with legs of lengths 9 and 11, hypotenuse of length c, and acute angles θ and φ.

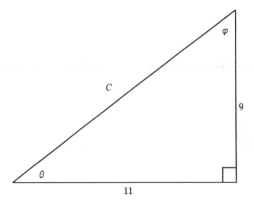

Choice A applies the Pythagorean Theorem to get $c^2 = 9^2 + 11^2$. We take square roots of both sides of the equation to get $c = \sqrt{9^2 + 11^2}$.

Choice B begins with the trigonometric ratio $\cos \varphi = \dfrac{\text{adjacent}}{\text{hypotenuse}} = \dfrac{9}{c}$. Thus, solving for c, we get $c \cos \varphi = 9$ and $c = \dfrac{9}{\cos \varphi}$. Further, since $\sec \varphi = \dfrac{1}{\cos \varphi}$, we get $c = \dfrac{9}{\cos \varphi} = 9 \sec \varphi$. Now, since $\tan \varphi = \dfrac{\text{opposite}}{\text{adjacent}} = \dfrac{11}{9}$, we get $\varphi = \arctan \left(\dfrac{11}{9} \right)$. Putting this together with our expression for c we get $c = 9 \sec \varphi = 9 \sec \left(\arctan \left(\dfrac{11}{9} \right) \right)$.

Choice C begins with $\cos \theta = \dfrac{11}{c}$, which we solve for c to get $c = \dfrac{11}{\cos \theta}$. Since $\tan \theta = \dfrac{9}{11}$, we get $\theta = \tan^{-1} \left(\dfrac{9}{11} \right)$. Putting this together with the equation for c, we get $c = \dfrac{11}{\cos \theta} = \dfrac{11}{\cos \left(\tan^{-1} \left(\frac{9}{11} \right) \right)}$.

45. B: If the three triangles are congruent and isosceles, the two base angles in each triangle are congruent. The interior angles of a triangle sum to 180°. Therefore, $0.5x + 12 + 0.5x + 12 + x = 180$. Solve for x.

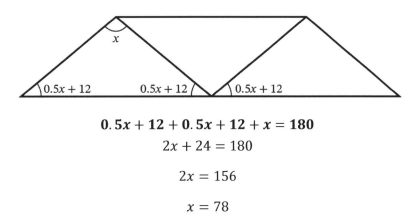

$$\mathbf{0.5x + 12 + 0.5x + 12 + x = 180}$$

$$2x + 24 = 180$$

$$2x = 156$$

$$x = 78$$

46. A: A triangular pyramid has four triangular faces. The arrangement of these faces in a two-dimensional figure is a net of a triangular pyramid if the figure can be folded to form a triangular pyramid. Choice B represents a rectangular pyramid, choice C is a triangular prism, and choice D is a square pyramid.

47. C: All regular polygons have rotational symmetry. The angle of rotation is the smallest angle by which the polygon can be rotated such that it maps onto itself. Any multiple of this angle will also map the polygon onto itself. The angle of rotation for a regular polygon is the angle formed between two lines drawn from consecutives vertices to the center of the polygon. Since the vertices of a regular polygon lie on a circle, for a regular polygon with n sides, the angle of rotation measures $\frac{360°}{n}$.

Number of sides of regular polygon	Angle of rotation	Angles $\leq 360°$ which map the polygon onto itself
4	$\frac{360}{4} = 90°$	$90°, 180°, 270°, 360°$
6	$\frac{360}{6} = 60°$	$60°, 120°, 180°, 240°, 300°, 360°$
8	$\frac{360}{8} = 45°$	$45°, 90°, 135°, 180°, 225°, 270°, 315°, 360°$
10	$\frac{360}{10} = 36°$	$36°, 72°, 108°, 144°, 180°, 216°, 252°, 288°, 324°, 360°$

48. 15: $\triangle ABC$ is similar to the smaller triangle with which it shares vertex B.
$AB = (2x + 1) + (x + 2) = 3x + 3$. $BC = 4 + 6 = 10$. Set up a proportion and solve for x:

$$\frac{3x + 3}{10} = \frac{x + 2}{4}$$
$$12x + 12 = 10x + 20$$
$$2x = 8$$
$$x = 4$$

So, $AB = 3x + 3 = 3(4) + 3 = 15$.

49. A: Since all of the answer choices are parallelograms, determine whether the parallelogram is also a rhombus or a rectangle or a square. One way to do this is by examining the parallelogram's diagonals. If the parallelogram's diagonals are perpendicular, then the parallelogram is a rhombus. If the parallelogram's diagonals are congruent, then the parallelogram is a rectangle. If a parallelogram is both a rhombus and a rectangle, then it is a square. To determine whether the diagonals are perpendicular, find the slopes of the diagonals of the quadrilateral.

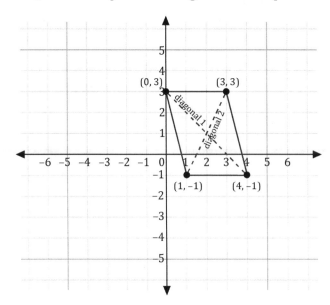

Diagonal 1   Diagonal 2

$$\frac{-1-3}{4-0} = \frac{-4}{4} = -1 \qquad\qquad \frac{3-(-1)}{3-1} = \frac{4}{2} = 2$$

The diagonals do not have opposite reciprocal slopes, so they are not perpendicular. Thus, the parallelogram is *not* a rhombus or a square. To determine whether the diagonals are congruent, find the lengths of the diagonals of the quadrilateral:

<table>
<tr><td align="center">Diagonal 1</td><td align="center">Diagonal 2</td></tr>
<tr>
<td align="center">$\sqrt{(4-0)^2 + (-1-3)^2} = \sqrt{(4)^2 + (-4)^2}$
$= \sqrt{16+16}$
$= \sqrt{32}$</td>
<td align="center">$\sqrt{(3-1)^2 + (3-(-1))^2} = \sqrt{(2)^2 + (4)^2}$
$= \sqrt{4+16}$
$= \sqrt{20}$</td>
</tr>
</table>

The diagonals are not congruent, so the parallelogram is not a rectangle. The polygon must be a parallelogram.

50. C: Since there are 100 cm in a meter, on a 1: 150 scale drawing, each centimeter represents 1.5 m. Therefore, an area of one square centimeter on the drawing represents 2.25 square meters in the real room. Since the area of the room in the scale drawing is 20 cm², the room's actual area is 45 m².

Another way to determine the area of the room is to write and solve an equation using the area formula for a rectangle.

$\frac{l}{150} \times \frac{w}{150} = 20$ cm², where l and w are the dimensions of the actual room:

$$\frac{lw}{22,500} = 20 \text{ cm}^2$$

$$\text{Area} = 450,000 \text{ cm}^2$$

Since this is not one of the answer choices, convert cm² to m²:

$$450,000 \text{ cm}^2 \times \frac{1 \text{ m}}{100 \text{ cm}} \times \frac{1 \text{ m}}{100 \text{ cm}} = 45 \text{ m}^2$$

51. D: The given conditions guarantee that the triangles are similar since both triangles have the same angles. But similar triangles with two pairs of congruent sides may still not be congruent. The diagram below gives an example of two triangles are plainly not congruent. Nevertheless, $\triangle ABC \sim \triangle DEF$ since there is a fixed ratio of 2: 3 between corresponding sides. This guarantees that corresponding angles are congruent. Further, there are also two pairs of congruent sides—one pair of length 6 and one of length 9. They are not, however, corresponding sides in the similarity relation. Thus, they will not work to demonstrate congruence of the triangles. For instance, if we try to show congruence by SAS, we have the two pairs of congruent sides, $\overline{BC} \cong \overline{DE}$ and $\overline{CA} \cong \overline{EF}$, but the angles between them, namely $\angle C$ and $\angle E$, are not congruent. The same happens if we try to apply ASA or AAS.

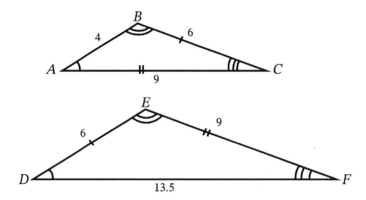

52. A, C: We begin with a diagram of an equilateral triangle $\triangle ABC$ with sides of 4 cm, as shown. Since it is equilateral, all three interior angles measure 60°. We drop an altitude $\overline{AD}$ from vertex A. Then, $\triangle ADB \cong \triangle ADC$ by HL since they have equal hypotenuses (4 cm) and common leg $\overline{AD}$. Thus, $\overline{BD} \cong \overline{CD}$, meaning the length of segment $\overline{CD}$ is 2 cm, and making segment $\overline{AD}$ a median. Since $\triangle ADC$ is a 30-60-90 triangle, its long leg, $\overline{AD}$, which is both an altitude and a median, has a length of $2\sqrt{3}$ cm, showing choice B to be false and choice C to be true. Further, the area of $\triangle ABC$ is $A = \frac{1}{2}bh$, half the product of its base (length of $\overline{BC}$) and height (length of $\overline{AD}$). This gives us an area of $\frac{1}{2}(4 \text{ cm})(2\sqrt{3} \text{ cm}) = 4\sqrt{3}$ cm^2, showing choice A to be true.

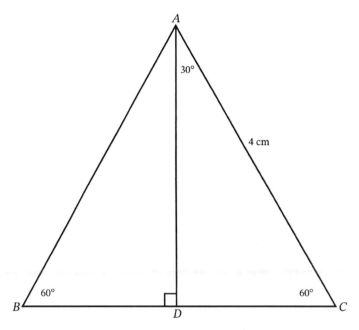

53. A: The given values make the Pythagorean theorem true, that is $5^2 + 12^2 = 13^2$. So, this is a right triangle. Let the base of the triangle be $5x$ and the height of the triangle be $12x$. So, the area is $A = \frac{1}{2}bh$, or $\frac{1}{2}(5x)(12x) = 30x^2$.

Statistics and Probability

54. C: When rolling two dice, there is only one way to roll a sum of 2 (rolling a 1 on each die) and 12 (rolling 6 on each die). In contrast, there are two ways to obtain a sum of 3 (rolling a 2 and 1 or a 1 and 2) and 11 (rolling a 5 and 6 or a 6 and 5), three ways to obtain a sum of 4 (1 and 3; 2 and 2; 3 and 1) or 10 (4 and 6; 5 and 5; 6 and 4), and so on. Since the probability of obtaining each sum is inconsistent, this is not a random selection.

55. B: One way to approach this problem is to first consider the number of arrangements of the five members of the family if Tasha (T) and Mac (M) must sit together. Treat them as a unit seated in a fixed location at the table; then arrange the other three family members (A, B, and C):

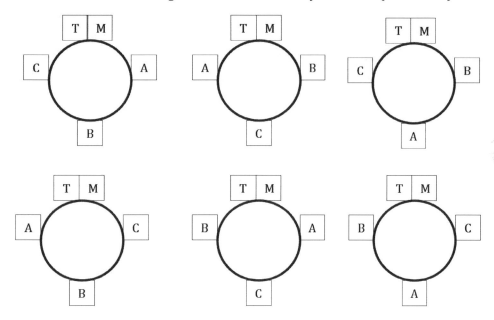

There are six ways to arrange four units around a circle as shown. Any other arrangement would be a rotation in which the elements in the same order and would therefore not be a unique arrangement. Of course, Mac and Tasha are not actually a single unit. They would still be sitting beside each other if they were to trade seats, so there are twelve arrangements in which the two are seated next to one another. In all other arrangements of the five family members, they are separated. Therefore, to find the number of arrangements in which Tasha and Mac are *not* sitting together, subtract twelve from the possible arrangement of five units around a circle. There are $(n-1)!$ ways to arrange n units around a circle for $n > 1$. So, $(5-1)! - 12 = 24 - 12 = 12$.

56. A: The range is the spread of the data. It can be calculated for each class by subtracting the lowest test score from the highest, or it can be determined visually from the graph. The difference between the highest and lowest test scores in class 1 is $98 - 23 = 75$ points. The range for each of the other classes is much smaller.

57. B: There are three ways in which two women from the same department can be selected. Two women can be selected from the first department, or two women can be selected from the second department, or two women can be selected from the third department.

Department 1	**Department 2**	**Department 3**
$\dfrac{12}{103} \times \dfrac{11}{102} = \dfrac{132}{10,506}$	$\dfrac{28}{103} \times \dfrac{27}{102} = \dfrac{756}{10,506}$	$\dfrac{16}{103} \times \dfrac{15}{102} = \dfrac{240}{10,506}$

Since any of these is a distinct possible outcome, the probability that two women will be selected from the same department is the sum of these outcomes:

$$\frac{132}{10,506} + \frac{756}{10,506} + \frac{240}{10,506} = \frac{1,128}{10,506} \approx 0.107, \text{ or } 10.7\%$$

58. D: A fair coin has a symmetrical binomial distribution which peaks in its center. Since choice B shows a skewed distribution for the fair coin, it cannot be the correct answer. From the frequency histogram given for the misshapen coin, it is evident that the misshapen coin is more likely to land on heads. Therefore, it is more likely that ten coin flips would result in fewer tails than ten coin flips of a fair coin; consequently, the probability distribution for the misshapen coin would be higher than the fair coin's distribution toward the smaller number of tails. Choice A shows a probability distribution which peaks at a value of 5 and which is symmetrical with respect to the peak, which verifies that it cannot be correct. Furthermore, in choice A, the sum of the probabilities shown for each number of tails for the misshapen coin is not equal to 1. The distribution for the misshapen coin in choice C is skewed in the wrong direction, favoring tails instead of heads, and must therefore also be incorrect. Choice D shows the correct binomial distribution for the fair coin and the appropriate shift for the misshapen coin.

59. D: A score of 85 is one standard deviation below the mean. Since approximately 68% of the data is within one standard deviation of the mean, about 32% (100% − 68%) of the data is outside of one standard deviation within the mean. Normally distributed data is symmetric about the mean, which means that about 16% of the data lies below one standard deviation below the mean and about 16% of data lies above one standard deviation above the mean. Therefore, approximately 16% of individuals have IQs less than 85, while approximately 84% of the population has an IQ of at least 85. Since 84% of 300 is 252, about 252 people from the selected group have IQs of at least 85.

60. B: Determine the probability of each option.

For choice A, this is the total number of students in the tea circle of the Venn diagram divided by the total number of students surveyed:

$$\frac{42 + 12 + 7 + 26}{250} = \frac{87}{250} = 34.8\%$$

For choice B, this is the total number of students in the hot chocolate circle and in at least one other circle divided by the total number in the hot chocolate circle:

$$\frac{31 + 7 + 26}{31 + 7 + 26 + 56} = \frac{64}{120} \approx 53.3\%$$

For choice C, this is the number of students in the intersection of all three circles divided by the total number in the overlap of the coffee and hot chocolate circles:

$$\frac{7}{7+31} = \frac{7}{38} \approx 18.4\%$$

For choice D, this is the number of students outside of all the circles divided by the total number of students surveyed:

$$\frac{11}{250} = 4.4\%$$

Choice B has the greatest probability.

61. C: To get one red bead and one green, we must either draw a red bead first and a green bead second, or a green bead first and a red bead second. Since these events are mutually exclusive, we can add their probabilities to get the probability of their union (i.e., the probability that one or the other happens). Recalling that $P(A|B)$ is the conditional probability of event A given event B, we apply the multiplication rule for dependent events to calculate:

$$P(\text{red first and green second}) = P(\text{red first})P(\text{green second}|\text{red first})$$
$$= P(\text{red from blue box})P(\text{green from red box})$$
$$= \frac{6}{10} \cdot \frac{2}{8}$$

$$= \frac{3}{5} \cdot \frac{1}{4}$$

$$= \frac{3}{20}$$

$$P(\text{green first and red second}) = P(\text{green first})P(\text{red second}|\text{green first})$$
$$= P(\text{green from blue box})P(\text{red from green box})$$
$$= \frac{4}{10} \cdot \frac{2}{6}$$

$$= \frac{2}{5} \cdot \frac{1}{3}$$

$$= \frac{2}{15}$$

Thus, the probability of getting one red bead and one green bead is $\frac{3}{20} + \frac{2}{15} = \frac{9}{60} + \frac{8}{60} = \frac{17}{60}$.

62. 131: Use a Venn diagram to help organize the given information. Start by filling in the space where the three circles intersect: six customers ordered all three items. Now, use that information to fill in the spaces where two circles intersect. For example, fourteen customers ordered both pumpkin bread and cranberry muffins, and six of those were the customers who purchased all three items, so eight customers bought pumpkin bread and cranberry muffins but not eggnog pie.

Once the diagram is completed, add the number of orders from each portion of the diagram. The total number of customers was $34 + 19 + 51 + 9 + 8 + 4 + 6 = 131$.

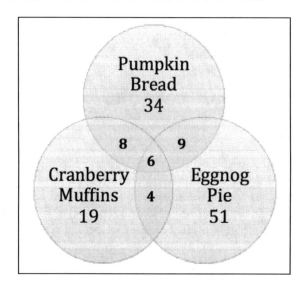

63. B: The average number of females per age bracket is the total number of females divided by 4, or $\frac{297}{4} = 74.25$. The number of volunteers at the animal shelter is 13% of the total number of volunteers (626), which is $0.13(626) = 81.38$. The difference in the number of male and female volunteers is $329 - 297 = 32$, and the difference in the number of people over 60 and people under 21 is $187 - 118 = 69$. The greatest quantity of the answer choices is the number of volunteers at the animal shelter.

64. C: 65 of 118 volunteers under the age of 21 are male. So, the probability that a male is chosen is $\frac{\text{number of } 0-20 \text{ year-old-males}}{\text{number of } 0-20\text{-year-olds}} = \frac{65}{118} \approx 0.55$.

65. D: If each of the five groups will contain four boys and four girls, there must be twenty boys and twenty girls in the class. Since the order of the boys and girls does not matter in the group, the situation represents a combination. The number of ways to select four boys from a group of twenty boys is:

$$_{20}C_4 = \frac{20!}{4!\,(20-4)!} = \frac{20!}{4!\,16!} = \frac{20 \times 19 \times 18 \times 17 \times 16!}{4!\,16!} = \frac{20 \times 19 \times 18 \times 17}{4 \times 3 \times 2 \times 1} = 4,845$$

The number of ways to select four girls from a group of twenty girls is:

$$_{20}C_4 = \frac{20!}{4!\,(20-4)!} = \frac{20!}{4!\,16!} = \frac{20 \times 19 \times 18 \times 17 \times 16!}{4!\,16!} = \frac{20 \times 19 \times 18 \times 17}{4 \times 3 \times 2 \times 1} = 4,845$$

Since each combination of boys can be paired with each combination of girls, the number of group combinations is $4,845 \times 4,845 = 23,474,025$.

66. B, C: Choice A has the numerator $7 \cdot 12 \cdot C(17,2)$ which overcounts the ways to choose the four students to be officers with both classes represented. For instance, if we consider the group of officers consisting of juniors J_1, J_2, and J_3 and senior S, the approach in choice A will count this group three times: first, by choosing J_1, then S, then $\{J_2, J_3\}$; second, by choosing J_2, then S, then

$\{J_1, J_3\}$; third, by choosing J_3, then S, then $\{J_1, J_2\}$. In fact, the overcount is so great that the fraction in choice A evaluates to about 2.94, which is impossible since a probability cannot exceed 1.

Choices B and C both take correct approaches. Choice B takes the sample space to be all assignments of 4 members to specific offices. Choice C takes the sample space to be all choices of which 4 members will serve, but without deciding which member gets which office. But both approaches correctly calculate the size of their respective sample spaces. Then both correctly subtract the elements of their sample spaces that include only juniors or only seniors, and then correctly calculate the probability by the formula (favorable outcomes) ÷ (total outcomes). So, the answers in B and C are equal.

Additional 4 Praxis Practice Tests

To take these additional Praxis practice tests, visit our bonus page:
mometrix.com/bonus948/praxmath5165

How to Overcome Test Anxiety

Just the thought of taking a test is enough to make most people a little nervous. A test is an important event that can have a long-term impact on your future, so it's important to take it seriously and it's natural to feel anxious about performing well. But just because anxiety is normal, that doesn't mean that it's helpful in test taking, or that you should simply accept it as part of your life. Anxiety can have a variety of effects. These effects can be mild, like making you feel slightly nervous, or severe, like blocking your ability to focus or remember even a simple detail.

If you experience test anxiety—whether severe or mild—it's important to know how to beat it. To discover this, first you need to understand what causes test anxiety.

Causes of Test Anxiety

While we often think of anxiety as an uncontrollable emotional state, it can actually be caused by simple, practical things. One of the most common causes of test anxiety is that a person does not feel adequately prepared for their test. This feeling can be the result of many different issues such as poor study habits or lack of organization, but the most common culprit is time management. Starting to study too late, failing to organize your study time to cover all of the material, or being distracted while you study will mean that you're not well prepared for the test. This may lead to cramming the night before, which will cause you to be physically and mentally exhausted for the test. Poor time management also contributes to feelings of stress, fear, and hopelessness as you realize you are not well prepared but don't know what to do about it.

Other times, test anxiety is not related to your preparation for the test but comes from unresolved fear. This may be a past failure on a test, or poor performance on tests in general. It may come from comparing yourself to others who seem to be performing better or from the stress of living up to expectations. Anxiety may be driven by fears of the future—how failure on this test would affect your educational and career goals. These fears are often completely irrational, but they can still negatively impact your test performance.

Elements of Test Anxiety

As mentioned earlier, test anxiety is considered to be an emotional state, but it has physical and mental components as well. Sometimes you may not even realize that you are suffering from test anxiety until you notice the physical symptoms. These can include trembling hands, rapid heartbeat, sweating, nausea, and tense muscles. Extreme anxiety may lead to fainting or vomiting. Obviously, any of these symptoms can have a negative impact on testing. It is important to recognize them as soon as they begin to occur so that you can address the problem before it damages your performance.

The mental components of test anxiety include trouble focusing and inability to remember learned information. During a test, your mind is on high alert, which can help you recall information and stay focused for an extended period of time. However, anxiety interferes with your mind's natural processes, causing you to blank out, even on the questions you know well. The strain of testing during anxiety makes it difficult to stay focused, especially on a test that may take several hours. Extreme anxiety can take a huge mental toll, making it difficult not only to recall test information but even to understand the test questions or pull your thoughts together.

Effects of Test Anxiety

Test anxiety is like a disease—if left untreated, it will get progressively worse. Anxiety leads to poor performance, and this reinforces the feelings of fear and failure, which in turn lead to poor performances on subsequent tests. It can grow from a mild nervousness to a crippling condition. If allowed to progress, test anxiety can have a big impact on your schooling, and consequently on your future.

Test anxiety can spread to other parts of your life. Anxiety on tests can become anxiety in any stressful situation, and blanking on a test can turn into panicking in a job situation. But fortunately, you don't have to let anxiety rule your testing and determine your grades. There are a number of relatively simple steps you can take to move past anxiety and function normally on a test and in the rest of life.

Physical Steps for Beating Test Anxiety

While test anxiety is a serious problem, the good news is that it can be overcome. It doesn't have to control your ability to think and remember information. While it may take time, you can begin taking steps today to beat anxiety.

Just as your first hint that you may be struggling with anxiety comes from the physical symptoms, the first step to treating it is also physical. Rest is crucial for having a clear, strong mind. If you are tired, it is much easier to give in to anxiety. But if you establish good sleep habits, your body and mind will be ready to perform optimally, without the strain of exhaustion. Additionally, sleeping well helps you to retain information better, so you're more likely to recall the answers when you see the test questions.

Getting good sleep means more than going to bed on time. It's important to allow your brain time to relax. Take study breaks from time to time so it doesn't get overworked, and don't study right before bed. Take time to rest your mind before trying to rest your body, or you may find it difficult to fall asleep.

Along with sleep, other aspects of physical health are important in preparing for a test. Good nutrition is vital for good brain function. Sugary foods and drinks may give a burst of energy but this burst is followed by a crash, both physically and emotionally. Instead, fuel your body with protein and vitamin-rich foods.

Also, drink plenty of water. Dehydration can lead to headaches and exhaustion, especially if your brain is already under stress from the rigors of the test. Particularly if your test is a long one, drink water during the breaks. And if possible, take an energy-boosting snack to eat between sections.

Along with sleep and diet, a third important part of physical health is exercise. Maintaining a steady workout schedule is helpful, but even taking 5-minute study breaks to walk can help get your blood pumping faster and clear your head. Exercise also releases endorphins, which contribute to a positive feeling and can help combat test anxiety.

When you nurture your physical health, you are also contributing to your mental health. If your body is healthy, your mind is much more likely to be healthy as well. So take time to rest, nourish your body with healthy food and water, and get moving as much as possible. Taking these physical steps will make you stronger and more able to take the mental steps necessary to overcome test anxiety.

Mental Steps for Beating Test Anxiety

Working on the mental side of test anxiety can be more challenging, but as with the physical side, there are clear steps you can take to overcome it. As mentioned earlier, test anxiety often stems from lack of preparation, so the obvious solution is to prepare for the test. Effective studying may be the most important weapon you have for beating test anxiety, but you can and should employ several other mental tools to combat fear.

First, boost your confidence by reminding yourself of past success—tests or projects that you aced. If you're putting as much effort into preparing for this test as you did for those, there's no reason you should expect to fail here. Work hard to prepare; then trust your preparation.

Second, surround yourself with encouraging people. It can be helpful to find a study group, but be sure that the people you're around will encourage a positive attitude. If you spend time with others who are anxious or cynical, this will only contribute to your own anxiety. Look for others who are motivated to study hard from a desire to succeed, not from a fear of failure.

Third, reward yourself. A test is physically and mentally tiring, even without anxiety, and it can be helpful to have something to look forward to. Plan an activity following the test, regardless of the outcome, such as going to a movie or getting ice cream.

When you are taking the test, if you find yourself beginning to feel anxious, remind yourself that you know the material. Visualize successfully completing the test. Then take a few deep, relaxing breaths and return to it. Work through the questions carefully but with confidence, knowing that you are capable of succeeding.

Developing a healthy mental approach to test taking will also aid in other areas of life. Test anxiety affects more than just the actual test—it can be damaging to your mental health and even contribute to depression. It's important to beat test anxiety before it becomes a problem for more than testing.

Study Strategy

Being prepared for the test is necessary to combat anxiety, but what does being prepared look like? You may study for hours on end and still not feel prepared. What you need is a strategy for test prep. The next few pages outline our recommended steps to help you plan out and conquer the challenge of preparation.

STEP 1: SCOPE OUT THE TEST

Learn everything you can about the format (multiple choice, essay, etc.) and what will be on the test. Gather any study materials, course outlines, or sample exams that may be available. Not only will this help you to prepare, but knowing what to expect can help to alleviate test anxiety.

STEP 2: MAP OUT THE MATERIAL

Look through the textbook or study guide and make note of how many chapters or sections it has. Then divide these over the time you have. For example, if a book has 15 chapters and you have five days to study, you need to cover three chapters each day. Even better, if you have the time, leave an extra day at the end for overall review after you have gone through the material in depth.

If time is limited, you may need to prioritize the material. Look through it and make note of which sections you think you already have a good grasp on, and which need review. While you are studying, skim quickly through the familiar sections and take more time on the challenging parts.

Write out your plan so you don't get lost as you go. Having a written plan also helps you feel more in control of the study, so anxiety is less likely to arise from feeling overwhelmed at the amount to cover.

STEP 3: GATHER YOUR TOOLS

Decide what study method works best for you. Do you prefer to highlight in the book as you study and then go back over the highlighted portions? Or do you type out notes of the important information? Or is it helpful to make flashcards that you can carry with you? Assemble the pens, index cards, highlighters, post-it notes, and any other materials you may need so you won't be distracted by getting up to find things while you study.

If you're having a hard time retaining the information or organizing your notes, experiment with different methods. For example, try color-coding by subject with colored pens, highlighters, or post-it notes. If you learn better by hearing, try recording yourself reading your notes so you can listen while in the car, working out, or simply sitting at your desk. Ask a friend to quiz you from your flashcards, or try teaching someone the material to solidify it in your mind.

STEP 4: CREATE YOUR ENVIRONMENT

It's important to avoid distractions while you study. This includes both the obvious distractions like visitors and the subtle distractions like an uncomfortable chair (or a too-comfortable couch that makes you want to fall asleep). Set up the best study environment possible: good lighting and a comfortable work area. If background music helps you focus, you may want to turn it on, but otherwise keep the room quiet. If you are using a computer to take notes, be sure you don't have any other windows open, especially applications like social media, games, or anything else that could distract you. Silence your phone and turn off notifications. Be sure to keep water close by so you stay hydrated while you study (but avoid unhealthy drinks and snacks).

Also, take into account the best time of day to study. Are you freshest first thing in the morning? Try to set aside some time then to work through the material. Is your mind clearer in the afternoon or evening? Schedule your study session then. Another method is to study at the same time of day that you will take the test, so that your brain gets used to working on the material at that time and will be ready to focus at test time.

STEP 5: STUDY!

Once you have done all the study preparation, it's time to settle into the actual studying. Sit down, take a few moments to settle your mind so you can focus, and begin to follow your study plan. Don't give in to distractions or let yourself procrastinate. This is your time to prepare so you'll be ready to fearlessly approach the test. Make the most of the time and stay focused.

Of course, you don't want to burn out. If you study too long you may find that you're not retaining the information very well. Take regular study breaks. For example, taking five minutes out of every hour to walk briskly, breathing deeply and swinging your arms, can help your mind stay fresh.

As you get to the end of each chapter or section, it's a good idea to do a quick review. Remind yourself of what you learned and work on any difficult parts. When you feel that you've mastered the material, move on to the next part. At the end of your study session, briefly skim through your notes again.

But while review is helpful, cramming last minute is NOT. If at all possible, work ahead so that you won't need to fit all your study into the last day. Cramming overloads your brain with more information than it can process and retain, and your tired mind may struggle to recall even previously learned information when it is overwhelmed with last-minute study. Also, the urgent nature of cramming and the stress placed on your brain contribute to anxiety. You'll be more likely to go to the test feeling unprepared and having trouble thinking clearly.

So don't cram, and don't stay up late before the test, even just to review your notes at a leisurely pace. Your brain needs rest more than it needs to go over the information again. In fact, plan to finish your studies by noon or early afternoon the day before the test. Give your brain the rest of the day to relax or focus on other things, and get a good night's sleep. Then you will be fresh for the test and better able to recall what you've studied.

STEP 6: TAKE A PRACTICE TEST

Many courses offer sample tests, either online or in the study materials. This is an excellent resource to check whether you have mastered the material, as well as to prepare for the test format and environment.

Check the test format ahead of time: the number of questions, the type (multiple choice, free response, etc.), and the time limit. Then create a plan for working through them. For example, if you have 30 minutes to take a 60-question test, your limit is 30 seconds per question. Spend less time on the questions you know well so that you can take more time on the difficult ones.

If you have time to take several practice tests, take the first one open book, with no time limit. Work through the questions at your own pace and make sure you fully understand them. Gradually work up to taking a test under test conditions: sit at a desk with all study materials put away and set a timer. Pace yourself to make sure you finish the test with time to spare and go back to check your answers if you have time.

After each test, check your answers. On the questions you missed, be sure you understand why you missed them. Did you misread the question (tests can use tricky wording)? Did you forget the information? Or was it something you hadn't learned? Go back and study any shaky areas that the practice tests reveal.

Taking these tests not only helps with your grade, but also aids in combating test anxiety. If you're already used to the test conditions, you're less likely to worry about it, and working through tests until you're scoring well gives you a confidence boost. Go through the practice tests until you feel comfortable, and then you can go into the test knowing that you're ready for it.

Test Tips

On test day, you should be confident, knowing that you've prepared well and are ready to answer the questions. But aside from preparation, there are several test day strategies you can employ to maximize your performance.

First, as stated before, get a good night's sleep the night before the test (and for several nights before that, if possible). Go into the test with a fresh, alert mind rather than staying up late to study.

Try not to change too much about your normal routine on the day of the test. It's important to eat a nutritious breakfast, but if you normally don't eat breakfast at all, consider eating just a protein bar. If you're a coffee drinker, go ahead and have your normal coffee. Just make sure you time it so that the caffeine doesn't wear off right in the middle of your test. Avoid sugary beverages, and drink enough water to stay hydrated but not so much that you need a restroom break 10 minutes into the test. If your test isn't first thing in the morning, consider going for a walk or doing a light workout before the test to get your blood flowing.

Allow yourself enough time to get ready, and leave for the test with plenty of time to spare so you won't have the anxiety of scrambling to arrive in time. Another reason to be early is to select a good seat. It's helpful to sit away from doors and windows, which can be distracting. Find a good seat, get out your supplies, and settle your mind before the test begins.

When the test begins, start by going over the instructions carefully, even if you already know what to expect. Make sure you avoid any careless mistakes by following the directions.

Then begin working through the questions, pacing yourself as you've practiced. If you're not sure on an answer, don't spend too much time on it, and don't let it shake your confidence. Either skip it and come back later, or eliminate as many wrong answers as possible and guess among the remaining ones. Don't dwell on these questions as you continue—put them out of your mind and focus on what lies ahead.

Be sure to read all of the answer choices, even if you're sure the first one is the right answer. Sometimes you'll find a better one if you keep reading. But don't second-guess yourself if you do immediately know the answer. Your gut instinct is usually right. Don't let test anxiety rob you of the information you know.

If you have time at the end of the test (and if the test format allows), go back and review your answers. Be cautious about changing any, since your first instinct tends to be correct, but make sure you didn't misread any of the questions or accidentally mark the wrong answer choice. Look over any you skipped and make an educated guess.

At the end, leave the test feeling confident. You've done your best, so don't waste time worrying about your performance or wishing you could change anything. Instead, celebrate the successful completion of this test. And finally, use this test to learn how to deal with anxiety even better next time.

Review Video: Test Anxiety
Visit mometrix.com/academy and enter code: 100340

Important Qualification

Not all anxiety is created equal. If your test anxiety is causing major issues in your life beyond the classroom or testing center, or if you are experiencing troubling physical symptoms related to your anxiety, it may be a sign of a serious physiological or psychological condition. If this sounds like your situation, we strongly encourage you to seek professional help.

Tell Us Your Story

We at Mometrix would like to extend our heartfelt thanks to you for letting us be a part of your journey. It is an honor to serve people from all walks of life, people like you, who are committed to building the best future they can for themselves.

We know that each person's situation is unique. But we also know that, whether you are a young student or a mother of four, you care about working to make your own life and the lives of those around you better.

That's why we want to hear your story.

We want to know why you're taking this test. We want to know about the trials you've gone through to get here. And we want to know about the successes you've experienced after taking and passing your test.

In addition to your story, which can be an inspiration both to us and to others, we value your feedback. We want to know both what you loved about our book and what you think we can improve on.

The team at Mometrix would be absolutely thrilled to hear from you! So please, send us an email at tellusyourstory@mometrix.com or visit us at mometrix.com/tellusyourstory.php and let's stay in touch.

SCAN HERE

317

Additional Bonus Material

Due to our efforts to try to keep this book to a manageable length, we've created a link that will give you access to all of your additional bonus material:

mometrix.com/bonus948/praxmath5165